Drunks, Drugs & Debits

Galt Publishing

Drunks, Drugs & Debits:

How to Recognize Addicts and Avoid Financial Abuse

Doug Thorburn

PUBLISHED BY GALT PUBLISHING
P.O. Box 7777, Northridge, California 91327-7777

"Just Say No To Addicts" is trademarked by Doug Thorburn.

Address the author c/o Galt Publishing

MBTI is a registered Trade Mark, Consulting Psychologists Press
Inc., Palo Alto, CA

CFP® and Certified Financial Planner® are marks owned by the
Certified Financial Planner Board of Standards, Inc.

Publisher's Cataloging-in-Publication
(Provided by Quality Books, Inc.)

Thorburn, Doug.
    Drunks, drugs and debits : how to recognize
addicts and avoid financial abuse / by Doug
Thorburn. -- 1st ed.
    p. cm.
    99-97269
    ISBN: 0-9675788-3-3
    Includes bibliographical references and index.

    1. Substance abuse--Popular works.
2. Alcoholics--Family relationships. 3. Addicts--
Family relationships. 4. Employees--Substance
abuse.   I. Title.

RC564.29.T46 2000   362.29'13'0973
                             QBI99-1610

Printed in the United States of America

2000

First Edition

10   9   8   7   6   5   4   3   2   1

For John Galt

This book could not have been written without the help of numerous individuals, acknowledged at the end. I invite you to read it.

Table of Contents

Table of Figures

Preface

"The devil puts a pillow under the head of a drunk."
—Scottish Proverb

My name is Doug. I'm not an alcoholic or other drug addict. I got lucky. Others, through the fate of genes inherited, were not. This book is dedicated to those unlucky ones, the alcoholics and other drug addicts. It's also dedicated to their victims, including their closest friends and lovers, who have not been given the tools required, either to diagnose the disease or assist in the healing process. The victims include not only immediate family, but also everyone with whom the addict comes into contact: co-workers, employers, employees, renters, and landlords. They also include those who are victims to violated contracts and against whom frivolous lawsuits are brought, not to mention motorists and law enforcers, both risking their lives. It's dedicated as well to healers: the caring and concerned doctors, therapists, nurses, psychiatrists, priests, ministers, rabbis, chaplains and others in their quest to serve humanity.

Foreword

By G. Douglas Talbott, M.D.

While there have been numerous books written on alcoholism and substance abuse, this one, *Drunks, Drugs and Debits,* is extraordinary and unique.

Financial expert Doug Thorburn looks at the devastating effects of substance addiction from the viewpoint of a non-alcoholic, codependent individual. He emphasizes the financial chaos wrought by this destructive disease.

This is a book that examines the catastrophic penalties that alcoholism and other drug addiction extract from individuals. It opens to many people a new way to recognize, diagnose and deal with the many faces of substance addiction.

Being the son of an alcoholic father and having been in a long-term romantic relationship with an addict, the author approaches the disease from a personal, painful and intimate viewpoint. He also utilizes multiple case studies and personal histories that helps one recognize the signs of alcoholism and other drug addiction. This allows the reader to view such situations in his or her own life from an entirely new perspective. The Thorburn Substance Addiction Recognition Indicator is a particularly helpful tool.

Written by a layman for the layman, this book nevertheless has a very sound scientific basis. The connection of the genetic foundation to the disease and the altered neurochemistry of the brain resulting in a predisposition to addiction in certain people, is spelled out in refreshingly simple terms. Recognizing signs of addiction allows contemplation of one's own roles and relationships in connection with possible addicts.

The perspective of addiction and the media is fascinating and references to possible addiction in major historic figures who have caused untold misery captures the imagination. The comparisons of denial versus ignorance are powerful and wonderfully illustrated with case reviews. The need for accountability through the process of experiencing pain and consequences is emphasized in profound ways. Doug also gives entirely new approaches and insight into recovery methods for the non-addict.

Only superficially described in other books, the idea and method for separating one's finances with the goal of avoiding further financial abuse is yet another excellent tool. Yes, the author presents concepts and ideas that currently are, at the very least, controversial from an addiction medicine standpoint. He nevertheless demonstrates knowledge of a variety of therapeutic approaches to this primary, psychosocial, biogenetic disease. Sir William Osler described syphilis as the great imposter of the last century, mimicking many of the symptoms of numerous other diseases. Such could be said for the disease of addiction today.

Although I believe not every statement, theory, or observation made by the author is uncontroversial, his views and new approaches are substantial contributions. The field of addiction needs this book and will benefit greatly from this thoroughly researched and documented work.

G. Douglas Talbott, M.D., FASAM, FACP
Past-President, American Society of Addiction Medicine
Vice President, International Society of Addiction Medicine
Team Physician, Atlanta Braves
Consultant, National Football League
Consultant, National Basketball Association

Introduction

I awoke, my body aching from the hard, uncomfortable bench where I had laid, I supposed, for a couple of hours. I checked myself over and finding no obvious injury began looking around at my bleak surroundings. Through the cold steel bars I saw uniforms, similar to the ones worn by those that brought me the previous evening. I cautiously glanced at the others in the room, seeing only hardened faces staring back. The stench of alcohol emanating from each of them, it seemed, was overwhelming.

I briefly thought how lucky I was to be alive and began to ponder my misfortune. What had led me, a successful 41-year-old financial professional and never before in trouble with the law, to this deplorable condition? It was coming back to me slowly. I reflected on the abuse I had endured for much of the previous two years of which I had absolutely no understanding. I wondered at the injustice of arresting the wrong person. I speculated as to how others could be so blind to the truth.

The answer, I later found, was simple. I was in love with a substance addict. Being naïve and unaware of the signs and symptoms of substance addiction and the destructive behaviors of which addicts are capable, I unwittingly became an enabler. I had slowly become enmeshed in a nightmare that turned into the most devastating experience of my life, but also the most pivotal.

The mental anguish and emotional abuse foisted upon me, including landing in that dark jail cell, ironically did not end the relationship. That ended several months later when she left me, doing what is known by recovering addicts as "pulling a geographic." The addict moves, hoping things will change, despite the fact they are taking the addiction with them.

By that time, mostly recovered from this traumatic ordeal, I had learned enough to write a six-page newsletter for my tax and financial planning clients, alerting them to financial problems an addict can create in both their own and others' lives. It was partly cathartic, but mostly an attempt at sharing my limited knowledge. I contemplated the response the article generated, praised highly by recovering addicts yet viewed relatively indifferently by non-addicts. I slowly realized the average person doesn't have a clue as to how to detect when substance addiction is creating havoc in his or her life or what to do about it when they do. I began reading books, in addition to continuing a process of learning from numerous recovering addicts while attending meetings of both Alcoholics Anonymous and Al-Anon, a support group for the non-addict. I realized that an understanding of this horrific affliction and its catastrophic effects on others required far more than merely a few pages in a client newsletter.

While most believe that addiction is a problem, it is far more wide-spread, destructive and serious than they imagine. While not intended as the final word on substance addiction, what follows is empirical evidence taken from my own story, as well as others. This kind of evidence has led to many scientific breakthroughs, including, for example, to the idea of vaccination and to the discovery of aspirin and numerous other drugs. These writings are meant to provoke thought in you, the reader, and to serve as impetus for further study. The use of anecdotes (historical as well as others culled from numerous interviews) is intended to add to our knowledge of substance addiction and the behaviors it can cause. With the aid of the tools presented, you may find yourself reevaluating your own experiences.

This book is an attempt to show others how to recognize substance addicts. We fervently hope to reverse the commonly accepted myth that addicts can say no to drugs, instead informing why and how the non-addict, along with addicts in recovery, must finally "*Just say no to addicts.*" With the exception of some necessary but basic comments on the biology of addiction, I hope to do this in language the lay person can relate to and easily understand. I have attempted to remove anything with an overly certain tone, since this field is filled with exceptions. So for example, if "invariably" still slips in, keep in mind I recognize there's almost always (invariably?) an exception. Because of the tremendous misinformation and misunderstanding of addiction, it is recommended that this book be read in the order presented.

There are very few books that focus on the non-addict dealing with addicts. This one is unique in suggesting there is only one formula to extricate oneself from becoming or remaining a victim. This is to:

1. learn how to tentatively diagnose addiction,
2. assume the cause of destructive, unethical and/or criminal behaviors is substance addiction (unless proven otherwise), and
3. "uncompromisingly disenable" meaning that we stop picking and choosing exceptions to "tough love," ceasing to "help" the addict in any and every way possible.

1

Addiction and Financial Abuse:

A Primer

Lori[1] is an extremely bright, successful self-employed client of my income tax/financial planning practice. Her income had plummeted from a couple of hundred thousand dollars annually to less than $50,000 in the last few years, barely enough to make the payment on a home she had purchased in Southern California in the early 1990s. I had only recently become aware of some of the signs of substance addiction, including the existence of seemingly inexplicable problems in one's financial life. I wondered who the addict might be in Lori's life and had a good idea that it wasn't her. I had begun to realize substance addicts can so seriously impact others that it just might show up in her behaviors, including a deteriorating financial situation. When she came to my office to have her tax return prepared, I started asking questions.

I'd written the article on alcoholism and financial disaster for my client newsletter several months before. Lori had glanced at the title, but hadn't read it since she "didn't know" any alcoholics. I suggested that since the vast majority of alcoholics and other substance addicts can lead superficially normal lives, hold jobs and even have spouses or significant others and children, everyone knows at least one or even several. "No," she protested, "not family, friends, employees, peers or even acquaintances. Nobody." I responded that she'd eventually encounter one. I told her that understanding addicts' behavior had already helped me save money and preserve sanity in both my business and personal life. Suggesting she at least skim the article, I then dropped the subject and began preparing her tax return.

To give you some background, I've always viewed myself as more than just a tax preparer. As an Enrolled Agent I negotiate and do battle with the

---

[1] *All names and many of the details in previously unpublished stories have been changed.*

IRS as appropriate, essentially walking in clients' shoes through the audit and collections process. As a Certified Financial Planner licensee, I organize and integrate the jumbled fragments of clients' financial lives, including tax strategies, investments, retirement, estate planning and insurance for risk management. I use all available tools to assist clients in the production, maximization and preservation of income and capital.

I previously took this view further than have many, when I recognized the difficulty people have in producing income when they dislike their work. I became certified to administer the Myers-Briggs Type Indicator®, which helps determine natural personality style and perception, judgment and skill preferences. I also learned Temperament Theory which, describing core needs and values, define one's source of self-esteem. These had turned into powerful tools in assessing clients' innate income producing talents and skills. I had helped to redirect some clients' entrepreneurial and professional energies. Creating long-term satisfaction in this manner often led to substantial increases in income.

It was quickly becoming apparent that my early understanding of substance addiction could prove to be an even more powerful tool to help clients. I had observed several addicts seriously impacting non-addicts in financially devastating ways. The damage was tornado-like, causing some with whom they came in contact utter financial ruin, yet only marginally affecting or even skipping others. This recognition was to blossom into the single most helpful instrument for the protection of income and savings that I have ever found. While failing to choose a life's work in which they are truly happy can adversely impact their own financial lives, they often self-correct or, when the lack of congruity is pointed out, are thrilled to discover where their true talents lie. Addicts, I learned, were incapable of recognizing the need to change behavior. They negatively impacted both their own and the lives of others without the latter even being aware they had become victims.

Unlike natural disasters such as tornadoes, which complete their damage within minutes or hours, substance addiction can last decades, totally unrecognized by even those living with it day and night. While natural disasters can be insured against, there is no insurance against the random financial and psychological devastation caused by substance addicts.

I draw upon my own experience, having lived with an addict/father for 20 years. More significantly, I later became romantically involved for 3 years with a beautiful and highly intelligent woman who turned out to be an addict. After barely surviving that relationship, I was determined not to let it happen again. To better understand the woman, who (up to that time) was the greatest love of my life, I began attending Alcoholics Anonymous (AA) meetings. I ended up going to hundreds of 12-step meetings (both AA and Al-Anon, for spouses and other significant persons of alcoholics), speaking with dozens of recovering alcoholics and reading all the books on the subject that I could find.

Unintentionally, I expanded the scope of my tax and financial counseling practice to help clients understand what is often the origin of their financial (and non-financial) nightmare. I began assisting clients and friends in sidestepping the abusive behavior of substance addicts. The motivation to write this book evolved out of my success in assisting clients, many with experiences similar to mine yet with little or no understanding of their cause. Perhaps most profoundly, the drive came from a desire to help addicts, who are generally wonderful individuals in sobriety. I slowly began to realize that addiction is one giant paradox: that to help addicts, recovering addicts and non-addicts alike must uncompromisingly disenable. Yet to do this, we must first learn to recognize the practicing addict. This book was expressly written not only to enlighten others how to identify likely addicts, but also to guide in helping the addict "bottom out" far earlier than he otherwise might.

At least 1 out of 10 adults is a practicing substance addict. These addicts affect most of the population at any point in time. When I see signs of addiction, I have learned to be more suspicious and inquisitive. Several minutes into preparing Lori's return, I remembered she had lent money to a business partner. The partner had also been a client of mine and I had a hunch she hadn't filed tax returns for a couple of years, at least not through me. This pattern of extreme procrastination is a sign of chaos frequently found in the lives of substance addicts. Since a bad debt can sometimes be deducted as a capital loss, I asked how the loan repayment was going. I watched an outwardly calm, serene lady, become enraged. She ranted, "I lent her $100,000 over the last several years, totally trusting and believing in her. She isn't working hard enough to ever pay me back and acts like she doesn't even owe me the money!" "Lori," I said, "there's your alcoholic."

Now granted, there are some non-addicts who don't file tax returns for years at a time (or repeatedly file after extension deadlines). There are others who borrow large sums of money they never re-pay. But when the two are combined, a pattern of financially irresponsible behavior emerges. I have found through experience that the likelihood of addiction substantially increases with each additional irresponsible action. Lori looked at me quizzically and said, "She drinks a few glasses of wine every night...." I indicated that many recovering alcoholics report that they drank only wine and only at night, while others made sure that no one else saw the extent of use. Some create a far greater level of intoxication by combining the drug alcohol with prescription pills or illegal drugs, neither of which is readily observable. I explained it's not necessarily the amount consumed, but rather the relationship a person has with the substance and how it affects his life, behaviors and character that really matters.

Those who have a relationship with substances engage in bizarre, destructive and often unethical or criminal acts. These are due to distorted perceptions caused by the effect of the chemical on the brain. Distorted perceptions, by definition, result in impaired judgment. Impaired judgment in turn generates observable phenomena. This includes egocentric self-centered behavior,[2] an unshakable belief that the substance is not the source of the addict's problems and an all-consuming effort to insure access to his drugs. The bizarre and criminal actions can occur even while stone cold sober or temporarily abstinent. This is due either to brain injury from chronic use or the need to set the stage for such use. One of the great paradoxes of the affliction is that irrational behavior occurs randomly, whether using or not. This can make addiction difficult to identify, particularly in the early stages.

Putting other pieces of the puzzle together, Lori became reasonably certain her partner and best friend of 20 years was an alcoholic. She recognized the "Jekyll and Hyde" nature of the affliction, realizing the irresponsible and self-centered alcoholic was not the person Lori knew lay underneath and loved. I offered some suggestions on protecting herself from further financial abuse, including terminating the partnership in a tax-advantaged manner.

A few weeks later Lori called to thank me. She told me that she had been unable to sleep for two years without waking at 2 or 3 a.m., furious and despondent over the fact that her "best friend" shopped when she should have been working for the partnership and saving to repay her debts. Having identified and, more importantly, explained the problem, she told me she was now able to let it go, knowing she would likely never be repaid. For the first time in years, she said she was able to sleep through the night, feeling as serene and accepting of the unfortunate situation as one could be.

There were numerous and varied occasions where I found myself identifying practicing substance addicts by recognizing a pattern of behavior, even in people with whom I had little or no contact. A husband and wife client, Ephram and Nan, were both recovering alcoholics and illegal substance addicts with (supposedly) 10 years sobriety. I hadn't seen either since they had moved away several years earlier, but continued to prepare their tax returns by mail. Nor had I spoken with Ephram since the move, Nan having been my contact. I asked her how he was. "Oh, fine," Nan replied, but then confided in me that they had been arguing lately over petty things. He lost his temper more easily and seemed to be needling, even belittling her. I asked if he was using again, by this time realizing that a recovering addict not practicing the steps of the 12-Step Program

[2] *The ego's role in substance addiction is masterfully explained by James Graham, "The Secret History of Alcoholism," Rockport, MA: Element Books, 1996.*

might very well be. "Of course not," she replied too quickly, "he's fine, clean and sober."

Changing subjects, we discussed her business for a few minutes. Then Nan made another comment about her husband's behavior that justified my initial question. She told me Ephram was not keeping promises, including ones made to Nan and their daughter. Believing a recovering addict keeps promises and stays honest if sober, I asked, "Are you sure he's not using?" Irritated, Nan responded, "Of course not! I live with the man and I'm a recovering addict myself! I know what to look for—he's clean!" Realizing I had pushed too far, I said OK and got back to her half of the tax return.

Obviously, my questions about Ephram's sobriety must have gotten Nan thinking, because she then admitted that he was buying luxury items she felt they couldn't afford. They were having a tough enough time just making the house payment. Here was a possible financial sign of the impaired judgment of the practicing addict. Concerned, I told Nan, "If Ephram is using again he'll hide it, since if you find out, he knows you'll leave him. This would end his game, since you're his psychological and sexual enabler. You know how addicts lie, cheat, steal and manipulate; you know they can sell ice to Eskimos. I could be wrong, but I think if you take another look, you'll find tangible proof that he's using." Sure enough, two months later she called to tell me he was discovered using uppers, downers and alcohol right under her nose, apparently for some time. Knowing that addiction affects every area of one's life, she felt that for her and her child's safety (and sanity) she had to give Ephram two choices: proven sobriety or the loss of his family. He made his choice. She left.

I realized that identifying active addicts by simply observing behaviors was not something others were doing. I began "diagnosing" addiction. When I shared my opinion with the non-addict victim, I was often met with disbelief, only to be told days, weeks or months later that my diagnosis was correct. I began seeing great significance and value in "diagnosing" addiction in protecting non-addicts from serious financial, psychological and sometimes physical harm.

I also recognized that many only gave lip service to "tough love." This requires refusing help for the addict in any way. It pays homage to the drunk who explains, "Those who helped me on my feet from the floor of the bar didn't help me. Those who stepped over me, did." It is difficult at best to truly give "tough love" of this magnitude and nature to someone we care about, without understanding the nature of addiction. We must learn how it distorts perceptions and impairs judgment, which explains why the addict is incapable of responding to anything other than what is here referred to as "uncompromising" tough love.

Chances are, you have had at least a brush with a substance addict without even knowing it. If you weren't seriously impacted, you were lucky.

However, many have been, without knowing the source of the impact. You may have been seriously injured psychologically, physically or financially and never realized the perpetrator of the damage was an addict. You may have gotten involved with someone who initially had every wonderful quality you dared hope for in a spouse, employee, tenant, landlord, employer or partner. You may have grown up with an addict, or parented a wonderful child who mysteriously turned against you, often in his or her teen years.

You saw all the good sides to this person you thought you knew and loved. For myself, I saw the best in both my father and Patricia, my fiancée. I had no idea what to make of increasingly bizarre behaviors of my relatively innocuous alcoholic father, nor the truly destructive behaviors in the woman who had become a central part of my life. I watched people gravitate toward her, and marveled how she could make friends with practically anyone. She was (when clean and sober) knowledgeable, caring, effective and efficient at her work. I fell in love with this woman who then slowly morphed into a monster created by her drugs. I would come home to a clean house and a hot meal. This slowly changed to a dusty home and dinner beginning later and later. Soon, there was food all over the kitchen with dinner at 10 p.m. and eventually no dinner at all, with food in other areas of our home being carted away by ants. The care and love I experienced progressively degenerated into unreasonable, irrational and hateful behaviors. The deterioration was just slow enough that I didn't initially make the connection to her use of alcohol and other drugs.

Many of you have experienced the same, slow change. You had already fallen in love, or become their friend and were unable to make sense of actions that contrasted sharply with their earlier style. Some of you finally made the connection between this and their drug of choice. You might have attempted to control the use of the substance, pouring it down the drain or flushing it down the toilet. You may have been physically abused for daring to interfere, even though you knew that the use of the drug was ruining the lives of the addict and everyone connected. What you may have missed was that their use of the substance is not the same as yours. Theirs is addictive; yours is not.

Have you ever hired a trusted employee who slowly began making mistakes that were covered up by co-workers? As the errors continued and blame was shifted, the work relationships deteriorated. Did you hire workplace psychologists who just could not identify the source of the problem? Were you perplexed as those problems escalated, even after firing several other employees? Have you ever had to issue a large refund, or has a customer, due to another person's errors for which you took responsibility, sued you? Or, as a co-worker, did you protect someone who was "having problems," only to find <u>yourself</u> demoted or fired? Have you worked with someone who cancels appointments, extends his lunch hour, misses deadlines or clearly wastes material and resources and when criti-cized, exhibited bursts of exaggerated or inappropriate emotions? You may have been dealing with an addict.

Have you been involved in an accident, only to have the other party lie, resulting in your insurance rates going through the roof? Have you been victim to a crime of violence or theft by someone you knew and, like the little boy who says, "Oh, my brother would never do such a mean thing," you were stunned when the crime was committed? When the inevitable apology came on bended knee, did you believe him? If so, you may have just enabled an addict and insured that you would be violated again.

Because we've never been given the tools to diagnose addiction, we would have no idea the perpetrator was an alcoholic or other substance addict and no understanding of the long-term consequences of addiction. James Graham, an expert on alcoholism, learned the hard way, as I did. In his groundbreaking book, "The Secret History of Alcoholism," Graham reports that another alcoholism author and counselor, Reverend Joseph Kellerman with the National Council on Alcoholism, thinks it takes the average spouse nine years "to tentatively diagnose alcoholism."[3] Think about it. If it takes that long for someone who lives, breathes and raises children with the addict, it may take 20 or 30 years for the uninitiated to tentatively diagnose addiction in friends or business associates.

Instead of nine years, one of the goals of this book is to teach how to identify addicts within days or weeks. Only then can we avoid the finan-cial disasters and heartbreaks resulting from getting tempted into relation-ships, contracts and friendships by "people of the Jekyll and Hyde vari-ety." The uncompromising tough love referred to earlier is, in fact, the only kind that can be offered addicts. All these suggested actions, how-ever harsh they may seem, are directed at bringing back the real person.

Alcohol and other drugs are not, in and of themselves, bad. Nor are addicts terrible people. <u>Alcoholism</u> and other drug <u>addiction</u> often lead to criminal, unethical, destructive, insane and horrifying behavior by the per-son we may know or love. **It is absolutely essential to understand that we're dealing with a chemical, not a person.** We cannot trust or reason with a chemical.

Historians should understand the role that addiction may play when interpreting events. Biographers would do well to become more cognizant of the cause and effect relationship between addiction and chaos in their subject's life, in order to offer an accurate portrayal of that person. But most important, <u>we</u> must comprehend the role of addiction in understand-ing the behaviors of those around us.

Wait a minute, you might be asking, what made this guy an expert in

[3] *Graham, Ibid., p. 28-29.*

addiction? He's not a licensed therapist or doctor, or even a recovering addict! You're right. My experience instead lies in the observations of my life, both professional and personal. Professionally, I've prepared over 15,000 tax returns, viewing financial details that few are privileged to see. I've had the opportunity to observe a high correlation between financial difficulties and substance addiction, something that may seem intuitively obvious, but only when we consider just the addict. The more perverse and destructive effects have been not to the addict so much as to those with whom he comes in contact (family, friends, employers, etc.).

This book is an attempt to make sense of man's most destructive affliction — substance addiction. It affects the physical, psychological, spiritual, social and financial health[4] of the addict and everyone else. It is reported by some in the health care industry, as much as half the health costs of the entire country result from substance addicts' overdoses, accidents and some 350 secondary diseases attributable to substances.[5] These effects have gone largely unmentioned or seriously understated. This is something believed to be a glaring omission in the area of income creation and growth, not to mention preservation of capital at both the individual and social level. Doctors and financial advisers alike have not been trained in this area.

My hope is to help improve the understanding of what may be the single greatest cause of family and business break-ups. Addiction may even be capable of destroying entire cultures and forcing others to remain in a relatively primitive condition. The connection will also be made between the affliction and perhaps 80% of all crime, including virtually all domestic violence.

The connection to financial disaster may be somewhat less, perhaps in the area of 50%, only because numerous other variables are present. These include the "creative destruction" of market forces (for example technological breakthroughs and competitive pressures) as well as government regulations capable of wiping out businesses and even rendering entire industries obsolete. Traffic fatalities too, have causes other than addiction, such as road and weather hazards, reducing substance-related deaths due to accidents to about 50%. This can also be said for financial problems resulting in bankruptcy. Bankruptcy attorneys report that as many as half of all bankruptcies are related to substance addiction in the debtor or close person in whom the debtor held trust.

There are many books on both recovery from addiction and recuperat-

---

[4] *Certified Alcoholism Counselor Terence Gorski calls it a "bio-psycho-social disease." I see it in slightly broader form as a "bio-psycho-social-financial affliction."*
[5] *Toby Rice Drews, "The 350 Secondary Diseases/Disorders to Alcoholism," South Plainfield, NJ: Bridge Publishing, 1985.*

ing from close relationships with addicts. There isn't one, however, by a layperson for the layperson that teaches the non-addict to recognize addiction and avoid or disentangle oneself from financial involvement with addicts. We hope to fill this void. We also offer something believed to be a unique guide to recovery, integrating spirituality with science.

But first, you need to identify a few of the possible addicts in your life. The quiz that follows provides an indication of possible substance addiction and will be fully described and explained later. Take a moment now to answer these questions regarding someone in your life who may have caused you the sort of problems we've just described. As you continue reading, you may wish to think back to this person and refer to this indicator. Please note that answering "yes" to one or more questions does not automatically make someone a substance addict.

Figure 1 - The Thorburn Substance Addiction Recognition Indicator -Short Version
For use by the non-addict to protect himself

	YES	NO
1. Does s/he smoke?		
2. Has s/he had *recurring* financial difficulties?		
3. Does s/he have loose sexual morals, including serial adultery?		
4. Are there other non-substance compulsions dangerous to self or others, including gambling, sexual or compulsive eating disorder?		
5. Does s/he have *intense* mood swings, erratic behavior or indications of any psychological disorder or mental illness? *		
6. Are others *frequently* overly cautious, "walking on eggshells" around him or her?		
7. Does s/he have a *pervasive* "the rules don't apply to me" attitude? *		
8. Is s/he a *supremely* good liar? *		
9. Has s/he made false accusations with malicious intent? *		
10. Are there any signs of a *massive* over-inflated ego?		
11. Has s/he been convicted of any felony?1*		
12. Should s/he have been convicted of any felony?1*		
13. Does s/he have *severe* problems at work and/or home due to his/her behavior?		
14. Does s/he engage in destructive behaviors that others *often* cover up? *		
15. Does s/he *habitually* blame others for his/her circumstances? *		
16. Has s/he ever pushed others into committing crimes/unethical behavior? **		
17. Is s/he *often* belligerent or nasty, or *frequently* engage in intimidation tactics to get his/her way in seemingly unimportant matters? *		

	YES	NO
18. Is s/he *often* extremely sarcastic in a mean-spirited way, or *regularly* belittling of others? *		
19. Does s/he engage in *repeated* verbal or physical abuse? *		
20. Have there been *recurring* promises to "never do it again," whatever "it" may be?"**		
21. Does his/her family have a history of substance addiction?		
22. Is there now (or was there ever) a high tolerance to alcohol?		
23. Does s/he frequently have red or glassy eyes, or dilated or constricted pupils?		
24. Have you found "paraphernalia" that s/he insists is a friend's? *		
25. Does s/he frequently drink champagne, martinis, or hard liquor mixed with soda? *		
26. Does s/he *often* drink heavily before eating? *		
27. Has s/he ever said, defiantly regarding any substance, "I can stop any time I want?"**		
28. Does s/he hide or minimize the extent of use of any substance? **		
29. Does s/he ever push others to drink or use other drugs? **		
30. Does s/he have drinking or drug "buddies?"		
31. Does s/he gulp alcoholic beverages?		
Totals		

*= Any behavior which in and of itself points to what is believed to be a high (over 50%) probability of substance addiction in either the person or close other.

**= Any behavior which in and of itself points to a virtual certainty of substance addiction in that person.

1= For our purposes, felonies do not include "victimless crime" which are those neither party to the "crime" wants to report to the police. However, "victimless" does not mean harmless.

Even 2 or 3 of the non-asterisked "yes" answers should cause to to look for addiction. If more than 3 are answered "yes," there is a high probability of either active *substance addiction, or in the case of the recovering addict, imminent relapse. However, if questions 22 through 31 are answered in the negative, there may be a non-substance related mental disorder and/or severe codependency. While at first a codependent may be confused for an addict, when any 6 or more of these questions are answered "yes," along with one affirmative answer fropm the last 10, there is usually confirmation of substance addiction.*

2

How Common Are Addicts?

And how dangerous are they?

Substance addicts "inflict great harm on other people, in ways least sus-pected by the average victim....Other diseases...wreck bodies, but no other disorder does as much harm to those who come in contact with the vic-tim."

-- James Graham[6]

Since this entire book is about substance addiction, the term needs to be defined. Substance addiction may be defined as:

The psychological and/or physical dependency on alcohol or other psychoactive drugs, resulting in repeated negative consequences either to oneself *and/or others*, of which the user is incapable of seeing or grasping the magnitude, due to distorted perceptions caused by the substance's action on the brain.[7]

You're probably thinking, huh? What does this mean? It's simple, re-ally. Addicts themselves have problems (or create them for others) and are incapable of connecting these problems (negative consequences) to their use of substances. This is due to the fact that the drug affects the brain of the addict differently than the non-addict. Unfortunately, few observers recognize this, making it difficult at best to estimate the number of alcohol and other drug addicts. However, to help with assigning probabilities of addiction in specific individuals, we need an overall starting point. If we become financially (or otherwise) entangled with an addict, their problem becomes ours and any negative consequences will be shared. If we see a high probability of addiction before we become involved, we can often

---

[6] *Graham, Ibid., p. ix and xv.*
[7] *The psychoactive substances include the legal drug alcohol, prescription drugs (such as Valium, Vicodin and Demerol) and illegal drugs (such as cocaine, metham-phetamines and heroin). For reasons discussed later, tobacco and caffeine are not included.*

avoid the problem.

The number of alcoholics is estimated at between 15 and 30 million in the United States. That's about 7-15% of all adults. Add an additional several million who aren't even counted as alcoholics, but who are addicted to other drugs (legal and/or illegal).[8] Of these addicts, very few are in recovery. According to alcoholism expert Dr. LeClair Bissell, only 10% of alcoholics <u>ever</u> enter any effective treatment program[9] and few stay sober. Another expert, Arnold M. Ludwig, M.D., came to a similar conclusion in finding less than 10% of those in a typical substance recovery program stayed sober for the entire first 18 months after treatment.[10] The Rand Corporation in a 1980 report entitled, "The Course of Alcoholism: Four Years after Treatment," tracked a group of 900 alcoholic men over a 4-year period. Only 15% were in continuous remission the entire time.

Taking these estimates into account, it is reasonable to start with a 10% probability that any person we encounter is a practicing alcoholic or other drug addict. They may appear to be highly functional individuals, since 85% of adult alcoholics and 70% of adult illegal drug users (most of whom, we will find, are likely addicts) hold jobs.[11] Almost 12% of the American workforce reports drinking 5 or more drinks per occasion on 5 or more of the past 30 days.[12] Since alcoholics often minimize the extent of their drinking, it is suggested the aforementioned 10% figure is a conservative one.

Ten per cent may not sound like much, until we add those whom addicts severely affect. According to addicts in recovery, every addict adversely affects 3 or 4 others, at least one in a potentially lethal way. Therefore, at any point in time, 40-50% of the population is negatively affected by at least one substance addict, with 20% (10% addict, 10% addict-affected) seriously so. Those affected often exhibit some of the behavior patterns of the addict that can, in turn, adversely affect others. In the end, practically everyone may be impacted.

Not only that, but as addicts come in and out of non-addicts' lives, one can be affected detrimentally multiple times. The effects of the events associated with an addict can linger a lifetime, even while unaware of the underlying cause of what may have been horrific physical, mental and/or financial abuse. Most crime, for example, is rooted in substance addiction.

[8] *Most in the United States are today probably polydrug users.*

[9] *Graham, Ibid., p. 5.*

[10] *Arnold M. Ludwig, M.D., "Understanding the Alcoholic's Mind," New York: Oxford University Press, 1988, p. 51.*

[11] *National Institute on Drug Abuse, "Research on Drugs and the Workplace," NIDA Capsules, June, 1990, p. 1. (Reported in the National Council on Alcoholism and Drug Dependence, Inc., Fact Sheet, "Alcohol and Other Drugs in the Workplace.")*

[12] *Ibid.*

(For our purposes, crime is defined as violations of person or property, prosecutable or not.) The psychological affects of rape, embezzlement, theft or any other criminal or unethical behavior can be truly devastating. The financial losses are distant seconds when compared with the psychological devastation generated by broken trust and betrayal, not to mention the effect of the truly monstrous addicts such as Joseph Stalin, at the cost of millions of lives.[13]

The connection between crime and addiction is supported by a 3-year study of the 1.7 million prisoners incarcerated during 1996, conducted by The National Center on Addiction and Substance Abuse at Columbia University. They found that "1.4 million had violated drug or alcohol laws, were high when they committed their crimes, had stolen to support their habit, or *had a history of drug and alcohol abuse that led them to commit their crimes*"[14] (emphasis added). There's a good probability that the criminal has a "history of drug or alcohol abuse" if these other factors are present. If there is a history that has resulted in consequences such as incarceration, these individuals qualify under the definition of addiction, since they engaged in repeated chemical use despite negative consequences to themselves or others.

Only 1% of the adult population is incarcerated. About 80% of these are substance addicts, which is a conservative estimate according to recovering ex-con addicts. If substance addicts comprise 10% of the U.S. population, where are the other 9% (90% of all addicts)? Many of those not incarcerated have likely committed crimes, including physical harm, theft, fraud and violations of contractual arrangements for which they haven't been caught or jailed. Many have engaged in other unethical behaviors. Some may have already served time. They may have repeatedly committed violations of others' rights or broken private agreements such as familial, employment, debtor or tenancy arrangements *for which they cannot be prosecuted* but which are (in the broad sense of the term) crimes.

If 80% of all prisoners are addicts, then it is possible that substance addicts commit 80% of all crime. A broader definition of crime can include not only those for which the criminal isn't caught or can't be prosecuted, but also seriously unethical behavior that can adversely affect the lives of others. This hypothesis will be supported in discussing the nature of addiction and its effects. The focus will be primarily on the devastating results of the distorted perceptions of reality, impaired judgments and ego inflation symptomatic of the disease, which can lead to financial and other

---

[13] *Graham makes an incontrovertible case for Stalin's alcoholism, Ibid., pp. 155-187. Numerous friends who are former Soviet citizens confirm the diagnosis.*
[14] *The New York Times, Christopher S. Wren, "Drugs cited as major factor in crime," January 9, 1998.*

abuse. It will be further supported by stories of such abuse.

We all know that severe addicts live on Skid Row, die from cirrhosis of the liver, or kill others in automobile accidents. Few, however, recognize the countless other disasters for which addicts are so often responsible prior to this latter stage, because the signs of early-stage addiction are rarely noted. This is when the addict, functioning and competent, often commits crimes. He may also be the world's greatest salesman. He might engage in unethical behavior, such as serial adultery. Yet hardly anyone identifies him as an addict.

We often think they are only suffering momentary lapses in judgment when committing petty thefts, embezzlement and adultery (or falsely accusing others of such). When they psychologically and physically abuse their spouses and children, it is easy to think they'll get better if we only try to understand them or give in to whatever demands they make. We fail to connect these lapses to a drug addiction. Yet, observe one who physically abuses another or engages in patently irresponsible behavior, such as allowing a child to play video games in a casino at 3 a.m. so the adult can gamble; one likely observes the impaired judgment of an alcoholic or other drug addict. Repeated cheating on or yelling at the spouse and children for no apparent reason is one manifestation of an addict's inflated ego. If he is an addict, we are witnessing not a person but a chemical and its effects on the brain. If we understand addiction in its earliest stages, we can figure out why the unpredictable behavior of the addict never (or only temporarily) gets better, until there is abstinence and recovery.

Even if you don't think you know any alcoholic-addicts, anyone who does much driving regularly sees the effects of the addict's impaired judgment. Few know the regularity of which 5-10% of the population live and drive under the influence. Out of every 500 to 2000 incidences of driving under the influence, only one is caught and prosecuted for Driving While Intoxicated (DWI, or Driving Under the Influence, DUI).[15] Since the average addict is estimated to drive about 80 times per year while intoxicated,[16] he will get caught only once every 6 to 25 years, hardly an adequate deterrent. In a study conducted in Florida, 78% of traffic violators with a Blood Alcohol Content (BAC) over .10 per cent (legally drunk in all states, 16 of which now have a lower threshold at .08 per cent) were not even identified by the ticketing officer as DUI. According to this and other studies (in which researchers administered breath tests after officers had completed their investigations), more than 3 out of 4 people driving under the influ-

---

[15] *U.S. Department of Transportation, "DWI Detection and Standardized Field Sobriety Testing: Student Manual," Oklahoma City, OK.: National Highway Traffic Safety Administration, 1995, p. II-3.*
[16] *Ibid.*

ence and stopped by police officers for other moving violations were not suspected of DUI.[17]

Are these same individuals, who repeatedly violate other drivers' rights, just as likely to violate the rights of others when not driving? In my experience and by the testimony of almost every recovering addict, the answer is yes. They lie and we don't catch them. They cheat and they are not found out. They steal and we have no idea that anything was taken or who the culprit was. If they are caught (one out of 500 times?) the inevitable apology leads to forgiveness and the behavior is repeated. One of the traits of addiction that makes it especially difficult to identify is that the behaviors are erratically destructive. Until latter stage addiction sets in, we may see a productive, wonderful and apologetic human while between drinks or uses. Furthermore, we are not even looking for a connection to drugs, due to the belief that addiction is a question of underlying character.

Few are aware that possibly several friends and co-workers are substance addicts. We often are no more conscious of the violations of our rights and unethical behavior that occur right under our noses than we are of the addict driving in our midst. If we are aware, we are no more likely to connect the behaviors to substances than the arresting police officers who fail to identify a DUI. We have no knowledge of the severe price paid by the non-addict due to the addict's behavior, because it is so often hidden. We're simply not looking for addiction, because we don't expect to find it.

This non-recognition of addiction is not due to denial, as commonly believed. There is an almost complete ignorance of the appearances, symptoms and effects of addiction, particularly in its early stage. Alcoholic charm, friendliness and a wonderful wit lure us into romantic and financial relationships. Having known the addict during clean and sober moments, we later find it difficult to extricate ourselves from his clutches. It is hard to understand the addict is not the same person we thought we knew. We're not taught to identify addicts in school; instead, we learn that anyone can "just say no to drugs." It's sanitized and euphemized for adults in the media and polite society, where we're told, "John would be fine if only he didn't drink so much." Addiction has rarely been accurately portrayed in the movies or television, which often glorify the use of alcohol. Yet this early stage of addiction is when the addict is most dangerous to others physically, psychologically and financially.

We generally don't think that anyone with a job could be an addict. Lori's partner in the opening story was not on Skid Row or in jail. The partner has since gone on to conning others into lending her even more

---

[17] *Ibid., p. ll-4.*

money. She can't be prosecuted for theft, since technically, she hasn't stolen the funds. Yet, what else can it be called when she asks for loans with repeated promises to repay and doesn't? She was competent in early stage addiction, having built a reputation for good work. Haven't many of us said to ourselves, "Oh, she's in trouble just for now. If I help her out, she'll go on to do great things. I <u>know</u> she'll pay me back?" This is what my client Lori said to herself, having never been taught that these are some of the early signs of addiction. We will see that addicts exhibit such symptoms early, which can be used to protect our pocketbooks and mental health and, in the process, prevent us from enabling the addict.

Like Lori's partner, there are countless others who can't be prosecuted, since proof of intent (required to successfully prosecute many crimes) is hard to come by. My Significant Other addict, Patricia, was no exception. I paid for her children's private education <u>and</u> lent her money, believing she was a recovering addict struggling to properly raise two children. Little did I know she had relapsed, thereby lessening my chances of ever being repaid (not to mention the odds of her children benefiting from a good education). Due to the practical inability to prove intent and the fact that I voluntarily lent her money or spent it on her behalf, the non-repayment was a crime of false pretense, difficult to prosecute. Her drinking was, of course, perfectly legal, even though I never would have provided financial support had I known of her relapse and better understood the nature of addiction.

Although the drinking was legal, the behaviors resulting from the alcohol were often not. Not only did she drink and drive, worse yet, her children were sometimes in the car. She was involved in at least 6 accidents (3 quite serious) in just 2 years. Yet not one officer tested her for sobriety. No wonder I failed to pay heed to the now apparent clues; not even police suspected insobriety. This is not to demean the officers, because the ability of the practicing addict to con is exceeded by no other. It is unfortunate that all parties to a crash are not viewed with suspicion for possible DUI and tested accordingly. Patricia sued the other parties in two of the accidents. They had no idea she should have been held (in my opinion) for contributory negligence in at least one of the accidents (I believe she was high as a kite at the time).

Her children were adversely affected by the addiction. Besides risking their lives by driving with them under the influence, she tolerated exceedingly poor behavior on their part and even drank hard liquor and smoked dope with her young son. This poor behavior made finding a sitter for any period of time we wanted to ourselves an almost impossible task. Not only were her children not removed by Child Protective Services (CPS), she convinced them that everyone else inflicted psychological damage. She and the children consecutively trashed several residences, causing $5,000-$10,000 in damage at each. If you're a landlord, try prosecuting a tenant for such vandalism, especially if the tenant is a single mom who tells confabulated tales of woe, with children who have been taught to support such stories. She was not caught or prosecuted for child abuse, child endangerment, using illegal drugs, driving under the influence, vandalism, appropriating funds under false pretenses or any other crimes. If the average drunk is caught for DUI only once in 500 or 2000 times, the same may hold true for these other criminal behaviors.

She was among the (approximately) 80% of non-recovering addicts holding jobs. She was further financially enabled by her parents and, of course, myself. She did not experience the consequences of her criminal and unethical behavior. That is the reason she didn't seek recovery.

At the very least, we are all indirectly affected by addicts' behaviors. The damage one addict inflicts can, in fact, be monumental and injure practically all of us. Regardless of the police officers' behavior, Rodney King was high on alcohol and other drugs when he led them on a 100-mph car chase. When finally stopped, he violently resisted arrest.[18] Entire sections of Los Angeles burned to the ground, a billion dollars in property damage resulting due to one man's using, drinking and driving. He has since been ordered to enter an alcoholism treatment program due to repeated instances of legal trouble while under the influence. In the meantime, the results of such addicts' behaviors are reflected in our insurance rates and higher taxes for police, prisons and public health. It is possible that not only civil disturbances, but also even entire wars between countries have been caused (at least partly) by the behavior of alcoholics and other drug addicts.

Who is to say how Adolf Hitler might have turned out, had his father, Alois, not been a severe alcoholic. This may have contributed to Adolf's personality flaws. While being the son of a particularly deranged alcoholic could explain his incredibly destructive behaviors, according to a compelling study by psychiatrist Leonard Heston, M.D. and Renate Heston, R.N.,[19] Hitler himself became an amphetamine addict by 1937. This better explains his increasingly bizarre and reckless behaviors and willingness to take extraordinary risks. At the very least, this may have changed the course of WWII and contributed to (if not caused) the Holocaust. Hitler's biographer Albert Speer, in an introduction to the Hestons' study suggested, "It may be that amphetamine injections induced the recklessness which led him to run amok faster and faster...."[20]

According to alcoholism expert James Graham, Joseph Stalin was clearly

---

[18] *The videotape was edited by local television station KTLA, "to eliminate footage of Mr. King charging at the arresting officers," according to The Economist, March 14, 1998, "The Economist Review," p. 4.*

[19] *Leonard L. Heston, M.D., and Renate Heston, R.N., "The Medical Casebook of Adolf Hitler," New York: Stein and Day, 1980.*

[20] *Ibid., pp. 19-20. See the appendix for a brief synopsis of the Hestons' work.*

an alcoholic and responsible for the murder of at least 25 million fellow Soviets and a reign of terror lasting almost 30 years. Not just a fanatic or sociopathic actor shot Lincoln. John Wilkes Booth was an alcoholic-actor, while police officer John Parker's "need for a drink on the night of the assassination was so strong that he deserted his post outside the President's box, left the theater and went to a bar. When Booth left *his* bar and crept up the stairs leading to the President's box, John Parker wasn't there to challenge him."[21] Like Lincoln, fatally affected by two alcoholics, we have all been harmed to an extent difficult to fathom without understanding the action of the drug on the brain of the addict.

[21] *Graham, Ibid., p. 118.*

3

A Genetic Foundation

The creation of the bizarre

"Since the alcoholic is not going to have any spontaneous insight, and since the disease makes approach so difficult, it is crucial that the persons close to an alcoholic understand the nature of the problem."

— Vernon Johnson[22]

There is a physiological reason why addicts cannot stop drinking and why it so severely alters their psychological makeup. One reason is, they do not physically process alcohol the way non-addicts do. While not a classic disease in terms of the transmission of germs, it can be likened to diabetes. These result from a genetic predisposition. In the case of diabetes there is an inborn inability to properly process sugar. Improper processing of alcohol leads to alcoholism. It's possible that a genetically based shortage of various "feel good" neurotransmitters, leads to addiction in general. The difference is, while all of us must have sugar (or food that can be converted to glucose), no one needs alcohol and few need other psychoactive drugs.

The AA Big Book calls alcoholism an "affliction," although the founders of AA called it a disease in other communications. It is now recognized as a disease by some outside AA, albeit half-heartedly, while others remain unconvinced. A 1984 American Medical Association survey of physicians revealed that 80% of doctors believe alcoholism is not a primary disease, but instead symptomatic of a psychiatric disorder. Dr. LeClair Bissell sees us "groomed from childhood to believe that alcoholism is not really an illness, but is instead a sign of weakness. We [doctors] feel less that we are

---

[22] *Vernon E. Johnson, "I'll Quit Tomorrow," San Francisco, CA: Harper and Row, 1980, p. 5.*

diagnosing a disease than that we are accusing the patient...."[23]

What matters most is that there is agreement on its initial treatment by those in a position to help the addict. Uncompromising tough love is the treatment required before any other is possible. This is true regardless of whether or not it is believed to be a disease.

Though irrelevant in terms of determining the initial treatment, the disease theory is helpful in correctly diagnosing addiction. Without this, we can't even begin to treat the addict. There are clues to addiction that would not likely exist were it not a disease. For example, we would not expect rates of addiction to vary among those of differing ancestry, certainly to the degree we observe, were it not genetic. Nor would we expect psychopathological disorders to clear up, which we will show usually occurs once the addiction is arrested.

It's also essential that those providing longer-term treatment recognize it as a disease. This is important for at least two reasons. One, the care provider can watch for reappearance of symptoms, indicating relapse. Two, if it is treated as a character defect (or some other moral weakness), a recovering addict may think he can drink or use again. There seem to be a few out of every thousand who may be able to safely do this. However, we cannot predict who these might be. This is an exceedingly risky position on the part of those who would assist the addict to stay in recovery.

Some may prefer to call addiction a sickness or allergic reaction, like one would have to a bee sting. Just as most can be stung without a reaction, the same can be said for drinking and using other drugs. Some, however, react adversely to both stings and drugs, becoming worse with each experience. The difference is, no one sets out to be stung. As a matter of fact, those who react allergically make a point to avoid being anywhere near bees. On the other hand, the addict purposely drinks and uses, inflicting damage to their brain, their bodies and those closest and most dependent on them. This is not something healthy people set out to do, or continue doing, once these results become apparent. We can shed some light on the reasons for this self-sabotage by exploring the effect the substance has on the brain of the addict.

A clue to this may be found by studying the addict's responses to the questions, "Are you using; if so, how much and is the substance creating a problem in your life?" Chances are, he will never admit to using much (if at all) and will definitely not concede that it's the source of any problems. This is why addiction is called a disease of "denial." However, this word doesn't begin to do this affliction justice. "Denial" implies a willful attempt to not admit to something. This disease causes distorted percep-

[23] *Lucy Barry Robe, "Co-starring Famous Women and Alcohol: the Dramatic Truth Behind the Tragedies and Triumphs of 200 Celebrities," Minneapolis, MN: CompCare Publications, 1986, p. 135.*

tions, leaving nothing to admit. It is <u>far</u> grander than mere denial.

Some, including AA, suggest a self-administered test to determine whether one has a problem with alcohol. The questions are mostly subjective. Anyone desiring to make something besides the disease the culprit for his problems can easily answer, "No, I don't engage in that behavior." That's exactly what the addict will usually do. No addict's ego will allow himself or his substance to be blamed for problems or transgressions against others, until he's ready to get clean and sober. One of the AA questions,[24] "Is drinking making your home life unhappy?" can easily be answered in the negative since, obviously, it's not the substance that makes a home a hotbed of yelling and chaos but rather the nagging spouse, the disruptive children or the barking dog. Another, "Is drinking jeopardizing your job or business?" is likely to be answered, "Of course not! There's trouble because my employer's an idiot, my co-workers are jerks and my subordinates don't do what I tell them to do!" Regardless of the problem, the addict is incapable of seeing his part. This is why it goes well beyond "denial."

We will see that such questions can be answered yes only when the substance addict is allowed to suffer and experience a level of pain unimaginable to the non-addict. The pain of using must become greater than the pain from not using for sobriety to become possible. This suggests that addicts experience immense pleasure from using and literally "feel no pain."

There are two flaws with taking self-administered tests literally.[25] First, due to distorted perceptions that substances create in addicts, they are incapable of seeing they even have a problem. Second, if and when they finally admit to a problem, they will continue to drink as long as the benefits of drinking exceed their perceptions of the costs. Instead, we might want to view such tests as useful for planting a seed in the addict's mind as to the nature of his troubles.

These flaws distinguish addiction from every other disease. Those with other afflictions can generally see a problem once there is an effect on functioning and a diagnosis is made. Addicts cannot. Those diagnosed with other diseases attempt to get well, while the opposite holds true for those with addiction. The addict's ego will not let him believe the diagnosis until multiple crises occur in his life and sometimes, not even then. While

---

[24] From an AA pamphlet, "20 Questions," those used by John Hopkins University Hospital, Baltimore, MD. We will later analyze the questions and turn them on their head for use by the non-addict.

[25] Johnson, Ibid. On p. 21, Johnson states categorically, "It is impossible to find out the subject's behavior by questioning the subject." While he says that such questioning has been abandoned, we will see that some, hoping against hope for honesty, have not abandoned it in practice. Note Johnson's use of the term "impossible." We will find that an addict being honest about his own behavior is, truly, impossible.

the affliction is similar to many genetically based diseases, it is impercep-
tible to those both afflicted and affected, which make it decidedly unlike
others. When he finally does admit to it, he frequently refuses to take measures to get well, since the process of early recovery is so painful.

Even after they admit they are addicts, there are some who still believe
the substance is not the cause of their troubles. One man, by his own admission an alcoholic, was charged with driving under the influence 24 times,
convicted 18 times, sent to prison twice and had his driver's license permanently revoked. He just didn't see alcohol as a problem.[26]

It's not surprising that many refuse to accept the disease concept of alcoholism. As recently as 1989, recovering alcoholic Father Joseph C. Martin
wrote, "The validity of the disease concept is no longer questioned."[27] Yet
in 1995, author Peter C. Mancall wrote, "At the present time most physicians have moved away from what has been termed the 'disease concept of
alcoholism.' Clinicians now generally hold that alcoholism is a behavioral
disorder rather than an illness in a biological sense."[28] Many object to the
idea of calling it a disease because it follows that the afflicted cannot be
held legally or morally responsible for their behaviors.

Yet, the distinguishing characteristic of imperceptibility to the afflicted
requires that the treatment of addiction be a world apart from that of other
diseases. The paradox of the tough-love treatment causes some to believe
addiction is a moral weakness. However, tough love requires the addict to
accept all consequences of the addiction in his actions and behavior. After
all, his disease, in effect, makes the decision to take that first drink and sets
into motion all the subsequent events. He must reach a place where the
decision to overcome the disease is possible, which occurs only by experiencing consequences. This is a libertarian treatment, requiring total responsibility for one's condition.

If it were not a genetic disease, it must be environmental. However,
Psychiatrist Donald Goodwin provided clear and convincing evidence as
to the genetic foundation of the affliction.[29] (You may find yourself wading

---

[26] *"Career drunk driver sentenced to live close to alcohol sources," L.A. Daily News, from the Associated Press, Hillsboro, Ohio, January 4, 1998, regarding 50-year-old Dennis Cayse.*

[27] *Father Joseph C. Martin, "Chalk Talks on Alcohol," San Francisco, CA: Harper and Row, 1989, p. 43.*

[28] *Peter C. Mancall, "Deadly Medicine: Indians and Alcohol in Early America," Ithaca, NY: Cornell University, 1995, p. 5, citing Herbert Fingarette's "Heavy Drinking."*

[29] *Donald Goodwin, M.D., "Is Alcoholism Hereditary?" New York: Ballantine Books, 1988, pp. 98-115, in which the pivotal Danish adoption/brothers studies are reported.*

through the next few paragraphs, but it will be worth it.) Goodwin studied the children of alcoholics adopted by non-alcoholic non-relatives. He found that these children had almost 4 times the rate of alcoholism (18%) as that of a control group of adopted children whose biological parents were not alcoholics (5%). The children of alcoholics group had no exposure to their alcoholic parent after, at most, the first few weeks of life. There were no differences in regard to other types of psychiatric illnesses and life experiences except for incidence of divorce (which was 3 times greater for the children of alcoholic parents).[30] If there was any flaw in this monumental study, it was that it may have understated (perhaps by as much as half) the rate of alcoholics in both groups. The criteria for alcoholism used were the more obvious latter-stage symptoms (compared with early-stage) and the majority of those studied were under 30 years of age. There may have been a significant number of early-stage alcoholics who hadn't yet been identified.

The lower rate of alcoholism among the control group occurred despite the fact that the adoptive parents of that group had almost twice the rate of alcoholism (22%) as the adoptive parents of the biological children of the alcoholic group (12%). This was deemed a coincidence. If environmental influences were to blame for alcoholism, we would predict, in fact, _higher_ rates of alcoholism in the control group and perhaps even double that of biological children of the alcoholic group

Figure 2 – Alcoholism is Genetic

	Rate of Alcoholism of Adopted Child	Rate of Alcoholism of Adoptive Parent
Child of Alcoholic Adopted Out	18%	12%
Child of Non-Alcoholic Adopted Out	5%	22%

If environmental influences such as the rate of alcoholism of the adoptive parent held sway, we might expect the child of the non-alcoholic to be almost twice as likely as the child of the alcoholic to be an alcoholic, or

---

[30] *This was supposedly unrelated to the alcoholism, which is hard to believe. The divorced parties might be found congregated among early-stage addicts in some future study. The addict often exhibits an abundance of "alcoholic charm" during this early stage, along with behavior not so consistently objectionable. Many non-addicts happily marry this "fun-loving, charming and witty" addict.*

about 33% instead of just 5%.

In phase 2 of the study, Goodwin compared sons of alcoholics raised by their alcoholic families with brothers who had been adopted and raised by unrelated families (in whom the rate of alcoholism was closer to the 12% figure). If environmental influences such as alcoholism in the custodial parent were controlling, we might expect a 100% rate of alcoholism among sons raised by their alcoholic family and a 12% rate among the brothers raised by the unrelated families, or some such disparity. Instead, there was no difference in the incidence of alcoholism between the two groups of brothers. As Milam and Ketcham point out, these findings shatter the theory that alcoholism is learned behavior or that it has anything to do with environmental influences. What this means is, there would be more alcoholism in the children who are adopted by alcoholics if environment was a factor. Goodwin proved that children adopted from alcoholic parents have a far higher rate of alcoholism than would be expected. This supports Milam and Ketcham's findings that genetics is the determining factor, rather than environment.

Those who scoff at the disease concept may do so out of a deep-rooted desire to hold the addict accountable for his actions. Yet, we will see that such accountability is precisely the treatment necessary for the addict to recover and it is essential that this be recognized by the legal system. In the meantime, the extreme to which opponents of the disease concept argue is amazing. One writer argues that since 82% of the adoptive sons who had a biological alcoholic father were not identified as alcoholics (keeping in mind this study may have used a too-strict criteria for alcoholism), we cannot conclude there is a disease of genetically determined alcoholism.[31] If true, there are no genetically determined diseases, since we might, under this standard, need 100% incidence of inheritance to qualify a disease as genetic.

Now, we are going to hit you with a little technical mumbo-jumbo having to do with the physiological aspects of the disease. It is essential that this be understood, because as Gorski points out, it starts with biology. Please bear with me. By the way, you may find the chart that follows this section helpful.

Here is why there is unquestionably a genetic predisposition. It is, in part, a result of the inability of the liver to process alcohol's poisonous by-product, **acetaldehyde**, into the end-product **acetate** at a normal rate, caus-

---

[31] *Herbert Fingarette, "Heavy Drinking: The Myth of Alcoholism as a Disease," Berkeley, CA: University of California Press, 1988, pp. 52-53.*

ing acetaldehyde to accumulate.[32] On the one hand, acetaldehyde poisons the cells, especially those in the liver, heart and brain. On the other, it keeps the alcoholic partying and feeling fine due to an interaction with the brain's **neurotransmitters** that increase levels of an opiate-like substance called **isoquinolines**. These make the addict feel really good. Because of this, the addict seems to counter the painful effects of the buildup in acetaldehyde and eventual very unpleasant conversion into acetate. The non-alcoholic experiences this transformation into acetate quickly and the isoquinolines don't increase, so the discomfort from alcohol is more immediately felt. The pleasurable feeling from the effect on the brain's neurotransmitters isn't short-circuited by pain in the addict, thereby reinforcing the desire to drink. The feedback mechanism that tells non-addicts to stop and go to sleep, instead tells the addict that in order to feel good, he should just keep on using.

This is related to the fact that drugs induce the release of enormous quantities of the brain amines, especially dopamine, norepinephrine and serotonin. The brain that becomes accustomed to drugs causing increased neurotransmitter activity, eventually forgets how to release these "pleasure enhancers" on its own. This creates the physical need for the drug to provide the pleasurable feeling that the brains of non-addicts provide without chemical additives.

While the other psychoactive drugs are laser-like in their precision, combining with and resulting in the effective release of individual brain neurotransmitters, alcohol combines with many, further complicating the effects of this particular drug.[33] It inhibits **glutamate receptors** by as much as 80% after as few as 2 drinks in the space of an hour (resulting in a Blood Alcohol Content, or BAC, as low as .04 per cent). This leads to relaxation and general sedation, contributing to dis-coordination, one of the many causes of the 20,000-plus alcohol-related traffic deaths per year. (Ironically, this relaxation and sedation is what allows the drunk driver to often walk away unscathed from serious accidents, while the innocent die all around them.)

It also disables a particular glutamate receptor known as the **NMDA receptor**, decreasing the ability to form new memories. Experiments show a 30% reduction in the strength of synaptic connections essential in forming these memories (the technical term is LTP—Long-Term Potentiation) after only a single drink. This stabilizes near 80% impairment at a BAC of

---

[32] *Dr. James R. Milam and Katherine Ketcham, "Under the Influence: A Guide to the Myths and Realities of Alcoholism," New York: Bantam Books, 1983, pp. 35-39. The facts that more of this poison accumulates in alcoholics and that it lasts longer before conversion to acetate may explain many of the numerous secondary diseases and disorders alcoholics are subject to.*

[33] *The following discussion of the neuro-transmitters is adapted from Stephen Braun's brilliant and fascinating "Buzz: The Science and Lore of Alcohol and Caffeine," New York: Oxford University Press, 1996, pp. 49-59.*

.2 per cent (twice the maximum legal limit for intoxication). Since some degree of memory impairment occurs even after a single drink (prior to visible intoxication), observers can be understandably confused. This phenomenon may account for many of the alcoholic's distorted perceptions.

The inhibition of the glutamate receptor effectively interferes with the brain's accelerator, by making it harder for the brain to gain speed. Another neurotransmitter, the **GABA receptor**, is given increased sensitivity by alcohol, which is equivalent to an increase in the sensitivity of the brain's brakes. In other words, both of these are causing the brain to slow down. Are you still with me? Now, check this out. Alcohol binds with the GABA receptors, just as does Valium (and other "benzodiazepines"). The pleasurable feeling of calm that alcohol can provide is similar to the effect of Valium. The reason for the dangerous and deadly multiplicative effect of the alcohol and Valium combination is that they bind to different parts of the GABA receptor, warping the receptor to a far greater degree than either would if acting alone. This is the reason so many addicts take both drugs (they need very little of each for a good high) and why many die from combining relatively small amounts.

Alcohol boosts **dopamine** levels more modestly than amphetamines and cocaine, but enough to provide adequate stimulation to initially offset the depressant effects of the increased sensitivity of the brakes (the GABA receptor) and the disabling of the accelerator (the glutamate receptor). Just as we'll observe massive behavioral changes in the speedball freak (for example, John Belushi), who combines cocaine with heroin (the quicker-acting cocaine providing an initial boost followed by the depressant effects of the slower-acting heroin), we'll see such changes of usually lesser magnitude in the alcoholic.

Alcohol further results in the release of **endorphins**, the body's natural painkillers, thereby causing alcohol to resemble opium and its derivatives morphine and heroin (each of which are simply progressively stronger and more potent forms of opium). Alcohol acts, as well, in a way that is the functional equivalent of boosting **serotonin** levels. This is how Prozac works, alleviating depression and increasing self-confidence. Lab rats that have been bred to prefer alcohol to water have significantly lower levels of serotonin when sober than do rats that do not crave alcohol.

These disparate effects of alcohol should not surprise us, given the paradoxes in the behavior of various alcoholics at different times. Nor should we be shocked that probably most alcoholics, given the opportunity to use other drugs, become poly-drug addicts. They could be searching for the drug that affects the neuro-transmitter that they may innately lack. The use of such drugs further decreases their own natural ability to produce these neuro-transmitters. Addiction in the predisposed usually begins with whatever drug is most readily available: alcohol. The idea that marijuana "leads" to the harder drugs is a myth supported only by the legality and pervasive use of alcohol, which few wish to identify as the first drug of choice. Most substance addicts who move to other drugs continue to use alcohol. Significantly, as we have seen, it doesn't take much alcohol to distort memories and, therefore, perceptions. This may have a lot to do with their willingness to try other drugs which, in the predisposed, leads to addiction to those substances.

Figure 3 – Alcohol Takes a Shotgun Approach; Other Drugs are Laser-Like

	Disables Glutamate	Increases GABA	Boosts Dopamine	Releases Endorphins	Boosts Seratonin
Alcohol	X	X	X	X	X
Sedatives	X				
Valium		X			
Cocaine			X		
Heroin				X	
Prozac					X

Substance addiction is like light in the sense of having two properties and yet having neither. Light appears both as matter and non-matter (waves), while addiction appears both as physical chemistry and non-matter psyche. Having made it this far (whew!), you have seen that addiction has a physical (biological) component. We will now see the effect this has on perceptions (psyche).

Distorted perceptions and impaired judgment

The addict cannot see he has a problem with a substance because his perceptions of reality are distorted. By definition, this results in impaired judgment. The substance initially acts as a pleasure enhancer, providing a super-confident feeling. When problems arise, his distorted level of confidence causes him to view himself in a positive vein, resulting in a vacuum for others to appear in a negative light. In other words, when the addict feels better, you look worse. This fuels his egomania.

The particular distortions addicts experience are of fundamental importance[34] and explain the range of bizarre, destructive, unethical and criminal behaviors. The key distortion is a particularly perverse form of selective memory known as **euphoric recall**, the positive recollection of everything he does. This results in the addict remembering his good behavior but not his bad, or recollecting his poor behavior as being good. He remembers he was "the life of the party" when in fact, he was a blithering idiot; he remembers (and believes) he was driving safely, when the truth is, he was speeding recklessly. He truly believes he is competent at work or at raising children, when he is probably far less capable than he thinks, becoming incompetent in latter stages of addiction. While sober, if he could watch himself under the influence, he might see he has a problem. Unfortunately, few people videotape such events.

Vernon E. Johnson suggests that the distortions created by euphoric recall are the most devastating, "for it is the greatest single factor contributing to self-delusion." Addicts remember every one of their excessive drinking episodes euphorically, always grossly distorting the truth. "There is *no* time when they have been under the influence that they are able to recall accurately, and yet they go on believing firmly *that they remember everything* in complete detail."[35] The results manifest themselves everywhere in the addict's life.

One of the behavior patterns almost always symptomatic of addiction is the blaming of others for all their problems. Many attribute this blame to self-justification or rationalization. However, if the addict remembers that his own behavior is always only good or right and never bad or wrong, how can he be blamed for anything?

This distorted perception results in the belittling and rejection of others. It may even be the cause of hatred of other persons or whole groups. Whenever we observe the outward manifestations of such emotion, we can look to see if it has the distorted perception of euphoric recall at its roots.

The fact that addicts remember everything they did was good and nothing bad (and truly believe it) results in the super-inflated ego and god-like behaviors that James Graham brilliantly describes. Addicts are perfect, or so they think, because they don't remember otherwise. For these reasons video- and/or audio taping episodes of egotistical, nasty or other bizarre behavior can be a powerful tool in a professionally aided intervention.

---

[34] *This is derived from Johnson, Ibid., who beautifully presents, describes and explains the psychological and physiological paths to these distorted perceptions, pp. 35-47. Essential reading by the founder of the Johnson Institute in Minneapolis, MN, specializing in interventions and recovery treatment.*
[35] *Ibid., p. 43*

The addict's perceptions are further distorted by **memory repression**, which are psychologically induced periods of amnesia. Many are accused of having selective memories, but with substance addicts this becomes a high (excuse the pun) art form. He will remember his competencies, but not his failures. He'll remember lending you money, but not you paying him back. Nor will he remember the money you lent him. He'll remember you were late for an engagement once, but not his own numerous late arrivals. He'll remember that time you lost your temper, while he will fail to remember the countless times he lost his. He'll remember your promises, but not his own. We think he's lying, yet how can anyone tell such perfect, believable lies? His memory is faulty due to the poison in the form of acetaldehyde, that causes his brain to malfunction and to the rot that ego-inflation inflicts on his character.

The addict also experiences chemically induced periods of amnesia known as **blackouts**. This is not the same as "passing out." The addict appears to be totally functional, alert and aware of events and what he and others are doing; yet he will never remember anything that occurred. This is not because the events that happened during a blackout are forgotten, but rather because they are simply not stored in the brain. It's as if the NMDA glutamate receptors have all been turned off; there is nothing to recall. A recovering alcoholic friend says she was in a series of blackouts at her university, being high on substances practically every waking moment for a year. This left her, 10 years later, with almost no memory of anything that occurred during that time.

This can get really bizarre when we carry on under the assumption that the addict knows everything we experienced together or discussed, but doesn't. Accusations of lying are made and the madness begins—"Don't you remember I told you!"..."No, I don't remember a thing, you're lying!" When or for how long a blackout will occur is not determinable by measuring the consumption; there may have been very little, resulting in a blackout lasting several days. On the other hand, it may have lasted only minutes even though much was consumed.

If a blackout can occur with very little consumed, why not euphoric recall? Why not memory repression? Why can't an addict prone to violence have something triggered in his poisoned brain that causes him to commit some ghastly act, even murder, with very little of the substance used? This possibility may be pure fantasy, or it may explain much of what brings people into our criminal justice system. It may explain the behaviors of those who drink little, but for whom the drink is pure poison.

Whether the addict fails to remember something due to a blackout or repression, or remembers it incorrectly due to euphoric recall, doesn't really change the results: those around him are dealing with someone who <u>appears</u> to be blatantly lying. The non-addict may thus allow himself to react quite angrily. I, personally, used to become irate when I dealt with those I call "intellectually dishonest." Now I know, most of the people in my past who seemed dishonest really were alcoholics or other substance addicts, suffering from blackouts, memory repression, euphoric recall and ego inflation. Understanding this "reason why" gave me a head start in my own recovery and eventual elimination of anger. Such lies and other behavior on the part of the addict may become easier to deal with in one's own psyche, when it is understood that these are simply the patterns of alcoholics and other substance addicts.

Figure 4 – The Role of Euphoric Recall in Alcoholic Behavior

EUPHORIC RECALL* → Inflated Ego → Degrading of Others→ False Accusations

Inflated Ego →Sense of Invincibility → Reckless Behavior

→ Blaming Others for Own Problems → Belittling

→ "Lying" → Intellectual Dishonesty → Arguments over Actions and Events

→ Blaming Others → Hatred of Others, Both Close Persons and Groups

→ Reinforces Poor Behavior

→ "Little God" Behavior → Lack of Consideration for Others

→ Grandiosity

---

*   *Causes the addict to remember all he does as good or right and nothing as bad or wrong.*

Memory repression, blackouts and euphoric recall explain the distorted perceptions of the addict. These account for what is termed the addict's "denial," seeing what the addict only wants to see, not that which is too painful to acknowledge (including that one even has a problem). "Denial" is an unfortunate choice of words, since it implies a voluntary and willful action and that they really do know differently. As we have seen, they do not. The addict is literally incapable of seeing he has a problem due to the chemically induced alterations of memory and the subsequent generation of ego inflation. Yet, denial is treated as if it were both the crux of the disease and its most important effect. This leads some to believe alcoholics just aren't morally "strong." They "should know" they shouldn't drink or use other drugs.

What some call "denial," is really "distortion." This distortion of reality is far deeper and of vastly greater importance in explaining the affliction. This results in the manifestations that cause others unbearable pain, including an impairment of judgment that impacts every aspect of the addict's life and the many who cross his path.

The distorted perceptions combined with his resulting massive ego explain how and why the addict appears to hate those whom he would love if in his right mind. The appearance is that of creating distractions from his own behavior in order to take the focus off him. Let's remember, he doesn't think he's done anything bad or wrong. So, he cannot believe he is the source of his problems. Therefore, you become the source of his problems, not he; you must be the addict, not he. Underneath, at some subconscious level, he may know the truth about himself. Perhaps such "knowing" occurs in moments of clarity during periods of sobriety. This triggers self-hatred, which taints his view of others, resulting in severe repercussions on those around him.

The addict ego requires that they be bigger and better than everyone else, so they degrade and defile others in order to build themselves up. They may accuse even close persons of vile behaviors. John Nichols, the father of British playwright Beverley Nichols, repeatedly alleged that everyone in his family had syphilis.[36] He made such accusations even when sober. The well-known alcoholic writer, Ernest Hemingway, was openly contemptuous of other writers, calling one a "battle fatigue type." He spoke harshly of another writer, calling him "a liar with the inbred talent of a dishonest and easily frightened angel" and said that he was "behaving like an insecure sexual idiot." He also ridiculed the face of Sinclair Lewis, even while knowing Lewis suffered from a disfiguring skin disease.[37] Sinclair Lewis, an alcoholic in his own right, "ridiculed small-town businessmen in Babbitt, maligned women in Cass Timerberlane, and dozens of barely concealed public figures in Gideon Planish."[38] Another writer, alcoholic William Faulkner, according to an analysis by his brother of his seemingly innocuous portrayal of the fictionalized "Snopses," was really engaging in "'a massive put-down of a whole class of white Southerners.'" Graham points out that Faulkner's "alcoholism-dominated ego needed objects of debasement and ridicule. Rather than ridiculing his family or friends, this

[36] *Graham, Ibid., p. 14.*
[37] *Graham, Ibid., p. 85.*
[38] *Graham, Ibid., p. 90.*

alcoholic writer chose the entire Southern middle class."[39]

The idea that ego inflation causes the belittling and hatred of others holds true even on a personal level. I had long believed my father's racist sentiments stemmed from his alcoholism. Graham's thesis brilliantly explains my father's psychological makeup and perhaps that of millions of others with a racist point of view. Not all racists are addicts, but there are indications that most are or have been severely affected by one. Adolf Hitler (the son of an alcoholic) indulged in his racist manifesto even prior to his amphetamine addiction. A sober and recalcitrant former Black Panther, Eldridge Cleaver, realized, "If people had listened to Huey Newton and me in the 1960s, there would have been a holocaust in this country."[40] A friend of Governor George Wallace reported that "'One drink would set him off on a drunk...(and he) wasn't a very pleasant drunk, either....He became belligerent, wanting to fight anything that moved.'"[41] Although he never seemed to drink much, apparently he stopped completely when he realized, "It will cause him to lose control of himself...and something bad will happen."[42] He died "not drinking," with huge support among Blacks.

Although hatred and racism are bad enough, the addict's distorted perceptions of reality result in so much more. They explain inane arguments, while we think we're discussing issues with someone rational and intellectually honest. Yet, in the face of all evidence, they either really don't remember or what they remember is grossly inaccurate. Even if they are aware, their obsession is to preserve the availability of their substance and their inflated ego at all costs, even to theabandonment of relationships and truth.

It also explains why they eventually become incompetent not only behind the wheel of a car but at work, play, raising children and at life in general. How can it be any other way, when the addict is incapable of self-critical analysis, believing he does nothing wrong? Early on, when describing my view of the effect of the affliction on competence to recovering alcoholics, I'd say, "If 'incompetent' is too harsh a term, then they must be 'less capable,' at work, etc." I was corrected by several. An attorney who lost his license to practice and was rebuilding his life responded, "No, incompetent is correct." Another described how, for years, he managed 80 people, was never late for work, never missed a day and convinced both his supe-

---

[39] *Graham, Ibid., pp. 86-87.*

[40] *"Eldridge Cleaver's Last Gift: the Truth," David Horowitz, The Los Angeles Times, May 3, 1998.*

[41] *Dan Carter, "The Politics of Rage," New York: Simon & Schuster, 1995, p. 104.*

[42] *Marshall Frady, "Wallace," New York: Random House, 1996, p. 81.*

riors and those he managed that he performed 8 hours' work a day. In fact, it was work he could have done by his own sober testimony in an hour.

On the other hand, it explains competency and improved performance in specific areas in the early stages of the disease. Milam and Ketcham state, the only visible difference between the alcoholic and nonalcoholic in the early "hidden" stage of the disease is the "improved performance…when he drinks and a deterioration in performance when he stops drinking."[43] In nonalcoholics, there is improved performance in concentration, memory, attention span and creative thinking (probably due to the quick boost in dopamine levels) with very small amounts of alcohol (under one ounce). However, deterioration quickly sets in, perhaps because of the offsetting effect of the inhibition of the NMDA glutamate receptor (the target of sedatives) and increased sensitivity of the GABA receptor (targeted by Valium).

It is baffling that many great rock musicians, writers and talented actors perform magnificently early in their careers, seemingly despite the extent of their alcohol and other drug use. Ironically, it explains the phenomena we so often see: the rocketing success of the young drug user and the inevitable crash that follows. These are addicts in the first stage of their affliction, the burn-up stage. They move from success to success, varying only in how long the good life lasts. It always ends when the addiction moves into its second and eventual final stages, in which either recovery or death must occur. Nobody has ever adequately explained the stages of addiction to young people, or that while some can use drugs recreationally, others cannot. With current medical technology, we cannot know who is destined to be an addict. They all feel they will be different, able to control the substance, even though in the end, the substance controls them.

Distorted perceptions explain impaired judgment. Before we can judge, we must first perceive. We do this by taking in information through the use of our senses (touch, taste, etc.) and/or the imagination, when we deal with abstractions. We then use these perceptions to form judgments. If our perceptions are distorted, our judgments are based on inaccurate information. For example, if we first distort our taste with an onion, then lick a chocolate ice cream cone, we will likely judge the flavor of chocolate ice cream to be bad. If an addict perceives that you have cheated on him, he not only makes an accusation that is false, but when you deny it, he will judge you a liar. The judgment itself becomes, by definition, impaired, explaining much of the bizarre behaviors of substance addicts. These behaviors can often be readily observable even in people we hardly know and something that can be turned into a powerful tool to protect ourselves from their grotesquely harmful behaviors.

The distortions of reality explain why it is literally impossible for thera-

---

[43] *Milam and Ketcham, Ibid., p. 57.*

pists to work with practicing addicts in any meaningful way. How can we arrive at the truth with the interference of euphoric recall, blackouts and memory repression, each resulting in everyone else being the cause of the addict's troubles? "Getting honest" requires diminished distortions. According to chemical dependency counselors, this can take several years' sobriety, during which time it is of little or no use working with an addict on a therapeutic level.[44] The problem is how can you tell if the addict is truly using, when he's conning the therapist along with everyone else?

Many addicts get sober long enough just for the visit to the therapist. Two high-priced therapists working with my significant addict and me hadn't the foggiest idea she was using. This contributed to a continuation of my enabling her, financially and psychologically, for well over two years longer than if the affliction had been explained at the outset. Had the enabling stopped, earlier recovery might soon have followed, resulting in far less damage to all of us (especially her children). Because they didn't diagnose her addiction, I became the scapegoat for her numerous problems. "You're controlling, you're too harsh, you set too many rules." Yes, when one lives in insanity, one tends to make too many precisianistic (read: picayune) and obsessive rules as over-compensation for the out-of-control nature of living with addicts. The therapists, failing to recognize this predictable reaction of some, gave mine all the excuses she needed to continue using.

Further exacerbating the difficulty the addict has in recognizing his problem, the substance numbs the pain, both physical and psychological. Even if he has a vague sense that the problem may be with him, how can he understand its depths or gain the desire to get clean and sober if he feels no emotional pain, resulting in the commission of yet further acts harmful to others?

This may be one of the factors that keep alcoholics drinking and falling off the wagon. They begin to get sober and remember some of the things they did (while events occurring during blackouts cannot be remembered, repressed memories can). They observe some of the affects of their behavior on close persons or themselves. This causes them to drink again,[45] once more deadening the pain of recognizing their incessant violation of others'

---

[44] *Some therapists may disagree with this assessment. My question is, how can they tell* which *practicing addict therapy might be helping when addicts* all *suffer from distorted perceptions? If they can help a few, that would be grand, but at what price to others who will use the fact they are getting counseling as a weapon against family, friends and co-workers?*

[45] *Susan Powter supports this thesis, in "Sober...and Staying That Way: The Missing Link in the Cure for Alcoholism," New York: Simon & Schuster, 1997, p. 73.*

rights, personal space and their own values.[46]

Other forms of addiction can dangerously affect others. However, the danger from non-substance addicts pales in comparison and scope to the danger posed by drug addicts. Yes, some compulsions (in particular, gambling and sex) may give one the ability to more easily generate false memories and confabulations. However, the numbers of those able to come close to the distortions of substance addicts, without also being one, are quite small. This is due to the biological effects of the foreign chemicals. When these are not ingested, what some call other "addictions" are referred to here as "compulsions." The compulsions that endanger others usually have their roots in substance addiction. In instances where they don't, this book may still be helpful in treating the condition.

There are "addictive types," who have many compulsions. There are many non-mind-altering, non-drug "addicts." These are not necessarily bad. I am, for example, "addicted" to learning. My wife is "addicted" to running. Some might call these hobbies, while others, who would negatively judge the extent to which learning or running is important to us, might consider us "addicts." If these were to seriously interfere with other normal activities and relationships, they might be considered problems, but still it is not addiction, without the vile behavior made so much easier with a substance. The 12-Step Programs state that it is addiction when your life becomes unmanageable. People's non-substance compulsions usually don't get in the way of their lives. Why? Because they're not medicating their brains.

Those who make the suggestion that other compulsions can be generically as dangerous to those around them have missed the point. The substance addict has, through chemically and psychologically induced amnesia and euphoric recall, distorted perceptions of reality. While non-substance addicts can create these distortions, it's so much easier with a drug. Learning and running don't release dopamine and endorphins for nearly as long as substances. More significantly, they don't diminish our brain's natural ability to produce such neurotransmitters.

Since blackouts, euphoric recall and memory repression are the perceptive means that create the insanity, blame, arguing, incompetence and overall impaired judgment, non-substance addiction is not as likely to create such devastation. Inflating one's ego by overpowering and belittling others is difficult without a drug. Destructive behaviors are much easier with distorted perceptions caused by a substance, allowing the addict to more easily engage in self-justification and anaesthetizing himself when he real-

---

[46] *Caroline Knapp points out the paradox: "Alcoholics drink in order to ease the very pain that drinking helps create....You hurt, you drink; you hurt some more, you up the intake." Caroline Knapp, "Drinking: A Love Story," New York: The Dial Press, 1996, p. 189.*

izes what he has done.

Other compulsions are often created, perpetuated or made worse by an actual substance addiction. The most dangerous (gambling, sex and over-spending) are often linked to a drug. This supports the compulsion with distorted perceptions, resulting in cross "addictions." While these compulsions can create mood changes, it's so much easier with the drug.

Relapse prevention specialist Terence Gorski points out that many early recovery addicts substitute (or continue in) compulsive behaviors, including gambling.[47] Recovering alcoholic-gambler Mike Brubaker, who has his own therapy/counseling firm in Casa Grande, Arizona,[48] told me he believes the percentage of gamblers who are active or "recovering"[49] substance addicts is probably about 50%. He sees both substance addicts and compulsive gamblers daily in his practice. Lower estimates I've heard of in the range of 20-30% probably refer only to more obvious latter-stage addicts and/or those in early recovery. Recognizing substance addiction is, as we're beginning to see, difficult in its earliest stages. This may be the reason so many cross-addicted compulsive gamblers are likely not diagnosed as substance addicts.

Treating other compulsions can be complicated by the fact that if psychoactive substances are being used, the primary source of the problem may be overlooked or ignored. Non-addicts may focus on the peripheral compulsive behaviors. The therapist attempting to treat non-substance compulsions enables the addict. He may hop from one compulsion to another, as the chameleon-like symptoms of the primary disease mutate. The primary affliction, psychoactive drug addiction, is frequently left to wreak havoc on the lives of the addict and those around.

Breaking the web of deceit

Ask an alcoholic if he's drinking. The answer will be no, whether he is or isn't. He may even be more convincing if he is drinking. Recovering

---

[47] *Terence Gorski and Merlene Miller, "Staying Sober: A Guide for Relapse Prevention," Independence, MO: Herald House/Independence Press, p. 120.*

[48] *Mike Brubaker with Ken Estes, "Deadly Odds: Recovery From Compulsive Gambling," New York: Simon and Schuster, Fireside/Parkside Books, 1994.*

[49] *The term is used loosely, since substitution of one compulsive behavior for another complicates and interferes with recovery from substance addiction. Gorski (Ibid., p. 124) argues that such behaviors allow the process of relapse to begin; hence, substitutions of compulsions clue us in that the addict is not in good, solid recovery.*

alcoholics and other substance addicts take reluctant pride in the fact that when using they could sell a lie to the devil. All that matters, by their own admission, is that the supply line is open for their next drink or fix. "When we drank," you'll hear at AA meetings, "we were insane. We lied, cheated, stole and manipulated. You couldn't trust us for anything, because all we cared about was our drug — king alcohol or queen cocaine (or other chemical of choice)." There is a compulsion to use in the addict that supercedes all else in their lives.

This clues us in on the methodology we must use to determine whether someone is a practicing addict. We will not get the truth from the addict himself. Instead, we must observe behaviors. When we later learn that someone is a practicing substance addict and look back at his bizarre behavior, we may conclude that if we observe such behavior in another, we may **be** observing an addict. This is elementary science — trial and error. If it behaves like a duck, chances are, it's a duck. With enough observations of similar behaviors, we can ascribe a probability of substance addiction. We can also listen to stories of recovering addicts describing their lives while using in gory detail and, when in good, solid recovery, with brutal honesty. For example, since we've learned that 80% of those who have committed crimes are likely substance addicts, we should be able to conclude that if someone has committed a crime, there is an 80% probability he is an addict. This is also true for those close to us, although it's something we don't want to believe. We might exclaim, "Oh, my Billy, he couldn't possibly be a substance addict!" Such a belief flies in the face of probability theory and reality.

A Schick Chemical Dependency Program booklet states, "...[it] does not require long years of intensive medical training to diagnose alcoholism easily. The diagnosis can be made just as accurately by an observant personnel manager, colleague or spouse."[50] Often, it's as easy as asking if any sane, rational human would engage in these destructive behaviors. The problem is, few have been properly trained to look for substance addiction. Even less believe their prognosis and hardly any act on it, by disenabling and allowing the addict to experience the negative consequences of his actions. This may be due to the lack of understanding the nature of the disease and the need for crises in the life of the addict.

We usually cannot observe how much an addict drinks or uses, because he rarely reveals its full extent. Addicts "minimize," exaggerating on the downside the amount of use. Police know this as, "I only had a couple of beers," usually meaning a six-pack and two or more shots of hard liquor. Some hide it completely, especially from those closest to them. I believe, in the case of my personal addict, she knew she had to hide her drinking. She

---

[50] *James W. Smith, M.D., "An Orientation on Alcoholism," Schick Chemical Dependency Programs, p. 35, no copyright date (probably written in about 1982).*

sensed that if I'd known, I would not have tolerated her behavior. She knew that without me she had no one to enable her, financially or otherwise.

There are many different places to observe alcoholic behavior. Less than 10% of the population consumes 50% of all alcohol;[51] it is likely that these 10% are alcoholics. One obvious place to look for them would be in bars. Bartenders confide that alcoholic patrons vary depending on location and day of the week. For example, resorts report that a quarter or less of their bar customers might be alcoholics, as is true for your local pub on Friday and Saturday nights (when social drinkers often hang out with their alcoholic friends). They're often early stage addicts, and still functional. On the other hand, you'll find that more than half the local drinkers on weeknights are alcoholics and close to 100% on weekdays (and tend towards latter-stage addiction). Any of them may be expert pool players and great storytellers. Sure of themselves, they often seem clear-headed and having a good time. They may be pumped up and arrogant. What you generally won't see or hear is the damage they've only begun to do to family, friends, landlords, creditors, employers and employees. That must be experienced either personally or anecdotally at AA meetings.

You'll rarely hear the cold, hard truth behind alcoholism and other substance addiction outside AA and other chemical dependency meetings. It was by attending such meetings that I was able to begin to grasp the immensity of destruction in the wake of addiction. Before, I thought no, this is my dear, wonderful, strong and intelligent friend and lover. She can stop drinking if it's creating problems in our lives; she just needs a little encouragement from me. After all, if I can stop drinking anytime, she can, too. These meetings taught me I was wrong and that addicts are all very much alike, different from non-addicts.

If you don't believe this, attend a series of AA and/or Narcotics Anonymous (NA) meetings. If you attend NA, note that the addicts there are no different from those in AA except that they tend to be more predominantly unstructured and anti-authority. Other than this distinction, since a drug is a drug to an addict, you'll hear only variations on the theme of demeaning, sordid, violative and often monstrous behavior. Consider the possibility the stories they don't tell are those most difficult to admit to and ones that might land them in jail if someone in AA violates the trust. The real stories can be far worse than the ones you hear.

Anyone can attend most AA and NA meetings.[52] You may want to at-

---

[51] *NIAAA, "Sixth Special Report to U.S. Congress on Alcohol and Health," USDHHS, 1/87, p. 3, reported in NCADD Fact Sheet:, "Alcoholism and Alcohol-Related Problems." Similarly, 20% of drinkers consume 80% of all alcohol.*

[52] *Some are "closed." The list of meetings in your area that is obtainable from an AA office or meeting will inform of this and other restrictions, such as men or women only, gays, etc.*

tend a variety of meetings, since each AA local group is self-regulated. They differ widely in tone, focus and style. Since you won't likely relate to every meeting, I recommend at least a dozen over a two-week period at different locales, easily found in any medium-sized or larger city. Everyone can probably find something of value whether or not they believe an addict has affected them. You are likely to conclude substance addicts have more seriously affected you than you realized, as did Lori in the opening story.

It's not too easy rid ourselves of that lingering hope in the back of our minds: my addict is different. Unfortunately, although we wish it were the case, he's no different from other addicts when using or in-between uses. There are variations in how dangerous they may be to others. The degree is difficult, if not impossible to predict. We're dealing with enormous variations in the effect of chemicals on the brain. It is essential to understand that we are not dealing with a person we know and love. We are dealing with a chemical. This is a monster; Dr. Jekyll turned into Mr. Hyde by the terrible effect these chemicals have on the brain of the addict.

After attending several AA meetings, I began to gain a deeper understanding of addiction. I was finally able to properly respond to my addict's worsening behavior. I then dealt with her unreasonable and argumentative accusations with, "I'm sorry, but I'm not going to argue with you. You're insane and I'm not. After 30 days of sobriety, I'd be happy to discuss this further." The only thing I'd change now is the timeframe. I'd give it a year or two clean and sober (perhaps longer in the instance of poly-drug use) before the addict is truly able to begin discussing important issues rationally. Always keep in mind that they can't fight you if you step out of the ring. Understanding this helps maintain sanity.

"Alcoholics should not have to wait until their lives are nearly destroyed by alcohol before their disease is recognized; they can be diagnosed in the early stages of the disease."

Dr. James R. Milam and Katherine Ketcham (1981)
"Under the Influence" (p. 96)

4

How to Recognize Addicts

Why we need to identify the addict

" The [recovering] alcoholic has no tolerance for the limelight. That's why we keep on harping on anonymity. Not just to protect the drunk from the stigma the public puts on it, but mainly to keep our darn-fool egos under control...."
—Dr. Bob S., speaking to Bill W.[53]

This quote highlights the importance of deflating the ego in recovery. As James Graham puts it, "alcoholism creates egomania." Knowing this helps to identify addicts.

Why do we want to be able to identify possible substance addiction? Many argue it's none of our business whether someone uses addictively. Yet, the financial, physical and emotional cost of addicts' behaviors is enormous. We want to know which motorists may be addicts, so we can get out of their way. We want to know which potential employees may be using, so we don't lose a business to theft, lawsuit or gross negligence. The same goes for potential employers who are addicts, so we don't invest our hearts, souls and careers. We wouldn't want to be involved with a company in which we, the employee are not treated fairly, or worse, being an owner-shareholder, as the business begins the long slide to bankruptcy.

Recognizing addicts can be helpful in all areas of our lives. We wouldn't want to be dragged into court and blamed for something they have done, or accused by an addict of something we didn't do. We don't want to hire a contractor for home improvements who takes the money and runs before completing the job. Why would we want to rent our home to an addict, only to have it trashed? Most important, we definitely don't want to waste time getting romantically involved with someone who is a practicing addict, knowing the potential for long-term emotional and financial catastro-

---

[53] *From a conversation between the co-founders of AA in the movie, "My Name is Bill W."*

phe.

The great paradox of the affliction is, we can only help an addict by not "helping." We do this by first identifying the addiction. Many recovering addicts have said, "If I had been enabled (helped) one more time, I would have been enabled (helped) to my grave." What this means is, the less we help, the sooner the pain needed to recover is experienced. Unfortunately, this excruciating pain sickens us as observers and so we try to prevent it. The problem is, we cannot know how much pain he needs. We may be stopping the pain five minutes before the miracle happens.

Gorski points out that in the pre-treatment period of recovery, during which the addict tries to stop using on his own and (typically) repeatedly fails, he does not really believe he has a problem. "They have not accepted their alcoholism because they have not developed consequences severe enough to convince themselves" they are addicts.[54] The reason for this is simple. We have stood in their way, deflecting the consequences.

Enabling is the act of protecting another from the consequences of his behavior. As one brilliant Al-Anon pamphlet points out,[55] enabling is a requirement for any substance addiction to continue, and hence is precisely what must be stopped as early in the progression of the disease as possible. Only then can addiction be arrested. This is the required initial treatment for addiction. Unfortunately, enabling is rarely stopped in its entirety without having a level of understanding offered here.

Perpetuation of alcoholism requires that others rescue the alcoholic by helping him get his job back or restoring him as a member of the family, thereby making him appear to be a responsible adult. The same concepts apply to the teenage addict, at a time when an addict's active drug career usually begins. We rescue him from assorted trouble at school, help with his car insurance and other expenses, attempting to make life seem normal. The Al-Anon pamphlet continues, "As everything was done *for* him and not *by* him, his dependency is increased, and he remains a child in an adult suit. Others have removed the results, effects and problems caused by drinking. They have cleaned up the entire mess made by the alcoholic. Persons other than the drinker suffered the painful results of the drinking. This permits him to continue drinking as a way to solve his problems."[56]

The reason most people don't stop enabling is because few really un-

---

[54] *Gorski and Miller, "Staying Sober," Ibid., p. 110.*

[55] *Reverend Joseph I. Kellerman, "Alcoholism – A Merry-Go-Round Named Denial," Al-Anon Family Groups, 1969, pamphlet, p. 8. This is by far the best pamphlet I have seen published for any of the 12-step programs and is at least partially responsible for having awakened me to the fact my addict was in principle, no different from any other.*

[56] *Kellerman, Ibid.*

derstand addiction. Without understanding that the disease distorts perceptions (through euphoric recall, blackouts and memory repression), it is difficult to comprehend how devastating the consequences must be for the addict to become aware of his problem. Therefore, few non-addicts act early in the progression of the disease. Most enablers either never stop the enabling or do so only reluctantly after repeated attempts at helping. They may finally give up because of lack of funds or the energy needed to come to the rescue yet one more time. Only then do the chances for permanent sobriety improve substantially.

The consequence of continued enabling is that the addict physically deteriorates, culminating in damage to the brain and other internal organs. Gorski and Miller write, "the damage itself interferes with the ability to abstain."[57] Therefore, the longer the enabling, the longer the use of substances continues, which then results in greater damage and difficulty in staying sober. Because of this, as few as 1 in 7 ever achieve permanent recovery.

The key to recovery is the non-addict's offer of pure, uncompromising tough love. By the recovering addicts' own testimony, this is the only kind of love understood by practicing addicts and, more importantly, the only kind that works.[58] Tough love involves allowing the addict to experience every consequence of every action, no matter how painful it may appear. Talk, while helpful in interventions, is not the sort of feedback that gravity provides. Pain is the addict's only effective teacher and the only appropriate pre-intervention feedback. We must accept the fact that we are not smart enough to know where the addict's tolerance for pain ends, allowing pain to perform its magic.

How can someone learn better judgment when they are offered protection from the consequences of their poor behavior? Few can be "saved" by observing and learning from the experience of others or by being given orders not to do this or that, even by those with good intentions.

Since the signs of addiction are unknown by most, society would experience far less of its disastrous repercussions were it to allow everyone, addict and non-addict alike, the dignity of experiencing consequences. Non-addicts, too, would more quickly learn whatever lessons needed. Happily, there are many clues to addiction. Once these clues are known, we can feel more comfortable with the idea that the intended recipient really needs that dose of medicinal tough love. If nothing else, we can step out of their way (as some of the martial arts implore), allowing the negative energy of

---

[57] *Gorski and Miller, "Staying Sober," Ibid., p. 64.*

[58] *Knapp, a recovering alcoholic, states she doesn't think anyone can achieve sobriety "until you simply have no other choice...until you are simply in too much pain...to go on."*

the addict's impact to resonate within and be used against him. By doing so, we may better protect ourselves from the addict's behaviors.

Behavior patterns of possible addicts we don't know

Intoxicated drivers

While not always obvious, the behavior patterns of addicts are usually erratic and volatile. This is an extremely important clue, since we can see this in people we don't know and whose faces we can't see. This is most helpful when it comes to driving. In this area, more than anywhere else, the addict endangers our livelihood and even our lives.[59]

All right everyone, buckle up. We're going to spend some time discussing road behavior of those under the influence. We'll do this for several reasons. The best statistics that show the degree substances cause actual harm to others involve drinking and driving. The financial impact of dangerous driving can be devastating. More importantly, the bizarre and dangerous behavior on-road is simulated off-road, providing valuable clues to addiction.

It is important to recognize that there is a good chance that anyone who repeatedly drives while legally intoxicated is an alcoholic. The average addict does this about 80 times per year, while there is reason to believe the average non-addict does so no more than a few times in a lifetime, certainly after college years. The same is probably true for other drugs. Therefore, the odds that someone who is arrested for DUI is an addict is very high (and likely 100% if arrested a 2nd time for this offense).

Driving is the riskiest activity in which most of us engage. The 40,000 fatalities on the road each year dwarf the number of murders and even accidental deaths from other causes. Since about half of road fatalities are alcohol or other drug-related, many fatal accidents might be avoided if we

---

[59] *Some of the methods of spotting drunks are from an outstanding traffic school course, an at-home course, the study guide for which is "Responsible Driving," by Everett R. Amundson, p. 32-33 (manual, Whittier, CA: Everett R. Amundson, 1995). Others were gleaned from discussions with Motorcycle Officer Medrano, Sergeant Page and Officer Mott, Drug Recognition Experts with the Los Angeles Police Department.*

were able to identify impaired drivers.

We can start by understanding the effect of various quantities of alcohol on Blood Alcohol Content (BAC). When "one drink" is mentioned in this section, we are referring to a 12 ounce can of beer (5% alcohol), a 5 ounce glass of wine (12% alcohol) or one shot with 1 1/2 ounces of 80-proof liquor (about 40% alcohol). One drink does not refer to a Long Island Ice Tea (which can be 17 drinks, depending on who makes it). Typically, in a 180-pound man, one "drink" raises the BAC by slightly over .02 per cent in one hour. This can vary depending on the amount of food in the stomach, health and sex of the drinker. Even the mood, elevation above sea level and carbonation or "bubbliness" of the drink can have an effect. The liver burns up .015 per cent BAC per hour regardless. You may be surprised to learn our 180-pound friend must consume 5 drinks in an hour to reach a BAC of .09 per cent (just over the legal DUI limit in 16 states).[60]

It gets more surprising. Say our guy has 12 "drinks" from 10 p.m. to midnight (not uncommon for a heavy drinker) resulting in a BAC of .25 per cent. Immediately, from the start of drinking, the liver starts doing its thing and by 8 a.m. has burned up .15 per cent of the alcohol. Since his BAC has dropped only to .10 per cent, even without an early morning "eye-opener," he could (and should) be arrested for DUI on his way to work. In another 4 hours, with a BAC still at .04 per cent, it will take only a half a bottle of lunch time wine to put him back over the legal threshold.

The BAC increases at .03 per cent per "drink" in a 120-pound person, something to be kept in mind when observing female drinkers. Consider also that the drinks mixed and poured by alcoholics usually pack an extra punch. "Normal" for them may be 2 drinks (or more) in our formula.

---

[60] *Since 5 drinks elevates the BAC to about .11 per cent, and the liver's action brings it back down by .015 per cent, he'd end up at just over .09 per cent after one hour.*

Figure 5 – Amundsen's Blood Alcohol Content/ Weight Chart [61]

No. Drinks	Body Weight in Pounds								
	100	120	140	160	180	200	220	240	*Not Legally Under the Influence*
1	.04	.03	.03	.02	.02	.02	.02	.02	
2	.08	.06	.05	.05	.04	.04	.03	.03	
3	.11	.09	.08	.07	.06	.06	.05	.05	*Driving Ability Impaired and Dangerous*
4	.15	.12	.11	.09	.08	.08	.07	.06	
5	.19	.16	.13	.12	.11	.09	.09	.08	
6	.23	.19	.16	.14	.13	.11	.10	.09	
7	.26	.22	.19	.16	.15	.13	.12	.11	*Definitely Under the Influence and Deadly*
8	.30	.25	.21	.19	.17	.15	.14	.13	
9	.34	.28	.24	.21	.19	.17	.15	.14	
10	.38	.31	.27	.23	.21	.19	.17	.16	

HOW TO USE THE CHART

1. Determine your weight category (use the lower weight if you fall between the categories).

[61] Amundson, Ibid., p. 26. His instructions have been modified from subtracting one drink per hour in instruction 3 and a BAC of approximately .07% in the example.

2. Determine the number of drinks you will have, or have consumed.

3. Subtract .015 per cent BAC per hour of drinking.

Example: A person weighing 160 lbs. Drinking six beers in 3 hours would have a BAC level of approximately .09%. This amount is significant and will cause judgment errors. Considered "legally" intoxicated in 16 states.

A good starting point for the probability of whether someone is driving under the influence (DUI) can be found in time and day. According to conversations with Los Angeles Police Department Drug Recognition Experts (DREs), at least 5% of drivers are DUI on weekday nights and 10% on weekend nights. Twenty-five per cent have a BAC over .04 per cent on weekend nights. Over-confident and aggressive behavior is common even at this "low" level. Medically speaking, some level of impairment starts at .02 to .035 in every person, a fact that led Sweden, Belgium, Czechoslovakia and Finland to reduce the legal BAC to .03 per cent or less.[62]

The key to identifying those under the influence lies in two actions of the drug alcohol. One of the effects of impaired judgment (probably from a combination of the release of both dopamine and endorphins) is a feeling of invincibility, which leads to greater risk-taking than sober individuals would normally engage in. Additionally, while those under the influence (especially of depressants) may be able to control one thing or engage in one task, they cannot control the many operations required while driving. This is the reason law enforcement officers give suspected drunks multi-task instructions, such as requesting proper identification and registration, while at the same time asking where he's going. If the suspect stops to answer the question and forgets some or all of the items requested, looking confused, he's probably DUI.

Keep in mind, DUI stands for "Driving Under the Influence." We have been referring to alcohol these last few pages, but "influence" can also include other drugs. DREs have various ways of recognizing other drug use. An easy way to spot users of some drugs is to measure pupil size. The diameter of the iris (the colored part) is about 12 millimeters (mm). The pupil (the dark part) is 2.5 to 6.5 mm in normal adults (slightly larger in children) depending upon light conditions, or about 1/5 to a little over 1/2 the diameter of the iris. If it's less than 2.5 mm, "pinpoint" sized, opiate (e.g., heroin) or non-therapeutic levels of opioid (e.g., Demerol) use is evident. There is evidence of marijuana or heavy alcohol use at 6-7 mm in light. Eight to ten millimeters (pupils as "big as the moon"), taking most of the diameter of the iris, is evidence of non-therapeutic stimulant (cocaine

---

[62] *James E. Royce and David Scratchly, "Alcoholism and Other Drug Problems," New York: The Free Press, 1996, pp. 58-60.*

or amphetamine) use.[63] While this is a wonderful tool for identifying non-tolerant and occasional use, according to addiction expert Forest Tennant, M.D. most addicted (tolerant) users exhibit normal pupil size. Furthermore, such users may fail to show <u>any</u> of the physical signs of substance use and being under the influence.[64] Unfortunately, the only unequivocal physical proof of use in many is blood or urine testing. This is the reason we must look to <u>behavior patterns</u> in identifying substance addiction, using physical signs (when available) only for supplemental verification.

For example, behavior patterns can show up as a feeling of invincibility that is demonstrated by excessive speeding and lane changes. The lack of multi-tasking ability leads to inconsistent speeds and intermittent braking, whether or not the cause is apparent. The "I am God" attitude leads to tailgating and cutting in line at on ramps and elsewhere. This is where the addict says, "Get out of my way; I'm more important than you."

Even when stone cold sober, some of us engage in these and other erratic driving behaviors. However, the *probabilities* are higher that the person committing these acts is DUI. Combine any three of these and odds are we're observing a DUI in progress (or an addict, in-between uses). If you know what to look for, clues needed to get out of their way can be found several times a day. This may give one an extra edge at avoiding the financial, physical and emotional strains resulting from injury, or even death due to car accidents.

The National Highway Traffic Safety Administration (NHTSA) conducted a study of driver behaviors and level of BAC at night, applying probabilities to being DUI. Some of these are found in Figure 6 on the following page.[65]

There are many other erratic behaviors, never subjected to a study that could provide clues to which drivers may subject us to danger. Now remember, one of the things we're looking for is the inability to multi-task (DREs refer to this as testing for the ability to "divide attention"). A DUI

---

[63] *Sergeant Joseph M. Klein and E.W. "Ted" Oglseby, "Street Narcotic Enforcement," Fullerton, CA: Joe Klein Seminars, 1997; author's attendance at Joe Klein's Seminar on Drug Abuse Recognition.*

[64] *Forest Tennant, M.D., Dr. P.H., "Identifying the Cocaine User," W. Covina, CA: Veract, Inc., 1997; Tennant, "Medical Uses and Legal Identification of Drug Use," videotape series, Veract, Inc.; author's discussion with Dr. Tennant.*

[65] *"DWI Detection and Standardized Field Sobriety Testing: Student Manual, Ibid., pp. V-5 to V-7. If more than one clue is detected, the NHTSA suggests that 10% be added to the higher of the probabilities detected for each additional clue. Some officers state that this is a simplistic and conservative way to estimate the odds of DUI. It is suggested that if 2 or more clues exist, we should add half the lower percentage to the higher probability clue observed.*

driver may approach a traffic signal, stop sign, construction site or other obstruction too fast or too slow. He may miss the stop point or simply ignore it. He may fixate on the centerline or the vehicle in front, hugging either as if they were guides. He may signal one way and turn another. He may move with the traffic flow ahead, ignoring the signal that just turned red. Getting lost in thought could explain the finding in the study that DUIs may have delayed reaction times at traffic lights.

Figure 6 – Driving Behaviors and Probabilities of DUI

Behavior at Night	Likelihood of DUI
Turning with a wide radius.	65%
Gesturing erratically or obscenely.	60%
Almost striking an object or vehicle, stationary or moving, such as passing abnormally close to a sign, wall or other car.	60%
Drifting, then swerving abruptly.	55%
Speed more than 10 M.P.H. below speed limit.	50%
Tailgating.	50%
Braking erratically and unnecessarily.	45%
Slow response to traffic signals, such as remaining stopped long after the light has turned green.	40%

Another effect is that feeling of invincibility, often taking form in reckless behavior. The DUI may cut off oncoming traffic by turning left. He might speed up not at the yellow light, but at the red. On two lane roads, he may pass with barely enough room for safety. I once had to slow from 65 to 45 MPH to avoid being involved in a head-on collision; the (probable) drunk was passing me at barely 70 MPH with a big semi quickly approaching in the opposite lane.

There may be outrageous behavior, such as continuing to tailgate even after being warned to back off (flashing the brake lights several times). Speeding on a highway with no one around may or may not be a clue to DUI. However, speed differentials between cars, where the addict's ego can be inflated ("I am bigger and better than you"), is a definite red flag. It is suspected that addicts (whether using or in between uses) comprise the vast majority of such dangerous road behavior and almost every instance of road rage.[66] By engaging in dangerous maneuvers and distracting others, they may also contribute to collisions even though they are not directly involved. This is not revealed in statistics.

The DUI lacks peripheral awareness due to impaired vision at a BAC as low as .08 per cent. He may fail to see the car running a red light to his left as he begins to move on a green light. As a result, he may contribute to an accident without anyone ever knowing he (perhaps along with the guy who ran the red) was drunk. After all, how many officers administer a sobriety check on the "victim," especially if hurt? Very few check the sobriety of either driver when both may (quite suddenly) appear totally alert due to the adrenaline rush from having been involved in an accident.

Based on mostly anecdotal information, the NHTSA reports that only 7% of non-fatal accidents are related to DUI. Yet, there's never been a rigorous study of participants in such accidents. One could ask, if roughly half of all highway deaths result from DUI, isn't it possible that half of all non-fatal accidents involve intoxicated persons? If the clue that "almost striking an object or vehicle" at night gives a 60% probability of DUI, there is no reason why actually striking an object or vehicle would be only 7%. Some Drug Recognition Experts suggest the published statistics seriously understate the problem and agree it may be closer to 40-50%. There's also a feeling that both parties involved in accidents are frequently DUI because sober drivers are often able to avoid these incidents.

In fatal accidents, only 75% of drivers are tested for alcohol and none for other drugs. The NHTSA believes that if there is no alcohol present, why bother looking for anything else. That this may be a low estimate, even among fatalities, can be supported by pointing to the NHTSA's own Field Validation Study of the LAPD Drug Recognition Expert program. DREs were tested for their ability to identify which drugs a person had in his system. They found that only 3.7% of the suspects who had used other psychoactive drugs had a blood alcohol content equal to or greater than .10 per cent (the legal limit at the time in California).[67] The vast majority of DUIs using other drugs, then, were not found legally drunk. This finding contradicts the NHTSA assumption that if the driver isn't drunk, he isn't drugged. Unfortunately, the DRE study didn't track the ratio of drugs without alcohol DUIs to alcohol DUIs. However, several officers have told me they believe that for every 3 or 4 under the influence of alcohol, at least one more is under the influence of other drugs with little or no alcohol in his system. We may conclude, then, that the fatalities resulting from DUI may be closer to the 60% the NHTSA study found were under the influence when objects or other vehicles were "almost struck."

Without specially trained DREs, who are able to recognize the physical signs and symptoms of other drugs as well as alcohol, most of the suspects who had a low BAC would likely have been released without being charged with DUI. Keep this in mind when friends tell others (who have been victimized by addicts), "You should have been able to see the drug use." How could you, when the vast majority of police officers, not trained DREs, often fail to detect it?

It is possible that the frequency of highway deaths due to the impaired judgment of substance addicts is under 80% only because so many other variables are present, such as weather and road conditions. If we eliminate these variables, it is reasonable to assume that since addicts commit 80% of crime, then 80% of traffic fatalities and lesser accidents could result from driving under the influence.

When a person has zero self-worth, he takes measures to prove to others that he is worthy of their attention. This may show up in various ways and could explain why those people driving flashy cars, utility trucks and sports utility vehicles (SUVs), especially in areas not needed, may more likely be addicts. LAPD DRE Unit Officer Sergeant Tom Page states, "You are what you drive; a car is an extension of one's personality." He suggested it is possible those driving these types of vehicles are more frequently driving under the influence than are others. There are plenty of reasons to drive SUVs other than to satisfy the addict's ego. However, Graham's thesis of ego-based behavior suggests that addicts, particularly those in early-stage prior to financial ruin, may have a greater propensity to own such big, flashy vehicles. One owner is quoted as saying, "It's hormones. We want to be bigger than the other guy on the road." Another says, "Guys look at you like you've got some testosterone. The No. 1 reason I bought this truck? I like the way I look in it."[68] These are clearly ego-based behaviors.

Some statistical support for this is found in the fact that SUVs are twice as likely as other vehicles to be involved in single vehicle accidents, including rollovers and running off the road. Granted, some of these accidents may be due to the higher center of gravity of these vehicles, which is the reason an Auto Club spokesman suggests SUV owners learn how to drive these types of vehicles before they buy them. However, he adds, "I don't know if (SUV drivers) are aggressive or overconfident in the vehicle's

---

[68] *The Wall Street Journal, "The Pride and Joy of a Texan Is a Very Big Truck,"* by *Fara Warner, March 29, 1999.*

ability but it translates to more dangerous behavior on the road."[69] Aggressiveness and overconfidence, as we have seen, are both indicative of possible substance use and therefore, addiction.

Now, not everyone driving a utility vehicle who tailgates and weaves through traffic has the disease of addiction. In the same way, if you smoke, you are not necessarily addicted to psychoactive substances; however, you are more likely to be than the rest of the population. The probabilities may be higher in one who is smoking, speeding and tailgating than one not engaged in those or other dangerous driving behaviors. Add these larger vehicles to the equation and the probabilities may further increase. One of the themes of this book is that addicts are far more dangerous to our well being than are others. We need to be alert to any and all patterns of behavior that give clues to addiction. The road behavior of addicts is among the most deadly. It may be our own life or that of a loved one we save, if we observe a possible candidate and exercise risk avoidance.

It is not that addicts intend to drive drunk. In between episodes, they often tell themselves they'll never again drive while using. But they do. Recovering alcoholic and fitness guru Susan Powter describes this, reporting how she kept telling herself she would never again drink and drive, yet repeatedly did so.[70]

If involved in an accident, in which you suspect the other party may be under the influence, you can request that he be tested. You must let your suspicions be known to the police upon their arrival. Just make sure you do not let the suspect out of your sight from the moment of impact, so you can honestly state he did not drink alcohol, pop pills, etc., after the accident. An experienced DUI suspect always "drank after." If we could obtain solid statistics as to the percentage of DUIs contributing to non-fatal accidents, this might lead to full-scale testing of all participants in serious incidents.

Many recovering addicts report that a DUI (or at least his last one) put them on the path to sobriety. The larger the number and more severe the crises, the greater the likelihood of hitting bottom. I like to help in the creation of such crises wherever I can, so I regularly call 911 from my cell phone to report suspected DUIs. Since a drunk is wielding a dangerous weapon, police tell me this is an entirely appropriate use for the emergency number. The state of Utah actually encourages this and hopefully others will follow suit. Perhaps then, we will stop more addicts early enough in their lives and we will read fewer articles like the following:

[69] *The Daily News, "Auto Club suggests tips for SUV owners," by Gregory J. Wilcox, March 6, 1999.*
[70] *Powter, Ibid., p. 68, p. 73 and p. 165.*

"Crash Driver Faces Murder Charges
"By Amy Collins, *Daily News* Staff Writer
"A Los Angeles man was charged Thursday with murder and drunk
driving in a crash that killed two Pepperdine University law students on
Pacific Coast Highway.... In the minutes before the crash Tuesday
evening, another driver called 911 to report that the van was driving
erratically....'She was still on the phone with us when he crashed....' The
van's driver...was convicted of drunk driving in Utah in 1992...[the
drunk] suffered a sprained ankle..."[71]

I have spotted many likely drunks in my rear-view mirror, weaving
through traffic at high rates of speed. Memorizing the color, make of car
and license plate number as they pass, I call 911 and follow as close and for
as long as it's safe. They have no way of knowing who reported them.

Unfortunately, the culprit is rarely caught. Police figure they're lucky if
they catch one out of a hundred who are reported. That's not enough. A
warning letter could be sent to anyone reported driving dangerously. The
probability is high that a person receiving more than one such letter is a
problem driver. After 2 or 3 of these letters, the local police could pay a call
to the owner of the vehicle. Experiencing a visit from the police won't
affect the behavior of most addicts, but may affect the behavior of at least
some, perhaps helping create the bottom for a few. If this were instituted
on a wide scale, the threat of such a visit may cause the behavior of many
addicts to change, perhaps saving more than a few lives.

Although drunks are dangerous to confront, a private person's arrest
(you may know this as "citizen's arrest") can be made in appropriate circumstances. Sergeant Page told me, "If a friend attempts to take the wheel
after obviously drinking to excess, he can be arrested for attempted DUI,
just as someone can be arrested for attempted burglary or murder." You
can tell a 911 operator that a person suspected of being under the influence
is attempting to drive away.

The more I know about addiction, the less likely I am to confront a possible addict without police presence. However, one morning I observed
several of the behavior patterns identifying addiction in a female driver,
including tailgating, speeding, etc. What I did could be dangerous, so I
don't recommend it.[72] I rolled down my window at a stoplight, she rolled
down hers (now I knew she had a problem) and I asked what she had been
drinking this morning. She told me it was none of my business and I responded, "You will be arrested for a DUI." She yelled an obscenity (something about suggesting I have sex with myself) and turned at the next street.

---

[71] *Los Angeles Daily News, December 12, 1997, p. 10*
[72] *"Don't do this at home," and, "Do as I say, not as I do."* :-)

A few blocks later I pulled over a motorcycle officer patrolling with radar. After telling him what happened, he noted where she turned, along with her car's description. A few days later I stopped to speak with him again. Turns out, he had just ticketed her for speeding. He said she was belligerent, but not under the influence. As a Drug Recognition Expert, he agreed with me that she was probably a get-started-at-lunch alcoholic, in-between drinks in the morning.

The most dangerous are those who show few signs of being under the influence until behind a wheel. Princess Diana's driver, Henri Paul, by most reports appeared stone cold sober the night of the tragic collision. When I heard he drove 90 MPH in a 30-MPH zone, I suspected he had to be high as a kite. Due to his appearance of sobriety (except for what may have been telltale glassy eyes), I guessed he was an addict. For 3 days, however, the media downplayed the possibility he had been drinking, blaming the Paparazzi. My diagnosis was vindicated when Paul's BAC was reported to be .178 per cent, well over twice the legal limit in 16 U.S. states. Only later did his well known "drinking problem" come to light. What, then, was he doing on the payroll of a large company as a professional driver and why didn't anyone stop him?

Probably because no one sensed he was impaired due to extraordinarily high tolerance, something all addicts have in the early-to-middle stage of their drinking or using careers. They can handle a lot more alcohol and other drugs than can non-addicts, who usually begin to feel sick at any BAC over .10 per cent. Addicts, on the other hand, may be able to handle 2 or 3 times that, with no ill effect. Non-addicts may slur speech and stagger at levels as low as .05 per cent BAC, while such physical impairments may not be visible in addicts until reaching levels much higher (as high as .24 per cent). What's truly incredible is, if Henri Paul weighed 200 pounds, he needed to consume 9 "drinks" in one hour to reach a BAC of .178 per cent.[73] Yet according to news reports, nobody saw him drinking, much less staggering or slurring his speech prior to the accident. (My suspicion that at least some saw him drinking but continued to lie for him, enabling his poor behavior even after death, proved accurate. A year later it was reported several knew of his condition; finally, in September, 1999, French magistrates ruled the crash was due to the fact that Henri Paul was drunk and on prescription drugs.)

We have noted that while addicts can experience improved performance in the initial stages of the disease, they tend to take greater risks. Improved performance would imply they should be better drivers. The studies only seem ambiguous. Amphetamines, for example, were shown to improve "reaction times and various measures of vigilance and psychomotor per-

---

[73] *Amundson, Ibid., p. 26 and 28.*

formance [Laties, 1962; Laties and Weiss, 1966]," while a small negative effect was a test subject's "tendency to take greater risks" measured at a small .5 per cent additional risk factor [Hurst, 1962]. However, a "retrospective study concluded that amphetamine abusers [read: addicts] had four times as many crashes than would be expected in the general population" adjusted for experience and mileage.[74] This seeming contradiction is resolved when we realize that addicts act differently, when they know they are being observed. Therefore, test subjects would be expected to act very differently when observed. I would suggest the excessive risks taken by addicts can only be measured retrospectively. The latter study, reporting substantially more crashes, implies gross impairment of the addict's ability to judge risks, greatly offsetting any improved reaction time.

Sometimes the clues that someone is legally drunk are obvious, yet nothing is done to prevent tragedy. Amundson[75] reports an incident of a drunk, Larry Mahoney, driving the wrong way on an interstate. He slammed into a bus with 63 teenagers and 4 adults, rupturing the fuel tank of the bus. Twenty-four teens and 3 adults died in the ensuing fireball, while Mahoney survived. His BAC measured .24 per cent, a level at which even an addict with high tolerance begins to display speech and stability impediments. This tragedy could have been avoided. He'd been bar hopping, so he could have been refused service. If police had been waiting outside the bar for drunks, the whole thing could have been prevented. Someone could have even stopped him from driving off (according to the report, someone "almost" did). Many people share the idea that "it's not my business." This is nonsense. What is the difference between his driving a vehicle and killing 27 innocent people and a couple of crazed kids shooting up a group of people at a Colorado high school? It is everyone's business.

Non-driving situations

The most common and readily recognizable clue to possible addiction in people in non-driving conditions whom we don't know is cigarette smoking. For some reason, smokers seem to be more prone to use alcohol and other drugs addictively than do non-smokers. However, smoking in itself is not a drug about which we should be concerned in the context of this book. Although releasing endorphins in the brain (with far less an effect

[74] *University of Wisconsin Law School, "Compendium on Drug Impaired Driving,"* 1996, p. 33, reporting a study by Hurst, P., "Amphetamines and Driving Behavior," in Gregory Austin (ed.), "Drug Users and Driving Behaviors," GPO, Washington, D.C., 1977, 9-10.
[75] *Ibid., p. 32.*

than the opiates), tobacco doesn't seem to cause distorted perceptions such as euphoric recall, etc., leading to the destructive behaviors that destroy the lives of others.

Be that as it may, the rate of smoking among practicing addicts is probably in the range of 90%. Many addicts stop after several years of sobriety, accounting for fewer smokers at AA meetings. (This cessation of a cross or substitute addiction is a helpful, if not necessary, component to building solid long-term sobriety, according to relapse prevention expert Terence Gorski and others.) Since about 25% of adults in the U.S. smoke, the probability of a smoker being a psychoactive substance addict is over 30%.[76]

Because there are no accurate self-administered tests for addiction, these assertions can't be proven. Accurate statistics require accurate reporting, a contradiction in terms in the field of addiction. The best we can do is to go on the belief that 10% of the population is made up of practicing addicts. Based on the best available reports, the odds of addiction in a driver smoking and acts of aggressive driving (which inflate his ego) are far higher than 10%. I suggest the odds are also substantially greater in a smoker similarly inflating his ego by yelling, or otherwise becoming visibly agitated in non-driving situations.

Addiction in those you don't know may affect you only temporarily although, when unlucky, a fleeting connection may seriously affect your whole life. The impact, however, by those you know is usually far greater.

Why it's difficult to identify the addict you know

They tell us that codependents belong in Al-Anon. They say, codependents have a problem in attempting to control others inappropriately.

And so they may, except their "sickness" and controlling, when compared with addiction is like comparing a cold to cancer. The non-addict doesn't wake up every day hoping to God he doesn't take that first drink, hit, fix or snort. He doesn't distort his perceptions with chemicals (possibly destroying both his life and those closest), yet continue to use despite

---

[76] *If the population consists of 10% psychoactive drug addicts, of whom 90% smoke then those who are both addicts and smokers comprise 9% of U.S. adults. If 25% smoke, then it follows the probabilities are 9/25ths of smokers (over a third) are also alcoholics or other drug addicts. In countries where a far greater percent of the populations smokes, this is not as useful a clue to addiction.*

tragic consequences. For a time, the non-addict may appear to be as sick as the addict. However, once educated, recovery comes far more quickly.

Yes, the chemically codependent person belongs in Al-Anon. He should also read self-help books, listen to Tony Robbins and other self-help tapes, eat healthy foods, breathe deeply and do whatever else helps his psyche to heal. More importantly, however, he belongs in AA. Hearing what it's all about from addicts gives a depth of understanding that cannot be gained anywhere else. This increases the rate at which we heal and our ability to stop enabling. It bears repeating that without experience, we lack the insight needed to help us understand that everything we do to enable the addict only hurts us both. Hopefully, this book will substitute for sad experience. Understanding addiction through the eyes of addicts helps us learn to identify those in our lives, thus making disenabling far easier.

The addict so seriously affects some that it is difficult to identify which is which. When I see someone acting crazy, as I did in my relationship with Patricia (my personal addict) in either a family situation or at work, I would give very high odds of addiction. I now know my behavior was a direct result of the lies, manipulation and repeated violations of my rights and boundaries. An outside observer would have been hard-pressed to identify which one was the actual addict. The therapists by whom we were counseled, one a $175 per hour child psychologist, had no idea Patricia was a practicing addict and viewed me as the source of the problem due to my reactive controlling behaviors. The therapists seemed to have no idea this is typical codependent behavior, in which one predictably becomes more controlling in compensation for the utter chaos elsewhere in his life. The control may become excessive in detail, while more important areas suffer. This is the reason observing control issues in a spouse or child may be helpful in diagnosing addiction.

I saw the way this worked with a couple of my clients, Ellen and Larry. I had diagnosed (tentatively) Ellen as an addict. She looked a mess, spaced out and catatonic. I wondered if her husband Larry (a wonderful funny guy, smooth, seemingly focused, alert and quite the conversationalist) had read my client newsletter articles on the subject of addiction.

Another client, Joe, was a co-owner of a corporation with Ellen and Larry. Joe was thinking about converting the corporation to a partnership. I suggested he should seek legal counsel for this, since Joe could become liable for acts of other partners if the entity were a partnership. I warned him that I believed the wife of one of the co-owners might be an addict, making liability exposure potentially lethal to their finances and explaining addicts can in no way be trusted. Joe, understanding my concern said no, none of the wives had a problem. On the other hand, he told me Larry had one. I suggested he take another look at Ellen, to which he responded with certainty, "No, she's fine; Larry's the alcoholic." Joe, seeing my astonishment, asked why I thought Ellen was the addict. After describing her appearance, he suggested, "You'd look a mess too, if your spouse repeatedly disappeared without warning for several days at a time." This was the first of a number of couples in whom I suspected substance addiction in one, only to find later, I had diagnosed the wrong spouse.[77]

It's easy to diagnose the obvious alcoholic on Skid Row. What we don't see is the devastating effects on people close to highly functional addicts long before they reach those depths. Very few forge that essential link between the undoing of the non-addict and someone else's addiction. The functional addict is not diagnosed and the non-addict begins, after a while, to look like an addict.

The movie, *The War of the Roses,* missed perhaps the greatest opportunity ever for showing this. If either spouse (played by Michael Douglas and Kathleen Turner) had been portrayed as an addict, the ensuing insane behavior would have made sense. As it was, we were led to believe the spouses were both just nuts. As we've found, we rarely see such crazy behavior without addiction on someone's part. When I've mentioned this to spouses of addicts, their response has often been, "That's my household. I'm living *The War of the Roses.*"

To the uneducated or casual outside observer, the codependent can appear to be as sick as is the addict. Psychological dysfunction in particular, may be more obvious in the non-addict because the drug often smoothes out the addict. Crime (in the broadest sense of the term) is often a direct consequence of the distorted perceptions caused by substance addiction. What makes it all the more confusing is the <u>non-addict</u> may commit the crime, although the addict usually lures him into doing so. Therefore, the correct attribution of such crime may be addiction. The difference is that when apprehended, the non-addict codependent will more easily see his deed for what it is, generally resulting in a much more abbreviated life of crime.

Terence Gorski defines codependence as, "A progressive pattern of self-defeating [behavior] that develops in response to living in a committed relationship with a chemically dependent person or other dysfunctional person."[78] He defines codependent as, "Anyone whose life has become unmanageable as a result of living in a committed relationship with an addicted person."[79] Since a "chemically dependent" person is technically one who suffers physical withdrawals when not using and "addicted"

[77] *When I explained the ugly effect Larry's alcoholism could have on friends and business associates, Joe decided to keep the business entity in corporate form.*

[78] *Terence T. Gorski, "Do Family of Origin Problems Cause Chemical Addiction?" Independence, MO: Herald House/Independence Press, 1989, p. 16.*

[79] *Gorski and Miller, "Staying Sober," Ibid., p. 172.*

means a <u>psychological</u> dependency on the substance, we should include both terms in our definition. The commonly accepted meaning of "committed relationship" might be expanded to include any family or "extended" family member, either biological, lawful, employment and other close persons, with whom there is regular interaction. This more-inclusive view better explains why some non-addicts develop symptoms that make them appear crazier than does the addict. Therefore, we re-define **codependent** as:

Anyone in a familial, employment or other close relationship with a chemically dependent or psychologically addicted person whose responses include very unhealthy reactions such as bizarre, destructive, unethical and/or criminal behaviors.

Addicts get their non-addict enablers to do things they would not do otherwise. This includes deception, manipulation and even theft or worse. In his book *Heartbreaker*, songwriter John Meyer described how Judy Garland (with whom he had a two-month affair) could make him crazy. "...She could make you do things you'd never dream of doing, make you lie, make you cheat, make you steal, dissemble, be false, be nasty, fill you with guile."[80] Knowing as much as we do now about addicts, this is not surprising. They may affect the non-addict in ways that go far in destroying their humanity and all sense of proper behavior, especially if very young. Many adolescent delinquents and/or their parents (one or both) may be addicts.

In the extreme case, this could explain a heinous crime committed by two boys, ages 10 and 11, in 1994. Five-year-old Eric Morse was dropped from the 14th floor of a Chicago public housing complex because he wouldn't steal candy for them. The young killers, who displayed no remorse, mouthed obscenities at reporters covering the trial. The fathers of both boys were in prison. We learned earlier that 80% of incarcerated prisoners are addicts, therefore giving these parents an 80% chance of addiction. One of the mothers repeatedly missed school-counseling sessions. This is an example of one of many behavior patterns that point to possible substance addiction. Finally, the other mother was a known drug addict.[81]

Children of addicts are all affected to a greater or lesser extent. Codependent grown children, like myself, are qualified to attend Adult Children of Alcoholics (ACA) meetings. While attending one of these meetings, I met a person who told me that his parents were not alcoholics, but

---

[80] *Reported by Robe, Ibid., p. 298.*
[81] *The L. A. Times, "Where did we go wrong?" by Alex Kotlowitz, author of "There Are No Children Here: The Story of Two Boys Growing Up in the Other America." My copy of the article is not dated.*

his grandparents were. I commented, "You must have lived with your grandparents for some time." He said, "No, I never lived with them." Intrigued, I asked, "Then why <u>are</u> you here?" He responded, "Because my parents lived with my grandparents."

It began to dawn on me how incredibly powerful this affliction can be. The grandparents' alcoholism had such great effect on the parents as to cause the grandchildren to seek help at ACA meetings. I realized that if I had children, they might seek such help.

My father was a wonderful man in many respects, as are most alcoholics. However, after attending just a few ACA meetings I realized that I had learned several poor behavioral lessons from him. I was impatient and relatively intolerant of others' opinions if I felt those opinions illogical. I thought yelling solved problems and that constant bickering between spouses was normal. This belief, by the way, kept me in an unhealthy marriage for 12 years.

This is the norm in families of addicts. As noted codependency expert Claudia Black writes, "In retrospect, most adult children who were raised in alcoholic homes remember the frequent arguing which took place in the home….about 'anything and everything.'"[82] I began to see that emotional growth of both addicts <u>and</u> their codependent non-addicts may be stunted. While the addict's is said to cease for as long as active addiction exists, the emotional growth of that addict's child (while not completely stopped) probably progresses at half the normal rate. This is not to say such behavior patterns are <u>never</u> exhibited in non-alcoholic relationships. They can be, but are far less likely when there is no substance addiction.

We have shown so far that it is difficult to identify the addict due to the confusion between him and the codependent. We have suggested that if there is crazy behavior, there is likely addiction somewhere; we just don't always know where. There are other challenges in identifying the addict. Tolerance is one of them. This allows the addict to easily fool those who look for obvious signs of inebriation or other drug use. Because addicts have high tolerance, we must instead look for behavioral clues to addiction. The addict may be crazy between drinks, yet "smoothed out" while using, as was Ray Milland's alcoholic character in the classic 1945 movie, *Lost Weekend*, or Nicholas Cage's in *Leaving Las Vegas*. The clue is found in behavior, when we don't see drinking or other substance use. Even young addicts, after getting high are sub-par when they "come down." As they get older, the drop in BAC brings them even lower, eventually leading to deep despair and depression. In latter stages, they can't even get up to "normal" with use and <u>really</u> "crash" after the drug wears off.

---

[82] *Claudia Black, "Children of Alcoholics — As Youngsters — Adolescents — Adults — 'It Will Never Happen to Me!'" New York: Ballantine Books, 1981, p. 146.*

Tolerance accounts for greater and more frequent use as the affliction progresses. This explains the story in which the employee finally tells his boss he quit drinking 6 months ago. The employer replies, "I only figured out you drank when you came in sober one day." All this means is, if you witness bizarre or other behavioral clues, you may be seeing an addict. The results of tolerance and secrecy of use can make observing the drinking a waste of time. Thus, behavioral clues are more important.

Another reason we may fail to identify addiction is because we automatically eliminate certain people from the realm of possible addicts. We think, for example, a 12 or 13-year-old is too young to be an addict. We would be wrong. Consider actress Drew Barrymore. She was drinking addictively at 8 years old. We think such an adolescent can't possibly use enough to trigger substance addiction. "This is just not true," exclaim many recovering addicts who, by their own testimony, drank addictively from their first use. The tragedy is that by failing to diagnose early, irreversible chemical changes may occur, especially in the brains of the young.[83] The trouble in linking abnormal behavior to this use is, while we believed the behavior predated the use, the reverse was true.

Determining whether someone else may be an addict is often frowned upon. It's considered an "accusation" rather than a diagnosis by those who do not understand that addiction is a bio-psycho-social-financial disorder. Yet diagnosis is essential in order to know that we cannot predict how destructive the behavior might become. We cannot identify if we don't suspect. As alcoholism expert James E. Royce puts it, "You won't find alcoholism if you don't look for it."[84]

We have seen that the addict is incapable of self-diagnosis. Therefore, "doing someone else's inventory," unfortunately viewed with disfavor in the 12-Step programs, is something we must do in order to protect ourselves financially (and otherwise). We need to develop a "probability profile" as to whether a close person is an addict, just as the National Highway Traffic Safety Administration has done (to a limited extent) for police officers sizing up drivers' behaviors. What is true for the police is true for us: the higher the probability we assign to a person being an addict, the more careful we must be. Mere suspicion of substance use was ruled by the Supreme Court to be potentially so dangerous to law enforcement officers, they were granted the power to pat down suspects. Knowing that the addict may be dangerous (and also knowing that by helping we can only harm) we need to be able to say, "I'm sorry, I will not give you any more money, because I may never get repaid. I will not become your part-

---

[83] Tennant, *"Medical and Legal Identification of Drug Use,"* videotape series, Part IV: *"Identifying the Covert Drug User," Ibid.*
[84] *Royce and Scratchley, Ibid., p. 176.*

ner, or believe you when you tell me you're not having an affair, for I may get AIDS. I will not let you drive with our child or share the same auto insurance, because you may drink and drive. I will no longer believe your excuses and stories, hire you or allow you to rent my home, because it's possible you care far more for your drug than for decency, honesty or anything else."

AA's twenty questions[85]

AA and other organizations suggest 20 questions to help a person decide whether he has a drinking or other drug-related problem. **These questions work for addicts only the moment before they've reached a point of complete surrender.** When "bottoming out," they can be helpful. Unfortunately, due to the distorted perceptions of reality, impaired judgment and numbing of psychological pain, the addict is incapable of answering these questions honestly unless ready to get clean and sober. Their subjectivity also makes this difficult. We will attempt to turn them into more objective and useful questions for the addict who seeks sobriety. More important for our purpose, non-addicts (or recovering addicts) can use these modified questions to determine when someone they care for may be a practicing addict. They can be used as warning flags about those with whom we are considering getting involved.

1. "Do you lose time from work due to drinking?" The addict, not yet ready for recovery, may respond, "Well, I get sick a lot, but not from drinking. I inherited a poor constitution from my mother," or some other excuse. Often, there is another illness, which is difficult to trace to alcoholism. Many diseases are secondary, such as bronchitis, colds and viruses. Later in their drinking career, alcoholism contributes to heart, kidney and liver problems[86] and even cancer. A higher incidence of accidents also results in lost time from work.

The likelihood of addiction is increased with an inordinate number of absences. Further, the scope of the question could be expanded to include others, especially younger addicts, by asking the same for school. However, alcoholism doesn't have to result in absence. One generic and objective question could be, "Is the work completed in a competent manner?" If it isn't, there may be an addict in your life.

Behaviors such as tardiness, absenteeism and incompetence are more

[85] *New York, NY: Alcoholics Anonymous World Services, Inc., pamphlet: "20 Questions."*

[86] *Beth Polson and Miller Newton, Ph.D., "Not My Kid: a Parent's Guide to Kids and Drugs," New York: Avon Books, 1984, p. 52 and elsewhere.*

typical of latter-stage addiction. Since early-stage addiction is often marked by over-achievement and extremely focused competence, many of these questions more likely identify behaviors of latter-stage addicts.

2. **"Is drinking making your home unhappy?"** This is an easy one for the addict to escape by using rationalizations (unconscious excuses), something at which the addict is expert. They rationalize why they miss work, why their family members are unhappy, why they didn't get a raise, why they did poorly in school, why they got sick. The addict never got sick because he drank <u>too much;</u> "Anyone would have gotten sick drinking on an empty stomach." He did poorly on a test not because he drank so much he couldn't study, but rather because the teacher asked questions that weren't in the book. Nor was his drinking the cause of the argument with his wife. It was her incessant nagging, the kids not doing as they were told and the dog's constant barking.

If there is yelling and screaming in the home, the probability that someone in the family is a substance addict is increased. If the cops have ever been called to quiet things down, this may even rise to 80%. Few domestic disputes occur after dark without alcohol or other drugs distorting the perceptions of one or more of the participants. Some disputes happen during the daytime where the substance isn't apparent. Many occur when the addict is between drinks, suffering the excruciating pain of short-term withdrawal.

3. **Do you drink because you are shy with other people?"** This question is also subjective, allowing the addict to make up excuses. "No, I drink because everybody else does." Worse yet, one reason that both alcoholics and non-alcoholics drink is to grease the wheels of social discourse. Therefore, this is a question to which many non-addicts may be able to honestly answer, "Yes." The more "reasons" (read: excuses) one has to drink, the more likely one is an alcoholic. However, reasons are not observable. We can simply ask, "Does my possible addict drink a lot?" but we will find that an addict's drinking or its extent cannot always be seen.

4. **"Is drinking affecting your reputation?"** Again, this is a question subject to rationalization. It allows for responses such as, "Of course not, it has nothing to do with my drinking. I was set up by my friend/employer/spouse/employee." A more objective question might be "Is your reputation going downhill?" However, an addict can still manufacture excuses to protect access to his drug(s) of choice. We, as observers, can be less biased. Although still a judgment, ours is more honest than that of any practicing addict's. If, in our opinion, we see a reputation going downhill, whether it's among her peers at school ("she's easy") or at work with fellow employees ("he makes a lot of mistakes"), we can add to the probabilities of addiction.

At this point, you may have answered "yes" to all these questions for someone in your life. Now get your pencils out and put on your thinking caps. If we're figuring that each question gives a 25% likelihood of addiction and we simply add the probabilities, we have already reached 100%. The problem is, addiction is overstated by just adding up probabilities. It is suggested that in many cases, reaching 100% requires that the addict admit to addiction, usually done only when the recovery process begins. For the sake of argument, let's say we assign a 30% likelihood of addiction to inordinate amounts of absences from work or school. This means (without further observations) there is still a 70% chance he's not an addict. Observing serious problems at home can reduce this number even more. If we assign a 50% likelihood of addiction to those problems, without adjustments we're left with only 20% likelihood that he's not an addict. Instead, let's take 50% of the remaining possibility of non-addiction and add that to the first 30%. Now, using these assumptions, there is an overall 30% + 50% of the 70% left over, or 30% + 35% = 65% probability of addiction. Whew! Did you get all that? Take a look at Figure 7 on the next page for a concrete example.

Probabilities are by their nature estimates and require subjective analysis on our part based on experience. Experience, in turn, leads to gradual improvements in estimates. When the estimated probability of addiction is 80%, we can conclude that in ten similar instances, addiction has been shown to exist eight times. With continuous observation and practice, we can develop our skills in addiction recognition and refine our estimates.

5. "Have you ever felt remorse after drinking?" This is impossible to answer "yes" to until the addict gets honest and remembers an episode for which he should feel remorse. Remember that blackouts and memory repression cause memory failure. On the other hand, he may think he remembers, but because euphoric recall results in self-favoring rationalizations, what is remembered is wrong. This both amazes and disgusts the observer, who may get lured into arguing with the addict about the extent of his rude or other destructive behavior the night before.

As an observer, one should be more interested in behavior for which there is no apparent remorse. If your loved one, schoolmate or co-worker repeatedly fails to exhibit remorse for various episodic and obvious atrocious behaviors, the likelihood of addiction may be increased by, say, 10% each time. This also may be true if the remorse takes the form of apologies or other amends, but the poor behavior is repeated again and again.

In the meantime, you can save yourself a lot of pain and anger by simply observing and performing your internal calculations of probabilities instead of arguing about poor behavior. If you're dealing with an addict, you may as well yell at a brick wall. Always remember, you're trying to argue with a chemical.

Figure 7 – Ratcheting Up the Probabilities of Addiction

Indications	Stand Alone Likelihood of Addiction*	Add to First Column**	Overall Likelihood of Addiction
Pattern of Financial Difficulties	25%		25%
Inordinate Work or School Absences	30%	30% of remaining 75% = 22.5%	47.5% (25% + 22.5%)
Serious Problems at Home	40%	40% of remaining 52.5% = 21%	68.5% (47.5% + 21%)
Blames Others for Problems	30%	30% of remaining 31.5% = 9.5%	78% (68.5% + 9.5%)
Hides Liquor	90%	90% of remaining 22% = 20%	98% (78% + 20%)

* These are only estimates at best. While we have a few good statistics in the area of driving "behaviors," we have nothing but anecdotes for non-driving behaviors. Use your judgment.
** This is one method. Another might be adding 10% to the highest likelihood for each additional indication.

6. "Have you ever gotten into financial difficulties as a result of drinking?" This is a great question and one of the reasons for this book. However, because he is incapable of early self-diagnosis, the addict will never admit that his financial (or any other) difficulties are a result of drinking or using. "Of course not," he would say, "the financial problems are from losing my job because my employers don't understand me." Or, "Yes, there are difficulties, but only because I bought that $40,000 car when I was getting plenty of overtime and it unexpectedly stopped," etc., ad nauseam. According to him, drinking results in fun, excitement, getting loose and having a good time; never the poor judgment that causes one to fall into severe financial straits. We need to make the question more objective: "Has the suspected addict gotten into repeated financial difficulties, or difficulties from which he has not been able to extricate himself in a reasonable period of time?" Granted, many non-addicts take risks that even addicts avoid. They sometimes fail at ventures. Many spend more than they earn. The question is, did they do something really foolish—and did they do it again and again? Many variables can make this a difficult call, but as with other debacles, look to substances first. When this is ruled out, only then should we look at other issues, many of which are due to the nature of our financial lives.

Another question might be, "Has a close person ever gotten into financial difficulties because promises, written or implied, were broken by the possible addict?" This is a crucial one, around which some of the later stories of financial abuse revolve. Suffice it to say if the answer is yes, there is very likely an alcoholic or other drug addict central to the problem. Another related observation is that non-addicts may subject themselves to levels of risk that they would never inflict upon others, while addicts often won't hesitate to do so.

7. "Do you turn to lower companions and an inferior environment when drinking?" An addict doesn't see his companions as "lower" or his environment as "inferior" when deep in his disease. It's up to us to assign a probability of addiction based on our opinion of his companions. We have a right to do this, in order to protect ourselves. We may also be able to help those we love and care about. The addict creates imaginative rationalizations for whom he keeps as friends, especially while drinking or using other drugs. Because the flock syndrome is often true for humans, there is a very high likelihood of addiction if he associates with an obviously criminal element.

Caroline Knapp points out that addicts surround themselves with co-conspirators whether or not we might consider them "lowlifes". Finding other addicts, they can rationalize, "Just look at how many other people drink the way I do, or drink even more."[87] The drinking or other drug use becomes normal and inconspicuous. The existence of co-addicts greatly increases the likelihood that the person we know is an addict. Knapp and numerous others have had many drinking companions who were, in many instances, considered their equals and not inferior.

It also may point to a person who grew up with drinking. Several friends and I all had an alcoholic parent, with many of us taking up heavy drinking as a consequence. That's part of the reason why at least one of us got involved with an addict—we never knew the difference between their drinking and our own. While it may have been, at times, abusive it was apparently not addictive.

8. "Does your drinking make you careless of your family's welfare?" This seems similar to question 6 to the extent that this applies to financial welfare. However, this may also relate to safety. My personal addict and her children moved from a nice home in an excellent location to a welfare tenement in a very dangerous area. Of course, drinking is never (as far as the practicing addict is concerned) the reason for such irrational decisions. When she got briefly sober, she couldn't move out quickly enough. Converting the question to, "Is the suspected addict careless of his family's welfare" implies a routine to such behavior, providing a decent question for our probability estimates.

9. "Has your ambition decreased since drinking?" This is another question the practicing addict cannot answer honestly until he is ready to bottom. It is also one that the non-addict has trouble assessing. Many people have bursts of energy with lulls in-between, which could be confused with addiction. Some addicts have an amazing ability to appear busy while accomplishing little or nothing. This makes their ambition difficult to judge. We can observe ambition indirectly, by concerning ourselves with determining whether goals, personal or at work, are repeatedly deferred. Where's the ambition in someone who has "retired" on little income and savings at age 45? This may indicate addiction. If some-

---

[87] *Knapp, Ibid., p. 144-145.*

one completes only an hour or two of work in an 8-hour day, addiction could also be suspected. Several recovering addicts have told me they excelled at this sort of sloth.

On the other hand, addiction experts Milam and Ketcham point out that performance improves in the early stages of addiction. Graham theorizes that ambition increases due to egomania. When these two points of view are combined, we have an explanation for over-achievement in these early stages. Therefore, one of the better clues to addiction is actually the opposite: is the ambition exploding while the ego inflates?

10. "Do you crave a drink at a definite time daily?" Few addicts answer this in the affirmative until, clean and sober, they admit not only to having had such cravings, but at all hours. While using, the addict may tell you, in his usual annoyed-at-you-for-asking style, "I just want a drink — is anything wrong with that?"

Craving is not something that can be directly observed or understood. The closest thing you can do to get a feel for craving is to imagine being held under water. Eventually, you'll do anything to get air. Or, imagine yourself in the Sahara desert without water. After a day or two you'll know what it's like to truly crave something. If you're thinking, "That's just the response of the autonomic nervous system," you're getting the picture.

If we could observe someone doing anything necessary to get his drug, we could conclude there must be a craving. However, while we can sometimes observe drinking, we'll rarely see him doing "anything necessary." Change this into one of several objective questions. "Does he <u>have</u> a drink at a definite time daily, such as cocktail hour?" "Is he drinking during daytime hours daily or often, particularly on work days?" "Does he start drinking Friday afternoon and keep it up all weekend long?" If any of these are answered "yes," we can dramatically increase our estimate of the likelihood of addiction.

11. "Do you want a drink the next morning?" There is a not-so-subtle difference between the phrases "want a drink," which the addict may be able to answer more honestly and "need a drink," to which he will not admit. By asking, "Does our possible addict drink the next morning," we can eliminate subjectivity.

If we see such use, we can erroneously ascribe addiction. I used to occasionally drink cabernet sauvignon on water-ski weekend mornings. I argued, "Many have champagne brunches, so why not wine?" I even tried to rationalize by thinking of it as a form of fruit juice. I'd often drink several beers in the afternoon. Alcohol has not made my life unmanageable, but such drinking may confuse the otherwise aware observer. Because I did such odd and even occasionally abusive drinking, I never gave a second thought to how others drank. This is one reason why some non-addicts unknowingly get involved with addicts. We really have no idea the drug affects others differently.

However, on one of those weekends, I observed one woman's personality changing during the course of the day. It turns out, she was adding vodka to her morning tea and smoking pot all weekend long. Such are the reasons we must ascribe probabilities to our observation and why, generally, a number of observable behaviors are necessary to assess addiction accurately. Even observing all-day drinking of wine may cause us to wrongly diagnose alcoholism if it is in, say, France or Italy, or the drinker's name is Winston Churchill. (Alcoholism expert James Graham diagnosed Churchill as not being an alcoholic).

The behaviors caused by addiction are so unpredictable that the reverse of the time of day in this question can hold true. Take, for example, one friend and client, Ray. He drove a well-known actress to and from work for several years. He'd wake up at 4 a.m. and guzzle 6-8 ounces of vodka with a little orange juice just to get his eyes open. While on his second super screwdriver, he got ready for work. Before 6 a.m. (when legal liquor sales begin) he'd bribe an attendant at a mini-mart to part with two 12-ounce cans of malt liquor. These, he would drink while negotiating a curving Santa Monica Mountain road, finishing just prior to picking up his client. After reaching the studio, Ray secretly drank yet another screwdriver. At around 10 a.m. he'd begin downing a dozen beers, all carefully disguised in Martinelli's apple cider bottles. After finishing these by 3 p.m., he felt so high that he rarely needed another drink for the rest of the day.

Few would notice this kind of behavior. We ordinarily look for heavy nighttime drinking when looking for an addict, expecting to find morning drinking added only in latter stage addiction. In Ray's case, he almost never drank at night and most were clueless to his true "breakfast."

12. "Does drinking cause you to have difficulty in sleeping?" The alcoholic will almost never blame his drug for tossing and turning all night. Instead, it's his spouse, the dogs howling, the workaday worries, the boss ticking him off all day and the kids annoying him all evening. As a matter of fact, he may believe the substance helps him sleep by knocking him out. This is not the best question, even for the objective observer, since many have trouble sleeping for a variety of reasons.

13. "Has your efficiency decreased since drinking?" This is difficult to observe, since addicts excel at hiding inefficiencies. Many recovering addicts admit they drank addictively from their early teen years, raiding their parents' liquor cabinet and getting other drugs through school connections. Having drank for so many years prior to one's working career, how do we assess (and especially self-assess) the effect alcohol has on efficiency? The excuse, "I'm getting older," will often suffice to allay concerns that it's the fault of the drug. Secondary diseases, too, spawned by alcoholism or other substance addiction provide ample excuses for decreased efficiency.

It's very difficult, even for an addict in recovery to look back and accurately assess his work. I asked a movie studio prop maker with a dozen years sobriety about her job performance while using a pharmacopoeia of illicit drugs. She said the drugs never compromised her competence. I suggested, "I doubt that, Diedre; you couldn't have been as competent when using." She again denied this. I altered the question. "Did you become more efficient at your work when you got clean?" She responded that she became "twice as efficient." Realizing what she said, she was puzzled. "Diedre," I said, "I know you're probably one of the best prop people in the business. Even when you were using, you were probably better than most. But look at all the addict studio workers you're comparing yourself with!" This explained her competency on the job—it was relative.

This can be a very poor question to determine whether someone is an addict, since in the early stages of addiction an <u>improvement</u> in performance when using may be experienced. Egomania, too, causes the addict to attempt to excel. Only in the middle to latter stages will we find increasing incompetence. In sobriety, there is a marked improvement in competency after the brain heals.

As is the case for virtually all of these questions, this particular one has been, perhaps inadvertently, designed to identify only the latter-stage addict. This is long after he has damaged both his own life and (too often) the lives of others. We must instead devise questions to diagnose early-stage addiction, both for our own good (so we may step aside from the addict's destructive path) and for his. This helps to set the stage for a bottom before the addict's life permanently disintegrates.

14. "Is drinking jeopardizing your job or business?" This is an easy one to which the addict can respond "no." "Of course it's not my drinking! My boss is an idiot, my co-workers are jerks and my subordinates don't do what I tell them! Besides, the work isn't providing enough challenges. I'm going to find a new job or business as soon as I can," grumble, grumble. Instead, objectively asking whether there are problems on the job may give clues to which we can ascribe a probability of addiction.

Remember Ray, the alcoholic studio driver? After 2 or 3 years of his heavy morning drinking, Ray was finally fired for attitude problems, with hardly a suspicion of drinking on the job. He never even missed a day of work.

Addicts can perform some tasks in an extraordinarily competent manner, including driving. Thank goodness, because if every addict was incompetent every time he drank and drove, remembering that the typical alcoholic-addict drives under the influence an average of 80 times per year, they would have killed all of us long ago. When I asked Ray why the actress, who must have suspected something, put up with it, he responded, he was *that* good a driver, even if other work skills left something to be desired. [88]

Red flags include a continuous change of jobs or a chain of failed businesses. However, such an observation must be handled with care, since there are some personality styles that thrive on change and variation. It may be difficult to discern non-addictive causes from the addictive. Look more to co-workers who, if they find difficulty working with our subject, may provide far better clues to addiction.

15. "Do you drink to escape from worries or trouble?" When an addict gets honest, this is not a bad question. They all drink or use to escape worries or trouble, at least in latter stage addiction. It's a vicious circle. Drugs distort perceptions that result in impaired judgment, manifesting in destructive behaviors that create trouble. The trouble causes worry and he drinks more. The addict cannot see this until brought to his knees by crises. Nor is this a particularly helpful question for the rest of us, since the reason for drinking is usually concealed. Besides, as many recovering addicts admit, they drank because that's what addicts do. They need no excuse.

16. "Do you drink alone?" This is the first truly objective question of the 20. It's not a bad one, but many non-alcoholics have been known to drink alone. The question might be better qualified by adding, "often, and a lot." Unfortunately, we observers may not know the answer or to what degree. On the other hand, if we find bottles or cans strategically placed in areas such as the trunk of a car or purse, we can pretty much guess he or she drinks alone and often. In such an instance, we have almost surely found an addict.

Conversely, many recovering alcoholics report they never drank alone. "What, me drink alone? That would have meant I was an alcoholic!" They always found drinking buddies.

17. "Have you ever had a complete loss of memory as a result of drinking?" An alcoholic might quip, "I can't remember." Seriously, just how does one know he's had a blackout? If he can identify it, surely this was not the result of drinking! Excuses given by addicts are ingenious; conscious recognition and acknowledgement of a permanent loss of memory

---

[88] *Asking what caused him to seek sobriety, Ray told me he had found God, although he couldn't think of what made him open to that in the first place. Suggesting there had to be a crisis to cause a need for change, a year later he finally realized that the loss of his job was that crisis. It's interesting, he had been sober a dozen years and still took that long to remember what precipitated the most important event of his life.*

comes slowly, if at all. Once several blackouts have been experienced the probability of addiction is nearly 100%. Unfortunately, this can only be observed indirectly.

If we get upset that our addict does not remember something, he's likely to respond with, "Oh, I remember now!" or some such lie, just to get you off his back. If many such incidences occur with sudden recovered memories, we may reasonably suspect blackouts.

18. "Has your physician ever treated you for drinking?" This is another (and along with question 20 perhaps the most pure) objective question. If answered yes, the probability of substance addiction is 100%. By that time, most aware observers will already know.

Most doctors understand little about alcoholism and other substance addiction. Twenty-five years ago, when many now-practicing doctors were in medical school, training usually included nothing on the subject. Today's required classes pertain to emergency medical treatment for those suffering withdrawal symptoms, with little or nothing on diagnosing the illness. Alcoholism expert Joseph A. Pursch, M.D., has called alcoholism the "4-2-1 disease: during *four* years of medical school, a student gets *two* hours on America's number *one* killer."[89] This corresponds with reports by many recovering alcoholics that even when honest with doctors about their drinking, they were told, "You don't have to stop drinking; you just have to learn to control it."

In an otherwise fruitless attempt to obtain literature on addiction published by the American Medical Association (AMA), I found a "Policy Compendium on Alcohol and Other Harmful Substances," a compilation of brief treatment, social and political viewpoints of various medical and public policy organizations. It has no reference to the use and misuse of prescription drugs, which result in some 100,000 deaths per year. Judging by the number of addicts who die from overdosing by combining "recreational" drugs, it is strongly suspected that they are far more likely to improperly combine prescription drugs than are non-addicts. This is an incredible omission.

The AMA's research reports, "Alcohol and drug use (are) responses to family violence victimization."[90] We have already seen, and will provide further testimony, that addiction precedes violence in virtually every instance. The AMA is confusing cause with effect in failing to recognize that addiction is a result of its genetic propensity to run in families, which leads

---

[89] *Reported in Robe, Ibid., p. 135.*
[90] *"Policy Compendium on Tobacco, Alcohol, and Other Harmful Substances Affecting Adolescents: Alcohol and Other Harmful Substances," Chicago, IL: The American Medical Association, 1994, p. 2.*

to the abuse. Further, the Compendium implies doctors can uncover substance addiction by asking the patient about his use of drugs. It does not mention the fact that the addict will minimize, hide and lie about his use. Yet, this can be learned from a brief discussion about honesty with almost any recovering addict.

We will later relate the story of Dr. Martha Morrison, psychiatrist and addict. She was repeatedly misdiagnosed by numerous psychiatrist colleagues as bipolar (manic-depressive),[91] or having some other psychopathological disorder or mental illness. If psychiatrists repeatedly misdiagnose, consider the extent of such errors by non-specialist M.D.s. Unfortunately, doctors won't recognize addiction until it has exacted an immense toll on both the addict and everyone around him. In the meantime, doctors do everything they can to "help" the addict. It bears repeating: everything we do to help addicts will hurt both them and us. In a sense, doctors may be the addicts' greatest enablers.

19. "Do you drink to build up your self-confidence?" This, again, requires too much subjectivity and honesty on the part of the addict who is not ready for recovery. Drugs clearly make him feel powerful and more self-confident. If there is a marked increase in observable self-confidence when known to be using alcohol or other drugs, a high probability of addiction is suggested. This can be difficult to observe, and especially tricky, since we often don't know when or how much the addict is using. If we observe notable ups and downs in confidence levels, such changes could be due to addictive substance use. This is, perhaps, the only clue to early-stage addiction in these 20 questions.

20. "Have you ever been to a hospital or institution on account of drinking?" Obviously, if answered yes, there is virtually a 100% probability of addiction.

The next 20 questions are from an Alcoholics Anonymous booklet called "For Women Only."[92] While still containing many subjective questions, they are more objective than the previous ones. Although supposedly "for women only," they are every bit as applicable to men as well. As with the last 20 questions, applying probabilities to these may be difficult. The reader may wish to judge using a sliding scale based on the severity of behavior. Two caveats: one, if any of these signs exist, get suspicious. Two, please keep in mind that AA's questions are for addicts who have hit bottom and

[91] *Martha Morrison, "White Rabbit: A Doctor's Story of Her Addiction and Recovery," New York: Crown Publishers, 1989.*
[92] *New York: Alcoholics Anonymous World Services, Inc., pamphlet: "For Women Only."*

are now open to being honest. Once again, our goal in examining these is to derive a better set of questions to help the non-addict identify addiction.

1. "Do you try to get someone to buy liquor for you because you are ashamed to buy it yourself?" Take out the words "because you are ashamed" and you've got a straight objective question which can occasionally be observed. Under the "any excuse will do" rule of addicts, she will find excuses to have someone else buy the liquor. For example, it's not ladylike; it's a man's job; I get propositioned at the store; etc.

2. "Do you buy liquor at different places so no one will know how much you purchase?" This can be converted to a more objective question by re-phrasing, "Do you go out of your way to buy liquor at different places?" or, "Do you often buy at different places?" If the original question is stated, the addict will likely provide such excuses as, "I get better prices buying it at different stores," or defensive remarks such as, "Why should I care if anyone knows how much I buy?" As for the non-addict, where the addict buys is probably as difficult to observe as whether she gets others to buy for her, since we usually aren't asked to be her purchaser.

3. "Do you hide the empties and dispose of them secretly?" This is objective, but not something about which the addict is likely to get honest. If the non-addict ever — let me repeat, <u>ever</u> — finds an empty bottle in an unusual place and there are <u>any</u> other attributes of addiction, the probability of addiction is nearly 100%. The practicing addict is absolutely brilliant with "reasons" as to why there might be a bottle in an unusual place. It may be simple, such as, "My friend came over and I just watched her drink and didn't even take a sip." Or, it might be an elaborate ruse, such as the one Patricia, my fiancée, gave me: "Oh, that empty bottle? That's from a year ago when I started drinking again, and then I stopped and didn't want you to worry about me, so I didn't tell you, but I'm fine now." Mm, hmm. (Read: yeah, right!)

4. "Do you plan in advance to 'reward' yourself with a little drinking bout after you've worked very hard in the house?" Again, this is something only the addict knows and is somewhat subjective. However, others can sometimes observe excessive drinking after working hard. This question can be applied to other people and situations by deleting the old fashioned "in the house." We often hear, "I've worked hard for this," or, "I work hard every day, so I deserve/need a drink after work." If there is a routine of drinking to at least a .12 BAC on frequent reward days or other "special occasions," or to .08 or greater every day after work (especially if on an empty stomach), there is a good chance of addiction. (Check the BAC/Weight chart to find the number of drinks required. It's a wonderful tool when we can see the drinking.)

5. "Are you often permissive with your children because you feel guilty about the way you behaved when you were drinking?" This can be modified and made useful by simply deleting everything after "because." There may be many reasons why a parent is overly permissive with her children, including difficulties in her own childhood. On the other hand, I closely and intimately observed over-permissiveness by an addict to the point at which there were virtually no boundaries. If it's so extreme that out-of-control children are the result, the likelihood of substance addiction in one or both parents is very high.

6. "Do you have 'blackout' periods about which you remember nothing?" If there is proof of a memory failure, with several friends supporting you, the addict may accuse you of conspiracy. Perhaps she'll even try to cover up the lapses in memory by taking an herb such as ginkgo biloba, a memory enhancer. This is the same as question 17 in the first set.

7. "Do you ever phone the hostess of a party the next day and ask if you hurt anyone's feelings or made a fool of yourself?" This is similar to question 5 in the first 20, "Have you ever felt remorse after drinking?" If you were the hostess, you should ascribe a high probability to your friend's addiction. Generalize this to, "Did you observe the person doing anything to hurt anyone at work, play, school, among friends, etc.?" If this is recurring, especially in adults and combined with other positive indications, there is a higher than average likelihood of addiction. It is rare that non-addicts repeatedly make fools of themselves or hurt their friends.

8. "Do you find cigarette holes in your clothes or the furniture and can't remember when it happened?" The addict is likely to attribute this damage to friends, some of whom may be addicts as well. "My friend sure has a drinking problem" is a refrain heard from many alcoholics who can see it in others but not in themselves. You might even be accused of being the one who "purposely" burned the holes. This is a very good example of an objective question, if we can identify the culprit. First, smoking increases the likelihood of other substance addiction; second, if there are such holes, there was likely a "nodding off" or some other lack of awareness that can often be attributed to the irresponsible and dangerous behavior of an addict. One statistic lends support to hypothesizing a 90% likelihood of addiction in such instances: the National Council on Alcoholism reports that "Alcoholics are ten times more likely to die from fires than nonalcoholics."[93]

---

[93] *Reported by Robe, Ibid., p. 402.*

9. "Do you take an extra drink or two before leaving for a party when you know liquor will be served there?" While the addict isn't likely to answer this honestly, it is a good test of addiction for the aware observer wise to such secrets. Generalize, by replacing "party" with "business meeting," "lunch date," "dinner date," etc.

10. "Do you often wonder if anyone knows how much you drink?" Chances are, this is too subjective a question to ask the practicing addict. Besides, addicts usually don't really care and, "It's nobody else's business."

11. "Do you feel wittier or more charming when you are drinking?" Although subjective, this may lead to some clues when observing introverts. Does the person "come out of her shell" when drinking or using? Are there repeated instances of such use and behaviors? This can be difficult to discern between overuse and abuse of substances vs. addiction, so this question shouldn't be given much credence. It's related to question 3, "do you drink because you are shy with other people?" and question 19, "do you drink to build up your self-confidence?" in the first 20 questions. For the same reasons as previously described, the excuse-making practicing addict cannot answer this honestly.

However, there is the matter of what James Graham calls "alcoholic charm." Alcoholics can charm their way out of (or into) practically anything. Ray, the studio driver, was once pulled over "stoned out of his mind." With his alcoholic charm and manipulation skills, he not only talked the officers out of the arrest, but also into allowing him to hire a tow-truck to bring him home. A non-addict is unlikely to be able to charm his way out of a DUI or other tricky situation.

Alcoholic charm is an attribute used when engaging in another alcoholic behavior, "serial sexual conquests." One recovering alcoholic told me he had no idea how he got so many women in bed when he drank. He said, "Frankly, I not only wouldn't do this now, but would probably fail miserably if I tried."

12. "Do you feel panicky when faced with non-drinking days, such as a visit to out-of-town relatives?" This is a terrific question for the addict beginning to get honest; however, most rationalize, "I can't stand the relatives" or some similar excuse. The non-addict, however, may observe a reticence to visit with relatives. If such visits get in the way of her drinking, picking fights is an excellent clue to addiction, since they can be used as an excuse to avoid future visits.

13. "Do you invent social occasions for drinking, such as inviting

friends for lunch, cocktails or dinner?" These are alibis to which active addicts would never admit. An objective, aware observer may see many such occasions and think nothing of it, having been prodded into sharing a busy social calendar.

One recluse who admitted to having a problem created a new rule: she'd drink only with company. Her empty social calendar became suddenly full Monday to Sunday. Similarly, I've known some addicts who always want to "party." Along with never drinking alone, drinking only with company is just one of many "rules" that addicts make in a futile attempt to control their problem. The trouble is, if one has to make rules for drinking, it's already a problem.

14. "When others are present, do you avoid reading articles or seeing movies or TV shows about women alcoholics — but read and watch when no one is around?" The addict may respond, "Of course, because those stories are so sad they make me cry, which I don't want others to see." While it may be difficult to find one secretly reading and watching, we might observe the addict's avoidance when present under the pretense of some terrific excuses. We may even see anger and resentment directed at us if we read or watch such programs. She who becomes enraged or sorrowful at the plight of alcoholics in the media often turns out to be one.

15. "Do you ever carry liquor in your purse?" If answered "yes," this perfectly objective question virtually guarantees substance addiction. Try catching it, however. If you get into her purse without getting killed, check the contents of pill bottles (if you've gone this far, have any pills you find analyzed) or shampoo, make-up and optical solution containers. Sounds strange, but my personal addict carried some of her purse liquor in an eye solution container. When I detected it, she denied it was liquor and, just to prove her point, proceeded to put it in her eye. Good thing for her she'd already anaesthetized herself.

The addict, of course, rationalizes. "I like to have liquor available, but I don't need it. I can stop any time I want." Until the addict has experienced enough crises, this question will fail to prove to her that she is an addict. For the rest of us, this can be generalized to, "Does she ever hide liquor or other drugs?" This is similar to question 3 above, "Do you hide the empties...?"

16. "Do you become defensive when someone mentions your drinking?" An observable phenomenon, the addict, denying she is ever defensive, rationalizes with a multitude of excuses, as she does for all her other objectionable and childish behaviors. Don't believe it. Put your trust in those behaviors. Anyone justifying her drinking or other drug use (if combined with any degree of destructive behavior) is very likely an addict.

17. "Do you become irritated when unexpected guests reduce your liquor supply?" While of little help for the addict performing self-diagnosis (who, me irritated? I'm not irritated!), others can observe it. If you comment on her irritation, she'll concoct excuses, such as the dog barked or the cat meowed. She might shift the focus of blame to the guests. "No, I'm not irritated about them drinking all my gin, but I do object to their behavior when they're here—can you believe the way they put down our dear friends when they weren't here to defend themselves? I just don't want to see them any more and, if we do, they can bring their own damned booze."

On the other hand, since she can easily buy more, irritation may not be evident. Replenishing the supply of shared illegal drugs is not as easy, in which case irritation may be more readily observed. Also, she may be taking legal pharmaceuticals, and not care if the alcohol has disappeared.

18. "Do you drink when under pressure or after an argument?" Her response might be, "You'd drink, too, if you had to live with him!" These excuses allow her to avoid realizing that she is the source of her own problems. If the drink really is "smoothing her out," we have a very likely middle-stage alcoholic. Also, made-to-order arguments can provide a great excuse to drink; therefore, such arguments are in themselves, clues.

19. "Do you try to cover up when you can't remember promises and feel ashamed when you misplace or lose things?" Typically, she denies that promises were made and accuses you of making them up. You may even be blamed for misplacing those items. She might deny that they were last in her possession, contrary to all evidence. Instead, "Does she cover up for unkept promises or misplaced items, deny having made promises and/or repeatedly misplace or lose things," is a better question for the observer. If so, there is very likely addiction.

20. "Do you drive even though you've been drinking but feel certain you are in complete control of yourself?" The response is likely to be, "Of course I can drive—I'm more focused and I didn't drink enough to impair my driving." To the extent the use isn't covered up and we use our BAC/Weight chart, an observer may get some inkling to the extent of drinking and driving. Non-addicts are never so self-assured to say they feel in complete control. On the other hand, advertised driver sobriety checkpoints may actually attract alcoholics. With their false sense of self-confidence, they can prove to others they're in control, thereby inflating their ego.

The instructions to the first 20 questions state that if any are answered in the affirmative, there may be alcoholism. If you respond "yes" to any two of the questions, chances are you're an alcoholic. If three or more, you are "definitely" one. We have seen that the practicing addict, who has not experienced pain from using that is greater than its pleasure, is literally incapable of seeing his problem. He makes every excuse possible to answer "no." Even when answering several questions in the affirmative, justifications run rampant. Therefore, it is an extremely rare moment when the addict can be helped by such questions. Only when that happens can other recovering addicts help him to get honest.

Most of our dealings with practicing addicts are prior to this event. The affliction must take its toll and the crises must reach a crescendo, forcing the addict to accept, ask or beg for help. Unfortunately, it can take as long as 30 or 40 years before crises force his hand, or before others have diagnosed the affliction and intervened. This is particularly true of those who use only one drug, such as alcohol; polydrug use often ends lives long before this. No matter what the time period, virtually everyone close is seriously harmed physically, psychologically and/or financially, as are many others no longer in the addict's life.

Our objective is to diagnose addiction far earlier, so we can avoid becoming one of the addict's victims. If we are already being affected, we need to stop the repercussions immediately. We must resolve to assist the addict in experiencing consequences of addiction so severe that we more quickly win back a person who may otherwise be a caring and decent human being.

As noted, it's far easier for the non-addict to honestly answer the above questions. Some of these questions are inherently weak, while others are highly subjective. A few are simply proof that an addict is already in the latter-stage ("Has your physician ever treated you for drinking?"), which is something we would already know. We need stronger and more objective questions that are designed to detect addiction in its early stage.

If we are to avoid their destructive behaviors, it is crucially important to recognize that our addict has symptoms similar to other addicts. The fact that they are far more likely to engage in such behaviors than are non-addicts indicates that the behavior is fundamentally different. If any suspicious behaviors are observed, exercise caution. Since predicting the timing and extent of dangerous behavior is, at best difficult and often impossible, once we conclude that a high probability of addiction exists, we need to protect ourselves.

This may sound paranoid, but addicts have an ability to deceive like no other. Bear in mind, they must inflate their ego, often through the exercise of power over others, and in extremely harmful ways. Moreover, they will do almost anything necessary to protect their right to use, often injuring others in the process.

It's also crucial to understand that addicts will modify their behavior if they suspect your scrutiny. Remember the study showing that while amphetamines improved reaction times in drivers, theoretically resulting in fewer accidents, a retrospective study concluded they had four times the number of crashes as they should? James Graham explains this with a brilliant analogy to physics. The Heisenberg Principle states, "The act of observing physical phenomena influences the target of observation. So it is with alcoholics."[94] Graham points to we non-professionals as having a distinct advantage over the professional, so long as we aren't obvious in our observations. This means, and let me emphasize:

Don't make comments about their use or possible diagnosis of addiction.

Keep suspicions to yourself until you are truly convinced there is a problem and are ready to act on that conviction.

We have been taught to look for symptoms of latter-stage addiction. Whenever it is said so-and-so became alcoholic at some middle or later age, we can be certain alcoholism that only now became obvious had existed long before. Yet in these latter stages, the addict is less dangerous to others. We are more alert to their disease and they are less competent at most things, including criminal behaviors. The early stage addict is least suspected and more competent and, therefore, far more dangerous. Fortunately, when we observe carefully and with suspicion, usually several symptoms will become apparent almost as soon as the drinking or other drug use begins. Such suspicion and subsequent disenabling would likely have saved the life of the little girl murdered at the hands of Jeremy Strohmeyer in a Las Vegas casino in 1997, not to mention countless others.

Father Joseph Martin points out, "We don't need a lot of book knowledge or fancy degrees to diagnose this illness" and asks that we not "become too enamored of learning, your own or anyone else's," including those with degrees who lack common sense. He points out the common sense of a five-year-old identifies addiction (even if he understands it less than do adults) in observing, "My mom and dad are always fighting and sometimes he beats her up."[95] As for those with degrees, Father Martin diplomatically states, "I have heard people in the alcoholism field ask questions they should never have to ask at all, because they have not yet grasped the idea of addiction."[96]

Most look for actual excessive drinking or drug use. As we've said,

[94] *Graham, Ibid., p. xi.*
[95] *Father Joseph C. Martin, Ibid., p. 74.*
[96] *Ibid., p. 85.*

this, by itself, does not always indicate addiction. If such use is found, we'll get a good idea whether addiction exists based on behavior. Keep in mind that destructive behavior can occur whether or not under the influence at the time of such behavior. While drinking, inhibitions are decreased in non-addicts, but addicts become very different people. However, we won't always see an addict's use. As in the case of certain particles in physics, whose existence can be inferred without actually seeing them, we must look for evidence of alcohol and/or drug use without the ability of such observation. More than one alcoholic has repeatedly waited until everyone else was sound asleep, only then drinking himself into oblivion.

Other addicts became anti-social when they had their first drink or snort, an event the closest family member probably never witnessed. These persons usually believe the anti-social behavior began prior to the substance use, yet they did not see the early drinking or using that actually predated the sociopathic behavior. The signs and symptoms may well be painfully obvious long before actually seeing excessive drinking, once we know where to look. These signs rest upon the quintessential fact that the addict's distorted perceptions inevitably result in impaired judgment, which always emerge in behaviors. *The best clues to addiction, then, are behavioral.*

Are you ready for a different set of questions for the non-addict? Here they are. Some are gleaned from the previous questions while others are new. It is essential to step outside the box of non-addictive thinking. Most can use and abuse and not become addicted, rendering them incapable of truly understanding what it is like to crave and be truly powerless over a substance. What non-addicts can do is learn how to recognize addiction, even if they don't fully understand it and then react appropriately. Keep in mind, these questions are for determining if there is a practicing addict in your life. Addicts in true recovery are some of the most honest people on the planet and, when questioned, are often the first to admit they are addicts.[97]

Now, I don't suggest there's an addict under every bed. The husband may have really lost the $100 like he said, instead of drinking it away; an employee may well have bloodshot eyes due to early morning swimming in an over-chlorinated pool rather than an early morning toke on a joint. We can't usually make a tentative diagnosis of addiction with only one indication; we generally need several positives to determine addictive use, at which point the caution flags should be raised and heeded. As a Certified Financial Planner licensee, I deal in risk management. Risk management is based on probabilities. If the probabilities are high for addiction,

[97] *If I think a person is a recovering addict I often test myself by asking, "Are you a friend of Bill W.?" (Bill W., with Dr. Bob co-founded AA.) If answered in the affirmative, he's in recovery. If the response is negative, I sometimes find a practicing addict.*

we must get out of harm's way. If he turns out to be an addict, he will almost invariably harm us, either electrocution-style or by keeping the burner on just low enough. Like the frog, we remain in the pot of water until we're figuratively boiled alive.

Signs and symptoms of addiction: questions for the observer

Over-achievement

1. "Are there significant attempts at over-achievement?"
This may seem like a very odd first question. However, James Graham has made the case for this as an early sign of addiction in his study of historical figures.[98] Some of the greatest spies, writers and actors were clearly alcoholics. Many successful businessmen and politicians are alcoholics or other drug addicts. Our focus must be to attempt an early diagnosis, when the addict may be exhibiting the classic signs of improved performance while most dangerous to others.

How can they have such great success, when addiction results in extensive physical deterioration and eventual brain damage? Simple. Things take time. Severe damage occurs with repeated and continued use. Dr. Martha Morrison became a full-fledged addict at the age of 12. She did well, even through medical school. She became a psychiatrist without anyone close to her knowing she was taking 20 different drugs a day. It is easily recognizable in the Skid Row bum, having proven his incompetence at work and life. This makes him unattractive and, therefore, generally harmless. A MD/psychiatrist like Martha Morrison may not be so.

Sir Arthur Conan Doyle said, through his alter ego Sherlock Holmes, one must fit the theory to the observable facts. No matter how far-fetched, the theory that best explains the phenomenon observed must be right. Early in my studies of addiction I suggested to numerous recovering alcoholics (who, at the time agreed with me) that the affliction manifests itself as incompetence. I was perplexed, however, by gradually finding a number of enormously successful and seemingly competent alcoholics. I just figured how much more competent they would be if only clean and sober. Then I considered the case of Ty Cobb.

Cobb was arguably the greatest baseball player ever, with a lifetime

---

[98] *Graham, Ibid. This question and explanations to behaviors I had observed but could not explain would not be possible without Graham's insight.*

batting average of over .400. He was a practicing alcoholic the entire time. Many suggest such highly successful people "become alcoholic." However, if alcoholism is a disease, then an alcoholic is an addict from early in his drinking career. How then, can the achievements of a Ty Cobb be explained?

It had not occurred to me that alcoholism could actually contribute to the addict's early success. Graham's theory, that the addiction drives the need to inflate the ego, requiring the acquisition of power over others, explains this. Such power may take the relatively innocuous form (when compared with some of the other power-seeking behaviors of addicts) of being the best, earning more than others, gaining fame and influence, controlling the audience or winning the game. Therefore, over-achievement, or attempts at such, would be common among addicts.

Lucy Barry Robe found that 22% of famous actresses and an astonishing 38% of famous actors were alcoholic-addicts.[99] Dr. Goodwin, the psychiatrist who conducted the Danish brothers study referred to earlier, found 30% of great writers were alcoholic, including 5 out of 7 American Nobel Prize-winning writers of this century.[100] At least in certain professions, over-achievement appears to increase the odds that we can ascribe to addiction.

This may explain the fact that addicts keep on drinking and using despite the negative consequences that inevitably occur. They keep hoping against hope for the same boost the initial intake gave them. They often report the first times were the best and that they keep searching for that elusive high, which may have even given rise to their fantastic early achievements.

Think of Edgar Allan Poe, Hemingway and Steinbeck; consider Thomas Paine and Congressman Wilbur Mills. All were enormously successful over-achieving alcoholics, many of whom later died of their disease or the secondary diseases that alcohol spawned. They don't succeed and later fall apart because they "became" alcoholic. They succeed because they often select an occupation at which they can wield power and influence. They find one at which they may become great,[101] allowing them to more effectively and quickly inflate the ego. Only later do they slowly and imperceptibly slip from the hidden stage of addiction into the more easily diagnosed latter stages, where it's most often first seen.

If there are practically any other affirmative responses to the remaining

---

[99] *Robe, Ibid., quoted in Graham, Ibid., pp. 8-9.*

[100] *Donald W. Goodwin, M.D., "Alcohol and the Writer," Kansas City: Andrews and McMeel, 1988, quoted in Graham, Ibid., p. 75. There is now an 8th, for whom I have no indication of addiction.*

[101] *As we will find later, people can become great at occupations consistent with their Temperament, making this a powerful tool for diagnosing addiction.*

questions, over-achievement should be viewed as possible first stage addictive behavior. The dangers such over-achievement can pose to others
were illustrated in the ZZZZ Best fraud case. Barry Minkow, one of the
most classic egomaniacs ever, convinced investors he had a multi-million
dollar business replacing carpets and rehabilitating office buildings, when
in fact there were merely contracts with the numbers doctored. After the
banks stopped funding what was, in effect, a Ponzi scheme,[102] he magi-
cally produced the needed cash by selling cocaine, even as he crusaded
against drug "abuse" on television. According to reports, he himself used
cocaine, keeping a large stash in his desk drawer.[103] Several of his associates were alcoholics. This may be guilt by association, but if it looks like a
duck and swims with other ducks, it's probably a duck. The scam cost
investors and lenders at least $100 million. Hence the need to become sus-
picious of some over-achievers. While there are many, we will not find
affirmative confirmations in non-addict over-achievers from the questions
that follow, as we might for Minkow.

Graham believes the alcoholic must boost his ego in compensation for
his drinking. Quoting David J. Pittman from his book, Alcoholism: An
Inter-Disciplinary Approach (Harper and Row, 1959), "The alcoholic must
prove he is better than his fellow man so that he will not have to feel so
guilty...when he is sober. Therefore, he must do things better than most
people...." While this may not be true of every addict (and there may be
other explanations for the behavior, such as euphoric recall), it may be the
case for those who are most dangerous to others.

Milam and Ketcham point out that "the only visible difference between
the alcoholic and the nonalcoholic [in the early stages of addiction] is improved performance in the alcoholic when he drinks and a deterioration in
performance when he stops drinking."[104] Small amounts of alcohol are
stimulating and energizing for both. However, the sedative properties of
alcohol quickly (usually in about 20 minutes) overcome the non-alcoholic,
eventually causing stumbling, sloppiness and incoherence. This does not
occur as quickly in the early-to-middle stage alcoholic, accounting in part
for their drinking more. The alcohol at this stage is therapeutic, making
the alcoholic feel "normal" and frequently super-human. This is true as
well for other addicts using stimulants (cocaine and amphetamines).

This early stage is deeply confusing to both observer and alcoholic, both
of whom have learned in school that alcohol is a depressant. Walk into any

---

[102] *Charles Ponzi was the 1920s con man who used new investors' funds to pay off
the old, giving the appearance, for a time, of 40% annual returns.*
[103] *Daniel Akst, "Wonder Boy: Barry Minkow — The Kid Who Swindled Wall
Street," New York: Charles Scribner's Sons, 1990, p. 113, 270 and numerous other pages.*
[104] *Milam and Ketcham, "Under the Influence," Ibid., p. 57.*

bar and tell me it's a sedative for those patrons. Here, you will observe the stimulating effect lasting far longer than a mere 20 minutes. The effect is very different on the alcoholic, who feels good for as long as the blood alcohol content (BAC) stays elevated. This may be due in part to alcohol's ability to inhibit glutamate receptors resulting in a sedation that causes a loss of inhibition. Perhaps more significantly, it offsets the sedative action by effectively boosting dopamine levels. This may be the source of the grandiosity and elephantine ego readily observable in alcoholics and stimulant addicts. Additionally, as we learned earlier, they don't feel sick from the poisonous effects of acetaldehyde as quickly as do non-addicts. In combination, these give the alcoholic the ability to party all night long. They may also work synergistically to create alcoholism.

It is only when the BAC begins to drop that performance falls apart and they begin to feel drunk and out of control. Towards the end of early- to middle-stage alcoholism, addicts discover "maintenance drinking," learning ways to protect themselves against the results of a drop in BAC by always keeping some alcohol on hand.[105] The careful observer may be confused over the fact that middle to latter-stage alcoholics are sick when they appear not to be drinking. These varying effects keep the observer confused regardless of the stage of addiction.

At best, it is difficult to confront suspected alcoholics not engaging in overt criminal behavior during the first stage. They would negate any diagnosis of their alcoholism, arguing that they are achievers, if not supreme achievers. They rarely get drunk or feel hung over, don't miss work or school, feel terrific when drinking or drugging, aren't violent and don't (yet) drink in the morning. The problem is, alcoholism doesn't begin when these behaviors start, any more than cancer begins when a tumor is 6 inches in diameter. The body predisposed to the disease already isn't processing alcohol the same way as the non-addict. Alcoholism (and probably other substance addiction) is triggered in this person, oftentimes with the first drink or use. This is an experience that changes his life.

Tolerance

2. "Does he have a high tolerance to the substance?"

No one question, including this, can definitively identify addiction. I know some large men who can drink a lot of alcohol whom I have not been able to diagnose as alcoholic. However, the early to middle career of the

---

[105] *Milam and Ketcham give an excellent explanation of this and improved performance, Ibid., pp. 57-61.*

classic addict requires an incredible amount to put him under. To some (certain occupations and cultures), this is a sign of manliness, machismo and virility. To others, it's a sign of possible alcoholism.

Tolerance is one of the best clues for early detection. There is little else to discern between the young addict and non-addict partying with their high school or college friends. The non-addict may begin to feel sick and tired after only a few drinks. The addict is energized and able to party all night long. He can drink everyone else under the table, and sometimes wonders aloud why others can't, even encouraging them to drink or use more. This is among the few clues for detecting the early-stage addict, since his life hasn't yet begun to fall apart.

Although we often won't observe it (since either we're not looking and/ or it's hidden), the addict may drink amounts we can't even fathom. As alcoholic actress Mary Pickford commented in 1942, "To an alcoholic one drink is too many and fifty aren't enough." Elizabeth Taylor had, by her own testimony, "a hollow leg. I could drink anybody under the table and never get drunk." Richard Burton, Taylor's twice husband and alcoholic in his own right, "almost drank himself into oblivion, in a futile attempt to keep up with Elizabeth." When Taylor entered the Betty Ford Clinic in 1983 for dependency on pills, it actually took her a couple of weeks to realize she was an alcoholic. "Just because I couldn't get drunk doesn't mean it wasn't poison for me."[106]

Many claim "it's not our business how much one drinks." Yet, we can more often "count drinks" in early-stage alcoholism than later, when the use is often hidden. Without the experience of pain from our early disenabling, followed by our loving intervention, there is little hope for early-stage sobriety and a life of non-abusive relationships. It is helpful then, not only to count drinks, but to also discern the amount of liquor in each (see BAC/Weight chart). The addict's consumption will usually shock the observer, which in conjunction with even one other symptom is sometimes enough to tentatively diagnose addiction.

It is only in the latter stages when the addict begins to lose tolerance. Eventually, as a result of severe physical damage (particularly to the liver), he gets high as easily as does the non-addict.

Smoking

3. "Does he smoke?"
Before you scream, "How prejudiced," or, "I know plenty of smokers

---

[106] *Robe, Ibid., p. 78.*

who are clearly not drunks," please keep an open mind. Consider the fact that we are looking for clues to confirm addiction in someone who, if verified, may pose a threat to us. The addict usually doesn't admit to addiction until, at the earliest, he is ready to get clean and sober, all the while damaging others along with himself. While there are plenty of non-addict smokers and many more who are not practicing addicts (check out the smoking habits of attendees at any regular AA meeting), the facts are these: over 90% of all alcoholics are heavy cigarette smokers,[107] yet only 25% of Americans smoke. It's math time again, folks. If addicts comprise 10% of the population and 90% of those are "heavy" smokers, haven't we just found 9% of the 25%? If these numbers are right, aren't over a third of smokers alcoholics? This doesn't even include addicts partial to drugs other than alcohol.

We must also modify the numbers for this (and many of these questions) when considering different cultures. For example, if the percentage of alcoholics is only 5% in a particular country, while those who smoke comprise 50% (as is the case in Japan), smoking isn't nearly the clue to other drug addiction as in the United States. However in California, where the percentage of smokers has shrunk to less than 19%, smoking may be a better clue than elsewhere.

Gulping

4. "Does he gulp alcoholic beverages, drink substantially more than others and/or always finish the last drop in the glass?"
An alcoholic cannot generally sip even a fine wine. They often <u>must</u> gulp, especially that first drink or two. Even when not gulping, they normally drink fast. This is because the addict does not drink a 1929 Chateau Lafitte Rothschild to enjoy its wonderful bouquet, the flavors of berries, chocolate, earthy overtones and velvety aftertaste. Rather, he drinks to get drunk.

It may even be unconscious. Caroline Knapp tells how she'd open "the first" bottle of wine, pour it and suddenly her glass was empty, "just like that." Then she'd proceed to fill it again. As she says, "I never consciously chugged the wine, it just happened, and all of a sudden I'd be bombed."[108]

If we observe this sort of drinking style, we can be fairly certain we're observing an alcoholic, especially if any of the other behavioral signs are

---

[107] *National Council on Alcoholism and Drug Dependence, Inc., "Fact Sheet: Alcoholism and Alcohol-Related Problems."*
[108] *Knapp, Ibid., p. 190.*

present. Even Knapp, a relatively high bottom drunk who didn't lose her job and all her net worth reports that she "rarely, if ever, drank moderately, even at the beginning."[109] Even though they will often take great pains to control their drinking using many different strategies ("a hallmark of alcoholic behavior"[110]), they will fail and this failure may be observable.

I was already aware of this symptom when an acquaintance named Dean arrived at a party I was attending with my date, Heather. I had shared my good wine with him on camping trips and noticed he never reciprocated. He was also the first and loudest to complain about my practicing addict's children's poor behavior on one trip. We were all supposed to bring our own bottle. Heather and I had brought a very good bottle of Cabernet Sauvignon, which sat newly opened on our table.

When I saw Dean arrive, I said to Heather, "Watch this. He's going to come over, say hello, introduce himself and rave about what a wonderful bottle of wine it must be because I have such great taste in wine...blah, blah, blah...and ogle it and do everything except ask for a glass." I told Heather I didn't want to offer Dean any, tiring long ago of the one-way traffic. Surprise, surprise; everything I said came to pass and Dean finally left us when it became apparent that we weren't going to share.

Excusing myself, I reminded my date not to give in if Dean came back, which I predicted he would. He did and Heather was, shall we say, too kind. I looked at the table and saw barely over half a bottle of wine left. Heather apologized and explained she just couldn't say no to such a nice guy (addicts can be so endearing when they covet what you have). Knowing by this time from my own spiritual awakening that it's impossible to get angry or overly upset when curious and that there is a reason for everything, I got inquisitive. I suggested we observe his drinking, since the possibility of addiction had never before occurred.

Dean, who looks like he weighs in at 160 pounds, drank at least 12 ounces of his 16-ounce clear plastic tumbler in about 5 minutes. He sipped the remaining few ounces over the next half-hour and then left the party. I suggested he may have run out of takers and went to get his own. While gulping to reach a BAC of about .06 per cent is not normally enough to diagnose addiction, with the other behaviors I'd observed over the years I'd suggest there should be a high degree of suspicion.

A propensity to finish the last drop is an additional red flag. In one case indicative of this, a woman and her date were at a table next to ours in a nice Italian restaurant. When the man excused himself briefly, she finished his drink. I also watched her face contort in a way that is difficult to describe other than to say that a Jekyll and Hyde transformation seemed to

---

[109] *Knapp, Ibid., p. 119.*
[110] *Ibid.*

have occurred.

Jail time

5. "Has he ever been convicted of any crime and spent time in jail?"
If so, according to our earlier analysis of the recent study of prison inmates, there's an 80% probability of addiction. If any other signs are present, the probabilities approach 100%. This type of addict must be treated with extreme caution, especially if incarcerated for any violent crime. While many addicts are not violent, others (the sort that frequently do time) are.

A recently released inmate and recovering addict told me that she felt 90% of her fellow prisoners were addicts. Another wrote, "If everyone [could be in AA], there would be no need for jails."[111] James Graham reported that a convicted killer stated, "If it hadn't been for beer and whiskey, I wouldn't be [in prison] today.....Ninety percent of the guys that are in here are pretty good people, but when they get hold of that bottle, it makes them feel like they are superman."[112] Confidence levels increase, even while accurate perceptions and good judgment diminish. As Graham has pointed out, the addict's ego requires the overpowering of others. He more often lands in jail when this manifests itself physically rather than only psychologically or financially.

A recent study of the mentally ill by the MacArthur Foundation found no difference in the level of violence between former mental patients and the general population.[113] While this finding was questionable, it clearly reported acts of violence nearly double among mentally ill people showing symptoms of addiction over those who didn't. This difference may be understated due to the omission of many that might be identified as addicts.

The propensity for crime among addicts took obvious form even in the former Soviet Union. Their totalitarian socialism no doubt treated criminals (those not in power) more harshly than in the U.S. Yet, the percentage of crimes found to have been committed by persons under the influence of alcohol ranged from 60% of all cases of theft to 90% of all those of "hooliganism." In some years it was found persons under the influence

---

[111] *"Alcoholics Anonymous: The Story of How Many Thousands of Men and Women Have Recovered from Alcoholism," New York: Alcoholics Anonymous World Services, Inc., Third Edition, 1976, p. 542.*

[112] *Graham, Ibid., p. 105.*

[113] *Sally Satel and D. J. Jaffe, "Violent Fantasies," National Review, July 20, 1998, pp. 36-37.*

had committed 100% of murders in entire regions.[114] As a rule, 80% of repeat criminals "systematically abused alcohol."[115]

The egomaniac addict's need to dominate others seems especially marked in young addicts. Consider the fact that most criminals get their start while young. They are brash, take risks, act like they own their victims and achieve ego satisfaction by controlling and overpowering them. In stage one addiction, they fuel the ego with competency and high performance whether in a legal or illegal business, profession or act.

Father Joseph C. Martin recounts the story of a young man in prison serving a 20-to-life sentence. He started attending AA because his cellmate did. He had no idea he would learn that if alcohol causes trouble, alcohol is a problem for him. After a few meetings, he pondered the fact he'd been drunk only three times in his life. "The first time he lost his arm in an accident with a machine. The second time he lost his family. And the third time he committed the crime that cost him his freedom. He concluded, correctly, that he is an alcoholic."[116] If getting high causes a person to engage in behaviors that could result in the loss of an arm, his family and/or his freedom, he is surely an addict. As Father Martin says, "What makes problems is a problem...[and] an alcoholic is somebody whose drinking causes serious life problems."[117]

One of the most confusing aspects of addiction is that while the addict may commit unspeakable acts when under the influence, he is most visibly sick between uses. This gets far worse as the addiction progresses.[118] It probably accounts for the fact that the reported incidence for most crimes occurring while the perpetrator is under the influence is only in the 40-50% range. Milam and Ketcham point out, "When the alcoholic stops drinking, all hell breaks loose. Blood vessels constrict, cutting down on the flow of blood and oxygen to the cells. The blood glucose level drops sharply and remains unstable. The brain amines, serotonin and norepinephrine, decrease dramatically. Hormones, enzymes, and body fluid levels fluctuate erratically. The body's cells are malnourished and become toxic from long exposure to large doses of alcohol and acetaldehyde," and because he stopped drinking, no longer has alcohol as his "major source of energy and stimulation and as an antidote for the ever-present toxicity."

"These chaotic events cause fundamental disruptions in the brain's chemical and electrical activity....the resulting pandemonium creates nu-

[114] *Stephen White, "Russia Goes Dry: Alcohol, State and Society," Great Britain: Cambridge University Press, p. 46.*
[115] *White, Ibid., p. 47.*
[116] *Father Joseph C. Martin, Ibid., p. 35.*
[117] *Ibid., p. 34-35.*
[118] *Milam and Ketcham, Ibid., p. 64.*

merous psychological and physiological problems for the alcoholic, including profound mental confusion, memory defects...paranoia, violent or fearful behavior...."[119] No wonder we can't link substance addiction to criminal activity. Too often, the crime occurs when the addict is not under the influence or is coming down, when suffering is at its worst. In many instances, by the time of the arrest the BAC has declined to seemingly inconsequential levels, or at least to those that do not indicate a heavy drinker or user of other drugs.

Even third stage addicts may be responsible for criminal behaviors in between uses. Recall the movies, *Lost Weekend* and *Leaving Las Vegas.* Smoothed out when the BAC was at obviously high levels, the main characters were blithering, nervous wrecks in-between drinks while the BAC dropped towards zero. Many spouses tell their addicted loved ones to "go have a drink," since these addicts are easier to deal with high than sober. It's as if they'd had a fight the night before with blows to the head, felt no pain and wake up sober but hurting. Although their cells and brain are in heated battle every time they use, inflicting damage to cells, the drug acts to numb the pain. It's also similar to undergoing an operation; the pain is felt only after the anesthesia wears off. It is possible that many crimes of passion are committed in-between uses.

Serial unethical behavior

6. "Should he be (but isn't) incarcerated for crimes such as physical abuse, burglary or mayhem, drinking and driving, stealing from you or making false, libelous or slanderous accusations, or engaging in any other unethical behavior in serial fashion?"

Many ignore such behaviors, or remove the keys, hide the purse, refuse to testify against him and/or believe his false accusations. If he should be convicted of such crimes, or you've pro-actively been making them difficult to commit, the probability of active addiction may be similar to those who've actually served time.

Experiencing consequences sooner results in a greater possibility of early recovery. Instead, the usual pattern is that close people, especially parents and friends, protect the addict from consequences. The result is an increasing likelihood of more obviously harmful behavior as the affliction progresses. We do not and cannot help by protecting.

---

[119] *Milam and Ketcham, Ibid., p. 64-65.*

From the earliest stages, addicts seem incapable of distinguishing acceptable from unacceptable behavior, or morality from immorality. Altered perceptions (from euphoric recall) cause them to remember everything they do in a positive light, regardless of how disgusting or unethical the behavior. Even without altered perceptions, they justify this behavior in order to gain access to drugs, regardless of the consequences. Either way, they are incapable of knowing or acknowledging right from wrong.

Graham points out that addicts often commit acts of violence and other criminal or unethical behaviors in serial fashion. Such behaviors promote the ego-inflation needed to fuel the addiction. Therefore, any repeated act that promotes and maintains power over others in any way is an excellent clue to addiction. Now, by no means are all adulterers addicts, any more than are all smokers. However, if a person commits adultery or other violations of contract or trust, the likelihood of uncovering active substance addiction increases.

Domestic abuse

7. "Does s/he commit domestic violence, verbally abuse others and/or engage in a tremendous amount of inappropriate swearing?"

Several police officers and chemical dependency counselors confide that domestic violence points to a nearly 100% probability of substance addiction. The question is, as in *The War of the Roses*, which one is the addict?

Substance addiction is a family disease. Chaos and insanity reign in the household or workplace of an addict. Those close to a practicing addict may become as crazy as does the addict; some, even more so. The addict may become violent, while the codependent may be driven to violence in response to the addict's lies and other destructive behavior. When growing up, many non-addicts learned violence as an appropriate response to perceived injustices. Therefore, while the existence of violence and/or verbal abuse is an excellent clue to addiction, it is by no means certain which player is the culprit.

More confusing, use of alcohol by the non-addict may increase during a period of elevated domestic insanity. Since the non-addict can become violent in such situations, we must look for other signs to determine which participant is which. This is not to remove blame from the violent or abusive non-addict. However, when the non-addict removes himself from the insanity and develops an understanding of the affliction, he will usually be quick to recover. Due to the nature of the affect of the chemical on the brain, the addict's recovery generally takes far longer.

A survey by Maria Roy, founder and executive director of Abused Women's Aid in Crisis, Inc. of 150 abused women, found 85% of violent husbands had either an alcohol or other drug problem. "These men were inclined to beat their wives at a higher frequency, either when under the influence of drugs (including alcohol) *or when sober,* and their violence was usually characterized by physical assault with or without a weapon, usually leading to serious injuries, and including sexual assault. Husbands in this group did not have to be drunk or on other drugs when committing a violent act; v*ery often, the assaults came during sobriety or when the effects of hard drugs had worn off*[120] (emphasis added). The most common drug used was alcohol. Eighty-five per cent of those husbands may have been addicts and the other 15% were possibly codependents.

According to a recent study, there is no evidence that men who complete domestic-violence counseling programs treat their women any better than men who have never taken such a course.[121] This suggests that such programs treat symptoms and not their underlying cause. One anonymous counseling center in the study reported that although it had counseled physical abusers for several years, they had seen only one recovery. The abusers only got worse in their repeated (serial) abuse and they all said, "You made me do it." They abused only family, never outsiders and when they were good, they were golden but when bad, monsters. The abuse followed a typical pattern of growing tension, hostility, verbal abuse and ultimately, physical attack. This was followed by the "honeymoon" in which they begged forgiveness. This center pointed out "many" domestic abusers are drug or alcohol "abusers" as well. By now, it should be obvious to we lay persons that the patterns described in the abuser were all suggestive of substance addiction.

When we think of domestic violence, most think of the husband committing acts against his wife and children. We should not be so constricted in our view. Several recent reports cited as many female violators as male.[122] Men just don't report it as often. This may be due to the fact that they aren't hurt as frequently or gravely, or they may be embarrassed to admit to any physical harm by a woman. The female partner also may commit acts of aggression against children. Children may then turn against their

---

[120] *Maria Roy, Ed., "Battered Women: A Psychosociological Study of Domestic Violence," New York: Van Nostrand, 1977, p. 39.*

[121] *Neil Jacobson and John Gottman of the University of Washington, and other studies interpreted in Margaret A. Hagen, "Bad Attitude," National Review, July 20, 1998, p. 38.*

[122] *1985 National Family Violence Survey, funded by the National Institute of Mental Health; 1986 study on U.S. family violence reported in the Journal of Marriage and Family; 1986 study on teenagers in the Journal for the National Association of Social Workers. Internet site at http://www.vix.com/pub/men/battery/battery.html.*

smaller siblings, behaviors which, if excessive, should be viewed as a sign of addiction somewhere in the family hierarchy.

Rage, almost always the predecessor to violence, is often symptomatic of substance addiction. Verbal abuse including put-downs, belittling and other disparaging language should be viewed with great suspicion. Excessive swearing may be a clue to addiction in that person or to someone close. Growing up, I was exposed to so much swearing that it became my own bad habit. A former client of mine, a high-powered attorney (earning $500 per hour in his prime) with whom I had a small misunderstanding, began swearing at me profusely over the phone. At that point, the possibility of addiction dawned on me. I confirmed my diagnosis with a lifelong friend of his, his drinking having indeed become a "serious problem."

Dishonesty

8. "Is there lying, false accusations, or statements that appear to consist of lies or intellectual dishonesty?"

Any degree of repeated lying about where he's been, how much he drinks, the real reason for the loss of his job or any other "problems" alludes to addiction. While many deceive, have affairs and blame others for their troubles, few do so as consistently, persistently and methodically as the alcohol or other drug addict. On one hand, blackouts, memory repression and euphoric recall account for the appearance of lying. On the other, there is no more underhanded way to exercise control over others than by lying. This is just another way to inflate that massive ego. They also may lie to protect their drug of choice and/or sources. As observers, we will unlikely be able to distinguish between these lies, but this is not necessary. As the degree of either suspected or actual lying increases, so does the probability of substance addiction.

The described effects of the written warnings given by pharmacies of various psychoactive drugs include impaired speech and memory, paranoia, psychosis, drowsiness, mental confusion and euphoria. Other physical symptoms warned about can include irregular gait, eye divergence and abnormal pupil dilation or constriction. These warnings should include lying and its progeny, intellectual dishonesty and false accusations, but do not.

In most cases, it starts immediately. In her book on child drinking, Nancy Woodward relates the story of an 11-year-old boy: "I knew in my mind that night, when [a girlfriend and I] got ready to go out, that we planned to buy booze. I had conned my mother into funds to go to a movie, which means that right there I had all the symptoms of alcoholism *because I was lying.* I had no intention of going to the movies. I was looking to get drunk" (emphasis added).[123] This does not mean every child who lies is a budding young addict, but again, the more consistent the lying, the greater the likelihood. It's also an excellent early-stage clue, if you can expose his lying. Unfortunately, addicts, young and old alike, are so adept at deceiving that not only won't you catch him, you may even apologize for daring to question his veracity.

As soon as a bold-faced lie is told, red flags should go up. Modern-day witch hunts, including crusades against pre-school teachers accused of committing atrocities against their young charges, are likely promoted by addicts. Taking the Buckey's McMartin Pre-School case as an example, a huge warning flag may have been that not one parent had a clue of horrifying abuse over a 5-year period during which it was supposedly occurring. Only an addict has the ability to convince others that such activity could take place without any solid evidence.

I later found that a female addict, Judy Johnson, who committed suicide 3 years later, made the original accusation. By that time, the ball was rolling and the madness of crowds took over. Granted, while crowd psychology takes on a life of its own, it is suspected that many incidences are initiated and carried through by addicts. Historians, once they begin to review events in the light of understanding addiction, may find addicts playing an instigating and continuing role in much crowd psychology. Without understanding substance addiction and, through trial and error, finding addiction where it has been suspected, this conclusion may seem absurd. However, comprehending some of the brain chemistry, along with repeatedly tracing the origins of destructive events to the behaviors of addicts makes it believable and, even, logical.

James Graham broadened and conceptualized this, finding addicts often make such false accusations to buttress their ego. These range from the most common, adultery,[124] to those by prosecutors and others against innocent people (Graham provides several well-known historical examples).[125] The recent child-abuse witch-hunts should prove no exception, but direct evidence will be difficult, at best, to obtain.

Those accused are frequently competent people, since there is little ego-gratification in attacking those known to be incompetent or guilty. The kind of attack "is determined by the social environment in which [the ad-

[123] *Nancy Hyden Woodward, "If your child is drinking...What you can do to fight alcohol abuse at home, at school, and in the community," New York: G.P. Putnam's Sons, 1981, pp. 34-35.*

[124] *Graham, Ibid., p. 59.*

[125] *Graham, Ibid., pp. 24-26.*

dict] functions."[126]   While some addicts use violence, particularly if deemed safe for them, others steal property. Those who make false accusations steal reputations. The form the attack takes is determined by the addict's Temperament (discussed later) as well as gender. Females resort to non-violent tactics more frequently due to lack of size and strength.

The classic case of lying by accusation is that of alcoholic Senator Joseph McCarthy, whose alcoholism, Graham suggests, explained his infamous behavior. Richard Rovere, in *Senator Joe McCarthy* (Methuen & Co., Ltd., 1960) denies McCarthy was an alcoholic, despite the report that, "His drinking prowess, until the last year of his life was, in fact, notable. He could 'belt a fifth,'...between midnight and five A.M., catch a couple hours sleep, and be at his office at eight or nine, ready for a hard day's work...." Graham points out that this description suggests McCarthy drank a lot, had high tolerance and didn't have hangovers early on, all indicative of alcoholism.[127]

Graham also alludes to the danger of bestowing power to alcoholic law enforcement officers and district attorneys. Alcoholic Charles M. Fickert, District Attorney of San Francisco, framed two labor leaders whom he knew to be innocent (Thomas Mooney and Warren Billings, each spending 23 years in prison) in what later became known as an American Dreyfus case. Alcoholic New York District Attorney and later Governor Charles Whitman sent innocent police lieutenant Charles Becker to the electric chair.[128] It is important to understand that these cases suggest, once an addict achieves a position of power, he is out of control and cannot help himself. We can use the signs of addiction to prevent addicts from gaining such authority, diminish it when attained and subsequently intervene. The same principles apply to the home, where an alcoholic abuses his power as head of household and to his work, where an alcoholic employer, employee or partner will do the same with whatever powers are conferred.

If we are to make this question more useful, we must stop our own lying, especially with children. If they hear us lie, we are teaching them to do so. If we ask them to falsely inform a caller that we're not home, we've taught them to lie and that lying is OK. Don't deceive, even about a marital problem or addiction in a spouse. It may not be something you wish to share, but they know something is wrong, whether or not you're truthful.[129]

---

[126] *Graham, Ibid., p. 19.*
[127] *Graham, Ibid., pp. 20-21 and 29.*
[128] *Graham, Ibid., pp. 24-26.*
[129] *M. Scott Peck in "The Road Less Traveled," New York: Simon and Schuster, 1978, pp. 59-63, has a magnificent discussion of lying and disclosure with children. Highly recommended.*

Erratic behavior

9. "Is he capricious in his use of power, or does he exhibit volatile, unpredictable and/or erratic behavior?"

Power is of little use to the egomaniac if the law is applied justly; rather, it must be used unpredictably and selectively. The egomaniac relates to W. M. Ireland's demarcation: "Power is nothing if it be consciously applied. The man who...punishes only the guilty, who absolves only the innocent, whose testimony is inexorably true, has no real power at all."[130] There must be *abuse* of power.

James Graham points out several forms this may take. Lying and falsely accusing others is one common abuse. The addict chief executive may capriciously fire his top people if they so much as look cross-eyed at him. Henry Ford II, whose victims fortunately included Lee Iacocca (who moved on to reinvent Chrysler), is a leading example.[131] Mass murderers randomly kill, even to the point of destroying those they depend upon. Joseph Stalin killed or incarcerated so many of his top aides that the Soviet Union was almost incapacitated before it entered WWII. The alcoholic head of household, in abusing his family, may favor one child over another. Unpredictably erratic, he alternates abuse and remorse.

On the less harmful side, this may take the form of what James Graham calls "unreasonable resentments." The addict may rant for days, weeks or months about some petty occurrence that non-addicts would simply shrug off. This gives an excuse to cut off ties with the perpetrator, whether a relative or an old friend. Power over family is thus maintained by forbidding or regulating contact with outsiders.

Undisciplined children

10. "Do the children lack boundaries?"

While children can be out of control in the absence of addiction, the more unrestrained their behavior, the greater the likelihood of addiction in the family. The challenge is in identifying the addict. It may be the child or parent(s).

Addicts frequently hide the chaos in their lives from others. In recov-

---

[130] *Quoted in Graham, Ibid., p. 12.*
[131] *Graham, Ibid., pp. 135-136.*

ery, they admit that their "lives have become unmanageable," a manifestation of chaos. Non-addicts, especially children, often unknowingly give
away the family secret if we simply observe their behaviors and keep in
mind the fact that the behavior of codependents often mimics that of addicts.

In the former Soviet Union, out-of-control behavior among children was
proven to be a sign of alcoholism in a parent. Researchers in Leningrad
found that in as many as 88 of every 100 families in which there were "problem" children, either or both parents were "problem" drinkers.[132] It was
reported that "the more the parents drank, the more likely that the juveniles concerned would have a criminal record."[133] This should not be surprising. The addict-parent, for all intents and purposes, abandons the children in order to carry on a love affair with a drug. The child, too, sees the
out-of-control behavior in the addict-parent's private life and varies it in
his own way. The results of this can reach horrifying extremes, as in the
aforementioned case of the two children dropping the 5-year-old from the
14th floor.

According to Polson and Newton, children react to the family addict by
adopting different dysfunctional roles.[134] Just as addicts vary in the manifestations of their disease, so do codependents in their reactions. Such roles
are not always obvious. The "Superkid" accomplishes almost superhuman
feats in an effort to offset the addict's poor behavior. Since some kids of
non-addicts are great achievers, family problems may be difficult to detect.
If, however, the addict is a sibling who gets a lot of attention (even in negative ways), hatred for him by the "Superkid" may be overt, since this is
attention the latter should be getting for his own successes and accom-
plishments. He may also avoid bringing friends to his home, in an effort to
prevent outsiders from discovering his family's imperfections.

The "Bad Ass Kid" is the more conspicuous. He imitates the druggie
sibling in everything except the drugs. He hangs out with a bad crowd,
gets bad grades and skips classes. Here's a kid who does everything the
addict does, but cannot get hooked because he simply didn't inherit the
addict genes. In an effort to take the focus of attention off the addict, he
gets into all sorts of trouble through outward rebellion. He seeks revenge
and is probably the type of non-addict most likely to be involved in criminal activities.

The "Family Clown" tries to defuse the family storm by performing or
being cute or cuddly in a vain attempt to keep the family laughing. The
"Passive Kid" withdraws physically and/or psychologically, hiding in his

---

[132] *White, Ibid., p. 41.*
[133] *White, Ibid., p. 46.*
[134] *Polson and Newton, Ibid., pp. 79-97.*

own fantasy world. All these children suffer terribly inside, adopting their own particular coping strategy. Any of these various manifestations should clue us in to the possibility of addiction somewhere within the family unit.

Financial difficulties

11. "Does he suffer repeated financial difficulties?"
Market-based variables can make it difficult to determine the underlying cause of the financial challenges one may face. However, repeated instances of overspending, over-indebtedness or loss of job/business is a sign of poor judgment, to which we may ascribe addiction.

Consider the egotistical drinker who insists on being the "big man," picking up everyone's tab at the bar, even though it's something he can ill-afford. He borrows to the hilt to spend on toys and extravagances, figuring he'll have no problem paying it back with the next big raise, commission or bonus. Such grandiose behavior is, by itself, an excellent clue to addiction, often creating the financial difficulties.

As we've seen, driving fatalities are usually caused by alcohol or other drug use, but may be caused by other variables. The same thing can be said for financial problems, such as the decline of industries, sudden increases in interest rates, sudden drops in asset values or the financial equivalent of "driver error" (i.e., simple mistakes). However, the sober individual is more likely to quickly correct and recover from such calamities than is the addict. Non-addicts are less likely to repeat errors that result in financial ruin. In discussions with clients and attorneys, it is suggested that the impaired judgment of addicts may cause as many as 50% of bankruptcies. These financial disasters may be those of addicts or others whom addicts adversely affected.

Covering up

12. "Are you protecting the possible addict from natural consequences by lying or otherwise covering or 'fixing things' for him?"
In other words, are you enabling? If so, you can probably take the "pos-

sible" out of addict. This includes excusing or ignoring the poor behavior of others with such comments as, "Oh, that's just the way Billy is." This is an area in which we can observe our own behavior to help determine the likelihood of addiction in another. We may lie about problems in the home,[135] including domestic violence. Spouses may lie about work absences or tardiness, giving every excuse except the truth (i.e. hangover). Parents sometimes even lie for their child, denying he is the source of a problem for which he is responsible. These well-intentioned parents defend their child from consequences meted out by school or worse, the law. They pay restitution required by government agencies. They may pay the child's auto insurance bill and tickets. Such enabling only helps to insure that young practicing addicts become older practicing addicts.

This can occur at work as well. For example, a fellow employee makes an inordinate number of errors or is rude to customers. Others helping to conceal such errors or behavior are enabling. All of these cover-ups are excellent signs of addiction in the enabled.

Authors Polson and Newton describe three kinds of "fixing" in their book on child addicts.[136] These "fixes" can easily be applied to adults. "Situational fixing" includes moving to a new neighborhood to change the child's "bad environment." This is equivalent to "pulling a geographic" (so-called by Alcoholics Anonymous) when done by the addict-parent. A work-related equivalent is moving the addict from one department to another, or the addict himself switching jobs. The trouble with a "geographic" is that no matter where you go, there you are.

Attempting to substitute good behavior for bad is called "fixing the behavior." Attempting to interest a child in new sports activities by buying him the equipment with which to support the activity is an example of such behavior fixing. The trouble is that no matter what constructive activity the child is engaging in, whether skiing, horseback riding, bowling, football or other activity, alcohol and other drugs are available. This is just as true for adult addicts. The source of the trouble is not being addressed. A work-related equivalent might be purchasing a new computer or other equipment specifically for a problem-worker, hoping this will improve his performance.

"Fixing the consequences" includes hiring the lawyer. Adults do this handily for children as well as for other adults. Co-workers fix consequences for fellow workers, excusing it as "sticking it out together." If we observe others — even whole groups — fixing consequences for someone, they may be protecting an addict. The trouble is, getting others to enable poor be-

---

[135] *Suzanne Somers does an admirable job describing this in "Keeping Secrets," New York: Warner Books, 1988.*
[136] *Polson and Newton, Ibid., p. 111.*

havior is a powerful way by which to exercise the control that fuels addiction. In the long run, by cooperating, we're not doing the addict (or ourselves) any favors.

We should be particularly watchful of enabling by people in positions near those with power and influence. **The higher an addict's social status, the greater the enabling, because the enablers have more to lose.**[137] In business, the enablers have their job and incomes to lose. In the entertainment industry, they can lose their job, income and prestige. In politics, at risk are job, income, prestige and power. Therefore, employees will lie for the addict, ignore their drunken incidents or behavior, cover up and even obtain their drug for them. *Do not think that because someone holds a high office in private or public life, we would all know he's an alcoholic or other drug addict. We would be* _less_ *likely to know this, since those near him, having more to lose, will do everything possible to protect his secret.* Such enabling can be the most valuable clue to possible addiction of those in power.

Enabling is the reason that so many talented people—Judy Garland, Marilyn Monroe, Richard Burton and John Belushi—die young; they were "helped" to their graves by those around them. Paradoxically, it is likely the reason binge alcoholic (and uni-drug user) Joseph Stalin maintained his power for as long as he did; nobody stopped him from drinking. Such enabling also makes it imperative that we look for behaviors other than direct evidence of use, as clues to addiction. This is particularly crucial when the subject holds high political or bureaucratic office. Since the behaviors of practicing substance addicts are so unpredictably destructive, those in such positions can become extremely dangerous. The higher the position of power and influence, the greater the damage that can be inflicted on innocent people.

Availability of substances

13. "Does he attempt to insure the substance is always available?"

The budding young addict will be the first to say, "Let's party," often supplying the booze or other drugs. Drinking (or drugging) is the focus of events and business meetings. He may have a fully stocked bar or a concealed vial. There may be a refusal or reticence to go to anyone's home where liquor isn't served or dope isn't used. The behavior of some addicts may become bizarre or even dangerous if concerned about the availability of their drugs.

---

[137] *This observation is made by Marianne E. Brickley, recovering alcoholic and ex-wife of Michigan's GOP Lt. Gov. James Brickley, quoted by Robe, p. 287, with further support for the concept on pp. 111, 120 and 150.*

Patricia (my personal addict) and I were heading out for a week's vacation. Patricia's 14-year-old son, Ross, threw a tantrum upon our departure, striking me. Living in an insanity of which I still had no understanding, instead of calling the police or just getting out of his way, I struck back. He then threatened me with a heavy glass lamp. I literally stared him down and lived.

By this time, I had found Ross with small amounts of dope on several occasions. Patricia invoked penalties that were never enforced, at times even coming to his defense. I later learned that Ross was already a heavy marijuana user and found evidence that Patricia was his supplier. Returning the favor, Ross lied for his mother. Addicts often enable each other if it is to their advantage.

In hindsight, I figure Ross probably threw a fit because his supplier and co-user was leaving for a week and he might not have his usual access to drugs. The behavior, a tantrum, was in itself a clue that something was wrong. Friends later told me they saw Patricia smoking dope and drinking vodka with her son, while I was working 80 hours a week during my busy season.

As we said, addicts engage in bizarre and dangerous behavior to insure availability of their substance of choice. One late night, supposedly in early sobriety, Patricia was allegedly beaten up while walking into a bar to use the restroom, as her two children waited in the car. This should have been enough to tell me she had relapsed, but at the time I was still naïve and ignorant of the extraordinarily high relapse rate of addicts in early recovery. She later admitted to doing a "minor deal" for some dope for her son, not for herself, of course.

Failing to see that a drug is always available should by no means lead us to believe there is no addiction. In fact, the ability to control or even discontinue use for extended periods may serve as false evidence that everything is OK. This is especially true for many early-to-middle stage alcoholics. A judge may threaten revocation of probation (as was the case for Robert Downey, Jr.), an employer with termination of employment or a spouse with divorce. Addicts may be successful at such times by exerting, what is for them, superhuman control. They will do anything and cooperate with anyone in order to protect their freedom to use in the long-term.

An analogy may be drawn to the temporary separation of a spouse due to family emergencies or work. Such separations can occur for a couple weeks or even months without major trauma. If the separation is due to death, however, there is agonizing and extended periods of grief.[138] This is the reason why addicts often "go on the wagon" for a time, yet rarely achieve

---

[138] *Gorski provides this terrific analogy in Terence Gorski, "The Role of Codependence in Relapse," Independence, MO: Herald House/Independence Press, 1991, audio cassette series.*

permanent sobriety.

Psychological disorders

14. "Does he have intense mood swings or the appearance of other psychopathological disorders including: 'nervous breakdowns,' narcissism, adolescent behavior in an adult, obnoxious behavior, borderline (chaotic) personality, unreasonableness, manic-depressive (bipolar disorder) or sociopathic behavior, paranoia, schizophrenia, psychotic or catatonic episodes?"[139]

Many therapists, seeking to explain volatile mood swings and other behavioral problems, look first for bipolar or other psychopathological disorders and/or mental illnesses. While these can be treated therapeutically or with medicine, substance addiction cannot. Yet, addiction can mimic all these disorders and illnesses, which therefore become symptoms of an underlying addiction. Only when the addiction is arrested can other problems be properly treated (if they haven't already dissipated).

Addicts exhibit abrupt mood changes, from depressed and withdrawn to hyper, manic and excited, for no apparent reason. The timing depends on when and which drug was used last, interactions of various drugs with each other and how the addict's particular brain neurotransmitters are affected. Often, these reactions take place in-between uses. The only difference (to the layperson) in observable behaviors of an addict and a bipolar is that if the addict cleans up, the depression and mania (eventually) disappear.[140] Even with as little as a month in recovery, the number of addicts exhibiting sociopathic behaviors (in a study by alcoholism expert Terence Gorski, discussed later) plunged from 90% to 10%.

Alcoholic actress Vivien Leigh was repeatedly diagnosed as bipolar (manic-depressive) even while she drank regularly and heavily. Alcoholism expert Charles L. Whitfield, M.D., said that although "she could have been suffering from both manic-depressive illness [bipolar disorder] and alcoholism, there would have been no way to know until one observed her alcohol- and drug-free for...one to three years."[141] Patty Duke's autobiography is suggestive of heavy drinking and other (legal) drug use as a trig-

---

[139] *Except for "nervous breakdowns," these were the psychopathological conditions ascribed by colleagues to fellow psychiatrist Martha Morrison, Ibid., reported on pp. 109-111 and 119. Nervous breakdowns have been ascribed to many alcoholic actresses.*

[140] *However, the difference in behaviors can be quite marked. The manic-depressive goes through month-long (or longer) states of either mania or depression before switching. The addict may alternate between states as frequently as hourly, but sometimes as long as months if he's maintaining a constant flow of drugs.*

[141] *Robe, Ibid., pp. 31; 142-145.*

ger for her bipolar disorder, a possibility Duke doesn't discuss. According to chemical dependency counselors, this disorder doesn't usually appear until the late teen years, well after most have had their first of many drinks. It's possible that other disorders such as sociopathic, schizophrenia and borderline personality might not only be mimicked but also triggered by heavy substance use and/or addiction.

While the percentage of bipolar, other disorders and the mentally ill are estimated by some to be 5% of the population, anecdotal discussions with (and books about) misdiagnosed recovering addicts may lead one to believe the percentage could be closer to 1 or 2%. The number of addicts, then, is at least two and as many as 10 times those having true (non-addiction related) psychopathological disorders or mental illness. Therefore, we should place the larger likelihood of the explanation for bizarre behavior on substances until proven wrong. We must always keep in mind, that although we want to help, we cannot, if there is addiction. Some chemical dependency experts have told me that the correct attribution of what appears to be the disorders or mental illnesses to substance addiction is in the neighborhood of 50%; perhaps after finishing this book, you may think that it's closer to 80%.

Psychiatrist Martha Morrison, M.D. relates how her moods would swing rapidly, moving from over-excitement, excessive energy and/or elation to deep depression, despair, despondency, self-pity, irritability, crankiness, nastiness, immature and child-like reactions or other bizarre behavior, including paranoia. To Morrison, an expert in addiction who treated other addicts, these bore no relationship to the innumerable and extraordinary amount of drugs she ingested, frequently exceeding a dozen different substances a day.[142] This inability to connect the behavior to the substance use suggests addiction cannot be self-diagnosed, regardless of the level of intelligence or expertise. If true, there may be a fatal flaw in one standard model of psychological counseling. Here, the psychologist asks the patient how the patient feels, what is wrong, etc. At the risk of over-generalizing, the therapist (in this model) acts only as a sounding board. Asking repeatedly, "Well, what do you think that means?" gives addicts the opportunity to blame others for their problems, with the tacit approval of the therapist. This may be the reason that recovering addicts who were in therapy during their using days usually view therapists as their biggest enablers.

Interestingly, one of the psychopathological behaviors, paranoia, may only be an appearance, an excuse to further the addict's capricious ends. Between 1934 and 1939, Stalin used paranoia as his excuse to purge (by death or imprisonment) half his elite officer corps and 60-90% of his Com-

---

[142] *Morrison, Ibid., p. 55 and numerous later pages.*

manders, Admirals, Marshals and other Communist Party members. His tools were (false) accusations of sabotage, insubordination, spying and treason. However, as Roy A. Medvedev points out about Stalin in *Let History Judge* (Alfred A. Knopf, 1971), the behavior is not that of a paranoid, but rather one of contempt. However, it looks like paranoia, which is an observable clue, while the reasons for the paranoia (contempt, etc.) are not. Similarly, Henry Ford II, after moving Lee Iacocca to tears in his expression of concern about the plight of Black Americans, raved to Iacocca, "Those goddamn coons...I hate them. I'm scared of them and I think I'll move to Switzerland, where there just aren't any."[143] Some of the other seeming psychopathological behaviors may be only ruses to control others, fueling their addiction through the exercise of power.

Changes of employment

15. "Have there been unexplained changes of employment or a number of different employers within a relatively brief period of time, or serious problems at work?"

Large numbers of changes in employment have been known to be a red flag to substance addiction (excepting seasonal or project-based businesses such as farming or movies). If these changes are due to problems at work, addiction is likely.

This is especially true since 85% of alcoholics and 70% of illegal drug users are employed.[144] Of course, before termination, addicts are probably the cause of many interpersonal problems in the workplace. This hypothesis is at least partially confirmed by a NCADD (National Council on Alcoholism and Drug Dependence, Inc.) report. A year after the employees at the Oldsmobile plant in Lansing, Michigan underwent treatment, man-hours lost "declined by 49 per cent, health care benefits [used] by 29 per cent, leaves [of absence] by 56 per cent, grievances by 78 per cent, disciplinary problems by 63 per cent and accidents by 82 per cent."[145] Note especially the grievances and accidents. These are particularly compelling numbers in view of the fact that many alcoholics may have gone undetected, while many in recovery (with only a year of sobriety) would still be in post-acute withdrawal. Recall that during early sobriety, many of the symp-

---

[143] *Graham, Ibid., pp. 135, 158 and 164-165.*

[144] *"NCADD Fact Sheet: Alcohol and Other Drugs in the Workplace;" National Institute on Drug Abuse, "Research on Drugs and the Workplace," NIDA Capsules, June, 1990, p. 1.*

[145] *Ibid.; D. Campbell and M. Graham, "Drugs and Alcohol in the Workplace: A Guide for Managers," New York: Facts on File Publications, 1988, p. 9.*

toms of active alcoholism often continue.

Statistics such as these lend support to the possibility that, absent other variables, 80% of automobile accidents are addiction-related. Additionally, the dramatic decline in grievances supports the findings that other interpersonal problems, including divorce, have their roots in addiction much of the time. If statistics existed for accidents resulting from carelessness by the jittery addict in-between drinks, there might be additional support for the idea that addiction, as opposed to simply use, is a significant cause of such accidents and problems. According to the same NCADD report, less than a third of one percent of employed persons are receiving treatment for alcoholism and other drug dependence.

Now, we need to get out the abacus. We've learned that 10% of the population is addicted and roughly 80% of these hold jobs. If only .3% of the employed (which is 3% of addicts) are getting treatment, we can omit those addicts undergoing treatment as being statistically irrelevant. We can just figure that one out of every 12 employees is an addict. With so many untreated employed addicts, it's reasonable to attribute most serious problems in the workplace (unaccounted for in the NCADD study) to them. The fact that they are reportedly 33% less productive[146] reinforces this idea.

If we see such problems, don't just ask if there is an addict; find him or her. These problems further surface in one report that found addicts five times more likely than non-addicts to file worker's compensation claims[147] and 3.6 times more likely to injure themselves or another person in the workplace. They are responsible for 40% of all industrial fatalities (a statistic remarkably similar to driving fatalities) and incur 300% higher medical costs and benefits.[148] One reason for injuries on the job could be the addict's prevailing obsession with their drug of choice. Not just when or how much, but with whom.

They are also conspiring to protect their use of the substance from anyone who might attempt to interfere. "Accordingly, a great deal of the active alcoholic's energy is spent constructing facades, an effort to present to others a front that looks okay, that seems lovable and worthy and intact."[149] This explains incompetence (or decreased productivity) on the job, espe-

---

[146] *STAND, Support Training Against Narcotic Dependency, Los Angeles Police Department handout, "Why STAND." Soviet research reported similar findings, suggesting the "efficiency" of the alcoholic worker was 36% less than that of non-drinkers, the equivalent of 93 lost workdays every year. Reported in "Russia Goes Dry," by Steven White.*

[147] *STAND, Ibid.; Thomas E. Backer, Ph.D., "Strategic Planning for Workplace Drug Abuse Programs," National Institute on Drug Abuse, 1987, p. 4.*

[148] *STAND, Ibid.*

[149] *Knapp, Ibid., p. 176.*

cially in latter-stage addiction. Recall how many students in middle school obsessed over their latest heartthrob, barely able to concentrate on the teacher or subject. This fixation is true in spades for the practicing addict, thinking about his relationship with the bottle or other substance and doing whatever it takes to protect that relationship. Remember what you will do to get air when your head is being held under water.

These facts are particularly important for small firms, few of which have Employee Assistant Programs or other tools to deal with the practicing addict, who has the power to destroy a small business. I was lucky. While losing a number of wonderful clients due to an employee-addict, my business did not fall apart. The most important clients lost were those with whom the addict had greater contact. Only one client told me he left because of the addict's behavior, which I naïvely attributed to a conflict of personalities. I later learned that his concern was the tip of a small iceberg (according to one report, there are 250 real instances of dissatisfaction for every one complaint). Such were the risks of being both a hands-off manager and totally ignorant of the effects of substance addiction.

If there are any complaints about an employee's behavior, whether from co-workers or customers, the possibility of substance addiction should be considered. Please note that the absence of aforementioned changes or problems may incorrectly lead us to assume there is no addiction.

Changing Partners

16. "Have there been unexplained or irrational changes of spouses or 'significant others,' or a number of different partners within a relatively brief period of time, or serious known problems at home?"

The same principles apply here as with problems at work. When we have a relationship with a substance, there cannot be a close and significant one with another human being. In the extreme, Caroline Knapp suggests that anonymous sex gives "the illusion of intimacy with none of the attendant risks, none of the aching vulnerability of sober sex."[150]

I previously thought financial difficulties were the main cause of divorce. I was really observing a side effect of substance addiction, which I now believe usually, underlies the financial difficulties. Graham quotes alcoholism authority Richard C. Bates, M.D., as estimating that 50 to 70% of all divorces involve alcoholism.[151] Up to 80% of all cases of divorce were attributable to the influence of alcohol in the former Soviet Union,

---

[150] *Knapp, Ibid., p. 74.*
[151] *Graham, Ibid., p. 60.*

where alcoholism was (and still is) epidemic.[152] It is probably not a coincidence that this is in the same ballpark as the 78% of workplace grievances at the Lansing Oldsmobile plant, reportedly due to alcoholism. Therefore, divorce may be an important clue to substance addiction in one party or the other. Since close persons can mimic the addict, it is possible untreated adult children of addicts may be at greater risk of divorce as well, a clue to possible addiction in a parent.

The divorces are, in part, due to the alcoholic's propensity not only to create financial problems, but to also commit domestic violence and other abuse. They may occur, as well, because of a greater tendency in addicts to commit adultery. Recovering alcoholic Conway Hunter, M.D. diplomatically points out, "Seeking companionship with members of the opposite sex outside of marriage is probably one of the most commonplace events that occurs in an alcoholic's life...."[153]

Lucy Barry Robe, in her study of famous women alcoholics, found that 86% of one sample group of addict women divorced at least once. Forty-five per cent of Robe's subjects married at least 3 times, while only 16% of all women do so.[154] These are very compelling statistics. It can be calculated that the probability of alcoholism in a woman who has been married three times is almost four times greater than one who has been married only once.[155] It would probably be higher, were it not for the fact that so many alcoholics die before having an opportunity to marry more often.

Absences and tardies

17. "Are there numerous absences from or tardies to work, school or home-life?"

Numerous absences or tardies increase the likelihood of addiction, particularly when they occur at the beginning of the week. Repeated hangovers, whether or not they result in missed work, suggest a very high probability of active addiction. This often provides management their first clue.

---

[152] *White, Ibid., p. 43.*

[153] *Dennis Wholey, Ed., "The Courage to Change: Personal Conversations About Alcoholism," New York: Warner Books, 1984, p. 201.*

[154] *Robe, Ibid., p. 267.*

[155] *Since the "all women" figure (16 out of 100) includes the alcoholic women sample (45 out of 100) and roughly 10% of the population is addicted, when eliminating the alcoholic women, we find that less than 12% of non-alcoholic women have been married 3 times. Therefore, the likelihood is almost 4 times greater (45% to 12%).*

Such absenteeism can give the spouse identical information, as can coming home at 3 a.m., or other "mysterious appearance." While we cannot see the ego, we can observe the effects of one that's inflated: arriving late gives a sense of power. "Look at me, I can arrive any time I want, because I am god-like." This egomania is, then, the source of the lack of consideration for others that addicts display, whether at work or play.

The National Council on Alcoholism and Drug Dependence, Inc., reports that absenteeism among alcoholics or problem drinkers is four to eight times greater than for other employees[156] and as much as 16 times greater among employees with alcohol <u>and other</u> drug related problems.[157] However, it is easy to confuse the addict with the non-addict, since "Non-alcoholic members of alcoholics' families use ten times as much sick leave as members of families in which alcoholism is not present." Furthermore, repeated school absences or tardiness, particularly in young children, may be a clue to addiction in the parent.

On the other hand, always being on time does not mean there is no addiction. There is some evidence that periodic drunks rarely, if ever, miss or are late for work. Recovering alcoholic-addict rock musician Grace Slick, known for her reliability, is a classic case of this.[158]

Defensiveness

18. "Does our suspect admit to using alcohol or other drugs extensively, but argue defensively, 'I can handle it,' or 'I can stop any time I want' and, if pressured, tells you it's none of your business?"

The inability to see that he is different from non-addictive drinkers in a potentially lethal way begins early in the addict's career. Non-addicts cannot handle the amounts of liquor or other drugs that addicts can. Non-addicts are able to stop any time they want, while addicts cannot. Use continues despite repeated and growing problems. At first signs of any trouble, addicts become very defensive about their use, while non-addicts will admit defeat.

Patricia, my personal addict, told me many times (once she admitted to her addiction) that events in her life were none of my business. When the money was rapidly disappearing from her checking account and I hap-

[156] M. Bernstein, J.J. Mahoney, "Management Perspectives on Alcoholism: The Employer's Stake in Alcoholism Treatment," *Occupational Medicine*, Vol. 4, No. 2 (1989), pp. 223-232.

[157] U.S. Department of Labor, "What Works: Workplaces Without Drugs," August, 1990, p. 3.

[158] Robe, Ibid., p. 96.

pened to notice, this too, was "none of my business." It turns out she had graduated to cocaine. Not only is addictive use the business of close persons, but so are the clues to such use, so they can step off the tracks when the train comes barreling through.

"Rules" for using

19. "Are there 'rules' for drinking or using, or is a known addict insisting that one particular drink (or other drug) can be tolerated?"

An addict cannot use <u>any</u> mind-altering chemical. If he says, "I can drink; after all, booze is not a drug!" or, "I can use pot; it's not the same as drinking!" or, "It's just beer," then you've got a practicing addict.

I'm a cabernet sauvignon aficionado. Patricia, whom I knew to be a recovering alcoholic (at the time, I had no idea what that meant), told me that it was all right to drink wine but not other liquor. I said, "No you can't! You're an alcoholic!" She responded, "No, wine is different."

This is one place where I learned a little bit of knowledge can be a dangerous thing. I knew I couldn't stop her from drinking; I'd learned as much from watching my father. Somehow, I knew to look for gulping and for behavioral changes while drinking. I didn't understand that the alcohol in wine was no different from the alcohol in other drinks.[159] Figuring I had no other choice, I proceeded to observe.

I observed sipping, not gulping and never saw her consume more than I drank. No behavioral changes were noted while drinking, although I saw such changes when she supposedly wasn't drinking.

I've asked recovering alcoholics whether they can sip a fine red wine. The uniform response was "absolutely not." Remember that to an alcoholic, alcohol, even in its most highbrow form, is meant for getting high and not taste. Then how could she have sipped all that time? By surreptitiously gulping vodka and adding Bailey's to her coffee, I later discovered.

She sipped wine, triggering the craving for more alcohol. With my inability to smell her alcohol, I had no clue and merely assumed she was experiencing chemical imbalances, as might occur with menopause or menstruation. Due to an adamant and uncompromising insistence that we always be absolutely honest with each other, she had me totally duped. This, along with the same demand of her children, was a fantastic set-up to insure that I wouldn't look too hard for dishonesty on her part.

[159] *Some drinks make me flush more quickly (certain white wines), some give me a rip-roaring headache (white tequila) and yet others give me a splotched hive-like reaction (some brands of vodka). I didn't know this is due to possible allergic reactions to different congeners (additives) and have nothing to do with the alcohol itself.*

One of the fundamental distinctions between addicts and non-addicts regarding their drinking behavior is that non-addicts don't need rules, because when, what or how much they drink is not an issue. "I only drink wine," is an example of many of the "rules" the addict makes up for himself. Other rules might be, "I never drink when I drive my kids," or, "I never drink before 5 p.m.," or, "I never drink when...." If you hear such rules, you are likely witnessing an early- to middle-stage addict attempting to control his drinking. This desperate attempt may last for years and, in the long run, becomes futile. Such rules erode and are eventually eliminated.

On the other hand, some alcoholics stick with one kind of alcohol for extended periods and even their entire drinking career. Many a recovering alcoholic says he drank only wine, or only Scotch, or only beer, denying he could be an alcoholic since he wouldn't drink "just anything." Some even insist wine or beer is not "really" alcohol (I believed a variation of this, thinking that somehow, fine red wine <u>could</u> be different). Alcoholism authorities Royce and Scratchley report on an upper-class hospital for alcoholics in which 15% of the patients never drank anything but beer.[160] The trouble is, we cannot determine with any certainty whether someone is or isn't an alcoholic just based on the amount consumed (which can be very little), or its particular form. It's the behavior that results from use that is relevant. An Italian consuming 14 ounces of pure alcohol in the form of wine over the course of a week is probably not an alcoholic. An American consuming half that amount in the form of vodka or Scotch every Saturday night and who then drives under the influence or engages in other destructive behaviors may well be.

Blackouts

20. "Does he have blackouts?"

Many authorities believe only an alcoholic (or other substance addict) has true blackouts (a complete blank in the memory).[161] Because addicts are brilliant at hiding the fact that they really don't remember, blackouts are very difficult for the observer to spot. They will blame anything but the drug for a lapse in memory.

Some authorities believe that while non-addicts can experience a blackout, it is often so terrifying that they will never drink or use as much again. The implication is, if the experience of using is so rewarding and pleasing

---

[160] *Royce and Scratchley, Ibid., p. 7.*
[161] *Smith, Ibid., p. 30.*

that it outweighs the fear of a blackout, the user is probably an addict. Therefore, if we detect more than one blackout, there is almost certainly, substance addiction. Also keep in mind that since blackouts can occur after as little as one or two drinks, this may be all that's needed to result in extraordinarily destructive behavior.

The observable evidence for these (as for euphoric recall) may come in the form of what appears to be lying. Since lying is a clue to addiction, the reasons for its appearance aren't relevant. If we see it, addiction may well be the explanation. Blackouts may also explain bizarre occurrences, such as a mysterious disappearance of the person. Travel is common during blackouts, with addicts having no idea how they got someplace when they "came to". They may also commit violent crimes while in this condition. Bizarre and destructive behaviors of addicts may be more often explained by alcoholic-induced amnesia than we can imagine.

Blaming

21. "Does he regularly blame others or 'circumstances' for his problems, or incessantly cry, 'Poor me'?"

Young addicts blame teachers and parents for problems and adult addicts blame their bosses, other innocent persons or "society." While the non-addict child or adult may occasionally do this also, this does not usually become habitual. Repeated instances should arouse suspicions.

The similarities of the enabling of the substance addict by the codependent and that of welfare addicts by society is remarkable. There may be good reason for this. According to perceptive and aware alcohol and drug social workers, as many as 80-90% of welfare recipients are addicts. The rest, are likely victims of addicts. The tools of control for the knowing enabler and that for society are also very similar. Just as an enabler robs the addict of the ability to rebuild his self-esteem by rescuing, society robs the same ability in the welfare addict through such rescues, euphemistically referred to as "putting a floor under" him.

It is suspected that most of those who play the "blame game" are addicts. They are incapable of accepting criticism without shifting blame. Now, we wouldn't ascribe addiction to everyone who sues a fast food restaurant for making the coffee too hot. However, someone who sues a bicycle manufacturer for being injured from riding at night without lights, may well be. The same could be said for someone hitting an employer with a wrongful termination suit, even though absent or late 300 times in two years. In other words, while not everyone who blames someone for something is an addict, there is a greater likelihood of addiction in those who do so repeatedly or in situations where the plaintiff really should have known better.

Diagnosing addiction in someone who plays this game is not easily done. This is because of the build-up of guilt and shame the non-addict may feel, due to the disintegration of the family or work environment. The non-addict may play rescuer or caretaker, cleaning up after the addict's messes, unaware that addiction is the source of the problem. This also results from the addict pointing the finger at everyone else, doing everything he can to convince others there's something wrong with them. If you feel you are to blame for the family problems or for the failures of your spouse or children, look for an addict. In addition, this can be done for society as a whole. To sum up, addicts tend to blame; less healthy non-addicts tend to accept blame and healthier ones tend to concentrate on solving their own problems, accepting what is offered them as challenges to be overcome.

Blame can take the form of complaining. Substance addicts are often the loudest and most vehement complainers in any group. Given their ability to talk people into doing things they wouldn't ordinarily with their alcoholic charm and gift of gab, they may well lead the crusade for increased handouts, or even more dangerous causes.

Several cult leaders have turned out to be addicts. This should not be surprising, since cult leaders are often criminals and 80% of criminals are addicts. For example, Jim Jones, an amphetamine and prescription drug addict and likely alcoholic,[162] led 900 men, women and children in Jonestown, Guyana to mass suicide in 1978. Addict Charlie Manson was able to convince his followers to commit murders. When leaving AA, Charles E. Dederich convinced some members to join his cult, known as Synanon which, according to its former members, engaged in such activities as brainwashing, wrongful imprisonment, kidnapping and even torture. He had, of course, relapsed long before.[163] D.C. Stephenson rose to the top of the Ku Klux Klan, creating a political machine that by 1924 controlled Indiana politics. One night he got drunk, summoned a woman to "join" him, raped her and was ultimately found responsible for her death. Like the dramatic rise and fall of individual addicts, the Klan's membership peaked at four million only to plummet, by the mid-1930s, to 100,000.[164]

---

[162] *Graham, Ibid., pp. 114-115.*

[163] *Graham, Ibid., pp. 122-125.*

[164] *A & E (Arts and Entertainment Network), "Ku Klux Klan: A Secret History," September 26, 1999.*

Illegal drugs

22. "Does he use illegal drugs, or heavily use legal psychoactive ones (sedatives, amphetamines or opioids) for extended periods of time?"

The use of illegal drugs is no different for the addict than legal ones. However, if someone (especially an adult) is willing to flaunt the law and risk jail for a drug, they are likely taking risks only an addict would. These addicts are often more easily diagnosed.

Our goal should be to first differentiate between friends and associates who may be users (and even abusers) from those of addicts, from whose destructive behaviors we need protection. This is difficult in the case of those using the drug alcohol and/or pharmaceuticals. It is hard to detect the difference between use, abuse and addiction to alcohol and yet, it's imperative to do so. It's even more difficult to distinguish among those using prescribed drugs. We don't usually think of doctors as pushers, prescribing drugs for addicts. Well, think again.

My first awareness that medical doctors know or understand little of this disease, resulted from observing Patricia's medical treatment. She supposedly suffered back injuries from two automobile accidents. (The accidents alone should put doctors on notice that they may be treating an addict.) The doctor prescribed Vicodin, a narcotic pain reliever. This is an opioid, or synthetic opium. Addicts call it "legal heroin." You don't give an alcoholic Vicodin (or any other psychoactive drug) without trying other remedies or, if the need for use is essential, prescribing a program of recovery immediately after. Otherwise, the addict is just getting an insurance- or government-paid-for buzz.

Seeing someone on Vicodin and alcohol is quite a sight. "Out there" and irrational, Patricia, who used both, exhibited virtually all the addictive behavioral traits described. I've since learned she was sloshed when she saw her doctor (apparently having her truly plastered moments when she wasn't home). Yet, it may have never occurred to him that she was an addict. Finally, proving that she was a practicing alcoholic, I called her doctor and informed him. The prescriptions stopped that very week. Explaining why she was no longer given Vicodin, Patricia told me that the FDA was coming down hard on doctors who "over-prescribed." The problem in attempting to control access to the drug was soon evident: she switched to crack-cocaine, giving a clue that she and, perhaps many others, do not have the back pain to the degree they claim (if at all).

The fact is, doctors learn little or nothing of what may be the most common disease known to man, alcoholism. Even when they have some understanding, they often prescribe medication anyway, since they know the patient will just go to another doctor who understands even less.

Addicts get prescriptions filled in amazing and creative ways. Movie producer (and extraordinary over-achiever) Don Simpson ("Beverly Hills Cop," "Top Gun," "Flashdance" and "Days of Thunder") reportedly had several different doctors and a dozen different pharmacies filling his prescriptions. After his death from overdose, the autopsy found at least 10 different drugs in his system. Unfortunately, his wealth, friends, doctors and pharmacists enabled this brilliantly creative and productive genius to an early demise.

If it's discovered there are multiple doctors and pharmacists prescribing and supplying the drugs, there is almost certainly addiction. What doctors don't seem to understand is that the drugs themselves are not nearly as addictive as are the patients who take them. As Vernon Johnson put it, "We can take care of physical addiction with relative ease; the burden of the harmful dependency is psychological."[165] Many non-addicts take such prescribed drugs for a period of time and then stop using. Addicts simply continue to take them or graduate to others. The difference is, some people have a predisposition to addiction and others do not.

Doctors prescribe stimulants including *amphetamines* like Benzedrine, *depressants* (including barbiturates and tranquilizers) such as Valium and *narcotic painkillers* such as morphine, Percodan and Vicodin. Other legal versions include *caffeine* (an extremely weak stimulant), *alcohol* and *codeine*. The illegal drugs include *cocaine, mathaqualone* and *heroin*. The difference is not whether someone can become addicted (any person predisposed to addiction can), but in the strength and/or politics of the substance.

[165] *Johnson, Ibid., p. 8-9.*

Figure 8 – Types Of Drugs: Legal, Prescription and Illegal

	Stimulants	CNS Depressants	Narcotics
Legal	caffeine, alcohol*	alcohol*	alcohol*
Legal by Prescri -ption	Benzedrine, Dexedrine, Amphetamines. Adderal, Dextrostat, Ritalin	barbiturates, Fiorinal, Fioricet, Seconal, Nembutal. sedative-hypnotics: benzodiazepine, Valium, Miltown, Equinil, Xanax, Halcion, Restoril, clonazepam (and any other "...pam"), Librium, Librax, Dalmane, Ativan, chloral hydrate, Klonopin, Placydil.	opioids: codeine, Vicodin, Vicodin ES, hydrocordone, Lorcet, Lortab, Dilaudid , hydromorphone, Darvon, Demerol, morphine, Darvocet, Tylenol with codeine, methadone.
Illegal	Methamphetamine, Cocaine	Mathaqualone (quaaludes)	Opiates: Opium, Heroin

As discussed, alcohol has attributes of all three of these types of drugs, although considered by most a CNS depressant.

Hiding substance use

23. "Does he hide the use of a substance, or the extent of his use?"

If he does, there is a probability of substance addiction approaching 100%.

For the first 18 months of my relationship with Patricia, I didn't suspect drug use. When finally confronted, she denied (for another 6 months) that she was drinking. I had no idea that I should have been inquiring about other drugs as well. I found empty liquor bottles only twice, for which there were the usual creative excuses (see items 3 and 15 in the "For Women Only" questions). This led to my brief incarceration referred to in the introduction.

On March 10, 1995 (my one day off after working 80 or 90 hours a week), Patricia was clearly high as a kite. She'd switched for the day (apparently) from her usual vodka to whiskey and combined it with Vicodin. It was total chaos at home. Everything was a mess and her children were out of control, a result of the psychological abandonment all children of addicted parents experience. Yet I stayed. I thought, at first, it was because I loved her and didn't want to abandon her while she was disabled. I now realize, it was entirely due to my lack of understanding addiction. If I applied the tool of tough love, I would have left her right then and there.

By this time I was certain she was drinking on a regular basis. It was important that she admit to it so I could "demand" she attend AA. I hoped, as do so many, to regain the mind of the lady I loved. I didn't know this was something that couldn't be done without assuming addiction and offering a dose of uncompromising tough love. Things were so insane that at one point, I slapped her face, like a person trying to get someone to "come to" might do. Although this was wrong of me, it led to a necessary series of events. Oddly enough, this is not the reason the police were called.

After five more minutes of yelling and screaming, it suddenly dawned on me she must be hiding booze in her purse. Grabbing it, she fought me furiously. I didn't fight too hard for fear of harming her, but as we played tug of war she told her son to call 911. After some discussion with the police, I went to jail, telling the officers the whole way that they had the wrong person. I seriously considered not allowing her to bail me out later that night, figuring once sober she needed to see what she had done. That may or may not have helped her form a more permanent bottom (this one wasn't it) but, the next day, she admitted to being a practicing alcoholic. She later dropped the charges, perhaps realizing her commission of serial child abuse might surface in a court of justice.

Ironically, it was the battle over her purse and not the slap that caught her attention. If I proved she was lying, I'd uncover her secret. She needed (at all costs) to protect her King Alcohol <u>and</u> continue to dupe me into paying the bills, thereby enabling far more grotesque behavior than I was able to observe. There <u>was</u>, of course, booze in her purse as well as in numerous other hiding places around the house and car.

After attending only two AA meetings and struggling with sobriety for several weeks, she claimed she was fine and no longer needed AA. However, I found liquor in her purse again (this time, with her consent). Another time I found a bottle in her closet. She responded, "Wow, I must have put it in a place where it was easy to find, because I really wanted you to find it so I could get my act together and stop drinking." She always told me she'd stop "this time."

She didn't. The drugs, the insanity in which I was living and the child endangerment got much, much worse. It invariably will, as long as an addict continues to use any drug and (with very few exceptions) does not attend AA. Two months later, she switched to crack cocaine, possibly because her doctor may have said her liver couldn't handle any more booze.

There are innumerable ingenious places that addicts like Patricia hide their substance(s). Under the hood of a car or strapped to its underside, in toilet tanks or inside dust bags of vacuum cleaners, in the kitchen cabinet disguised in vinegar bottles, in waste baskets and even flower pots. More than one alcoholic has gone so far as to fill the windshield wiper fluid compartment of his car with rum and run the wiper tubes through a hole in the dash. You may see him sipping a little Coke. After hitting the wiper fluid button, voila! Instant rum and Coke. Anyone who hides his alcohol in such creative ways is, very clearly, an addict.

In fascinating stories of tragedy, Lucy Barry Robe reports the secret places famous women have hidden their drugs of choice. Judy Garland's third husband, Sid Luft, found "small envelopes of Seconal and Benzedrine hidden everywhere: Scotch-taped inside the drapes...under the carpets...[in the] bedsprings; in the lining of Judy's terrycloth bathrobe; tablets and capsules buried deep in her bath powder and secreted under her books."[166] Many women use sedatives and tranquilizers in lieu of alcohol because they have the same effect on the brain[167] and you can't smell pills. As renowned alcoholism expert Dr. Joseph A. Pursch has pointed out, "If a fashionable lady gets stoned from a pint of Scotch a day, you can smell it and everybody knows it. But if she has one martini and two or three pills, she can still get zonked and nobody will suspect."[168]

---

[166] *Robe, Ibid., p. 160.*
[167] *Robe, Ibid., p. 157, quoting Dr. Stanley E. Gitlow.*
[168] *Robe, Ibid., p. 158.*

Society columnist Igor Cassini reported that after the death of his alcoholic-addict wife, Charlene Wrightsman Cassini, "We discovered the apartment, particularly her closets, littered with all kinds of pills, hidden in vases, under linens, stuffed in her shoes and the pockets of her clothes."[169] Marianne E. Brickley (recovering alcoholic and ex-wife of Michigan's GOP Lt. Gov. James Brickley) tells that she'd do anything to secretly insure she'd have a liquor supply. Apparently being watched, she'd "charge a gown at a chain department store, then return it at another store in the chain for cash...Then I'd use the refund money to get gin."[170] Actress Mary Pickford hid gin in the Listerine bottle in her "well-stocked" bathroom.[171] Marilyn Monroe instructed a one-time alcoholic assistant, "When I ask you for a glass of water, bring me vodka." The assistant was relieved. She wouldn't be the only one sneaking alcohol all afternoon at a publicity engagement.[172]

Stanley E. Gitlow, M.D., another alcoholism expert, coined the term "sedativism" years ago to describe the cross addiction to alcohol and other sedative-hypnotic drugs. These include everything from the barbiturates (Seconal, Nembutal), to tranquilizers (Valium, Librium) and other drugs such as Miltown, chloral hydrate and Quaaludes. Unfortunately, doctors still prescribe such pills to those they know to be heavy drinkers, not to mention alcoholics who hide their drinks behind closed doors. The trouble is, these drugs bind to the same neurotransmitter receptors that alcohol does, but in a non-competitive way: they bind to different sites on the same receptors.[173] These chemical actions result in *Potentiation*, the effect of one drink combined with one pill, equaling "an enhanced effect of as high as six to eight [drinks], depending on the person, the drug involved, and the dose."[174] Dr. Gitlow reports that one-half of alcoholic women may have sedativism, including two-thirds under age 30. In 1983 Betty Ford said, "An estimated 80% of women alcoholics are also dependent on one or more prescription drugs," which include both the sedative-hypnotics and synthetic opiates.

The belief in Al-Anon is to stop looking for the hidden booze; it's none of our business and we should just take care of ourselves. I believe by making it our business, we are taking care of ourselves. When we find addiction, we offer the addict two choices: sobriety, or uncompromising disenabling. Whichever choice is made, we are taking care of ourselves.

---

[169] *Robe, Ibid., p. 387.*
[170] *Robe, Ibid., p. 287.*
[171] *Robe, Ibid., p. 222-223.*
[172] *Robe, Ibid., p. 109.*
[173] *Braun, Ibid., pp. 52-59.*
[174] *Robe, Ibid., p. 157.*

Hospitalization

24. "Has he ever been to a hospital or other institution on account of drinking or using other drugs?"

If so, he is a substance addict. If there are *any* signs of current addiction, he has almost surely relapsed. This is especially true if there has been several years of recovery. Addicts in early recovery may still exhibit some of the behaviors of active addiction, which may continue until the addict regenerates damaged brain cells, rebuilds his own brain's ability to increase neurotransmitter activity and regains some sense of self-esteem. However, we must remain suspicious. Insobriety should be assumed in any addict who has stopped attending AA meetings and demonstrates any of their old behaviors. For as long as there are issues to sort through, AA is almost always a significant aid, if not essential component to recovery. If we are to be with an addict where we have our emotional and/or financial well being at stake, we have every right to know if he's attending meetings and to conduct random alcohol and other drug testing.

Poor diet

25. "Does he have a poor diet, with little food consumed, possibly resulting in serious illness?"

Some alcoholics seldom eat, due to all the calories they consume from drinking. These empty calories result in hundreds of secondary diseases and disorders, including repeated colds, viruses, bronchitis,[175] pneumonia,[176] hepatitis, diabetes, cirrhosis, jaundice and ulcers (common to early-stage alcoholics due to increased secretions of hydrochloric acid). It frequently instigates or exacerbates serious illnesses such as liver, heart and other organ diseases and/or failures, hepatitis and many more.

According to Lawrence Lamb, M.D., alcohol damages the small intes-

[175] *Polson and Newton, Ibid., p. 52 among many other pages, point out the child addict can experience repeated episodes of these diseases.*

[176] *James W. Smith, M.D., Ibid., on p. 35 points out the mortality rate is "far" higher in alcoholics than in the general population. My significant addict informed me early on that when she was young, she had repeated episodes of pneumonia and bronchitis. This should have served as a warning to me when she again began to suffer from these illnesses during our relationship.*

tine, where many enzymes are formed to aid in digestion. With fewer enzymes, much food enters the colon undigested, causing gaseous distention and fermentation, resulting in diarrhea.

Cancer is another serious illness that very few, including doctors, associate with alcoholism. According to Milam and Ketcham, alcohol may induce cancer by irritating cells directly and by damaging the liver, making it less able to do its job of breaking down and eliminating poisonous (carcinogenic) substances. It also causes nutritional deficiencies, further weakening the body's ability to ward off cancer. There are several other likely mechanisms at work as well, including a synergy with tobacco, which greatly increases their separate actions. Most cancer epidemiologists know all this. Incredibly, this is "not widely recognized by the medical profession."[177] All these effects may apply to other psychoactive drugs as well.

There is also a possible connection between drugs and sexually transmitted diseases. This is due to the feeling of invincibility resulting in needle sharing, multiple sex partners and unprotected sex. In the former Soviet states, up to 90% of syphilis and 95% of gonorrhea cases were associated with alcoholism.[178]

Using different diseases to diagnose substance addiction must be done carefully in conjunction with the other symptoms outlined. There may or may not be addiction. Also, confusion results from attempting to distinguish between the afflicted and seriously affected codependent. The latter can emulate the addict in both behaviors and illnesses.

Early deaths, which suggest disease, occur far earlier among alcoholics. The median age of death among women has been in the 70s during most of the 20th century. Yet, the median age of death among famous female alcoholics, according to statistics culled from Lucy Barry Robe's study, was barely over 50 during the same period, with over two-thirds having died by age 62.

Genetic and occupational observations

26. "Is he the child of an alcoholic or other substance addict?"

This alone, increases the odds by a factor of almost four that he is an alcoholic. Since the Danish brothers study required the addict to be in latter-stage addiction for him to be termed alcoholic, it is possible that the actual rate among such children may be as high as 40% rather than 18%.

---

[177] Benjamin Kissin and Maureen M. Kaley, "Alcohol and Cancer," in *The Biology of Alcoholism,* ed. Kissin and Begleiter, vol. 3, p. 481, cited in Milam and Ketcham, *Ibid.,* p. 90-91.

[178] White, *Ibid.,* p. 45. Here and elsewhere, what the source author calls "alcohol abuse," this author has taken the liberty in re-wording as alcoholism or other drug addiction. It is believed proper, considering the definition proposed.

The evidence proffered in question 27 below supports this, as does the fact that the control group found the general population was only 5% alcoholic (we argued both the 5% and 18% figures could be doubled). There are no statistics on other drugs, but due to the action on the various neurotransmitters, there is good reason to believe the odds may be similar.

27. "Is he a parent of an alcoholic or other substance addict?"

This is simply the reverse of the previous observation. According to two studies of women alcoholics, 41% and 49% had at least one alcoholic parent.[179] By the time they are parents with alcoholic children, their own alcoholism has had time to develop into a more easily observed latter-stage addiction, unlike the children of alcoholics (as did those in the Danish brothers study). These figures may be the more accurate ones when looking for familial clues to addiction.

28. "Is his ancestry one which has not yet developed as much a resistance to addiction as have others (not having, through evolution, filtered out the addictive genes to as great an extent as those of other ancestries)?"

People with Northern European ancestry are at greater risk of addiction than are those of Mediterranean descent. People of North American Indian, Eskimo and non-Mediterranean African descent are at even greater risk. This is simply an unfortunate fact of evolution that will be discussed later, in depth.

29. "Is he engaged in certain occupations and professions that seem to have a greater probability of attracting addicts?"

Lucy Barry Robe, psychiatrist Donald Goodwin and other researchers report that a far higher proportion of famous actors, actresses and writers are alcoholic-addicts than would be expected by chance.[180] While there is reason to believe the probabilities are somewhat less among those less famous due to the over-achievement factor, it's doubtful the likelihood is as low as the statistical norm of 10%. Remember, Graham posits that early stage addiction, usually beginning in the early teen years (well before most decide on their life's work), requires that addicts inflate their ego. Certain occupations allow their participants to exercise power over others. This can take form in power over minds (writing, philosophizing), power over one's audience (acting) and power over people (politicians, bureaucrats and law enforcers). This is particularly inviting for the addict in occupations where the exercise of such power can be selective.

---

[179] *Robe, Ibid., p. 172.*
[180] *Robe, Ibid., quoted in Graham, Ibid., p. 8-9; Donald W. Goodwin, M.D., "Alcohol and the Writer," Ibid., quoted in Graham, Ibid., p. 75*

Many have noted the high incidence of alcoholism among former battle-field heroes, attributed to the "stresses and strains" of being such. Pointing out that this is nonsense, Graham suggests the alcoholism precedes the courageous behavior and is, in fact, its root cause, based on the need to boost the alcoholic ego.[181] His thesis is supported by an U.S. Navy study that found an astonishing 46% of their recruits have "an identifiable history of problem drinking" *at the time of enlistment.*[182]

Professions that offer easy access to drugs may attract more addicts as well. Medical doctors, psychiatrists and pharmacists have reportedly high incidences of substance addiction. Keep in mind, any published statistics may, for obvious reasons, report rates of addiction among such professionals that are far lower than in real life. Addicts may be supremely competent when they must to satiate their ego, especially through work. Recovering addicts have reported that they have performed entire surgeries during blackouts, much in the same way that alcoholic pilots have flown Boeing 747s. The problem one pilot experienced was, he had to ask the co-pilot where they were headed after awakening from a blackout in mid-flight. (A surgeon might have it easier once he's started working on the organs at risk.) Easy access to drugs may also take the form of flexible schedules, allowing them to knock down 3 or 4 drinks during lunch along with everyone else, as found in many sales occupations.

These particular professions attract certain Temperaments[183] that may have a greater predisposition to experimentation, which leads to active substance addiction. The construction industry is filled with addicts, for reasons that may have to do with personality type and flexibility of schedules as much as the need to inflate one's ego.

30. "Is he male?"

Evidence from the Danish brothers study and Native American reservations suggest that male alcoholics outnumber female by 2 to 4 times. On the other hand, spousal abuse has been reported to be close to even between males and females when incidences of estimated non-reported abuse are added to the equation. Since it is believed that addicts commit virtually all abuse, addiction between the sexes may be about equal.

Anecdotal evidence supports the hypothesis that the number of female alcoholics may be greatly underreported. There is reluctance on the part of authorities to diagnose or report female addicts because such "behavior" is not tolerated as easily as male drunkenness. Since females often start drinking later, the onset of easily diagnosed alcoholism may be sooner for men. Females may more frequently mix their alcohol with prescription

---

[181] *Graham, Ibid., p. 120.*
[182] *Father Martin, Ibid., p. 73.*
[183] *This will be discussed in depth in a later chapter.*

drugs that, with the legitimacy of a doctor's prescription, also makes the diagnosis less likely. Finally, the craziness observable in some women may be attributed to "that time of the month," or "change of life," again making it harder to attribute addiction.

Potpourri

31. A potpourri of questions and observations that require little comment:

A. "Is he belligerent or nasty while drinking?" A subcategory of mood swings or volatile emotional states deserving separate recognition.

B. "Does he 'push buttons', especially in a very mean-spirited way?" When addicts drink, they know exactly where to dig and when the codependent is most vulnerable.

C. "Does he engage in extreme sarcasm?" This is an especially good clue when sarcasm is one of the "buttons."

D. "Does he engage in 'double-think,' in which everything is turned around?" The addict is not rude, you are. The addict is not insane, you are. The addict does not lie, you do. Etc. This may often take the form of what appears to be intellectual dishonesty, or "twisted logic," but really isn't. It results as much from the distortion caused by euphoric recall as from a need to control. Related to question 8 mentioned earlier.

E. "Is he a hypochondriac?" As we have shown, many addicts really do have other illnesses. However, some are hypochondriacs. This may extend to an exaggerated concern over their children's health in order to obtain drugs for themselves in their child's name.

F. "Does he push others to drink or use drugs?" "Come on, Joe, have another," is a tool used by addicts to make it appear that their drinking or use is no different from others'. This is related to the propensity to hang out with fellow addicts.

G. "Does he push others to commit crimes or engage in unethical behavior?" A magnificent example of this was found in the recent book and 1998 movie, "A Simple Plan," in which two alcoholics suggested the commission of a crime into which a non-addict allowed himself to be drawn.

H. "Does he often have red eyes, flushed face or 'drinker's nose'?" This affects a select few and only with certain drugs. It's important to recognize that some addict's eyes never turn red, while the eyes of some non-addicts do so with as little as .04 BAC. I, personally, suffer from facial flush including red eyes at low levels, very discomfiting indeed. Some Asians, who experience this due to the lack of a gene to properly process alcohol, are reported to have a very low incidence of alcoholism. Even if the predisposition to addiction otherwise exists in such individuals, they may not continue drinking due to the discomfort experienced. However, some continue to use despite this condition.

I. "Does he often have glassy eyes?" Check out Marilyn Monroe's bedroom eyes in her movies. She looks sexy with those glassy eyes. We now know she was drinking on the job. Aside from alcohol, marijuana causes glassy, red eyes, while stimulants can result in a glazed or tired look, due to lack of sleep.

J. "Does he often have dilated or constricted pupils?" As was previously discussed, pupils less than a fifth in diameter of the iris are indicative of opiate use. Slightly over half the size of the iris in the light signals heavy alcohol or marijuana use. Anything larger in adults is an almost certain sign of non-caffeine stimulants in non-therapeutic doses.

K. "Have you ever found drug paraphernalia (or empty bottles) that 'belong to a friend'?" This is an excellent clue for parents of suspected child or adolescent addicts. Many household items can be used as paraphernalia, any one of which would generally raise no suspicions while several in conjunction should. These include roughly 6-inch paper squares, little balloons (filled with something or not), big or unusual-looking spoons, Q-Tips, razor blade(s), lighter(s), metal wire, little coin-sized bags or cellophane baggies, artificial sweetener, tin foil and small pieces of folded newspaper containing baking soda.

L. "Does he have martinis or other drinks designed to increase the rate of absorption into the bloodstream?" The carbonation in champagne or soda water results in a higher blood alcohol content by opening the pyloric valve into the small intestine (rather than the stomach) where absorption is more rapid. In addition, alcoholics tend to hide the amount of alcohol in mixed drinks, often making them far stronger than those of non-addicts. I remember my Dad's drinks as super-strength gin-and-tonics, probably containing more gin than tonic.

M. "Does he drink heavily before eating?" Food in the stomach delays absorption of alcohol and is, therefore, anathema to the hard-core alcoholic.

N. "Does he sleep on the job or in class, or sleep excessively at unusual hours?" Methamphetamine and other stimulant addicts often stay awake for days at a time only to experience a crash, resulting in extended periods of sleep. Being awake all night after being up all day can be a clue.

O. "Does he eat or shop for food at irregular times, such as 3 a.m., while working a fairly normal job, or when not working?" I once went to a supermarket in a well-to-do area at about midnight and observed, almost exclusively, what some might call "freaks and weirdoes," buying "munchies" and alcoholic beverages. The clientele was so scary looking that I haven't shopped "after hours" since.

P. "Does he use gum, mouthwash or perfume excessively?" These enable the addict to hide the smell of alcohol and other drugs. For example, I have one client who has been in non-stop financial turmoil for years. He has two ex-wives and has been intermittently seriously ill during this period. Addiction didn't occur to me until a friend of his suggested that he masks alcohol with a heavy dose of cologne.

Q. "Does he have a short attention span?" It isn't always what is commonly called Attention Deficit Disorder.

R. "Does he wear 'druggie' clothing or hair style, or listen to 'druggie' music?" Even at 17, this may be a good indicator. At 40, it almost surely is.

S. "Does he have certain facial attributes, including a puffy face, heavy bags under the eyes or premature aging?" When combined with sun and smoking, premature heavy wrinkling can result. As with every other clue viewed in isolation, there may be other causes.

My failing to take this into account once cost my client and me $10,000 in unexpected taxes. He had asked me to calculate the tax cost of not rolling over a 401-K distribution to an IRA. Due to his aged and wrinkled look and the fact he was retiring, it didn't occur to me to confirm his age as being over 59 1/2. He wasn't. I computed the tax without penalty for early (before age 59 1/2) withdrawal. He decided to pay the tax (in itself, a clue to addiction). We agreed to split the additional cost because he acknowledged, in sobriety, that he might have decided (due to alcohol-induced distortions) to take the withdrawal despite the penalty and tax.

T. "Does he have 'druggie' or alcoholic friends and drinking buddies?" Birds of a feather really do hang out together. This is especially important to recognize in children. Kids don't "get in with bad kids and then start using drugs," as is so commonly believed. Remember that an addict is an addict *first*. Addict kids *seek out* other addict kids. Having found an enabler, older addicts frequently find troubled or irresponsible people that they can control. These are often other addicts who look worse off or use more addictively than themselves and serve as a sort of cover for their own use.

U. "Does he have an unusual communications style, such as speaking in short, inarticulate or unintelligible sentences, "stream of consciousness," or in a god-like pontificating style?"[184] One who pontificates (often a stimulant addict or alcoholic, as opposed to an opiate or psychedelic drug user) may get his way by intimidating others. The inarticulate style is a sign of confusion, sometimes resulting from polydrug use.

---

[184] *For Type and Temperament experts: The addict speaking in a "stream of consciousness" is likely to be a Perceptive Type. The addict who pontificates is more likely to be a Judging Type. The communication style of the addict may be one of the best clues to his overall Psychological Type and Temperament. This can provide crucial information for reasons discussed in the chapters, "Predicting a Predisposition to Addiction" and "Improving the Treatment of Drug Addiction," along with the professional appendix on Type and Temperament.*

V. "Does he have loose sexual morals?" Because the drug inflates the ego of the addict, it cuts off the spirit and conscience, leading to behavior that demonstrates a complete lack of self-esteem. Addicts derive ego-satisfaction from serial sexual conquests. This may take the form of adultery as a method of destroying a marriage, or as a substitute for more serious criminal activity. Frequently, a form of (or actual) prostitution ensues. In addition, these sexual behaviors allow the addict to exercise control over others, which may also result in an inflated ego. It would not be surprising if half or more of all prostitutes and adult film stars were found to be addicts.

W. "Does he have dangerous, non-drug-related compulsions?" Some of these have their roots in alcohol or other drug addiction. Such compulsions are signs of impaired judgment, which generally results from distorted perceptions, often caused by substance addiction. These include compulsive gambling, spending and sexual activity. This may also include eating disorders; however, this might also be related to sugar imbalances in the system. It can be argued that food, in a sense, is a drug. Many alcoholics are extremely overweight, some suffering from hypoglycemia or diabetes, which may lead to an unhealthy intake of sugar in both food and alcohol.

X. "Has there been a sudden loss of interest in what was a central hobby, sport or other activity?" This is an important clue to watch for in teenagers.

Y. "Does he have an inability to keep a schedule, with no internal discipline?" This is related to the question of tardies and absences.

Z. "Are people around the possible addict overly cautious, uncomfortable or uneasy with each other?" This is a good question for either a family or work unit. Many codependents report that for years they felt like they were walking on eggshells around the addict.

AA. "Are there repeated promises to 'never do it again,' whatever 'it' is?" This can include any negative behavior including drinking too much and abusing others. The promises are repeated because the subject does it again and again. This may be considered a subcategory of the questions about lying and "should be incarcerated."

BB. "Does he have telephonitis?" This is a behavior described by Graham and Robe, in which the addict controls others by regulating when they speak by calling at all hours of the day or night.

CC. "Does he have reverse-telephonitis?" In this behavior, the addict hangs up repeatedly in a display of power, cutting off others at will. My personal addict excelled at this behavior.

DD. "Does he fail to wear seat belts regularly or engage in other such unnecessarily risky behavior?" This is a sign of feeling invincible, resulting from the poor judgment of the practicing addict. The chances of addiction are greatly increased with the lethal combination of smoking, using a cell phone, not wearing a seatbelt and aggressive driving.

Figure 9 - The Thorburn Substance Addiction Recognition Indicator
For use by the non-addict to identify possible addicts

	YES	NO
1. Does s/he smoke?		
2. Has s/he had a pattern of *recurring* financial difficulties?		
3. Does s/he have loose sexual morals, including serial adultery?		
4. Are there other non-substance compulsions, dangerous to self or others, including gambling, sex, or a compulsive eating disorder?		
5. Does s/he have a pattern of erratic behavior, including the random wielding of power?		
6. Is s/he in an occupation that allows for ego-gratification beyond norms?		
7. Has s/he ever had more than one blackout (a complete loss of memory or events)? *		
8. Does s/he sleep on the job or have other odd sleeping habits?		
9. Does s/he have a short attention span and appear "scattered" or not focused?		
10. Does s/he have a senseless "stream of consciousness" style of communication?		
11. Has there been a sudden loss of interest in a central activity?		
12. Does s/he have an inability to keep a schedule?		
13. Have there been a series of accidents, whether fire, motor vehicle, work-related, near drowning or any combination of these?		
14. Does s/he have out of control children?		
15. Is s/he *frequently* tardy to or absent from work, school or social engagements?		
16. Does s/he engage in "doublethink", in which everything is turned around ("twisted logic")?		
17. Does s/he have *intense* mood swings or indications of any psychological disorder or mental illness?		

	YES	NO
18. Is there now (or was there ever) an *intense* drive to over-achieve?		
19. Are others *frequently* overly cautious, "walking on eggshells" around him/her?		
20. Does s/he have a *pervasive* "the rules don't apply to me" attitude? *		
21. Is s/he a *supremely* good liar, or have a pattern of intellectual dishonesty (being untruthful about something that appears to be an opinion)? *		
22. Has s/he made false accusations with malicious intent? *		
23. Are there any signs of a *massive* over-inflated ego?		
24. Has s/he been convicted of any felony? 1*		
25. Has s/he committed a felony for which s/he was not caught? 1*		
26. Does s/he have *severe* problems at work and/or home due to his/her behavior?		
27. Does s/he engage in destructive behaviors that others *often* cover up? *		
28. Does s/he *habitually* blame others for his/her circumstances? *		
29. Has s/he ever pushed others into committing crimes/unethical behavior? **		
30. Does s/he engage in *repeated* unnecessarily risky behavior?		
31. Is s/he *often* belligerent or nasty, or *frequently* engage in intimidation tactics to get his/her way in seemingly unimportant matters? *		
32. Does he <u>hate</u> others, whether as individuals or as classes of people (i.e. racism)?		
33. Is s/he *often* extremely sarcastic in a mean-spirited way, or *regularly* belittling of others?		
34. Does s/he *continually* "push buttons"?		
35. Does s/he engage in *repeated* verbal or physical abuse? *		
36. Does s/he *habitually* have telephonitis, calling others at all hours?		

	YES	NO
37. Does s/he *often* hang up on others?		
38. Have there been *recurring* promises to "never do it again," whatever "it" may be? **		
39. Does his/her family have a history of substance addiction?		
40. Is s/he the parent of an alcoholic or other drug addict?		
41. Does s/he have Native American, Afro-American or Northern European ancestry?		
42. Is there now (or was there ever) a high tolerance to alcohol?		
43. Does s/he frequently have red or glassy eyes, or dilated or constricted pupils?		
44. Have you found "paraphernalia" that s/he insists is a friend's? *		
45. Does s/he frequently drink champagne, martinis, or hard liquor mixed with soda? *		
46. Does s/he often drink heavily before eating? *		
47. Has s/he ever said, defiantly regarding any substance, "I can stop any time I want?" **		
48. Does s/he set rules for use of substances (such as time of day or type of substance)? *		
49. Does s/he use illegal drugs or legal ones other than alcohol for extended periods? *		
50. Does s/he gulp alcoholic beverages?		
51. Does s/he hide or minimize the extent of use? **		
52. Is s/he in an occupation that allows freedom to use substances in business settings?		
53. Does s/he use gum, mouthwash, breath mints or perfumes *excessively*?		
54. Does s/he take pains to insure the availability of a substance? **		
55. Does s/he ever push others to drink or use drugs? **		

	YES	NO
56. Does s/he have "drinking or drug buddies"?		
57. Does s/he wear "druggie" clothes or listen to "druggie" music?		
58. Has s/he ever been institutionalized for alcohol or drug problems? **		
59. Does s/he have a serious illness and/or a pattern of poor diet?		
60. Is s/he a hypochondriac about his/her own health or that of their children?		
Totals		

*= Any behavior which in and of itself points to what is believed to be a high (over 50%) probability of substance addiction in either the person or close other. Keep in mind, in certain cultures some of these behaviors may be considered normal, and may not accurately reflect addiction.

** = Any behavior which in and of itself points to a virtual certainty of substance addiction in that person.

1 = For our purposes, felonies do not include "victimless crime," which are those neither party to the "crime" wants to report to the police. However, victimless does not mean harmless.

Two or three of the non-asterisked "yes" answers should cause us to look for addiction. If more than 3 questions are answered yes, there is a high probability of either active substance addiction or, in the case of the recovering addict, imminent relapse. However, if what we might call "validating" questions 42 through 51, 54-56 and 58 are answered in the negative, there may be a non-substance related mental disorder and/or severe codependency. While at first a codependent may be confused for an addict, when any 6 or more of the non-validating questions are answered "yes," along with one affirmative answer from the "validating" ones, there is usually confirmation of substance addiction. Without at least one of these special validating questions answered positive, I'd cap the liklihood of substance addiction at 85%.

Drinking or using drugs does not, in and of itself harm others. Many people drink or use and never harm a soul; even some addicts may never hurt anyone else. Therefore, whether someone is an addict is really not our business, barring behaviors destructive of others. It may be troubling that someone wasting his life in an opium den might otherwise be a productive human being, but that's their choice. However, what is crucial and often misunderstood is he has no right to live off the income and assets of others. If he wants to live in an opium den, he can do so at his own expense and no one else's, unless someone cares to "help" him, a notion we have hopefully dispelled. Eliminate the handouts, the welfare and medical care, except by the voluntary assent of individuals. Those who would "help" will likely in the long run, result in very few starving or living on private charity for extended periods.

Before we discuss the specifics of disenabling, it is essential that we explore why so few really understand this affliction. Given the awesome damage and pervasiveness of substance addiction, this is surprising. It may cause even knowledgeable observers to underestimate the likelihood of addiction in a particular individual. By comprehending the reasons so few understand it, we increase the odds of successfully diagnosing addiction.

"He that is not aware of his ignorance
will only be misled by his knowledge."

Richard Whately (1787-1863)
Archbishop of Dublin

5

Denial vs. Ignorance

Non-addicts are told they are "in denial" about addicts who harm them. They ascribe reasons besides alcoholism or other drug addiction for the addict's behaviors. The question is how can someone be in denial about something they have never been taught? The sin is not denial; the sin is ignorance.

Addiction has never been truthfully and accurately taught in the schools. Children are told, "Just say no to drugs." Teenagers are warned, "When you're old enough, drink in moderation or not at all." As adults we're implored, "Don't drink and drive." All this is great advice, except it's preaching to the choir. Addicts can't say no to drugs, drink in moderation or drink and not drive. That is what addicts do.

As grown-ups, instead of plainly discussing addiction, we euphemize. We quickly hush those revealing the "family secrets" and look over our shoulders to be sure no one overhears. We can't possibly understand the telltale signs of addiction (and its pervasiveness), because we think it's only "us." Instead of accurately diagnosing the problem, we say, "He acts a little funny," "that's just Johnny," or, "he has a problem with his demons." Yet, when an actor cuts off his finger to show his girlfriend his devotion and she says "go to hell," while he heads for the hospital to have it reattached, this is not just a "problem." This is addiction.

Television, movies and other media offer a wonderful opportunity to instruct and teach a wide audience, yet have rarely portrayed addiction truthfully. Worse yet, therapists and doctors frequently misdiagnose, with the disease masquerading as practically all the psychopathological disorders and mental illnesses. With addicts bamboozling those in the medical profession, how can the rest of us do any better?

Addiction and therapists

"I never knew a person become insane who was not in the habit of taking a portion of alcohol daily." — English Clergyman Benjamin Parsons[185]

There have been numerous inroads made in understanding areas of the arts and sciences from those outside the specific field. An example is Daniel Brooks, a zoologist at the University of Toronto. Contrary to the belief among virtually all geologists that the Amazon River always flowed east into the Atlantic, he discovered that it flowed west into the Pacific millions of years ago, before the Andes rose. Freshwater stingrays of the Amazon were assumed to have descended from Atlantic rays that swam up-river. Brooks found that parasitical worms infesting the Amazon rays were closer to those infecting Pacific rays, offering biological evidence for a geological phenomenon that experts had hardly begun to hypothesize.

Psychologist David Keirsey points out that "breakthroughs in the behavioral sciences often come from outside the field." Psychologist Carl Jung's ideas were given new life almost by accident as a result of lay person Isabel Myers re-discovering his "Psychological Types" and with her mother, Kathryn Briggs, devising a questionnaire for identifying different personality types.[186] Unfortunately, many therapists view the Myers-Briggs Type Indicator and Keirseyan Temperament Theory, powerful tools for understanding healthy human behavior, with disdain and as "pop" psychology. Coming from outside the field, we may receive a similar response. We have already questioned the "mental health" model of addiction and proper treatment. Now we're going to review a bit and re-visit such treatment through my own and others' experiences. We'll see why it's imperative to suspect addition as the source of other problems first. We'll also address treating the non-addict.

Every field has its early great original thinkers. In the case of alcoholism, George E. Vaillant qualifies. Regarding alcoholics he said, "Personality and perceptions about the past [are] so markedly [affected] that the true facts of an alcoholic's life can often be discovered only by prospective study."[187] Since most therapists use historical perspective and the like (in which the patient is counseled to look to his past), Vaillant may be suggest-

---

[185] *"Anti-Bacchus: An Essay on the Crimes, Diseases, and Other Evils Connected with the Use of Intoxicating Drinks," 1840, cited in Milam and Ketcham, Ibid., p. 81.*

[186] *David Keirsey, "Please Understand Me – II," Del Mar, CA: Prometheus Nemesis Book Company, 1998, p. 3.*

[187] *George E. Vaillant, "The Natural History of Alcoholism Revisited," Cambridge, MA: Harvard University Press, 1995, p. 2.*

ing that the practicing (and maybe even recovering) alcoholic cannot be successfully counseled using such methods.

My significant addict (Patricia) and I counseled with therapists for most of our tumultuous 2 1/2-year relationship. Never suspecting active substance addiction, the therapists tried counseling and reason, a waste of time and money since one cannot counsel or reason with a chemical. They suggested that we present a uniform front in disciplining her children, having no idea she was in cahoots with them to insure an adequate flow of alcohol and other drugs. The therapists accused me of being over-controlling, not something the addict, virtually always the greater control freak in any relationship, needs a licensed therapist for. This also gave Patricia much-used ammunition to blame me for the kids' problems. These well-meaning therapists offered ways for all of us to cope and deal with each other, which would have been fine, were we all sane and rational human beings.

Practicing addicts have distorted perceptions. Blackouts and memory repression result in massive black holes in their memory banks. Anything recalled is distorted in a self-serving positive light due to euphoric recall, regardless of how negative the behavior. They lie about their use both to themselves and others. There was no recognition of any of this by the therapists. They were clueless to possible active addiction, even though they had been made aware of the fact she'd been a practicing addict for much of her life. Looking back, using our Substance Addiction Recognition Indicator, there were innumerable clues to relapse. The therapists were not trained to look for biological origins and resulting alcoholism as the source of problems we were experiencing.

At AA meetings, I heard the recovering alcoholics admit they are, when using, the world's greatest con artists. I realized I had been seeing (without understanding) conning on an unparalleled scale, not just of me, but also the therapists, teachers, school counselors, family and friends. If you recall, the Graham-Heisenberg principle states that addicts alter behavior when under observation. Since the signs and symptoms of addiction are behavioral, this makes conning the therapists easy. They are at a distinct disadvantage compared with those in a position to make extended clandestine observations, who understand the indications.

However, if there are any problems, addiction should be suspected as the primary disorder. That is likely the reason the patient has sought the services of a therapist. If I were a therapist, the first question I would ask a new patient would be *who* is the addict in his life. It may be someone now or in the distant past; a lover, parent or grandparent; a co-worker, employer or employee. It may be the patient himself. If 80% of crime is related to substance addiction, is it unreasonable to assume a similar percentage of psychological problems and what may appear to be mental disorders are actually related to, or caused by, substance addiction?

We should not condemn the entire mental health field. However, while there are some great therapists who understand the affliction, many do not. Polson and Newton relate a story of "parents who spent over $150,000 on a series of psychiatrists, psychologists, emergency rooms, medical hospitals and mental hospitals trying to find out what was wrong with their daughter....Not one professional ever told them their daughter had a drug problem."[188] If all of these professionals missed the correct diagnosis, what are the odds that any other professional would get it right?

On the other hand, perhaps they did diagnose correctly and chose not to mention it. This wouldn't be surprising, since there seems to be an amazing lack of awareness of addiction as the primary affliction.[189] They may have been thinking (as the Mental Health Model of addiction dictates), "drug use is the symptom of other psychiatric problems; if I address and help to resolve those problems, the drug use will stop, so I don't have to tell the parents." However, addiction is the primary disorder, "because it is the source of other symptoms."[190] The addict, informed throughout therapy that underlying problems cause the addictive use, figures once he's cured he can go back to using, which can account (at least in part) for relapses. He is not made to deal with the fact that he can never use again if he wants to put a stop to his own destructive behaviors.

Many diseases are initially misdiagnosed. The likelihood of correctly diagnosing substance addiction is far less favorable. As The Betty Ford Clinic's President John Schwarziose explains, addiction is a "totally misunderstood disease."[191] Addiction experts Polson and Newton suggest the results are that "many professionals try to treat the symptoms of the disease — emotional problems, family problems, school problems — rather than the disease itself."[192] This is like treating an AIDS patient for weight loss.

Since therapists using some variation of the failed "mental health model" of addiction attempt to psychoanalyze why the addict uses (ascribing some psychopathological disorder to his use), they ignore the incontrovertible evidence that addiction is a primary disease, physiological in origin. Let's go back to school for a minute and review the physiological process. The alcoholic liver converts alcohol into acetaldehyde more quickly and then into acetate more slowly in alcoholics, causing a build-up in acetaldehyde. This is the poison that irritates cells, hampers cellular activities, reacts explosively with other chemicals, causes permanent cellular damage, inhib-

---

[188] *Polson and Newton, Ibid., p. 175.*

[189] *Polson and Newton, Ibid., p. 172.*

[190] *Polson and Newton, Ibid.*

[191] *Interview with Larry King and Betty Ford, "Larry King Live," CNN, October 27, 1997.*

[192] *Polson and Newton, Ibid., p. 52.*

its synthesis of proteins in the heart muscle resulting in impaired cardiac function and leads to bizarre chemical reactions in the brain.[193] In other words, it messes you up.

The brain's chemical reactions center on the blocking of enzymes that inhibit brain amine activity. Brain amines are neurotransmitters, responsible for relaying information from one neuron to another. Such neurotransmitters include the aforementioned serotonin, norepinephrine and dopamine. Not being naturally inhibited, serotonin (the target of Prozac) and dopamine (the target of cocaine and amphetamines) in particular, make the addict feel better than he would if he only experienced the negative effects of the buildup of acetaldehyde. The addictive process is thus begun.[194] Therefore, addiction begins as a biological phenomenon or impairment of the body's ability to function normally. There is irregular processing of alcohol and a possible absence of normal levels of dopamine, serotonin, endorphins and other neurotransmitters in the brain, and/or a desire for more than is normal due to inborn Temperament. This biologically different processing of alcohol results in alcoholism, adversely affecting the psychological health of the addict and causing destructive social behaviors. Since a "disease" is defined as a particular destructive process in the body with a specific cause and characteristic symptoms, alcoholism is properly characterized as a disease.

We cannot (yet) see the biological processes, nor can we see inside the addict's brain to observe his internal psychological make-up and distorted perceptions. We can, however, observe the resulting impaired judgments, as evidenced by social and other behaviors, which are generally exhibited only by addicts in serial fashion. Such behaviors should cause us to suspect addiction and to diagnose and treat accordingly. With proper treatment of the disease itself, these symptoms disappear. Those supporting the mental health model treat only symptoms, masking and thereby perpetuating the disease.

Remember psychiatrist Donald Goodwin? Recall that over 25 years ago, he showed that alcoholism was almost four times more likely to occur in children of alcoholics separated near the time of birth from their parents and raised in non-alcoholic families than in children of non-alcoholic parents raised by either alcoholic or non-alcoholic stepparents. He also compared children of alcoholics with the children of non-alcoholics, finding no difference in the incidence of psychopathological behavior, depression, anxiety neurosis and personality disturbances.[195] Alcoholism and other drug addiction are not environmental in origin. They are not symptoms of

[193] *Milam and Ketcham, Ibid., pp. 34-37.*
[194] *Milam and Ketcham, Ibid., pp. 36-37 and 206.*
[195] *Goodwin, Ibid., pp. 98-115.*

an underlying psychopathology. They <u>create</u> them.

Even if there are other issues, they cannot be righted unless the substance use first stops. Vernon Johnson called alcoholism a "primary condition" that "blocks the lasting effect of any health care which might be delivered immediately to the physical, emotional, or other complications. If there is a fatty liver, for example, nothing lasting can be done to reduce that condition until the dependency is lifted off....If there is an existing emotional disorder, no lasting or effective therapy can be delivered until the dependency itself is corrected."[196] Graham succinctly states that most of the behavior of alcoholics while drinking "are not subject to psychological analysis since they are greatly influenced by the pharmacological effects of a psychoactive substance."[197]

This continues even into sobriety. Gorski and Miller discuss the symptoms of Post Acute Withdrawal, effectively any period in-between drinks lasting up to 18 months and occasionally much longer. These include an inability to think clearly, memory problems, emotional overreactions or numbness, sleep disturbances, physical coordination problems and stress sensitivity.[198] These symptoms mimic some of those of active addiction, which is why at the very least it's difficult for therapists to work with addicts in early recovery. This is made especially challenging by the fact that most addicts "slip" and the 18-month clock must be started all over again. Some knowledgeable therapists refuse to work with addicts until there is at least two and as many as six years of proven sobriety.

Therapists who try to work with addicts would see that they are brilliant with stories including excuses for behaviors and beliefs and with faking their own recovery, if only they understood addiction. Johnson talks about experienced counselors taken in by the alcoholic who admits that he has a problem, promising to do anything and everything the counselor suggests. The therapist and family try to help the addict, having no idea the alcoholic continues to be inwardly defiant. At best, he gains nothing from anyone else's "help;" at worst he uses it to justify his drinking and behaviors.

Addiction expert Dr. Forest Tennant suggests that regular alcohol and drug testing should be required of the addict who truly wants help. With sobriety, most issues and disorders gradually clear up. Any others can be treated with full confidence that real help is being provided to a truly recovering addict.

The professionals counseling Patricia and me were not the only ones who misdiagnosed. Most working with psychiatrist Martha Morrison, M.D.

---

[196] *Johnson, Ibid., pp. 48-49.*
[197] *Graham, Ibid., p. 122.*
[198] *Gorski and Miller, "Staying Sober," Ibid., p. 59.*

got it wrong, too. Morrison relates this in her illuminating self-study, "White Rabbit."[199] Hardly anyone saw the extent of her drug use from the age of 12, through medical school and even as a practicing psychiatrist. She actually counseled addicts for two years, all the while herself a practicing addict. At no time did she believe she was anything like "them." From medical school on, she had access to every legal drug possible, along with an array of illegal substances through an extensive network of suppliers. Her family doctor said when she was very young and surrounded by a loving family, "She may go down a dark alley but she'll always be smart enough to turn back."[200] He was wrong. As a practicing addict, it got to the point where she would "do anything—I mean anything—to get quantities of [cocaine]. I would have killed if anyone had gotten in my way."[201]

Addicts, however intelligent they may be, are not "smart enough to turn back," because it has nothing to do with intelligence any more than upbringing. It has to do with the biological chemistry. This is true regardless of other factors. The only thing that gets them "smart" is excruciating pain from personal crises.

At the tender age of 17, Morrison's brain was distorting perceptions by her daily use of speed (methamphetamine), eating "astonishing...amounts of nonprescription stimulants and [prescription] drugs like Vivarin, Nodoz, Robitussin, and Romilar with codeine. I tripped on mescaline, psilocybin, THC, and PCP on numerous occasions. I still ripped off my mother's Darvon [a mild, commonly prescribed painkiller that is one of the addict's substitutes for heroin], smoked dope before I went to school in the morning, and often dropped acid at school."[202] At the time, she never smoked less than 3 joints a day and once ingested the equivalent of 60 joints in 3 days, all on top of her normal use of other drugs. To the uninitiated, the level of use is staggering.

As an over-achieving early-stage addict, she got mostly straight A's through medical school. Many look to the work at school for signs of a problem in a student. Since there wasn't one, she was "functioning." There seems to be an unstated belief that the problem will resolve itself or, if it doesn't get any worse, it's labeled OK. But it always gets worse. The disease of addiction is progressive. As we've learned, work (and school) is the last thing to go. The inflated ego must compensate for the zeroed-out self-esteem by keeping work, school or perhaps a life of crime in order. In the meantime, the addict uses up his own energy and others' trust by lying, covering up and insuring access to his drug. Hence, his personal life

---

[199] *Morrison, Ibid.*
[200] *Ibid., p. 43.*
[201] *Ibid., p. 40.*
[202] *Ibid., p. 37.*

falls apart before work or school.

Morrison fooled everyone, being the "experienced con artist" that she was. She played "the 'good little girl' game to the hilt" as the youngest patient ever admitted to the adult psychiatric ward at the University of Arkansas Medical Center in Little Rock. She quickly learned who she had to brown-nose to get out. It took her "ten days to convince the staff that I had simply fallen in with the wrong crowd. I told them I had learned my lesson [and that] I never really enjoyed taking drugs anyway."[203]

As soon as she got out, she "dropped a fistful of acid and mescaline tabs, ate some Benzedrine and Dexamyl, and smoked several joints."[204]

A psychiatrist who reported her as "angry, hostile, uncooperative, and psychotic" had committed her.[205] Shortly after, she was diagnosed as a paranoid schizophrenic and, even after a bad reaction to Thorazine (a drug used in its treatment), the psychiatrists still "failed to diagnose correctly and comprehend that I was a junkie, not a psychotic."[206] Morrison was variously called obnoxious, wired and unreasonable. She was misdiagnosed as narcissistic, obsessive-compulsive, paranoid, schizophrenic, psychotic and catatonic.[207] One psychiatrist friend of Morrison's diagnosed her as bipolar, urging her to seek treatment and try lithium. The problem was that at the time, she was regularly (almost daily) ingesting Demerol, Mepergan, cocaine and other stimulants, Tenuate, Ritalin, Fastin, Valium, Ativan, Serax, Percodan, Cogentin, Artane, marijuana, alcohol, codeine and Tylox.[208] Non-users haven't even heard of many of the drugs that addicts put into their bodies.

Even when diagnosing addiction, medical professionals may display a profound misunderstanding of the disease. Alcoholism expert Arnold M. Ludwig, M.D., informs that seemingly innocuous mind-altering minor tranquilizers such as Librium and Valium "have been widely used [by psychiatrists] to treat anxiety in alcoholics" at hospital emergency rooms and alcohol detoxification centers for those in withdrawal.[209] This is a practice that, according to counselors, continues today. Yet, severe behavioral disorders can result from the use of any psychoactive drug by an addict. Furthermore, one drug may lead to a craving for another. Ludwig and colleagues demonstrated in their studies of alcoholics and craving that "al-

---

[203] *Ibid., p. 51.*
[204] *Ibid., p. 51.*
[205] *Ibid., p. 49.*
[206] *Ibid., p. 53.*
[207] *Ibid., pp. 109-111 and 119.*
[208] *Ibid., p. 117.*
[209] *Ibid., p. 43 and 50. I understand, however, one Valium is not only helpful but, apparently, life-saving in the event of delirium tremens (the "D.T.'s") in alcoholic withdrawal.*

most any drug that produces effects resembling those of alcohol may stimulate the desire for alcohol."[210] This is the reason that tranquilizers "serve to keep the embers of craving alive, continually reminding otherwise abstinent alcoholics what it feels like to be mildly intoxicated."

Psychiatrists, trained in prescribing drugs for psychopathologcal disorders, have a particularly difficult time helping patients without administering even more drugs. One psychiatrist with whom Dr. Morrison worked prescribed large doses of an anti-depressant, even after she told him she was taking heavy doses of drugs that he knew to include depressants.[211] Unfortunately, we cannot help by giving addicts more drugs to replace or offset the effects of others, or legal drugs to replace illegal ones.[212] We can learn to recognize addiction and allow addicts to experience the full consequences of their behaviors.

While there has been some improvement in the diagnosis and treatment of drug addiction, it's obviously been uneven and sporadic. The 24 classroom hours of instruction in addiction that most doctors receive today is still far too little for a disease that has been found to be the number one killer. With so little education and no first-hand knowledge, it's difficult for non-addicts to believe that drugs could become the central focus of one's life. They can't comprehend powerlessness over a substance and how it makes an addict behave. How else could they be so easily convinced by the addict that they either don't do drugs or have cleaned up their act over and over again?

While Morrison points out that drug addiction often went unrecognized and untreated in the late '60s and '70s, she admits it is disturbing that "drug addicts are frequently misdiagnosed and mistreated to this day [1989]."[213] Story after story attest to the fact that not much has changed. "My therapist was my biggest enabler," is an opinion shared by almost every AAer who dealt with a therapist prior to sobriety.

Complicating matters, almost half of all therapists are themselves highly credulous by nature, having a need to be genuine and with the highest integrity. Their first instinct is to believe an addict who says, "I'm clean

---

[210] *Ludwig, "Understanding the Alcoholic's Mind," 1988, Oxford University Press, Inc., p. 43. He modifies this with the proviso that the drugs be taken under conditions that promote drinking. He goes on to point out that "any excuse will do" for an alcoholic to drink, depending upon which Pavlovian connections the particular alcoholic has made to various external stimuli, totally unique to each alcoholic. Since we have no idea which stimuli will have this effect, this modifier is irrelevant.*

[211] *Ibid., p. 121.*

[212] *According to some psychiatrists and those in recovery, administering minimal doses of some drugs may help a few addicts. Others disagree, arguing that the fires of desire are thereby fanned. Such a discussion is beyond the scope of this book.*

[213] *Ibid., p. 59.*

and sober." These therapists (if psychologically healthy), would never lie, cheat or steal, and expect the same from others. This style of person is termed the "Idealist" by the father of Temperament theory, David Keirsey, or "iNtuitive Feeler" (NF) in the nomenclature of the Myers-Briggs Type Indicator, a personality indicator.[214] The strength they bring to psychology is their need to help others, while credulousness is their Achilles' heel when confronted by the pathological liar in the addict. Psychologists, perhaps more than most others, have a deep-seated desire to help their fellow man. After all, that's why they become psychologists.

This was the case for a charming and caring "Idealist" therapist named Beverly. With a degree in English, a double minor in theater and sociology and a graduate degree in marriage and family counseling, she is obviously extremely bright. No stranger to addiction, she believes that at least 90% of all 5 to 10-year-old patients at the psychiatric hospital where she worked had at least one addict parent.

Despite all this education and experience, she was not prepared to diagnose Robert as an alcoholic, especially since he had a very high-paying and prestigious job.

Beverly told Robert she was looking for a responsible, sensitive, religious, honest and successful businessman. They went to her church on their first date. Robert let Beverly know he was the top selling estate planner and investment advisor in his company. An overachiever, he told Beverly he was also a land developer and reserve police officer. He had made his first million by age 25. He insisted on complete honesty and valued that above all else. He seemed to care deeply for people, especially family, even paying his mother's rent. He'd been divorced a year from a woman who "suffered from mental illness, was a witch, slapped me all the time and cared about nothing but money." He had only recently completed the final property settlement and now paid his ex-wife $3,000 per month alimony. He was a member of a community service organization of men who painted hospitals and helped boys in the ghetto. He lambasted those who bounced checks or didn't pay bills on time, labeling them "irresponsible." This included Beverly's roommate of two years, for whom Robert later showed revulsion.

Although he seemed a bit cocky and full of himself at times, Bev fell in love with Robert. He was teary-eyed when he told her no woman had ever

---

[214] *Isabel Briggs Myers and Mary H. McCaulley, "Manual: A Guide to the Development and Use of the Myers-Briggs Type Indicator," Consulting Psychologists' Press, Inc., 1993, p. 257. According to Keirsey, Idealists comprise only 10-12% of the population, yet are disproportionately represented among psychotherapists and others in the people-helping-people professions. Type and Temperament are discussed in depth in the chapter, "Improving the Treatment of Drug Addiction."*

before made him a home-cooked meal. He occasionally exhibited volatile behavior, once getting upset with a sales clerk after being asked for his ID. He sometimes acted silly, stealing food off others' plates. After such mis-behaviors, he'd promise he'd never yell, act obnoxious or otherwise mis-behave again. Then they'd go to church together, where he'd ask her and God for their forgiveness.

Robert encouraged Beverly to quit her job so she could pursue her dream, which was acting. He told her parents that when they wed, he'd add her to his company medical plan (he was appalled when he learned she had no coverage). He convinced her family no man had ever loved her as much. When she began to poke a hole or two through his elaborately detailed stories of his past and present life, her family would come to his rescue. Beverly found herself up against her own family, making it difficult to do anything other than believe him.

Shortly before they married, Robert told Beverly's ex-husband to stop sending child support. He had plenty of money and suggested the sup-port go into a college fund. He offered to pay an expensive auto repair just before their wedding day. At times, things seemed too good to be true and she asked numerous questions. He responded in extraordinary detail. Not expecting her fiancé to lie to her and with full support from her family, Beverly quit work and married Robert.

Unfortunately, if things seem too good to be true, they usually are. Near the end of their honeymoon, Robert went into a rage over some little thing her son had done and went so far as to snap at Beverly's mother, with whom they visited briefly. A week later, purely by chance, Beverly met Robert's ex-wife, Ruth. Contrary to his story, Ruth had never been paid a dime and the property settlement had not yet been completed. Robert had ruined Ruth's credit and even helped cause the loss of her home to foreclo-sure. Adding insult to injury, they had barely divorced before Beverly mar-ried him. She began to see a role reversal between Robert and this "witch" when she discovered that the check for her car repair had bounced. She saw **more** rubber checks in the next couple weeks than she had seen with her roommate over a two-year period.

Fearing the worst, Beverly ran a credit check on her new husband. She discovered the man who "didn't owe anybody any money" had an abys-mal credit history, including a dozen tax liens and several personal judg-ments. She learned that the land development company, for which he had "very professional-looking" T-shirts made, was non-existent. Irate (yet now fascinated), she found that the "community service organization" was a cult of men in which there were bizarre rituals and heavy hazing, includ-ing nude dancing. Not only did he not have his financial house in order; he didn't even have liability insurance on his car, let alone the medical insurance he'd promised her.

If she had been trained to look, she would have found clues to potential problems prior to marriage. One was an admission to having been convicted as a juvenile for drug dealing and using (see questions 24 and 49 of the Thorburn Substance Addiction Recognition Indicator), which he supposedly no longer did. While detecting no direct evidence of alcohol or other drugs, there were occasional violent mood swings (question 17). After almost breaking up several times, he'd always "see the light," experiencing yet another healing from God (question 38). There were numerous memory lapses (question 7) which Beverly attributed to his busy work schedule (question 18). He obsessed about guns and, supposedly having a concealed weapon permit (almost impossible to get in Los Angeles), carried a loaded one (question 30). Robert spent lavishly (question 2), but Beverly thought he had tremendous wealth. Although a licensed therapist (an MFCC, or Marriage, Family and Child Counselor), she hadn't been taught these might be clues to active addiction.

Realizing she'd been conned and despite having no job, she soon mustered up the courage to leave. Due to her religion, she made a concerted effort at reconciliation, trying marriage counseling for 6 months. He conned this counselor, too, who believed his problem stemmed from a "chemical imbalance." During one session, trembling, he made a bizarre confession about a dishonorable military discharge at the age of 19 due to his arrest for selling drugs. Checking on the story, Beverly discovered he'd never even been in the military. Towards the end of the counseling, Robert was given the MMPI (the Minnesota Multiphasic Personality Inventory, one of psychologists' tools to uncover psychopathologcal disorders) and scored "psychopathic deviant" (PD spike, with a T-score over 65).

He admitted to being addicted to sex, spending and nicotine. Amazingly, he finally confessed to being a closet alcoholic, drinking heavily every night after Beverly went to bed, but "only to help him sleep." Beverly finally gave up trying to reconcile with Robert.

What makes the problem even more difficult to identify is that the practicing addict cannot see that he is one. It's easier to convince others you are not an addict if you believe it yourself. Ask an addict if he's using and he isn't, he'll answer no; ask if he's using and he is, he'll answer no and be more convincing. He truly believes he does not have a problem with the use. Since he may know you'll think he's an addict and try to interfere, he'll minimize the extent of use or deny it completely.

Morrison relates that as a psychiatric resident in training, she became aware she was having blackouts, but had no idea they were a symptom of her alcohol and narcotics addiction. Yet, part of her training "involved teaching substance-abuse classes to medical students and consulting on drug-related cases."[215] Using all her intelligence to hide her addiction, she

---

[215] *Morrison, Ibid., p. 106.*

never got caught using or passing bad (narcotic prescription) scripts. Even her husband, who knew she smoked marijuana and drank, was unaware of the extent of destructive and reckless behaviors to which the use of other drugs would take her, including carrying speed and narcotics through customs on a trip to Europe. Morrison's husband, along with other non-addicts could not understand the nature of addiction without being taught.

The constant hiding and secrecy of the addict produces stresses, as this form of betrayal among close persons always does. The excuses of both users and enablers covering up for users are legend. Morrison's husband found several empty Southern Comfort bottles in her laundry basket. Confronted, she explained she was collecting them to make candle lamps. Even upon finding her crumpled on the floor barely breathing next to a needle, he wouldn't take her to the emergency room for fear of ruining her career. If he, a professor of physiology and (apparently) a brilliant man, would make excuses and enable her drug use, anyone will, unless they understand that by doing so they are only hastening the addict's death, along with their own more gradual destruction.

Doctors like Morrison have gone on to create clinics where this knowledge is taught. But these things take time. Often a generation must pass before a new paradigm becomes commonly accepted. It was only 17 years ago when one of her doctor-friends thought Morrison was bipolar, when in reality she was "hyperactive and paranoid from the cocaine and other stimulants, and depressed and sluggish from the narcotics."[216] Unfortunately, this sort of misdiagnosis is still common. The recovering addicts themselves tell us as much, if we would only listen. Because the 12-Step program teaches that for the addict to remain clean and sober he must get and stay completely honest, I would trust many recovering addicts with my life. Yet we all-too-often believe the user who says he's not using, even though, looking carefully, he exhibits many signs and symptoms of active addiction.

Terence T. Gorski, an innovator in relapse prevention therapy, diplomatically states that the people who really understand this affliction are Board Certified Addictionologists and Certified Alcohol and Drug Abuse Counselors. The implication may be that uncertified therapists often understand little or nothing of addiction. They seem not to know of Gorski or his astonishingly compelling study of early recovery alcoholics. Gorski gave large numbers of alcoholics the MMPI on the 5th day of sobriety. It should not surprise us that over 90% scored high on the social deviancy scale, with a likely diagnosis of anti-social personality (sociopathic), or compulsive rule-breaker. He gave the same test to the same group of recovering alcoholics 20 days later (25 days into sobriety) and found a staggering

---

[216] *Ibid., p. 122.*

decline in those seemingly afflicted. Less than 10% scored high enough on the social deviancy scale to be considered possible anti-social personalities.

Psychologist friends told me that Patricia, my personal addict, was sociopathic. Yet, I asked, how could they know? If Gorski's study is any indication, they cannot, until there is a period of proven sobriety. This research supports my early skepticism, based on what were, at the time, limited observations and stories of recovering addicts at AA meetings.[217] More support is given by the finding by John M. MacDonald, M.D., who reported in *The Murderer and His Victim* (Charles C. Thomas, 1986) that "the only psychological disorder found more frequently among criminal offenders than in the general population were sociopathic [antisocial] personality disorder, alcoholism, and drug dependency."[218] If 90% of alcoholics are sociopathic among the general population of addicts and 10% of the population is addicted one may wonder, how many true non-alcoholic sociopaths are left?

What causes these sociopathic and other disorders in addicts? Simply put, addiction causes brain damage. According to Gorski, 73% of addicts have measurable cerebral cortical atrophy (damage to the frontal lobes of the brain) resulting in early recovery difficulties. This accounts, at least in part, for the almost impossible task of getting and staying sober. Gorski compares this with sex addicts, compulsive gamblers, runners (who get the so-called "runner's high") and compulsive spenders, none of which have any measurable brain damage. Since alcoholism is a bio-psycho-social disease, he argues that substance addiction is not just another compulsion. In his view, the brain atrophy is the biological component, giving rise to the other symptoms.

Compare an addict's brain with that of a non-addict's a day after drinking enough to equalize their levels of blood alcohol. The genetically sensitive (addictive) person has much more brain damage. A few days later, the non-addict's brain has healed, while the addict's has not. This causes him to go into the next drinking episode with a damaged brain. This is possibly due to the slower processing of acetaldehyde, the poisonous chemical that stays in the systems of addicts far longer than in non-addicts. Personality disorganization results, changing behavior and leading to social and relationship problems. According to Gorski, every addict exhibits emotional and mental problems that register on the MMPI as a personality disorder. The trouble is that therapists are giving the MMPI to addicts without knowing they are addicts. This causes them to diagnose psychopatho-

[217] *The information in this and the following six paragraphs were gleaned from Gorski's audiotape series, "The Role of Codependence in Relapse," Ibid.*
[218] *Graham, Ibid., p. 103.*

logical disorders without even finding the substance addiction. The assumption should be reversed. If there are psychopathologcal disorders reported on the MMPI, substance addiction should be assumed until and unless proven otherwise. If Gorski's work is correct, we will more often be right in this assumption. Acting upon this is safer than proceeding as if there is no substance.

The problem is, the MMPI is not measuring psychopathologcal disorders in the brain of an addict any more than the brain of a stroke victim,[219] it's measuring neuro-impairment to the frontal lobes of the brain, or brain damage which is allowed to continue because of incorrect diagnoses. The addict's obsession and compulsion, according to Gorski, is to use a toxic drug that damages the frontal lobes, destroying cognitive powers. It disrupts a person's thinking and feeling functions, or judgment, distorting their ability to be responsible for their behavior. Their brains are toxic and cannot respond to traditional forms of therapy well into sobriety. Yet Gorski implies, all too many therapists ignore the signs of addiction and attempt to treat the patient in the time-honored, therapeutically accepted way. He points out that the therapist can only damage the practicing addict (or one in early recovery) by using traditional methods of psychotherapy. By removing addiction as the culprit, the therapists are doing further damage to close persons. Believing their loved one is being treated for a primary pathology by the therapist or being properly medicated by the psychiatrist with yet another drug, the close person remains in the dark about addiction and has no reason to end or change the relationship with the addict.

If 15% of the population has serious psychopathologcal disorders and 10% are substance addicts (all showing some form of personality disorder), it is possible that two-thirds of the former are really substance addicts. The addicts are, therefore, receiving seriously defective treatment for their core problem and primary affliction. Many stories of recovering addicts support this conclusion. Since substance addiction mimics the psychopathological disorders and mental illnesses, this shouldn't be a surprise.

Addiction experts James E. Royce and David Scratchley also support this idea. They point out that tests, including the MMPI, from which one could infer "that one is an alcoholic because of personality problems," have generally been "administered during the first ten days of sobriety." They also report that James R. Milam and Rae H. Farmer repeated such tests and found that 70% to 80% of the psychopathological disorders found during the first 10 days of sobriety <u>disappear</u> after 3 months.[220]

---

[219] *Some therapists may argue it is measuring traits exacerbated by drug use. If drug use resulted only in decreased inhibitions as for non-addicts, I might agree. However, it results in a <u>change</u> of personality in addicts.*

[220] *James E. Royce and David Scratchley," Ibid., p. 132.*

We can also view this from the other side. Gorski reports, the disorders least common among codependents or non-addicts are the following: borderline (which is the need for or love of chaos in one's personal life), narcissistic (self-centered) behaviors, histrionic (attention seeking) behavior, paranoid (suspicious) behavior and antisocial (compulsive rule breaking) behavior.[221] These are disorders with which many practicing addicts are diagnosed, except addiction isn't "discovered" until later, in recovery. It should not be surprising that codependent non-addicts are rarely diagnosed with these disorders: they're not addicts and, therefore, rarely exhibit the symptoms.

The incredibly high percentage in Gorski's sample of addicts in early recovery testing positive for antisocial behavior supports this inference. Alcoholics Anonymous itself speaks to the narcissism (self-centeredness) of the addict with their theme song (sung to the tune of Cielito Linda, "i-i-i-i, i-i-i-i-i-i-i-i, me-me-me-me-me-me-me-me-me-me-me, i-i-me-myself and I") and the acknowledgement by all recovering addicts that theirs is the most self-centered disease on the planet.

We would think that the following description was describing addiction. This is from the 16th edition of the Merck Manual (an important text for psychologists) of 1992, page 1546: such persons

> "characteristically act out their conflicts and flout normal rules of social order. These persons are impulsive, irresponsible, amoral, and unable to forgo immediate gratification. They cannot form sustained affectionate relationships with others, but their charm and plausibility may be highly developed and skillfully used for their own ends."

Sound familiar? It continues:

> "They tolerate frustration poorly, and opposition is likely to elicit hostility, aggression, and serious violence. Their...behavior shows little foresight, and it is not associated with remorse or guilt, since these people seem to have a keen capacity for rationalizing and for blaming their irresponsible behavior on others."

This seems to be a near-perfect description of some addicts.[222] Continuing,

> "Frustration and punishment rarely modify their behavior or improve their judgment and foresight. Owing to impulsivity, [this person]...may attempt suicide if his aggressions become turned inward instead of being directed against others...."

---

[221] *Terence T. Gorski, "Do Family of Origin Problems Cause Chemical Addiction?" Ibid., p. 20.*

[222] *Particularly those of the "Artisan" Temperament, as we will find in the chapter, "Improving the Treatment of Drug Addiction." Addicts of this Temperament manifest behaviors that lead many into politics or prison.*

This description is of antisocial, psychopathic or sociopathic personalities.[223] The trouble is, it also describes many behavioral manifestations of substance addiction.

The following is another description, from Taber's Cyclopedic Medical Dictionary, Edition 13:

> "A group of mental disorders characterized by disturbances of thinking, mood, and behavior. There is an altered concept of reality and in some cases delusions and hallucinations. Mood changes include inappropriate emotional responses and loss of empathy. Withdrawn, regressive, and bizarre behavior may be noted."

This is the description for schizophrenia. The trouble is, once again it describes the behavioral abnormalities that characterize many substance addicts.

On those occasions where there is an underlying psychosis or neurosis, it stands little or no chance of being treated if the substance addiction is not treated first. Psychiatrist Herbert S. Peyser, M.D., wrote in "Alcoholism: A Practical Treatment Guide," that alcoholism must be "the first thing to be attacked [by the knowledgeable caregiver], and *there is no treatment for other conditions until this is under control*" (emphasis added).[224]

This may have been true for Actress Vivien Leigh, Mayo Methot (Mrs. Humphrey Bogart number 3), poet Edna St. Vincent Millay, actress Mary Tyler Moore, Susan B. Anthony, Ph.D. (grandniece of suffragette Susan B. Anthony), actress Frances Farmer and writer Mary Ann Crenshaw. They were all given the wrong primary diagnosis.

A psychiatrist diagnosed Methot as paranoid and schizophrenic. She died at age 48 of acute alcoholism.[225] Millay was diagnosed with anemia requiring hospitalization. She died at age 58 of a heart attack, with a bottle of wine in her hand.[226] Moore's cardiologist husband Robert Levine, M.D., told *People Magazine* that she was not alcoholic. Moore now considers herself a very lucky recovering alcoholic.[227] In a classic description of the Mental Health Model of Addiction, Anthony's psychiatrists told her, "Your sickness makes you drink. It is a symptom of your underlying problems. When we uncover the roots of your neuroses, we'll find out why you drink, and your drinking will take care of itself." Many other physicians diagnosed numerous emotional and physical problems. She got sober a few

---

[223] *From a letter to The Wall Street Journal, August 28, 1998, from Thomas H. Coleman, M.D., describing President Clinton's character defects.*

[224] *Cited in Robe, Ibid., p. 139.*

[225] *Robe, Ibid., p. 278-279.*

[226] *Robe, Ibid., p. 280.*

[227] *Robe, Ibid., p. 381.*

years later and her problems dissipated.[228] Psychiatrists all over the country variously diagnosed Frances Farmer as paranoid, schizophrenic, manic-depressive, catatonic and multiple personality. A diagnosis of alcoholism was not made, despite being drunk at work and repeated arrests for drunken brawls and drunk driving. In one of the most tragic cases of misdiagnosis ever, she was eventually committed to an insane asylum and, finally, given a lobotomy, before dying at age 57.[229]

Mary Ann Crenshaw wrote the best selling *The Natural Way to Super Beauty*, while drinking alcoholically. She was repeatedly misdiagnosed by physicians, psychiatrists and diet doctors, despite exhibiting symptoms including hypoglycemia, agitation, suicidal thoughts, insomnia, severe stomach pains, migraines, nausea, frayed nerves, blackouts, hallucinations and violent mood swings. She was prescribed Valium, Fiorinal, Placidyl (similar to Valium), Percodan, Librax, Navane (an anti-psychotic), Cogentin (to counteract the side effects of Navane), Phenobarbital, codeine and numerous other drugs. Diet doctors told her she could drink all the hard liquor she wanted. Despite all this, she got clean and sober and most of the symptoms disappeared.[230]

The trouble, as Dr. Kenneth H. Williams said in 1983, is that doctors still have "a long way to go" in recognizing that "alcoholism can look like, or almost mimic, any other mental disease," and that it can also "produce or mimic many other physical diseases."[231] The American Medical Association, in describing one of the symptoms of alcoholism as "an uncontrollable desire to drink," omits <u>any</u> description of the behavioral signs of alcoholism or how it affects those near the addict.

Treating addiction as a compulsive disorder has never worked. Nor has attempting to treat other underlying psychological problems as the primary disorder that "drive the alcoholic to drink." This is why, prior to 1935, when psychologists had given up on helping alcoholics, over 95% relapsed, apparently dying as practicing addicts. Yet the view that psychological problems are the primary disorder which causes alcoholism was resurrected and given a scientific name, the Mental Health Model of Addiction, which made it seem it had been subjected to rigorous testing when it had not. This Model survived well into the early '60s, even as recovering alcoholics themselves (through AA) admitted they drank simply because they are alcoholics. The Model fell into disuse, but has been brought back in the '80s and '90s. Gorski artfully states, "The new interest in adult chil-

---

[228] *Robe, Ibid., p. 137.*
[229] *Robe, Ibid., pp. 14-15, 27, 31, 140, 185-186, 243, 370 and 378.*
[230] *Robe, Ibid., pp. 162-167.*
[231] *Robe, Ibid., p. 167.*

dren of alcoholics and codependency is bringing many family therapists and psychotherapists into the addictions field. Many of these professionals are well meaning but do not have the basic knowledge of chemical addictions or how to treat it successfully. Others...look at the similarities between chemical addictions and other compulsions and jump to the conclusion they must all be the same thing in different forms."[232] *If psychological disorders caused chemical addiction, there would be many recovering addicts who could again drink or use socially.* Instead, there are almost none. The Mental Health Model fails in its most fundamental prediction.

Perhaps one in 1,000 purported addicts have been known to safely resume the use of psychoactive chemicals after recovery without psychopathological disorders reoccurring. These observations completely blow the Mental Health Model out of the realm of possibilities for the vast majority of substance addicts. If there are some truly bipolar people who "self-medicate" with drugs because of their manic-depression, or demonstrate sociopathic or borderline personalities before the drugs, they are in the minority. For example, heavy drinking may have preceded Patty Duke's well-known bipolar disorder. Her (likely) alcoholic business managers fed her Bloody Marys at the age of 13 or 14. She later took Phenobarbital, Percodan, Thorazine, Stelazine, Valium, Seconal and other tranquilizers and in her twenties repeatedly got drunk, to the point of being "hung over most of the day because I drank most of the night."[233] It is perhaps not coincidence that bipolar disorder usually shows up (according to mental health professionals) in 18- to 20-year-olds, after most begin their drinking and drugging careers. We increase the odds of helping the addict by assuming addiction is the source of all other problems, until proven otherwise.

The Model also predicts that psychological disorders cause other compulsions, failing to distinguish these compulsions from substance addiction in terms of either treatment or harm. Compulsive shopping, gambling and hand washing do not cause brain damage. Substance addiction does. They do not distort perceptions of reality with blackouts and euphoric recall. While gamblers, for example, can be as dangerous as substance addicts without a substance to feed the gambling, this is rare. Non-substance compulsions and "addictions" are not, overall, as dangerous.

---

[232] *Gorski, "Family of Origin Problems," Ibid., pp. 44-45.*

[233] *Patty Duke and Kenneth Turan, "Call Me Anna: The Autobiography of Patty Duke," New York: Bantam Books, 1987, pp. 90-91, 155, 169, 174, 196, 200-201, 203-205, 239 and 310. Patty Duke wonders if the anti-psychotic drugs Thorazine and Stelazine triggered her manic-depression. A careful reading of her book suggests the possibility that alcohol and other drugs may have not only played a role, but instead that she may have been misdiagnosed. Interestingly, she denies ever taking "drugs," obviously considering only street drugs as "drugs."*

Even when, on the odd occasion the non-substance addict is as destructive, totally different treatment is required.

Therapists have the same problem when counseling codependents. They often claim that the non-addict's "problems" must be promptly addressed. However, first things first. Just as addicts must stop the use of substances prior to exploring other issues or any psychopathologies that may exist independently of addiction,

Non-addict codependents must be educated about addiction before
successfully addressing their issues.

The non-addict must learn to recognize addiction. He must understand that harm may come to both himself and the addict by doing <u>anything</u> to protect the addicted from consequences. This allows him to *uncompromisingly disenable* with love and without guilt. Only then can he look at his own problems.

Therapists often address patients' issues without first exploring the likelihood they either might be addicts or at least seriously affected by one. Remember that addiction can cause symptoms in both the addict and codependent. Some of his perceptions and judgments may be distorted and impaired just from the natural response of codependency. No amount of counseling can treat an illness when addressing <u>only</u> symptoms. If you're swimming among sharks, you're not thinking about anything other than getting eaten. The bottom line is, before counseling can be truly successful, the non-addict should be removed from the relationship physically or mentally through detachment.

However, we must first distinguish between the addict and the codependent, so we know who to treat and for what. Psychopathological symptoms in the codependent are very different from those of the addict. Commonly, codependents are avoidant (socially fearful), dependent (overly reliant on others), compulsive (rigidly obeying rules), passive-aggressive (compliant but angry) and self-defeating (constantly setting themselves up for failure).[234] In a crazed couple, each blaming the other for their problems and "accusing" the other of addiction, comparing the apparent disorders can provide necessary clues for the aware therapist or other observer to determine the difference. Only then can the proper treatment for each be prescribed: tough love for the addict and removal of the codependent from the relationship. Gorski has found there is often a "spontaneous remission of codependent symptoms when the person is no longer in a com-

---

[234] *Gorski, "Do Family of Origin Problems Cause Chemical Addiction?" Ibid., p. 20.*

mitted relationship with an addict."[235] This should not come as a shock, considering the weight lifted off the codependent.

The codependent must understand the role that the chemicals play in the abuse, the lies and other criminal behavior of the addict. He can't begin to understand this role if the chemical use is downplayed, ignored or not diagnosed at all. However, once he does, he can more easily disenable with a clear conscience. It also helps him to know that the addict did not engage in destructive behaviors because of anything <u>he</u> did, or more importantly, out of hatred for anyone other than himself. The addict engaged in the destructive behaviors because that is what addicts do. Knowing all this, the codependent can ultimately recover far more quickly than can the addict. Unfortunately, as we will see in the next section, euphemistic and inaccurate portrayals of addicts in the media create a tremendous obstacle to understanding addiction.

Euphemizing addiction

As a species, we have long cleansed ourselves of our human failings so as not to blame, accuse or otherwise make someone appear "bad" in the eyes of others. Peter L. Bernstein, in "Against the Gods: the Remarkable Story of Risk,"[236] discusses John Graunt's compilation of births and deaths in 17th century London and his observation of "one Casualty in our Bills, of which though there be daily talk, [but] little effect." This casualty, or cause of death, was a kind of syphilis and Graunt wondered why the records showed so few died of this, while so many had long suffered. He concluded "most of the deaths from ulcers and sores [of which there were many] were in fact caused by venereal disease, the recorded diagnoses serving as euphemisms." Graunt noted that only "hated persons, and such, whose very Noses were eaten of, were reported...to have died of this too frequent Maladie."

As with this sickness of yore, we have, for too long, hidden substance addiction in the dark recesses of family histories. In countless instances, we have buried death under the technically correct but generically false cause. The Centers for Disease Control estimates that the number of deaths causally linked to alcohol is up to four times greater than traditional esti-

---

[235] *Gorski, audio-tape, "The Role of Codependence on Relapse," Ibid.*
[236] *Peter L. Bernstein, "Against the Gods: the Remarkable Story of Risk," New York: John Wiley and Sons, 1996, pp. 80-81.*

mates.[237] Milam and Ketcham point out that the deaths of early stage alcoholics are rarely attributed to alcoholism, when in fact the vast majority of
"accidents" (the greatest cause of death among the young) are probably
attributable to addiction. One study reported that as few as 10% of deaths
actually due to alcoholism are reported as such, the balance to accidents,
suicides, drowning, cirrhosis, cancer, cardiovascular and other diseases.[238]
My father, for example, died of a hematoma to the brain. While alone, he
got drunk, fell and struck his head on the corner of a television, resulting in
the hematoma. If records showed the underlying cause of death, his would
have been among several hundred thousand each year from substance
addiction (particularly alcoholism) in the United States. Instead, it was
"hematoma caused by accident."

The stigma of alcoholism and other substance addiction resulting in
euphemisms and family secrets explain (at least partially) why so little is
understood of this horrible affliction. If people die of everything other
than alcoholism, why should we bother to learn about it? As a result, as
Graham points out, "alcoholism is probably the most under-studied of all
complex subjects."[239]

It starts with celebrities. Even when talking about obvious addicts, talk
show hosts avoid the term alcoholic or addict. They tell us that famous
people chop off various body parts to show love, or throw up over pizzas
at restaurants in front of dozens of people and then pass out. They describe screaming and swearing matches in public. We're told how they
cavort with prostitutes and others while married, engage in stalking and
carouse all night and come in late for work. Yet society excuses their behavior with, "He was abused as a child," or "She's suffering from Johnny
dumping her and the loss of her part on her TV show." Sometimes it's
simply, "that's just who Billy is," and we should put up with his "oddities"
and "unusual characteristics" because he is famous or powerful. As a result, many think that if they stopped this aberrant behavior, they'd be all
right. No! Only when they stop using alcohol and other drugs, can these

[237] *The Centers for Disease Control of the U.S. Public Health Service developed the
concept of "Alcohol-Attributable Fractions" (AAFs) in a report entitled, "Alcohol-
Related Disease Impact," by J. M. Schultz, D.L. Parker and D. P. Rice, 1989. AAFs
provide an estimate of deaths causally linked to alcohol. Using this method, there are
about 4 times the number of alcohol-related deaths than using the traditional method of
deaths directly attributable to alcohol. However, they seem not to have linked murder to
such attributions, nor did they include other drugs. They may still be underestimating
the extent of the problem.*

[238] *Milam and Ketcham, Ibid., p. 83, citing the unpublished data of W. Schmidt and
R. E. Popham, "Deaths in 1823 Male Alcoholics, Corrected for the Expected Mortality in
Each Subgroup," 1978.*

[239] *Graham, Ibid., p. xiii.*

behaviors (eventually) end. First things first. We should pay attention to recovering addicts, who prescribe to their fellow drunks and druggies that if they "stop using, your life will improve." It's the only prescription that works.

There is one euphemizing, misleading phrase that may serve to explain the public's ignorance of the nature of addiction:

"Drug Abuse."

Abuse implies voluntary, willful action. Yet, it is used to describe much of what is actually addiction. Grounded in one's biological make-up, addiction is not voluntary. I have voluntarily abused alcohol, as have many others who are (apparently) not addicts. Non-addicts have a choice. The addict does not, especially after the first drink, due to cravings and the particular effect of the substance on their brain, biological in origin. Nor do addicts have a choice about the behavior the substance causes. By definition, in addicts it causes misbehaviors.

Never being sure they can limit themselves to just one drink and unable to predict what they may do when using, is not abuse. It is like cancer. We are, ultimately, powerless over both. No one voluntarily uses something over which they are powerless, causing behavior in which they (in their right minds) would never normally engage. The idea that they can control the use of the drug is exacerbated when terms such as "abuse" are used. If it could be controlled, an addict would, at the first signs of problems, stop using. As a matter of fact, non-addicts subconsciously think, "If he really, truly wanted to stop or control it, he would." The truth is, the addict cannot stop until an appalling level of pain is experienced, eventually causing him to admit he is powerless to control his use or resulting behaviors.

Addiction and the media

As in polite society, addiction in the media is often only recognized euphemistically, or in many cases not at all. In an advice column,[240] a questioner asks about a good friend and former co-worker who excessively bad-mouths the company after being terminated from employment. Asking if there is a way to get her to stop, the advisor responds that if he tries, he will lose her friendship. Instead, it's suggested that he discuss it rationally and explain that while she might have reason to be upset, he believes the job is right for him. Let her vent and then help her find a more suitable

---

[240] Ken Lloyd, "Help friend get past slamming ex-employer," *The Daily News,* January 26, 1998. Lloyd is a Ph.D. specializing in organizational behavior.

job.

As we have seen, this is an approach that will possibly enable and have him banging his head against a wall.

The first thing is to ascertain if she might be an addict. Constantly haranguing her old company and having been "terminated" (blaming others and having problems at work) are both clues to substance addiction. He should find out the reason for termination. Did she fail to show up for work, particularly on Mondays? Did she pick arguments with other employees? Does she have "family problems" or financial problems? Is there emotional volatility or other behavior that could be explained by substance addiction?

The response should hinge entirely on this. If there is a high probability she's an addict, it is suggested that there is nothing one can do except to stop the psychological enabling by being her sounding board and friend (not to mention any financial enabling). Step out of the ring so you don't prevent her from reaching whatever bottom she needs, collaborating with others if appropriate to perform an intervention. If it is determined she is not an addict we may find an addict in her life, to which her woes or attitude are a codependent response. It may be a significant other person or even the employer. If her complaints are credible, perhaps it's time the querying employee seeks other employment.

Ignoring the possibility of substance addiction is standard practice in advice columns and talk shows. Yet, if addiction-related, these problems cannot be fixed or dealt with in a mature and rational manner. Such immaturity is, in itself, a clue to addiction. Many recovering addicts and addiction counselors believe the addict is emotionally "stuck" at the chronological age when regular use of substances began. This is usually, as we have seen, quite young.

The media engages in incomplete and/or erroneous reporting of addiction in numerous other ways. It minimizes the degree of the problem, as in the case of Ventura County Superior Court Judge Robert Bradley, arrested five times for behavioral problems associated with drinking. One newspaper article reported the Judge admitting to having an alcohol problem for 10 years.[241] The article later quotes him as saying he "recognized it about 20 years ago," a far cry from ten. At his last arrest, his blood alcohol content was at .22 per cent. Yet another article reported that Bradley said he'd drunk 4 to 6 beers on the occasion,[242] which if consumed within one hour would result in a BAC of .06 to .09 percent in a 200-pound person. Obviously, he drank more than a six-pack. Fortunately, an officer saw him fall-

---

[241] *Daily News, "Judge's 5th arrest blamed on 'pain'," May 20, 1998.*
[242] *Daily News, "Judge faces new drinking charge," May 23, 1998.*

ing off his bicycle rather than driving a car.

The excuses for drinking were pervasive in media accounts. In cases such as these, the media doesn't simply state that he may be (or is) an alcoholic-addict. This is not entirely their fault or choice; it's the result of the legislature and libel laws, along with a desire to not proffer opinions. However, the media repeats Judge Bradley's own excuses for drinking "more in the last year," by quoting him as blaming his divorce and job situation. The uninitiated may be tempted to say, "poor man, give him another chance and when things get better he'll stop drinking." It didn't explain that his drinking probably <u>caused</u> his divorce and precarious job situation. The fact of being protected and enabled by his job didn't help.

It had been reported previously that "judges convicted of one DUI violation typically receive a private admonishment, the most lenient form of discipline."[243] The Judge is done no favors by being offered such leniency. The attorney's duty is to defend his client even though he is doing him great harm. He misleads others in explaining that his client "has had this problem for quite awhile and has been actively involved in trying to beat it."[244] While saying he's "trying to beat it," the unhappy result is, he may be insuring access to the next tavern. We cannot know if he's truly "trying to beat it" without being inside his brain. We can, however, observe his behavior and easily conclude that he has not even taken the first step.

The minimization of use and excuses were partially offset in articles where the term "battling alcoholism" was used. Media reports of substance addiction, unfortunately, deteriorate from this level. Alcoholism is rarely mentioned in stories of violent crime, and then mostly towards the end. In one story of a murder-suicide, in which the gunman shot his wife, then killed his 3-year-old son along with himself, it was reported in the <u>16th paragraph</u> (about two-thirds of the way through) that he "had a drinking problem."[245] It reported in the 5th paragraph "he had been involved in a bitter argument with his wife recently in which he threw an ax through a window." To better educate the public about the tragic consequences, it should be reported clearly and early that there is evidence of substance addiction without misinforming and downplaying by using terms such as "drinking problem" and "drug abuse." This may help people to realize addiction comes first, the crime second. Spouses and parents may then become aware of the risks in not taking quick and decisive action when addiction is suspected.

The lack of understanding was clearly evident in reports of a fatal stab-

[243] *Daily News, "Penitent judge returns to work after 2nd arrest," January 6, 1998.*
[244] *Ibid.*
[245] *Daily News, "Man shoots wife, kills son, 3, self," November 26, 1996.*

bing in the normally crime-free Stevenson Ranch section of the Santa Clarita Valley, north of Los Angeles. A mother had been confronting her son about his drinking. They "occasionally" argued and he "often" got drunk. According to neighbors, "he didn't appear to have a job" (the parents having enabled their son's behavior by supporting him).[246] Nowhere did it explain why this happened "in such a nice neighborhood" or the reason he often complained about his aching liver.

Very often, addiction is not reported, due in part to the euphemizing by friends and family. It was evident that entertainment lawyer William John Billick, who killed his 18-month-old twins and himself in February 1997, had symptoms of addiction. The stories reported that he was distraught over his wife's plans to leave, taking their children. They had been fighting for several hours. Billick had been arrested for a previous incidence of spousal abuse, but the case was dismissed when his wife told police her injuries were minor and that she would not cooperate in the prosecution. Under a "no drop" policy, the City Attorney's Office often continues prosecution, but declined with Billick since he had no prior criminal history and the couple was undergoing marriage counseling. The error was that he was not in treatment for possible alcoholism, in yet another case of the therapist and City Attorney's office apparently missing the point, despite these and reported violent tendencies in a prior marriage. Grief-stricken friends, reportedly shocked, couldn't understand what could drive him to kill his children.

Not every addict becomes this destructive. However, it proves the impossibility of predicting his behavior. With perceptions distorted and judgment impaired while blaming everyone and everything else, anything can and often will occur. Yet nothing I read[247] reported that Billick might be an alcoholic. However, a friend of mine, who knew the Billicks, told me that in his opinion, William Billick was a raging alcoholic. It's possible he was never before in trouble with the law because, like so many others, well meaning friends and colleagues had repeatedly bailed him out.

A far better reporting job was done of the tragic murder-suicide of comedian Phil Hartman by his wife Brynn. Here, the cocaine "problem" was recognized on the front page. However, despite the fact that Mrs. Hartman had reportedly been in a Malibu rehabilitation center five months prior, this "problem" was not labeled addiction. Euphemistic terms such as, "She had returned to cocaine use," or, "She and Phil had argued about it" and "She struggled with the cocaine problem and difficulties in their marriage,"

---

[246] *Daily News, "'Dial 911...My son stabbed us'," June 23, 1997.*
[247] *Daily News, "Father mad at his wife, kills twins," February 24, 1997, and "System was unable to save twins lives," February 25, 1997.*
[248] *Daily News, "Storybook lives end in tragedy," May 29, 1998.*

were used instead.[248] It was never explained that people don't argue about a substance unless its use is having a serious impact on their lives. If so, there's a good chance that addiction is the primary source of any difficulties. Nothing else can be resolved until the user is abstinent and in recovery. Until then, total separation (with restraining orders, if necessary) is appropriate, or one can end up with the all-too-horrible Hartman tragedy. Without administering painful consequences, attempting to talk to, or reason with substance addicts, is to no avail. When we believe there may be addiction, we <u>have to</u> act in such a way that recognizes and completely accepts the fact that,

We cannot predict how destructive the behavior of a practicing addict may become.

Two days later an article spoke of Hollywood's "bad habits" being hard to break, "even for" stars with wealth.[249] "Even for" would have more accurately read, "especially for" such stars. Addict stars (and others in positions of prestige, power and wealth) can shield themselves from the negative consequences, increasing the likelihood of continued use. In addition, such wealth and power fuel the ego, leaving little opportunity for recovery. Addicts often build wealth during early-stage addiction. Worse yet, actors, writers and others earning residuals and royalties are kept afloat even into the final stage, further delaying recovery and increasing the likelihood of an untimely demise. Lucy Barry Robe wrote convincingly in her study of the stars that money is the addict's biggest enabler, often "helping" the wealthy addict to his death. It's even easier for the good-looking; money flows easily to a Marilyn Monroe, a Tony Curtis and millions of attractive non-actor addicts like Patricia. Having money and/or being beautiful are enormous handicaps to overcome when one is an addict.

The use of the term "habit" is another unfortunate choice of words. Nobody would say a person with diabetes or cancer has a "bad habit" and yet, we say this about a person with the disease of substance addiction. Although one meaning for "habit" in Webster's is "addiction," this use would be better relegated to non-chemical compulsions in order to differentiate between the two. There is an infinite gap between the "habit" of tapping one's fingers annoyingly and substance addiction. It's unfortunate that the English language has so many words that fail to distinguish between different concepts. Such radically disparate meanings should be described with distinct symbols. Another definition for "habit" is "some-

---

[249] *Daily News*, *"Hollywood's bad habit: Drug abuse persists in celebrity circles,"* May 31, 1998.

thing done easily, a practice or custom," giving a sense of something rather innocuous and voluntary. If we are to give a more accurate meaning to non-addicts, terms that compromise the true nature of addiction should be avoided and use of the term "addiction" for non-substance compulsions should be shunned.

All is not hopeless for the media. While the same article on the Hartman tragedy uses the term "abuse" and "addictions" interchangeably, at least the latter term is used. There were even two points made that were informative for the attentive reader. It quoted Lt. Frank Valdez of the LAPD's narcotics unit as saying that the reason drug use is "not going away is that the demand is still there." This is one of the few instances of reporting and statements by police that do not put the blame for addiction on the supplier, who is simply meeting demand.

The other point made was a quote by an anonymous 45-year-old comedian. "When I first got sober, I thought, man, I'm never gonna be funny again....that's really part of the delusion, that I was funny because of the drugs and alcohol instead of in spite of them." He added, "There are people who still believe that," suggesting addicts always believe they are more competent at their work (including the work of making people laugh) when using. This is a result of their distorted perceptions, at least after early-stage addiction, when the addict may indeed be quite competent in compartmentalized areas.

Sometimes the media overlooks addiction simply due to the age of the perpetrator involved in the tragedy. The murder of 16-year-old William Futrelle in March 1996, by classmate Joseph Burris was called "a descent into madness." Burris's childhood was reported as being shattered by the death of his father. Why is it assumed that the death of a father would lead to a life of crime, when this does not occur with countless other children who lose a parent? Yet, this was the reported cause of his behavior. It was also revealed, "Within months, his conservative grooming gave way to baggy jeans, gold chains and a new hairstyle one relative described as 'inexplicable'....Joe began drinking, having sex, smoking marijuana, experimenting with heroin and cocaine...."[250] It should be obvious by now, they got the description of the behavior reversed: the drugs came first, followed by the "inexplicable" hairstyle and other histrionic behavior.

This is not dissimilar to media accounts of alcoholics who "drank because their lives were in disarray." Whether young or old, the excuse given for using or the order in which it occurred — problems, then use — always seems the same. According to the media, the addict indulges in response to life's problems, an utterly false claim that the addict's family, friends and non-addiction-trained therapists support. **If life's problems resulted**

---

[250] *L.A. Times, "Dad's Death Crushed Granada Hills Youth," October 7, 1997.*

in addiction, we would all be addicts. What is not recognized is, early-stage addiction leads to a predictable progression in which addicts (due to distorted perceptions and consequential impaired judgment) engage in increasingly bizarre and criminal behaviors. The addictive use simply becomes obvious when it reaches media attention. To the trained observer's eye it was there all along, albeit in more subtle ways.

Another problem in diagnosing addiction first is often due to the duration of the early stage. This can last a long time when addiction is only to alcohol. While some suggest the first stage usually lasts 8 to 12 years, there are instances of it lasting far longer (50-60 years in the case of Joseph Stalin, who used his massive power over others to fuel his addiction and keep him in early-stage alcoholism for his entire life). Surprisingly, maintaining addiction in seemingly controlled fashion for a long time has not always been to the disadvantage of the consumer and humanity. There are instances of extraordinary entrepreneurs and creative geniuses (Thomas Paine, Herbert Spencer and Beethoven come to mind) in apparent extended early stage addiction, ironically bringing tremendous good to the world. The personal lives of many of the greatest actors and writers may have been falling apart, while ego-fueled addiction drove them to success after success. However, polydrug use, causing potentiation, works to compress disasters. One may not entirely facetiously suggest that other drugs be offered to assist the addict in more efficiently and speedily hitting bottom. Addicts are perfectly capable of building great businesses and wealth sober, even if this may no longer be an insatiable need as their ego deflates.

The portrayal of addiction in books and movies

There are many excellent books describing substance addiction and recovery. However, tragically few pages are devoted to the affect the addict has on those around him. There may be two reasons for this glaring omission. One: therapists, as we have seen, have been trained to diagnose and treat psychopathological disorders, <u>not</u> biological (disease-caused) disorders. As such, they focus only on treating the person's psyche. Two: addicts (along with therapists) write most of the books describing addicts' behavior. They rarely know how devastating their effect on others has been, because their minds protect them with euphoric recall, memory repression and blackouts. They are thereby prevented from remembering everything, perhaps to reduce the likelihood of suicide when sober. As Vernon Johnson puts it, they could go into "irreversible emotional shock" from remembering too much.

The books that portray addicts as insensitive, irrational, self-centered monsters in their private lives frequently tiptoe around the fact that they are addicts. Even when it's eventually made obvious, the blame for their behavior often lies elsewhere. B. D. Hyman, daughter of actress Bette Davis, comes close to identifying, yet still doesn't quite get, the true source of the problem in the unauthorized biography, "My Mother's Keeper."[251] She describes her mother's behaviors and attitudes throughout the book as "bizarre, capricious, controlling, obsessive, self-centered, accusatory, nationalistic, insensitive, belittling, histrionic, hateful, blaming, sadistic, inconsiderate, chain-smoking, grandiose, paranoid, manic-depressive, volatile, moody, abusive, cruel, inappropriate, pompous, illogical, arbitrary, temperamental, irritable, erratic and rude." She believes these were related to her need "to prove who's *strong* enough to win."[252] Nothing else made sense without this "missing ingredient....the importance she attaches to fighting for its own sake."[253] What eludes Hyman is that this was Davis' particular method of feeding her alcoholic-starved ego.

Yet, there were vast numbers of clues to addiction. While reading along, imagine yourself an acquaintance of Davis'. You might observe only one or two symptoms, yet it will become obvious even those should be heeded. Think about people that you know who exhibit just a few such signs. Unimportant though they may seem, these clues could be grave warnings that you're dealing with an addict (just like Bette Davis). If you were to not pay attention, you could come to great financial or other harm.

The signs of addiction included **reverse telephonitis**, in which she hung up on her daughter on innumerable occasions throughout their stormy relationship. She repeatedly charged her daughter's husband of adultery in a game of **false accusations**, citing a "*very* reliable source,"[254] while at the same time suggesting her daughter engage in **unethical behavior** by spicing up her marriage with a little affair now and then.[255] In a variation of racism (**hating** whole classes of people), she despised men, calling them utterly useless, "the shits" and other **foul language** (terms she often used). She had an "instinct for attacking only people who were vulnerable,"[256] including, on repeated occasions, her own grandchildren. This is a form of **intimidation** and something that finally caused Hyman to disassociate with her mother.

[251] B. D. Hyman, "My Mother's Keeper: A daughter's candid portrait of her famous mother," New York: William Morrow and Co., 1985.
   [252] Ibid.., p. 277.
   [253] Ibid.., p. 279.
   [254] Ibid.., p. 130.
   [255] Ibid., p. 133.
   [256] Ibid., p. 165.
   [257] Ibid., p. 168.

Davis had **repeated financial problems** despite her stardom status and pay scale, because "she loved to spend money and did so like a drunken sailor,"[257] her lawyer-manager even "lending her money when she was broke."[258] She **ate little** and stuck with her **"rules for drinking"** for much of her life. She never drank after dinner (what use would that be when food sucks up all the alcohol?), never drank white wine ("that's for alcoholics"), and never drank (until late in her career) while working ("that's unprofessional"). Describing her Mother's drinking behavior, Hyman explains, "You can get shit-faced at breakfast and drink all day, which Mother does, but it doesn't count unless you drink after dinner. People who drink after dinner are 'real drunks.'"[259]

Although Hyman clearly identifies both Joan Crawford and Davis' fourth husband, actor Gary Merrill, as alcoholics, she's hesitant to call her mother one. She describes what we know as the alcoholic's **rule-breaking behavior** and **numerous accidents** when writing of her mother's belief that she was an expert driver, "despite a record-breaking history of citations for running red lights, over-shooting stop signs, speeding, illegal parking and a seemingly endless succession of fender-benders. She even drove through the back wall of a friend's garage by putting the car in the wrong gear"[260] and at one point drove over Hyman's foot. Yet, she doesn't mention the fact that her mother even drank until page 49, barely clueing us in to the importance of alcohol in her life. Hyman, as a young teen, hands mother "her usual Scotch, on the evening before the new housekeeper was to begin work," to which Davis glowingly remarks, "'God, you're an incredible girl! I'm almost sorry that the new woman's starting tomorrow.'"

She mentions Davis' **relationship with alcohol** a second time 67 pages into the biography when she quotes her as saying, "I need a drink," and a third time when Davis orders a couple of double Scotches waiting for a suite.[261] The next time her drinking is mentioned, "she got roaring drunk, insulted some very nice people, swore at the top of her lungs and tried to force grown men to do a Maypole dance."[262] These were the sort of behaviors her mother always engaged in anyway, with virtually all the activities and attitudes cited above having, by now, surfaced. Yet, her behaviors were still a "mystery" to Hyman, who appears to be a woman of reasonable intelligence. Even at 34 years of age, she told her mother, "[I have] no

[258] *Ibid., p. 180.*
[259] *Ibid., p. 155.*
[260] *Ibid., p. 47.*
[261] *Ibid., p. 76.*
[262] *Ibid., p. 114.*
[263] *Ibid., p. 208.*

idea what your problem is."[263]

Finally, half way through the book, she describes a social event in which Davis has "**pre-drunk**" before a party and then at the party downs three drinks (probably double Scotches) with everyone else still on their first. She gives her son-in-law a Miltown (a tranquilizer) for a headache, which was "probably strong" because it was Davis', while she "**gulped down**" double Scotch after double Scotch. All this was before appetizers were served,[264] when "Mother was getting drunker by the minute." Ms. Davis had consumed at least 6 double-Scotches by the time dinner was laid out, enough to elevate the **BAC** of a 120-pound person (when drunk over the course of 2-3 hours) to **about .30 per cent**, which is comatose for many.

Still, with all this liquor, Hyman failed to make the connection between the drinking and her mother's behavior. A comparatively peaceful period of a couple years (during which she was courted by a man in whom she was especially interested) abruptly ended with "an increasingly serious drinking problem...she not only drank in the morning, she was actually drunk by 10:00 A.M. and stayed that way until bedtime."[265] **Chain-smoking** her cigarettes, **she set "her own bed on fire a few times** in her life."[266] Constant complaining about everyone and everything led Hyman and others to believe the "real problem" was the attention paid to others (and not enough to her), or some other nonsense. Davis would engage in **massive misrepresentations, exaggerations, half-truths and confabulations** and Hyman couldn't understand how her mother "could delude herself so thoroughly."[267] In one of her numerous disgusting displays of bad behavior, she not only **accused others of lying** but told her grandson, "You're a damned liar, just like your mother always was!"[268] Hyman had no idea "how anyone could be so unkind to a child (she) professed to love."[269]

The difficulty in identifying alcoholism as the underlying source of all her mother's objectionable behaviors was due to the facts that Hyman (and everyone else) had never been taught to recognize the signs of addiction and because Hyman was a normal drinker. Alcohol doesn't do these things to non-addicts. Hyman could get plied on hot tea laced with brandy[270]

[264] *Ibid., p. 138-141.*
[265] *Ibid., p. 170. Alcoholics can be good for long periods of time if there's something they want. Pursuing the heart of a man, she controlled the drinking for a couple of years.*
[266] *Ibid., p. 195.*
[267] *Ibid., p. 234.*
[268] *Ibid., p. 211.*
[269] *Ibid., p. 204.*
[270] *Ibid., p. 92.*

and be none the worse for it. She, along with 90% of the U.S. population, could take it or leave it. She could drink normally, getting looped now and then, and go on with life in a normal fashion without abusing anyone. While Hyman loved others, she had no idea how incorrect her assumption was that "mother loved me more than anything else in the world."[271] She simply didn't understand the love relationship the alcoholic-addict has with the drug.

Nor did she lend any importance to the fact that Davis took the **tranquilizer** Miltown and may have used the **sleeping pill** Nembutal on a regular basis, mentioning the latter only peripherally in the course of describing one of her numerous "mock suicide" attempts. She **threatened** her own young children several times a year with **suicide** when they weren't obediently towing the line.[272] Davis **hid the drinking**, so most of the time Hyman didn't even see it. Her mother constantly fidgeted while cooking, nervously wandering from kitchen to guests to kitchen, and never allowing anyone else to enter. She was probably afraid someone would see her drink from a glass hidden behind a sugar or flour canister, with "a little orange juice in it just in case anyone should see it."[273]

She'd **rant and rave** the entire time about how she "slaved away" for all the ungrateful guests, finally emerging with macaroni and cheese. Hyman was extremely lucky that Davis, while committing unspeakably **abusive verbal atrocities** against Hyman's children, never got overly physical in the abuse. Small children should never have been left alone with Davis, even if one decided to maintain such an abusive relationship.

Compounding the difficulty in identifying alcoholism was the fact that Davis' professional stature was rarely compromised. She had been reduced to doing horror movies, as had Joan Crawford (Hyman hinted at the irony of monsters doing monster movies), but always seemed to rebound. Davis could always control her drinking when needed. Apparently, she was abstinent on the set until she neared the end of her career. She was also sober when conducting business with her lawyer-manager and when her alcoholic ex-husband's family or other people were present (in public or private) "who were of sufficient stature to impress her."[274]

Even at the very end of her and daughter Hyman's stormy relationship, she was able to appear rational exactly when it suited her purpose. Davis had a series of **strokes** that her **lifelong physician termed** "the direct result of many, many years of **alcoholism**."[275] In the hospital, unable to feed

---

[271] *Ibid., p. 266.*
[272] *Ibid., pp. 178-179.*
[273] *Ibid., p. 193, 227.*
[274] *Ibid., p. 157.*
[275] *Ibid., p. 269.*

her addiction, she was suffering through alcoholic withdrawal, itching so badly she'd scratch herself raw, unable to sleep and hungry, yet unable to eat. Nobody else, including all the doctors (except this same lifelong physician) had any clue as to the cause of these symptoms. This gives us yet another, sometimes life-saving, reason for being able to diagnose addiction. In withdrawal, she threw expletives and abuse at almost anyone who tried to help her, even at doctors and nurses. However, when a handsome young doctor and lifelong fan (who had nothing to do with her case) made his rounds, he stopped each day to see how Ms. Davis was doing. She always became a kind, considerate, primped up "wide-eyed, gutsy star."[276]

It's understandable why someone like B. D. Hyman could miss all these obvious clues to her mother's addiction. Like Hyman, I too, could "take it or leave it." This is one reason I never viewed the use of alcohol or other drugs as a problem. I received my education from those who said, "Don't use drugs," with the only result of such use being a horrendous headache (marijuana which, unlike some persons in high office, I inhaled) and a non-stop 2-hour talk with a friend (the effect of cocaine).[277] Both Hyman and I failed to forge the connection between alcohol and destructive behaviors, figuring that the people we saw were abusive with or without the substance. After all, if it doesn't make us crazed, why would it make others so?

As a 14-year-old, I failed to see the incompetence of grown-ups while they were under the influence. I figured I knew far less than would a 40-year-old. Booze and drugs were glorified during my adolescence in the late '60s and college years in the '70s. Why would I view it as a problem? The movie, *The Thin Man*, portraying a caring, considerate and competent private investigator named Nick Charles (played by William Powell), gave me a tremendous misconception of the affliction. Drinkers had such positive traits and abilities, including courage, humor and suave sophistication, ideals for the young addict and non-addict alike.

The only problem was, William Powell's character was pure fantasy, since a truly caring and considerate alcoholic (even if competent) is an oxymoron. Myrna Loy's portrayal of the beloved non-abused wife of the alcoholic was, too, an extraordinary illusion. My young mind knew no different; after all, to a boy, movies are real, aren't they? It shouldn't surprise us that the story's creator and writer, Dashiell Hammet, was an alcoholic (and alcoholic writer Lillian Hellman's significant other of thirty years).[278] Hammet combined an obvious latter-stage alcoholic, as evidenced by the

[276] *Ibid., p. 272.*
[277] *I do not plan on running for President or ever be a Justice on the Supreme Court.*
[278] *Robe, Ibid., pp. 299-302.*

extent of his drinking, with early-stage competence and with a non-alco-holic character in his concern for others. Perhaps Hammet chose to por-tray alcoholics as he would have liked to be seen by others, or as he may have thought he acted towards them. The more recent movie, *Arthur* car-ried on the tradition of portraying alcoholics as funny people and who like the rest of us, can care about and love another human being. While un-doubtedly true of Dr. Jekyll, this is totally inaccurate when referring to the practicing Mr. Hyde.

There are tragically few movies that accurately portray both the disease and the devastation it causes. This is unfortunate; movies could be the greatest educational tool of all. Most portraying addiction do a far better job showing the calamities that befall the afflicted than affected. Michael Keaton's character in *Clean and Sober*, for example, stole $50,000 from his partners and "borrowed" $40,000 from his parents, who had to mortgage their home, thereby enabling their son. This is something only an addict child could ask of parents. Here was a terrific opportunity to graphically illustrate the psychological and financial devastation wrought by such crimi-nal and unethical behavior, yet the movie failed to instill these points.

Viewers of the movie, *Leaving Las Vegas*, could have benefited greatly had it taken a few minutes to show what Nicholas Cage's character did to his employer to get fired and the misbehavior that cost him his family. Instead, it portrayed a month in the life of an addict at his bottom, ignoring the 20 or 30 years of failed relationships and financial devastation heaped on others during the long slide downhill. It was billed as a tragic love story, which it was, but not between he and the hooker. Such is the igno-rance of critics, who fail to point to the bottle as the object of affection.

Ray Milland portrayed a smoothed out drunk, writer Don Birnam, in the great 1945 classic, *Lost Weekend*. It was superb in its portrayal of the alcoholic-addict's ability to connive, con and lie. It depicted his childlike belligerence and nastiness when he didn't get his way. The movie painted his delusions, fantasies and supreme confidence when on the drug and his physical withdrawal and insanity when not. It recounted his early court-ship with girlfriend Helen St. James, played by Jane Wyman, during which he was able to control his drinking (just like Bette Davis). The representa-tion of desperation in getting his drink and the creativity of hiding places was excellent. The enabling by his brother was classic. He always had an excuse for Don's poor behaviors, covered up for him and gave him spend-ing money. When Don's girlfriend found a secreted bottle, he even pre-tended that it was he (Don's brother) who had a "problem" with drinking.

There was, however, a minimalist portrayal of the financial and psycho-logical devastation one would normally observe at this stage of addiction. Aside from a petty theft and occasional mooching, there was little damage to either his girlfriend or brother. Finally confronted by both in an early cinematic form of intervention, the viewer is led to believe he would easily become sober. We've seen how unlikely this would be for any addict, much less one in the latter-stage.

One movie that did succeed, brilliantly, in illustrating the psychological effects on close persons was *Shoot the Moon*, starring Albert Finney and Diane Keaton. The critics billed this 1982 drama as a movie about the breakup of a 15-year marriage. To my knowledge, it has never been referred to as an alcoholic movie and yet, it's one of the greatest ever. The reviewers failed to understand more profound meanings when they reported that Director Alan Parker arrives "at some telling revelations about what keeps people together and what drives them apart,"[279] unless they understood that "what" is frequently addiction, an unlikely insight. The movie superbly portrays the affect of alcoholism, ultimately causing the family's breakup. The "telling revelation" about what keeps people together may be civility, which does a gradual disappearing act from any family affected by an addict.

Shoot the Moon not only gives a feel for the impact of addiction, but also clearly shows the difference between addicts and those who use and abuse drugs. The Finney and Keaton characters both drink, the latter also smoking dope. Yet the difference between them is, while Finney's character is clearly an addict, Keaton's is not. The effect on the children, too, is exquisitely portrayed. The idea that addiction in either parent is prima facie evidence of child abuse was well supported. The question remains how bad is it?

A variation of such abuse was portrayed in the much-maligned Demi Moore flick, *Striptease*. Moore portrays a mother losing custody of her daughter to her legal pill-popping addict ex-husband who uses the child to help him steal wheel chairs. The addict, with the aid of his enabling father-attorney, pays off a judge to win the custody battle. Child abuse is evident with his daughter being an accessory to the father's crimes and watching her mother strip to raise needed funds for the custody battle. With Burt Reynolds playing a corrupt alcoholic Congressman, the movie chronicled the destruction by alcohol and other legal drugs. Some critics found the plot too incredible, yet I'm aware of a similar real-life case. Truth often outdoes fiction.

The best-known alcoholic movies would include, *When a Man Loves a Woman* and *Days of Wine and Roses*. The first stars Meg Ryan portraying a drunk with Andy Garcia as her supposedly enabling husband. He isn't as much an enabler as he is bewildered. One must watch very carefully to observe any adverse effect on their children. While the depiction of the

---

[279] *The editors of Consumer Guide and Jay A. Brown, "Rating the Movies," New York: Beekman House, 1985, p. 355.*

active alcoholism leaves much to be desired, the characterization of her recovery was far superior to any I've seen. Her distorted perceptions continued long after she stopped using. She moved from alcohol addiction to substitute compulsions, including heavy use of tobacco and coffee. She went from alcoholic non-relationships with her husband and children into a kinship with a fellow AAer that impaired her ability to re-start the most important relationships in her life. These are typical of early recovery. At one point she accuses Garcia's character of being a control freak. This leaves the viewer confused, unless he knows that a little controlling to an addict in Post-Acute Withdrawal seems like prison.

I was confused about this portrayal of early recovery until I connected it with writer Don Birnam in *Lost Weekend*. As his cells became adapted to the constant immersion in alcohol, so did Ryan's character. They both appeared sick, as one is in-between uses. The only difference was, she was in-between for months, abstinence slowly transforming into sobriety. Through these films I gained an elementary understanding of Gorski's Post-Acute Withdrawal or, as Milam and Ketcham call it, protracted withdrawal syndrome. The alcoholic may continue "to be depressed, shaky, and irritable many days, months, or even years after his last drink, and [is the reason] why so many alcoholics return to drinking after a period of sobriety."[280] They are really in-between drinks, accounting for the confusion and continued distorted perceptions and the non-addict's inability to distinguish active alcoholism from early sobriety.

Days of Wine and Roses, portrays the deterioration of two alcoholics, played by Jack Lemmon and Lee Remmick, along with their relationship. Only the very perceptive viewer will see the psychological abandonment to which every child of an alcoholic is victim. The psychological crippling that Jack Lemmon's character caused by destroying his father-in-law's greenhouse in a drunken rage was evident. The movie focused, as do most, on the effect of addiction relative to the addicts' own lives rather than those of others. It also confused cause with effect, as Remmick originally drank only to keep up with Lemmon before turning into a full-blown alcoholic herself. The end, however, was startlingly realistic. Lemmon's character got sober, while Remmick's sank deeper, with Lemmon realizing he could do nothing for her.

Another movie, *The Boost*, didn't limit itself to the effect on the addict. Starring James Woods as Lenny Brown and Sean Young as his wife, Linda, they slowly and inexorably fell into the abyss. The unique aspect is the portrayal of the psychological ruination of Lenny's employer to embezzlement, along with Lenny's rationalization for the theft. A tax shelter sales-

---

[280] *Milam & Ketcham, Ibid., p. 64.*

man in the mid-'80s, Lenny displays erratic behavior from the beginning, smoking and drinking wine. He blames others for his troubles and displays paranoia, cries the blues about his business and belittles himself. As he earns money he spends it like a big shot, even tipping out his last dollars to a parking attendant who had watched Lenny's car being repossessed. He invests funds he doesn't have, irrationally and over-excitedly takes unreasonable risks and jumps without looking into his "great ideas," which are all worked-over get-quick-rich schemes. Then he discovers cocaine.

The depiction of the differing effects the white snowy powder can have on various personalities is wonderful. His addict friend schemes and plays and the friend's addict girlfriend is "the world's biggest bitch."[281] Lenny gives up one drug only to move to the next, changing the "rules," while graphically showing that, to an addict, a drug is a drug. He repeatedly promises his wife to "knock off everything as soon as I put my plan into operation" and towards the end of the movie, beats her to a pulp when she merely steps on his drug. The movie's only weakness is, it doesn't show him gulping the wine or otherwise drinking to excess in the beginning, even though he is obviously (to the initiated) an alcoholic. One may conclude the other drugs merely hastened the personal and business disasters that alcohol would have taken many more years to cause. Recovering addicts have said as much: "Thank God for cocaine, so I could hit my bottom in 20 months rather than the 20 or more years it might have taken with alcohol alone."

The 1937 version of *A Star is Born* starred Fredric March as the failing drunk actor Norman Maine and Janet Gaynor as Esther Blodgett, an actress who becomes his wife. Already steeped in his addiction when the story begins, he enters the class of 15% of alcoholics who lose their jobs, as work begins interfering with drinking. As in most movies, the behavior and problems created by the 85% of alcoholics still working is not represented. Maine, an obvious latter-stage alcoholic perpetually drunk and now a has-been, promises to quit drinking (and to actually save money for a change) if Blodgett would marry him. His sobriety was shown as being without difficulty, withdrawal or resentment toward his suddenly successful wife, for whom he played secretary. In these respects, the story is deeply flawed.

When he finally begins drinking again, he does so in grand and con-

---

[281] *Lenny's values and Temperament (which will be explored in detail in the chapter, "Improving the Treatment of Drug Addiction") were magnificently displayed when he said, about his sales job, "I put a piece of my soul on the floor every time I do the song and dance." This makes him, probably, an "Idealist," while his friend and girlfriend are likely both "Artisans." Linda is most likely a "Guardian," loyal to the bitter end. She is not one whom we would expect to indulge in illegal drugs. However, as a matter of duty and obligation, Guardians would frequently follow the path of their Artisan spouses.*

spicuous fashion. When Blodgett wins the Academy Award for best actress, he climbs onto the stage uninvited and gives a vitriolic speech to the Academy for winning the "worst actor" award. She takes him home and, as she removes his shoes, putting him to bed in a classic early portrayal of enabling, she wonders, "If he could only start working again, maybe that would help him stop drinking." The movie portrays him sabotaging every chance he has at obtaining work. After a brief sobriety, he drinks yet again, resulting in a fight while gambling at the races, which lands him in jail. In some of the most profound enabling ever shown on the big screen, she pleads with the judge for leniency, telling him she'd be responsible for his behavior. Out of jail, Maine overhears Blodgett telling her director, it "may not be too late to go away with him and start over, somewhere," proposing they pull a "geographic." The director says, "It's your life you're giving up, Vicki," to which she responds, "So I can give Norman back his." Norman, overhearing this, guilt-stricken, feeling totally inadequate and self-esteem long since obliterated, commits suicide. It's perhaps the most heart rendering demonstration ever that we can't help the addict by assuming responsibility for him.

On a lighter note, a comedy that realistically portrays the symptoms of addiction and its consequences was *Stewart Saves His Family*, written and starring Al Franken of Saturday Night Live fame. Franken plays Stewart Smalley, in a wonderful parody of someone involved in numerous 12-step programs. Smalley is a classic unrecovered Al-Anoner,[282] having never learned to accept that he is powerless over events and people, always looking for a way to bail his family out of their alcohol and drug-related problems. The unusually good aspect of this film is the portrayal of his father, who is among the 85% of alcoholics remaining employed. The portrayal of the slow, punctuated and gradual slide into domestic insanity is outstanding. The depiction of the verbal abuse is excellent, along with the multilayered aspects of the affliction as a "family disease" in everyday life and varying situations.

This is perhaps the best movie made that mirrors growing up in alcoholic families, and is the lightest of the genre. Another member of Smalley's highly dysfunctional family is his chain-smoking, alcoholic-pothead brother who has his own bottom after being shot in a hunting "accident" by the father, who was drunk. Unable to connect the accident and alcohol, even the pain of almost killing his own son falls short of putting him on the path

---

[282] *He likely portrays an ENFJ as described by the Myers-Briggs Type Indicator, an externally structured "romantic Idealist" in Keirseyan terms. This specific Psychological Type is perhaps the most natural and prevalent enabler of all and one that pervades Al-Anon meetings far out of proportion to their numbers overall. This is discussed in the chapter entitled, "Improving the Treatment of Drug Addiction" and in the professional appendix on Type and Temperament.*

of sobriety. The family finally attempts an intervention, but fails. Other than the fact that most professionally led interventions today succeed in doing some good, this was a very realistic portrayal.

A number of alcoholic movies are so bleak, they are difficult to watch. These are not popular or terribly educational, portraying the latter-stage addict wreaking far greater havoc on themselves than on others. "Hopeless" hardly begins to describe the Albert Finney character, a tragic drunk, in *Under the Volcano*. This was the only 2-hour movie ever to take me 5 hours to watch, Finney's British character perhaps reminding me too much of my British father. The movie, *Sid and Nancy* portrays the sickeningly quick spiral of the hardcore drug addicts, punk-rocker Sid Vicious of the Sex Pistols and his girlfriend, Nancy Spungen. A comparison between the movies is illuminating, since the alcoholic in Albert Finney's character is far older than the drug-addicted Vicious, yet fairly equal in their degree of addiction. Real-life alcoholics usually live longer than hard-core drug addicts, as alcohol takes the addict on the slow road to self-destruction, spreading the pain of use more broadly and far longer.

A few movies have portrayed the incompetence of the latter-stage addict, who always believes he is the best at whatever he does, regardless of the truth. A sleeper of this genre was *Georgia*, starring Jennifer Jason Leigh as an addict singer and Mare Winningham as her extraordinarily gifted singing sister. Leigh couldn't sing, yet was still angered over the fact that the public flocked not to her, but to her sister. Leigh's character had her own core group of fans, however mostly in dark, dingy bars. This was noteworthy, due to the fact that addicts often support other addicts. Leigh was clearly envious of her sister's ability to attract large crowds, hating her for that and any other reason she could conjure, as the alcoholic must in order to try and increase her self-esteem through ego-inflation.

The story of AA's co-founder Bill Wilson in the TV movie, *My Name is Bill W.*, is an excellent biography of the stockbroker/investment analyst whose life turned into a living hell from drinking. Once again, James Woods starred as the title character, with James Garner turning out an outstanding performance as Dr. Bob. Failing to achieve sobriety in hospital after hospital, with the help of his wife, Bill W. finally realizes that he might stay sober by meeting and helping other drunks. The film shows that addicts truly need one another, because they understand each other's affliction better than non-addicts ever could. It also imparts the lesson that sobriety, once achieved, is the most important thing in the world for the addict, because everything else in their lives depends upon it. As noted addictions expert and doctor to numerous stars Jokichi Takamine, M.D., told Lucy Barry Robe, "Nothing comes before sobriety....if [the alcoholic] drinks,

---

[283] *Robe, Ibid., p. 451.*

everything else is academic."[283]

Of all movies, perhaps the greatest portrayal ever of both enabling behavior and the alcoholic egomaniac was in *Scent of a Woman*. It was yet another movie never billed as having alcoholism as its main focus. The anti-hero, Lt. Col. Frank Slade (magnificently played by Al Pacino in an Oscar-winning performance), is described by the critics as "abrasive, sarcastic, raging and bullying," but not alcoholic. Yet his alcoholic traits include drinking heavily from the outset (always "doubles"), gulping his drinks, yelling, belittling others (unless he wants something from the person), smoking and swearing liberally. He calls sex-talk 900#s (his daughter said, "He loves to talk dirty"), sexual innuendos pervade his speech and he pretends to like women above all else, yet speaks most highly of their genitals. He's a control freak ("touch me again, I'll kill you"). He even threatened a relative with his life for having called his weekend enabler by the name "Chuck" instead of Charlie (played by Chris O'Donnell), all the while doing the same thing himself, calling his in-laws by their wrong names. He was a war hero, and, in a case of classic alcoholic "invincible" behavior, started pulling the pins out during a grenade-juggling act. One blew up in his face, permanently blinding him.

Charlie, a college student, answered an advertisement by Slade's niece and her husband seeking a "sitter" for a Thanksgiving weekend trip, during which they would be leaving Slade at home. The enabling niece told Charlie to try and limit her uncle's drinks to four a day. Slade manipulated Charlie into taking the job, then lured him (using both charm and intimidation) onto a plane to New York for what was intended, by Pacino's character, to be a wild weekend ending in suicide. With classic alcoholic charm, he would be all sweetness and light when he wanted something, especially from the ladies. The contrast of this with the hatred of both self and others was a wonderful portrayal of the Jekyll and Hyde syndrome. He was pompous, grandiose, a superb dancer and overly concerned with how he looked. He could make people laugh and even talked a Ferrari salesman into letting Charlie take Slade for a ride. His alcoholic manipulation knew no bounds, as he then cajoled Charlie into letting him take the wheel (even though blind) for what was supposed to be a slow drive "just to get the feel of the car." After taking the car up to 70 mph on city streets, it's painfully obvious that Slade was unconcerned about the safety of Charlie or anyone else.

He was a magnificent liar, conning Charlie the whole weekend. The culmination of his alcoholic abilities occurred when he was able to manipulate Charlie's entire class and faculty. In his closing speech, he pompously presented the negation of consequences (by not being a snitch and informing on classmates for a vicious act of vandalism) as a path to principle, character and integrity. That one critic called this a "crowd-pleasing ending" speaks poorly about the state of crowd morals to the extent this reflects real life.

There are few other movies that portray addiction so accurately. However, the careful observer will note that in many movies, criminals are portrayed drinking and even gulping their drinks, but usually fail at connecting the dots between that and their behaviors. There is a desperate need for better representation of addiction and the behaviors it begets, something that cinema, perhaps, more effectively than any other medium, could best provide.

6

Scared Straight: Crises and Consequences

"Insight is almost always a rearrangement of fact."
                                                    Peter Knapp[284]

"Good character comes from good judgment. Good judgment comes from experience. Experience comes from bearing the consequences of poor judgment."
                    —A variation of Tony Robbins' observation.

Enabling as a property rights issue

The benefits and pleasures of using drugs are exaggerated from the viewpoint of the addict. The costs and pain are either not felt or, at the very least, minimized, which non-addicts find inexplicable without understanding the memory altering and brain-poisoning effect that drugs can have. The addict remembers everything he does in a favorable light. The pain of any negative action recalled in moments of clarity is numbed with further use, rendering him incapable of experiencing the full costs of his addiction. Such consequential costs of the addict's poor behaviors are dispersed, instead, to those with whom he comes in contact. Like radiated pain felt somewhere in the body other than at its source, these costs are often magnified and difficult to trace.

The damaging results of use are deflected to those who reap no benefit. The non-addict, due to his own unprotected and exposed sobriety, experiences the repercussions. Economists refer to such costs as "externalities."

[284] *Knapp, Ibid., p. 218.*

An example of these is the expense imposed by polluters when property rights go unenforced. When not required to compensate others for the costs of pollution, where is the incentive to minimize the polluting? The damage inflicted is usually well in excess of the value to the polluter. Likewise, the addict is not required to compensate others for the harm caused by his addiction. This results in the sharing of costs by imposing them elsewhere, allowing him to derive benefits greater than costs. He is, in essence, just like the polluter.

The benefits, such as the high, the rush and feeling of power (resulting from the biological boost in dopamine and other neurotransmitter activity) overwhelm any negative consequences he may experience. In the early stages especially, he often "just feels good," while succeeding in imposing practically all the costs of his addiction on others.

However, there is a difference. The polluter is a rational human being who, when subjected to marketplace discipline or facing legal sanction for violating others' property rights (the results of which would force him to bear the full costs of his own pollution), will usually change his behaviors. Forcing him to bear these costs is known (in professor of economics parlance) as "internalizing the externalities" or, in other words, making <u>him</u> pay. This requires the polluter to compensate those he adversely affects at a mutually agreed-upon price. If the total costs are greater than the benefits derived, this threat of business failure will force him to drastically reduce the pollution generated.

Unfortunately, the addict, who begins to experience these consequences only when the enabling ceases, may still ignore them for extended periods. The distorted perceptions created by the drug allow the addict to attach more value to benefits than costs, far exceeding those attributed by sober individuals. Hence, the addict must experience pain magnitudes greater (often catastrophic) than any non-addict before he attempts to put a stop to his "pollution."

Friends <u>should</u> tell on friends

The addict is not allowed to experience the natural costs or consequences of using when he is helped, or "enabled" by others. Without the feedback mechanism provided by disenabling, which would allow him to suffer, the addict does not have the opportunity to endure decimated finances, relationships and/or career. Not only is there no incentive to take corrective action, he cannot even see such action as being necessary. Even non-addicts with clear and undistorted perception must often go through these experiences, converting poor judgment into good. Enablers do not allow this to happen. Poor behavior is reinforced and persists, resulting in the drinking and using to continue unabated.

Dr. Semmelweis, a Hungarian physician, discovered the cure for childbed fever, from which 20% to 30% of all mothers and newborns perished during childbirth in early 19th century Europe. Identical symptoms were observed in a host of other operating-room deaths. The cure was very simple: he told doctors to wash their hands before operating or delivering. His fellow doctors refused to believe it could be that easy, or that their own hands were responsible for so many deaths. Despite the proof provided by statistics at his own clinic (where deaths were less than 1% of such procedures), other doctors did not emulate his practices until 30 years later when, finally, Louis Pasteur told doctors that Semmelweis had been right.

If lay people had known of Dr. Semmelweis' work, they might have, in a grass-roots sort of way, accelerated the intellectual process of accepting a new standard. As consumers, they could have insisted their doctors wash their hands before moving to the next patient. Today, we lay persons can speed up the process of accepting a new paradigm and recovery through the behavioral diagnosis of addiction and uncompromising cessation of enabling. We now know that everything designed to help the addict will only harm us both, so we must stop helping. We must learn that the identifying tags of addiction are often confused with other illnesses and mental disorders. We must insist that addiction be ruled out before treatment for any other sickness begins and that addiction must be treated in conjunction with other diseases.

Some suggest coercion as the best medicine for addicts. Psychiatrist Sally Satel wrote in a *Wall Street Journal* op-ed piece, "At the root of the problem are the misguided though well-meaning attitudes of many drug-treatment professionals. They believe in waiting until a drug user is 'motivated' to get help...telling addicts that treatment won't work until they 'want to do it for themselves.'"[285] Satel suggests force can work with addicts and we don't have to wait until addicts "want to do it." However, force *by itself* is not appropriate since addicts have an inalienable right to their own property, including their person. Nor is it helpful, since the addict will, in the end, always get his drug. In addition, Satel implies the use of illegal drugs is the problem. Yet, legal or not, drugs don't cause just anyone — or even most — to engage in behaviors that may be destructive to others Furthermore, it could be argued that the legal drug alcohol does far

---

[285] Dr. Sally Satel, *"For Addicts, Force Is the Best Medicine," The Wall Street Journal, January 6, 1998.*

more damage to the 10% of the population that will use it addictively.

While we do not have the right to force an adult addict who has not committed recognizable crimes into treatment, such treatment should be required once they are convicted. Keeping in mind that there could be an 80% probability of addiction if convicted of a crime, prisoners should be assumed to be addicts until proven otherwise. Since free choice works best in treating addiction, they too, can be offered a choice: treatment or lengthier imprisonment. Mandatory and regular drug tests should be required, with continuous drug-free results for a period of time both before release and as a condition of parole. The desire for freedom creates motivation. Dr. Satel points out that an addict is "someone whose behavior can be influenced by meaningful consequences."[286] It is suggested that the above are proper and moral consequences, which recovering addicts will appreciate the justice and fairness of.

We also have a right to choose with whom we live. A spouse or child diagnosed with addiction should be given a choice, too: sobriety, or separation from the family unit.

As Vernon Johnson points out, "It is crucial that the persons close to an alcoholic understand the nature of the problem. For they must take the initiative if the illness is to be arrested"[287] (emphasis added). They can assist the addict by allowing him to experience all consequences of his addiction. Many therapists, friends and employers wait for the addict to see the problem. Instead, by being pro-active (allowing consequences to be experienced through loss of jobs, spouses and children and incarceration, along with other sanctions for unethical or criminal behavior), the addict experiences the buildup of crises necessary to create a self-recognition of his own condition. As Johnson puts it, "The only way back to reality is through crisis." Crises, in turn, set the stage for successful intervention.

Peter C. Mancall, in his illuminating study of American Indians and alcohol,[288] relates what may be the world's first recorded case of successfully setting up a crisis and intervention. (Setting up a crisis is an offering of tough love, while intervention connects the dots between the drinking and consequences). A French traveler, Jean Bossu, hired an Indian hunter. One day, the hunter traded game he had just killed for brandy, and got very drunk. Bossu let the Indian know he would not put up with such behavior, and the Indian, atoning for his poor judgment, came back the next day weighted down with game for Bossu. Soon after, the Indian stole brandy from him and was fired. The hunter's wife begged for another

---

[286] *Ibid.*
[287] *Johnson, Ibid., p. 5.*
[288] *Peter C. Mancall, Ibid., pp. 1-4.*

chance. While Bossu appreciated the hunter's fine qualities, he wasn't one to take unnecessary risks (such as employing drunks). The wife persisted. After some negotiation Bossu, in cooperation with the hunter's wife, relations and friends, hatched a scheme.

The hunter became drunk again, but this time was set up to quickly run out of brandy. He was told by his wife and fellow conspirators to go to Bossu, who had more. Bossu said he would not give it for free and the hunter, having nothing else, offered his wife's services for a month. Bossu said that would not be in good taste, but that if he would sell his son as a slave, he would give a barrel of brandy in return. The hunter agreed and the pact was made in the presence of several witnesses.

When the hunter sobered up, his relatives told him of the horror that he had committed. He came crying to Bossu, wailing about being unworthy of living or of being a father. Bossu and the schemers explained to the hunter that his behaviors seemed bad only when he drank. This resulted in a sacred promise to never drink alcohol again in exchange for his son's release. Bossu later tested the hunter, sending others to offer alcohol, which the Indian refused (knowing that Bossu could track his drinking). The hunter had an obvious vulnerability to alcohol causing him to behave in ways that would later cause massive pain. Presumably, before a lot of brain damage had occurred, coercion from family combined with creative medicine effected a solution to this vulnerability. When forced to experience pain of consequences when sober, the result was prompt (and in this case instantaneous) reform.

Unfortunately, few if any who get stinking drunk their first, second or even hundredth time are given such a scare by a creative and anticipatory creation of crises. As many alcoholism experts have noted, the longer the use continues, the more difficult and tentative the recovery. Such pain can eventually reach levels that most of us would seek to avoid helping the addict to experience. Yet, if we fail to help the addict experience the consequences now, the pain required later always becomes greater.

An example of situations in which the pain can become too great for the rest of us to shoulder is having children removed from their addicted mothers (or fathers). However, given the fact that most of these parents have been addicted for years, it can take such horrifying consequences to effect the necessary pain. The idea should not be considered lightly, nor without a desire to see true healing and recovery. We must first acknowledge that an addict's preoccupation is with the substance, resulting in irresponsible behavior and a predisposition to blame problems on everyone but himself. This does not mix well with the numerous trials of growing up. We must accept the fact that good judgment, an essential ingredient to raising sound, healthy children, is non-existent when the custodial parent is an addict. These children usually experience abuse of the first order.

Many therapists in the chemical dependency field believe that female addicts are far more difficult to deal with than males, due to their greater propensity to be deceptive. This surprising behavior may have its roots in the fact that women "aren't supposed to have this problem." Many men in recovery say that it was a valid threat of divorce or loss of job that coerced them into sobriety. For women alcoholics, if this doesn't work, the fear or actual loss of children often does. Once an addict has achieved a period of blood-tested sobriety, she should be given the opportunity to reunite with her children, as long as there is a requirement that testing continues for at least a few years. We would, no doubt, end up with far fewer practicing female addicts, much safer children, far and away fewer juvenile delinquents and a huge reduction of the tragic consequences so prevalent in addiction, especially single-parent addict households.

However, anyone considering imposing this type of consequence should speak with recovering addicts (who have experienced this loss) and with chemical dependency counselors to determine the best approach. Due to the possibility of reverse blackmail or false accusations, kidnapping, or worse yet (but not unheard of) murder-suicide, it's questionable whether a warning should even be given. An intervention should be attempted when the children are removed, with the addict given a choice: proven sobriety and eventual return of custody or visitation rights, or restraining orders preventing any access to the children whatsoever. If this seems too harsh, keep reading.

This is particularly true of single-parent addict households. Many consider the rise of the one-parent household as the cause of many social ills. Mankind has evolved to become one of the few species on the planet where the parents are traditionally monogamous and often cohabitate for life, one of the reasons for our species' survival and success. Children mature best with a balance provided by non-addict parents of different styles, strengths and weaknesses. However, not all one-parent households are abysmal failures. Where the parent is not an addict, or is one but in good, solid recovery, juvenile problems are minimal in comparison with those in which the parent is a practicing addict. The anecdotal evidence is clear. Look at any child with serious problems or who has, himself, committed a serious crime. Very often we find an addict parent with even more severe problems. The major cause of failure in raising children is very likely addiction in one or both parents, regardless of whether there is one parent or two. On the other hand, an addict child is not a failure of a parent, although the perpetuation of active addiction by an enabling parent may be.

There is one instance where, understandably, a father stays in a marriage with an addict. Until the laws make it easier for the father to gain custody, he does not help his child by separating and, in fact, may cause him irreparable harm. If we can set the addict-wife up to be arrested for driving under the influence (as I once tried to do for Patricia), especially if her children are passengers, so much the better. Numerous recovering addicts say they drove drunk with their children, over and over again. However, unless either sobriety or paternal custody is virtually guaranteed, the father has little choice other than to stick it out for the sake of his children. Strategic planning, with the assistance of a recovering addict and/or knowledgeable attorney may be of great benefit in achieving the desired result.

Crises are precipitated in young addicts with great difficulty. The fact that we cannot help the addict by "helping" is true, regardless of age. Uncompromising disenabling when very young has saved many an addict's life. Unfortunately, as recovering alcoholic Conway Hunter, Jr., M.D., points out, "Some of the sickest people and the most enabling people are the parents of alcoholics. Their son, their daughter, can do no wrong, and they will love them to their graves. They will enable them to their graves' edge and then push them in."[289]

As with substance addiction, the surest cure for poor judgment of a serial nature, is to insure that consequences are experienced and that the pain of these are not spread to others.[290] With our new comprehensive understanding of addiction, we will now explore samplings of the systemic financial abuse by addicts of others and how, using our methods of recognition, such abuse might be prevented. Then, we will prescribe steps to extricate oneself from such abuse, if it has already begun.

---

[289] *Dennis Wholey, Ed., Ibid., p. 201.*
[290] *This is true among nation-states as well as individuals. A discussion of "institutionalized enabling" is found in the appendix.*

"It is the wit and policy of sin
to hate those we have abused."

Sir William Davenant (1606-1668)
English poet laureate

7

The Financial Abuse of Others

*"I eschew the...term '[drug] abuse' because I consider it both too broad
and too narrow. It is too broad because anyone can 'abuse' [drugs], and
it's too narrow because [addicts] do things that are far worse than the
excess consumption of [drugs]."*

—James Graham[291]

*"Truth is stranger than fiction, but it is because fiction is obliged to
stick to possibilities; truth isn't."*

—Mark Twain[292]

Parasite and host

We have seen that an addict's perceptions are distorted in grand fashion, worsening over time. The resulting impaired judgment eventually becomes evident in all areas of life, including work, play, the raising of children and financial affairs. Prior to this, by spreading the pain of consequences, addicts draw unsuspecting persons, regardless of relationship, into a descent often ending in moral, psychological and financial bankruptcy for all involved. Family member, friend, partner, employer, employee, landlord and tenant alike are unaware of the addict's tendency to destroy not only his own financial affairs, but also those of people with whom they come in contact, without regard to morality or ethics. In fact, the other person's financial affairs may be decimated by the behaviors of

---

[291] *Graham, Ibid., p. xvi. Graham used the term alcoholic in lieu of drugs and alcoholics in lieu of addicts in the original.*

[292] *Mark Twain, "Pudd'nhead Wilson's New Calendar," from "The Wit and Wisdom of Mark Twain," Philadelphia, PA: Running Press Miniature Edition, 1990.*

the crafty addict well before the latter's own finances are seriously impacted. Close persons, stunned by betrayal, may suffer emotional turmoil. Rendered immobile, they often continue to enable by doing nothing, resulting in a perpetuation of the abuse.

In interactions with addicts, mutuality, where both parties profit economically and/or psychologically, is not a factor. Instead, there is only parasite and "host" (or victim), user and used. While the host never chooses to be robbed of what he owns, parasite-like addicts use secrecy and deception as "hooks." This allows them to both physically and psychologically attach themselves to their hosts, taking needed sustenance while offering nothing in return. As Bionomicist Michael Rothschild puts it, parasites, "by latching onto their unwilling hosts...are able to extort profits that no mutually voluntary relationship would provide."[293] Healthy ecologies require interdependent mutualists such as the bee and the flower, where all parties to relationships and transactions benefit. Healthy economies, including family and business, need the same. One of the unheralded keys to avoiding the unhealthy relationship of parasite and host and stepping out of hook's way is to recognize addiction before becoming financially or otherwise entangled. The stories of abuse that follow will graphically show why such recognition is essential.

Family

Whether parent, child or spouse, the addict can wreak havoc on a family's financial structure. As is true for all abuse of others, it takes different forms and has varying degrees of severity depending on the relationship, the disease's action on the brain (which may be a function of the addict's Personality Type and Temperament) and the stage of addiction. Driven by an inflated ego, many early-stage addicts are financially successful. Like Lenny in the movie, *The Boost,* some spend all their earnings in substance-fueled displays of grandiosity. However, like Bette Davis, they can recover economically by sheer force of capacity to produce income (often resulting from their early achievements) until the disease destroys their ability to function, even at work.

Addicts in early-stage addiction are likely to wreak financial havoc on

---

[293] *Michael Rothschild, "Bionomics: Economics as Eco-System," Henry Holt and Company, Inc., 1990, p. 290. Originally published as, "Bionomics: The Inevitability of Capitalism." This book is an incredible work of art.*

others through conniving and trickery. In the latter-stage of their disease, the inability to stay employed may do even greater damage. Frequently, non-addicts let down their defenses when it appears the addict's behavior has improved, or when supposedly clean and sober. The trouble is that light at the end of the tunnel could be an oncoming freight train.

What follows are real stories accumulated from clients and friends. They could have been made up, but my imagination isn't good enough to invent tales as atrocious and repugnant as real life. These anecdotes are hard to find plausible and difficult to deal with psychologically, especially when the offender is a family member. By now, you probably accept that this perpetrator of contemptible behavior is not the person we know and love. Marty Mann, the first female member of AA, points out that while a few drinks might bring out what the non-addict really feels and thinks (due to the lowering of inhibitions), an addict's drinking produces a personality change that causes behavior very different from the real self.[294] If you still don't believe your addict will have absolutely no compunction against acting like those in the stories to follow, attendance at a few dozen more AA meetings and discussions with recovering substance addicts is suggested. Eventually, you will find that he is no different from the rest and will stop making the claim that your family member or friend, "Would never do that."

Children

Joe was a professed recovering addict. He cajoled his parents, aged 66 and 69, living on Social Security and a tiny pension, into lending him $50,000 to buy a business, a front-end alignment auto shop. They raised the funds by borrowing against their only asset, a fully paid-for home, expecting their son to make the $400 per month interest-only payments. He did so for the first three months and then lost the shop due to several errors in business judgment, including lacking a signed contract for the lease. To stave off foreclosure, the folks ponied up an additional $45,000 in payments over the subsequent 9 1/2 years.

The parents died within months of each other, leaving the $135,000 home encumbered by the $50,000 mortgage. After selling costs of $10,000, their

---

[294] *Mary Mann, "Marty Mann Answers Your Questions About Drinking and Alcoholism," New York: Holt, Rinehart and Winston, 1981, p. 13.*

net estate was $75,000. They bequeathed $1,000 to Joe with the balance to his brother. Joe was irate.

Although Joe may have had the best of intentions, it doesn't matter. As a practicing addict, his judgment was impaired. Nobody with his or her wits about them would pay $50,000 for a business without a signed lease. No sober child would force his parents to pay his debt, especially one they could ill-afford, while not making every effort to repay them.

Joe broke no laws. He couldn't be prosecuted for borrowing from his parents, making poor judgments or losing his parents' much-needed funds. Nor were any laws violated by complaining about the fact that his parents' deaths profited him so little. However, In the all-embracing sense of the term, the behavior was criminal even if the original intent was not.

Could the parents have known that he was neither clean nor sober? We seasoned observers no longer need to see someone drink or use to suspect a problem, having learned that we can determine probable insobriety by observing patterns of behavior. Ask any recovering alcoholic if he would ever request such a loan or take risks with parents' limited funds. He'll answer that he would, if he wasn't clean and sober or didn't intend to stay that way. Unfortunately, the parents were never given the tools with which to protect themselves from their own addicted son, nor help effect remission for their son's affliction, for which they would very likely have given their lives.

Tragically, this story is just one of many.

Jason's daughter, Roberta, asked for help in consolidating $26,000 in credit card debts. She'd been working as a supermarket clerk for 12 years, got behind on bills and "just never caught up." He reluctantly agreed and paid the bills in exchange for a promise to pay him back at a rate of $500 per month. If he'd known she had just lost her job, he might have used a fraction of the funds to help her with the dollar-a-meeting donation at Narcotics Anonymous, pocketing the difference.

Roberta's job had been steady for years. Jason had no idea that the vast majority of addicts hold jobs. She never even smelled of alcohol and kept little in her home. Yet, she was still experiencing severe "growing-up" pains at 29. He knew she smoked "some" marijuana, but so did lots of other young people in their late 20s. Even though earning a livable wage, Roberta was always "struggling to make ends meet," getting nowhere financially. She never admitted to making poor decisions regarding her massive debt load and the purchases that created it. She would say, "I needed the fridge; there was no other choice." She never considered buying a used one or having the old one repaired. Psychological health consists of realizing we always have choices and accepting the consequences. Believing we have none and repeatedly making poor decisions is a red flag of substance addiction. Jason had no way of knowing this, never having learned in school or anywhere else that if there is repeated poor judgment there are likely distorted perceptions, which usually result from substance addiction as opposed to, say, "growing pains."

Her mood swings ranged from hyper to subdued, to "crying the blues." These were later explained by methamphetamine and marijuana use. Roberta admitted that she almost always arrived at work a tad late, blaming her tardiness on traffic, problems with her pet or some other such excuse. Bailed out yet one more time, costing Mom and Dad $26,000, Roberta had no incentive to get clean and sober. They finally began to vaguely understand reality when Roberta had gone through the money, had paid off none of the debt for which the loan was intended and was practically homeless. Their comprehension of this was accelerated by the fact that they were being bled dry in retirement, so they finally refused to continue "helping." Having no funds and no job, she was forced to make a choice between the street and rehabilitation. Thanks to her parents' belated recognition that Roberta needed uncompromising tough love, she chose sobriety, a path she has stayed on for over five years. Her parents only wish it had occurred far sooner, more for their daughter's sake.

Some parents lose far more. For example, many take care to deed properties they solely own to themselves and adult children as joint tenants, thereby avoiding probate. The acquiring joint tenant owns half the equity for purposes the parents never intended, such as liens, seizure and bankruptcy. In one instance, a child incurred $100,000 in obligations due to non-filing of tax returns, which the government collected by filing a lien against the jointly owned property. The parents won the battle of probate only to lose half the equity in their $200,000 home to pay their son's income taxes.[295] Even if the son had become sober and responsible, it would have been too late: liens and eventual seizure cannot be avoided by transferring property back to the original owner. This may be viewed a fraud by not only the IRS, but also a bankruptcy court. These parents were out a lot more than probate ever would have cost.

Some stories are downright ludicrous. Randy Cassingham in his newspaper column, "This is True,"[296] reported a lawsuit in which Jane Prejean, 79, was sued by her son James, 49. "James says he promised to love his mother, but that was based on her promise to support him for the rest of his life. She said she cut off his financial support to force him to get help for his 'chronic alcoholism'." Fortunately for our justice system, the New York State Supreme Court threw the case out, ruling "a promise of love

---

[295] *It could have been worse. The government has the legal right to take the entire house when jointly owned. If, for example, there had been a $90,000 mortgage on the $200,000 home leaving only $110,000 equity, the parents would have lost everything except $10,000.*

[296] *Randy Cassingham, internet site "www.thisistrue.com"*

was not sufficient to establish the financial relationship as a contract."

Spouses

Spouses can cost even more, financially and/or emotionally. Lois had a few hundred thousand dollars in various liquid investments generating plenty of income. She married a disabled 50-year old, Bert, strictly out of love and not for his zero asset balance sheet. A year after they wed, Lois asked me the tax cost of drawing funds out of her IRA to help with her expenses. I suggested that instead, she use funds from her investments, to avoid creating additional tax from an unnecessary IRA withdrawal. She explained she didn't have that choice: Bert had absconded with all of the joint assets and disappeared.

After recovering from my initial shock, I got curious. I commented that I couldn't believe Bert would do such a thing. The only type of person who might would be an addict, although he certainly didn't "look like" one (even though by this time I knew not to judge a book by its cover). Lois told me, embarrassed, that Bert was a prescription drug addict. I suggested that his doctor was his pusher, to which she responded, "I was in denial. Everybody warned me about him." I said no, she wasn't in denial and even the doctor was conned. She was merely ignorant of what addiction is and the cold-blooded deeds of which an addict is capable. They don't teach this stuff in school.

It turned out Bert's "disability" was from an illness 10 years prior. I asked why, then, was he on permanent Social Security disability? Lois explained that he enjoyed milking the system for whatever he could. I commented that was itself, a sign of addiction and if he'd exploit the system, he might use an individual, even his own wife. His self-destruction, self-hatred and lack of self-esteem, resulting from doing little worthwhile for the last 10 years, led to his need to inflate his ego by destroying those who were dear to him. Doing what I could to help, I suggested that she limit both her income and tax by withdrawing IRA funds only as needed.

Once again, justice cannot be served. Converting joint funds to one's personal use is not a prosecutable offense. Bert remains among the 90% of addicts not incarcerated for engaging in what some would consider criminal behavior.

Another disastrous financial situation resulted, at least in part, due to my prior ignorance of the disease. Steve was a self-employed contractor, Liz, a salaried wage earner. Steve built their home, later borrowing $300,000 to pay off the original smaller loan and fund several construction projects on which he ultimately lost money. The home and lot cost only $200,000. The additional $100,000 was borrowed tax-free, something that can come back to haunt the borrower.

It did exactly that in the California real estate market collapse of the early 1990s and Steve and Liz's subsequent foreclosure. A foreclosure is generally treated as a sale for the amount of the unpaid loan, even though there are no proceeds with which to pay the tax. They were treated as having "sold" the home for $300,000 and had no money for the tax on the $100,000 gain. If they didn't repurchase a replacement home (costing at least $300,000 to avoid the full tax) within the then-required two years, they'd owe $35,000. Not having the funds to pay this, let alone purchase a new home, Steve told me that when things were looking up again, they just might be able to re-purchase. This wishful thinking came from the same perceptions that got them into the financial backwaters in the first place.

Shortly after filing a joint return, making them "jointly and severally" liable for the tax that would come due if they didn't buy a new residence, they filed for divorce. The two-year period expired and the return was amended, reporting the gain. The IRS goes after whoever has the funds or income to pay the tax. With Steve earning nothing, Liz was forced into an installment agreement. She was able to bankrupt the remaining balance after three years (which can be done if certain other requirements are met), but not before paying well over half the total amount owed.

Avoiding the payment of tax from a jointly filed return cannot be re-solved through the criminal justice system. Pursuant to a divorce decree, Liz could seek a judgment against Steve for his share. Unfortunately, ob-taining a judgment doesn't help if the defendant has no income or assets.

The tragedy was, had I prepared separate returns, each would have reported only his or her own half of the gain from the house "sale." Liz's liability would have been limited to her own share and bankruptcy might have been avoided. Having learned the signs and symptoms of substance addiction around the time of her bankruptcy, I now suspected, as you might, addiction. It took Liz several months to realize that my suspicions were true.

There were numerous clues to addiction prior to their marriage, 20 years earlier. For one, he was a convicted felon, having committed a crime for which his "buddies were really responsible;" he supposedly just took the rap. His father and brother were addicts, both having already died from the disease. He "experimented" heavily with illegal drugs, including "shooting up" during the '70s, developing hepatitis twice. While it may have been difficult to distinguish between the addict and non-addict in the psychedelic '70s, a non-addict would likely stop after the first hepatitis experience. Bear in mind, "substance addict" describes one who contin-ues to use despite negative consequences to himself and/or others. In ad-dition, there were intense mood swings. The morning after the frequent binges at their own parties, Liz "walked on eggshells" so as not to upset

Steve. Marrying him anyway, she had no idea her use of alcohol and drugs were somehow different from his. Are you getting an idea of the financial benefits in being able to recognize addiction?

The stories continue. Here's one of the tragic failures of our court system to mete out justice. After meeting at a bar, John and Mindy "had a good time" for a few months. Mindy was alluring, charming, witty, fun and quite the vixen. She told John it was medically impossible for her to get pregnant, leading him to use no precautions. He saw her do crank (methamphetamines) or coke occasionally, not really viewing such limited uses as a problem. Although naïve, since he didn't do or need it, he had no idea that others might. Within just a couple of months, John became concerned over Mindy's "volatile" behavior and her habit of twisting positive statements into negative ones. He was bothered by what seemed like paranoia and a lack of trust. When he called off the romance, she told him she was pregnant.

John decided to go half way to doing the right thing, moving in with Mindy, hoping to "make it work." Over the next five months, he became even more troubled by her behavior. He couldn't go anywhere without her "permission," hearing paranoid "where were you's" for things like taking a side trip to the store on the way home. She admitted to suffering a "nervous breakdown" a few years earlier and to having been under a psychiatrist's care. They went to another shrink together, where she tried to take control, attempting to answer questions meant for John. Diagnosed with bipolar disorder and endometriosis, she was given a variety of drugs (including Paxil and the opioid, Vicodin) as treatment. She told the doctor, "I can't get out of bed in the mornings," so he gave her more drugs. The psychiatrist, despite all these clues, had no idea that, in addition to those prescribed, she used illegal drugs. John saw that she didn't eat much and when she did, it wasn't health food. Experiencing more roller-coaster highs and lows, he left again, eight months into the pregnancy.

John came back only a month later to see the birth of his little miracle and hoping to reconcile for the sake of this helpless child. The obstetrician, knowing about some of Mindy's prescriptions, said the baby was not addicted and miraculously OK (especially since mother was a 45-year-old). John wanted to marry, but couldn't when he discovered that she had a $20,000 tax lien from years before. His employer, a defense company with whom he had security clearance, might fire him had he married into such an unpaid government obligation. Mindy's parents then paid the lien so the two could marry. This was probably not the first time Mindy was bailed out by her parents.

The first couple years of marriage, although not uniformly nightmarish, were punctuated by occasional benders on crank, sometimes for a full week. John finally put his foot down, mandating no more drugs, including alcohol, for either of them. While he had no trouble giving up his alcohol, Mindy's drugs went underground. He later realized there was a staggering degree of concealment of an amazing quantity and variety of substances. As the insanity became worse, he'd occasionally leave, but always came back to the yelling and screaming. They had another baby, resulting from what he thought might be a pinhole in a prophylactic. I suggested the baby might not be his. He responded, "I don't want to think about it."

During this time, Mindy earned $50,000 per year as a legal secretary. After the 1994 Northridge earthquake, she was "unable to deal with the stress of the increased traffic" due to the closure of major freeways. She quit, collecting state disability insurance for six months. She went back to work as an executive assistant for a tax preparer and, later, an investment advisor. She was fired by neither, despite the fact that her attendance and tardiness were "poor to pathetic," late every day and sometimes taking lunches from which she didn't return.

When the children were ages 2 and 5, having tried unsuccessfully to get her to marital counseling sessions, John finally decided to leave for good. Mindy immediately quit her job and yet again collected disability insurance under the pretense of stress-related illness. Filing for divorce and custody, she sought both alimony and child support. If she had been working, alimony would never have been awarded.

During the divorce they were audited by the IRS and assessed $5,000 for back taxes. John was paying it off in installments, when a new tax professional said there had been an error. The assessment should have been only $500. To get a refund of tax already paid and put a stop to future payments, an amended return would have to be filed, requiring both to sign. Mindy refused. Earning $55,000 per year, he proceeded to spend $40,000 over the next three years on the tax bill, lawyers, court costs, psychiatric reviews and paying debts that she ran up (reported on his credit report), which risked the loss of his security clearance.

During a full-day psychiatric review over custody issues, *she* accused *him* of alcohol and spousal abuse. With proof of her failing drug tests, John arranged for testimony from friends and babysitters attesting to illegal drug use. Whenever Mindy got notice of witnesses testifying against her, which is required 15 days before the scheduled court date, she'd cut off involvement with those people. One included a babysitter who saw her mixing crank with chocolate milk (thereby making it difficult to detect) which the sitter grabbed from the 5-year old as he put the cup to his mouth. Mindy was able to get continuances and, after four court postponements and 14 months, the judge ruled the testimony and failed drug tests were too old to be relevant to the case. By now, any witnesses to her behaviors were Mindy's new friends and unknown to John. The judge also determined, off the record, that drug "abuse" is no reason to take kids away from their mother, as long as "abuse" isn't occurring with the kids around her.

The daughter has learned that "people stay up all night, and that's OK."

Mindy rear-ended someone with her children in the car after being "cranked up" for several nights straight. The 8-year old is responsible for waking and feeding the 5-year old. Mindy parties all weekend, frequently doesn't take the kids to school on Mondays, invariably brings them late on Tuesdays and sometimes just sleeps all day. While she was passed out one afternoon, the kids found the car keys and were turning on the ignition when a neighbor fortunately intervened.

When I asked John about domestic violence on his part, he responded, "If you put a meek, mild dog in a corner and beat it with a stick, eventually you'll get a violent reaction." His dog is still relatively meek; she hit him with an umbrella once and he responded by pushing her. Many others might have done far worse, becoming among the possible 15% of domestic violence abusers who are not substance addicts.

Mindy is going to die because of parental, friend and institutional enabling. She will bring others down with her, as she destroys the lives of her ex-husband and children, the greatest victims of the enabling. Her parents probably enabled all her life. John enabled, having no idea what he was getting himself into or what he was doing. As an abuser of alcohol at times in his life, he had no way to distinguish between his own and addictive use. Massive institutionalized enabling has followed. She receives state disability. The court gave her custody of the children, whom she repeatedly endangers and abuses. John pays her alimony and child support, which would be more aptly called, in this instance, "drug subsidy and addict support."

There were a number of clues to Mindy's addiction prior to John getting entangled romantically, familially and financially. They met in a bar, she smoked and she "occasionally" did illegal drugs. He quickly learned her emotional state was volatile, she was paranoid and had been under a psychiatrist's care. Any one of these by itself might not have given even 50% odds, but combined, the clues pointed to almost certain addiction.

As obvious as this may seem to us, as developing drug addiction recognition experts, it's not apparent to most. Even for the initiated, the addict's control over use early on in romantic, friendship and financial relationships allows it to frequently resist detection. The charm, wit and feigning care of the addict is extremely seductive to the unsuspecting.

Addicts often lead seemingly normal lives. Recovering alcoholic Caroline Knapp writes of her own experience that despite cigarettes, coffee and an obsessive attitude toward *The New York Times* crossword, her public persona was healthy. She exercised, worked every day and even ate healthy foods. As she points out, "It sneaks up on you so subtly, so insidiously, that you honestly don't know you're falling into its grip until long after the fact."[297]   This is exactly why it is said the disease is "cunning, baffling and powerful." Lina and her husband Raymond found this out the hard way.

They were in their 30's when they married. There were few obvious signs of problems until four years later when they had a child. By the time the child was 5, Lina sought a divorce, citing Raymond's verbal abuse, physical threats, repeated instances of going out with his buddies and arriving home on weeknights at 3 or 4 a.m., along with a lack of connection to her. A jury of her peers unanimously decided in her favor, giving grounds for the separation.

Since this was a northeastern state that has at-fault divorce laws, a second trial ensued over financial and custody issues. After a year of discovery, she'd spent $100,000 in attorney fees (on a $30,000 per year salary), at which point she told her lawyer she couldn't pay any more. He continued pro bono, telling her he couldn't stand to see her lose everything to someone he politely called a "worthless good-for-nothing." She's since racked up the equivalent of another $100,000 in legal services. Raymond, despite the ability to do a lot of the legwork himself, has spent $90,000, on his $110,000 per year salary. There has been tremendous financial suffering in both families, having lent money to defray costs.

The subtlety and insidiousness of the affliction does not respect boundaries. While there were very few indicators we would have expected to appear by his early 30's, there were some that would have, for us, raised the caution flag. When dating and at her house for dinner, he'd gulp his first beer and drink another with his meal. Although not always drinking more than this, he always <u>had</u> to have his beer. If she ran out, regardless of the weather, he'd be visibly agitated and would drive, in what might be very dangerous icy conditions, to buy a 6-pack. There were also less obvious indications. He was late in filing his income tax returns for two years, but owed little (less than $1,000) when he filed. He'd been married once before, but so have many. These would have been enough to barely raise suspicions by themselves, but when combined could alert us to at least a possibility of addiction. There was very little else she could identify as alcoholic behavior during the first few years of their marriage.

After they had their child, his observable consumption increased to a 6-pack of beer in the evening. While this was not earth shattering, he also began having apparent blackouts, missing days at work and "freaking out" if anything went wrong. Little things were magnified to unreasonableness. If she was late five minutes once, she was "always late." If friends had to cancel plans, he inflated his ego with the control manifested by un-

---

[297] *Knapp, Ibid., p. 18.*

reasonable resentments, vowing never to see "those people" again. He was always right, she was always wrong. Yet when she sought a divorce, he's the one who insisted on a psychiatric evaluation. No wonder, since neither the psychiatrist nor a special referee (a highly regarded attorney acting as arbitrator, appointed by the court to offer a recommendation of custody) found evidence of alcoholism. Although failing to comment on what they diagnosed as narcissism and compulsive faultfinding, the psychiatrist did verbally object to Raymond's attempt to control the counseling. The therapists were, of course, looking for the stereotypical drunk with evidence of drinking immediately before the interviews. Early stage drunks are too smart for that. The slow yet inexorable decline of Raymond has caught Lina and her family like quicksand, as they sink deeper into a financial quagmire.

Parents

Addict-parents can cause well acknowledged psychological problems, as the adult children of alcoholics' (ACA) movement shows. What has not been pointed out is how alcoholic parents can cause their children financial problems, even after the addict dies.

Robin lived in a subsidized low-income housing project in the '40s and '50s because her father hid income from the IRS, held several social security numbers and spent all his money on booze and girlfriends. He'd take dares in bars that he could steal anything from anybody, including a classic theft of an entire lawn with 100 shrubs from a hospital, which he then installed at his home. At the age of 5, Robin was taught to lie to police about the cashmere sweaters and expensive perfume her father shoplifted for his girlfriends. This started Robin on a life-long cover-up, always being rewarded handsomely for lies and, later, under the tutelage of her alcoholic father, successfully shoplifting herself. To this day, she has to remind herself she cannot take things in stores without paying for them.

Shrinks labeled her dad as bipolar. The truth was, he was doing uppers, downers and alcohol. He once spent some time in the "best" recovery hospital and, upon release (this time leaving the lawn) made a quick visit to the nearest bar, left and immediately wrapped his car around a pole. People would occasionally get wind they'd been conned by this master of natural con artists[298] and, unable to get him, they'd go after Robin's mother, who attempted to make restitution. He "worked the system" to the max, always using all his sick days. After he was fired for stealing from his company at age 45, he managed to convince doctors and authorities he was permanently disabled and collected Social Security disability (SSI) under one of his false numbers, for the rest of his life.

Even when he was working, Robin's mother worked to put food on the table, since his paycheck never made it home. All through this, Robin thought her father was wonderful, showering her with gifts for cooperating in one or another of his countless escapades. Dad died, leaving her mother destitute and unable to receive Social Security, since he hadn't earned enough for eligibility under his own number (she refused to even attempt to collect under a false number). She always took pride in not divorcing him. Robin supports her mom to this day, as the financial effects of drug addiction reverberate through the generations.

Different people react in radically differing ways to addiction. Robin's father was likely a "player."[299] As a practicing alcoholic, he became even more of an antisocial incessant rule-breaker than his nature would normally dictate, delighting in his ability to out-maneuver the system in tactically brilliant ways.

Daniel's father, Jay, on the other hand, was a security-conscious, high-salaried, chief financial officer for a major steel company.[300] Jay was, so far, last in a long line of alcoholics. At age 10, during Prohibition, Jay was beaten if he didn't get the taste of the liquor in his parents' still just right. He went to work for the steel plant at age 20 and quickly rose in ranks. He was threatened with termination if he didn't get sober in his mid-40s and was institutionalized in a sanitarium for two years. He came home drunk the first day back on his job and never really stopped, until his liver almost gave out a couple of years before he died. His employer didn't do him, his family, his friends and themselves any favors by not firing him.

Jay was purportedly sick with TB, when he was really just a simple drunk. Because of feigned concern over his own condition, he forced Daniel to go to work at age 13. At age 16, when his dad entered the sanitarium, Daniel was told he had to quit school and work full-time to support the

---

[298] *According to Robin, who is familiar with Psychological Type, her father was likely an ESTP. Type-watchers will recognize the behaviors as magnified by substance addiction. This is described in the professional appendix on Type and Temperament and, especially, by Keirseyan Game Theory as explained in the chapter entitled, "Improving the Treatment of Drug Addiction."*

[299] *This is one of the Artisan "SPs" in Temperament. See the footnote above.*

[300] *He was probably a Guardian "SJ" in Temperament. See the footnote before the last one.*

family. This was all for appearances, since dad continued to receive compensation. This money was hidden and nobody knows to this day what happened to it. In the meantime, his family lived in near-poverty conditions relative to the real family income.

The affliction is so unpredictable in its affects as to defy logic. Daniel's dad received an MBA from a major university. Despite the high income, Daniel had to quit school to support the family. During his adolescence, friends were not allowed in the home, since dad came home too often drunk at mid-day to wreak his anger on the family and guests. He controlled everyone in this way, including his wife who, out of fear, never reported numerous beatings. Daniel thinks his mom died from a stress-related illness at age 60, a result of staying married to someone who likely needed to lose both his family and job if there was ever any hope of getting sober.[301] While leaving nothing to Daniel, Jay admitted on his deathbed that he "had been a terrible father." He would have been a better one, had someone only known to uncompromisingly disenable and subsequently intervene in his disease early on. This would have allowed him to fall fast and hard of his own alcoholic weight, others avoiding his trajectory so as not to be dragged down with him, allowing him to experience maximum pain from the consequences of his addiction.

We must learn to respond to the addicts in our lives, especially family, with the only kind of love addicts understand. "I love you very much. In fact, I love you so much I'm going to allow you the dignity of experiencing all the consequences of your addiction. At first, this will hurt me far more than it will hurt you, since you've anaesthetized the pain. Eventually, hopefully before dying, the pain of consequences will help you to realize that your use of drugs is the source of all your other problems. The only path to a better life is to stop distorting your perceptions and impairing your judgment by drinking and using."

Partners

The same is true for non-family, especially work associates, since so many become—or already are—our friends. I was long baffled by the fact that the formation of partnerships has often been followed by the destruc-

---

[301] *We will see later that this is exactly the kind of love a Guardian ("SJ") in Temperament would likely need offered, without which there is little hope for permanent sobriety and an abuse-free home life.*

tion of many of these friendships, the partnership failing amidst tremendous rancor. Often the explanation has been substance addiction of one or more partners.

The story at the beginning of this book was a particularly illuminating one. My client was the best friend and business partner of the addict. She had no idea, despite seeing her practically every day for years, that her friend couldn't be relied upon to repay debts or perform her role as a partner, due to her addiction. If it weren't for my intervention, the money might have continued to flow from "host" to "parasite" indefinitely, or until my client ran out of funds.

Oftentimes, the criminal-like behavior becomes more overt. There may even be embezzlement, though the law won't view it as such when a partner does the embezzling. Delbert and James provide a tragic example. Delbert partnered with James because they'd been good friends and James knew the electrical business inside and out. James had possession of the books, while Delbert occasionally wrote checks. Delbert's first clue to a problem was when a large check bounced six months after the formation of the partnership. He asked for the books and, after a brief delay, was (amazingly) provided with them. An analysis found $30,000 missing from the account. Confronted, James was "baffled" and unable to explain where the money went. Delbert pressed further, at which point James got hostile and threatened to quit. Seeking to minimize further damage and now realizing there was something seriously amiss, Delbert terminated the partnership. Needless to say, Delbert never got any part of the missing funds.[302]

There were numerous clues before the financial entanglement, but Delbert had no idea these meant his good friend was an addict. Even if he had, he would never have dreamt his friend would steal from him. As is true for many of these stories, the fact of addiction didn't even dawn on him until it was suggested. Every time, the lights go on and the eyes open wide, with an understanding and acceptance developing over the course of several minutes, days or months. It is quick when, at some subconscious level, there is already suspicion. However, with substances glorified in the media and movies, with negative inferences to the addict's effect placed on himself and strangers (and rarely on friends or family), these suspicions are usually buried. We just can't believe our friend or family member, including our extended family at work, would ever negatively impact us in such horrifying and destructive ways. Yet, that is what addiction is all about.

All Delbert knew about actual use was that James "occasionally" snorted cocaine and drank "a little". But there were plenty of behavioral clues.

---

[302] *I took a deduction for him under the business theft loss provisions of the Internal Revenue Code, thereby minimizing the total loss as best we could.*

James admitted to financial difficulties and was "always out of cash." Delbert once watched James give ice cream to his daughter for dinner and there never seemed to be much in the way of "real" food in his friend's home. There were marital difficulties, with James having a well-known disdain for his wife's wealthy parents. Delbert knew James sometimes hung out with questionable characters, at least one of whom subsequently went to prison.

Any one of these would have been enough to put us on alert. Combined, we can see clear signs of the impaired judgment best explained by the distorted perceptions borne of substance addiction. When the partnership began, Delbert found even more. There was increased emotional volatility, an inability to take criticism and financial problems causing James to ask Delbert for $1,000 to help with a house payment. Delbert also found out that car repossession was imminent. While Delbert was busy naïvely doing the work of the partnership, James sank deeper into his affliction unbeknownst to Delbert, who then shared the consequential financial pain.

This series of events strained relations between Delbert and his wife. She saw signs of his partner's lack of honesty that concerned her and, due to other normal codependent responses to his friend's chemical dependency, she sought marital counseling. Never did the therapist suggest possible addiction in their lives, even though she was informed all about the partner and partnership problems that were, for the most part, responsible for bringing them to this state. Rarely do we make the connection between substance addiction and the commission of criminal and unethical acts against known persons. Yet, if we find addiction, we will often witness such acts and, when we see such behavior, addiction is likely.

The law will not prosecute a partner for the improper conversion of partnership funds any more than a daughter for failing to repay a loan. Nor can you prosecute an addict for ruining your business. One example of this was the case of two women who shared ownership with a dozen others in a cooperative antique store, one in which funds for business overhead were pooled. Jackie met Sharon, a new member of the cooperative, at their monthly meeting held at a Denny's restaurant. While everyone else ordered soft drinks, Sharon ordered wine, flippantly asking, "Am I the only one here who drinks?" She didn't gulp and, in the course of an hour, had only one glass. Although not specifically on our Indicator, a possible clue to future problems lay in ordering wine at a luncheon in a cocky style, especially at Denny's.

A friendship developed due largely to Sharon phoning Jackie every day, often several times and occasionally at odd hours. To save money, Sharon suggested they split a booth at antique shows. Jackie began making business decisions taking both their needs into account, such as which shows to sell at, booth locations and costs. The partnership ended after three months of ruined business during what should have been peak season.

There were many clues, but Jackie, despite knowing what I went through with my addict, didn't attribute the bizarre behavior she saw to Sharon's substance of choice, wine. As it turned out, Sharon had gone "drinking" with her friends every Friday night for years. She stated numerous times, "I can drink a lot of wine, but not the hard stuff" and, "I have to go home and have a drink." Yet, she minimized her use with such comments as, "I only drink a little, once in a while," or "I only have one glass to untangle my nerves when I get home" and the classic, "I don't really <u>need</u> to drink."

Jackie heard Sharon blaming of others for problems, including a difficult financial predicament, chalking it up to character and the challenge of being a single mom. Sharon was always complaining about the tremendous adversity in her life, the source of this victim mentality not understood. She couldn't seem to hold a job prior to becoming self-employed, with the story of her last lay-off "not quite adding up."

When on the phone with Sharon, the daughter often screamed for attention. Jackie would have thought that Sharon was beating the 5-year old were it not for the fact that's difficult to do with one hand on the phone. Sharon often dropped the child off at her parents' or sister's, both of whom, in hindsight, enabled her behavior by caring for the child while Sharon went out drinking.

Right at the beginning of their weekend shows together, Sharon brought cheap jug wine and drank it all day long. But this was the weekend, so it was OK; after all, "only alcoholics drink on weekdays." There were occasional bizarre mood swings and behavior, culminating at a show where they rented a hotel room together. She was irate because there was a Hispanic convention and wouldn't go out to the pool because of "all those Mexicans out there." She sat in their room and drank wine. Later, when leaving for the show, she spilled the wine in her car. She went berserk over the loss of the wine, yet didn't seem to be the least upset over the stinking red mess on the seat and floor.

Jackie's goods were selling while Sharon's were not, so she disappeared for two hours, leaving Jackie to tend the wares. Returning drunk, she yelled and swore at customers, ruining business for both, along with those of the booths nearby. As I reminded Jackie of my experience with my addict, the irresponsible, bizarre behaviors and edginess suddenly began to make sense to her.

While this was a relatively inexpensive lesson in terms of direct damage done by the addict, Jackie's business never really recovered. The association with Sharon made it difficult to get good locations at events. Business acquaintances and friends shunned her for months. Just a few of the pre-existing signs would put us on notice that we may be dealing with an addict, however strenuous the denials. At one point, Jackie asked Sharon, "Is this the way you solve all your problems—you go home and drink?" Not receiving an answer until months later, Sharon responded in an incredible display of compartmentalized long-term memory: "You really hurt my feelings when you asked if I go home and drink to solve all my problems — I'm no alcoholic!" Jackie learned that she needed to be the judge of that, in order to protect herself.

Probably the best example of addiction affecting multiple parts of a person's life is the story of Kay and her personal monster, Jacob. This story is so good in demonstrating the various destructive aspects of addiction that we will do something very different here. After each part of the story, we will reveal the likely (and in some cases, confirmed) truth behind the odd behaviors; in essence, we will peer inside the brain of the addict. We'll call this "**TOMI**," or, "the Truth Of the Matter Is...." While separately, the behaviors are not necessarily suspicious, several in combination point to possible addiction. Some of these behaviors are not actual symptoms, but rather red flags warning us that we may find symptoms if we simply investigate further. There are many other straightforward badges of addiction in the story that need no comment.

Kay and Jacob met in San Diego, while she was wholesaling supplements to his newly opened retail vitamin store. Although very business-like, his office seemed in disarray with phones ringing unanswered, papers all over and much unopened mail. Having disdain for such disorganization, she declined his invitation to dinner. Learning of Kay's favorite restaurant through her partner, Jacob had a formal invitation sent, asking her to meet him for lunch. Thinking this pretty classy, she acquiesced.

During their meal, he told her that he had previously owned several businesses, but kept only a pharmacy in Florida. Regularly flying back and forth, he needed help with his new enterprise. He suggested that her outstanding ability to sell and communicate with others could blend profitably with his marketing ideas for nutritional supplements. He learned that she was well off financially and also knew many prosperous people through her parents, who owned a large sporting goods chain. Since sports enthusiasts are usually health-oriented, he suggested that selling vitamins through sporting goods stores might be a profitable new niche. Enamored of his charm, good looks and creative intelligence, she gave more information about her wealthy family than maybe she should have given. [TOMI: Addicts are brilliantly creative at finding just the information they need, using this to take you into their confidence and later turning it against you.]

A few days later she learned that a check he had written for the supplements bounced. Confronted, he shifted blame onto the bank, accusing them of, "once again, screwing up" his account. "It's important you trust me," he said, a statement that would be oft repeated, along with his hatred for dishonesty. "Come to the bank with me to straighten this out."

After Jacob screamed at the bank manager, Kay suggested that he relax. He quickly broke down, apologizing. "I'm so sorry, I'm so stressed. I need help in my business; maybe you know someone; all this travel is killing me." After a lengthy private meeting in the bank manager's office, the manager told Kay it was the bank's error. Jacob immediately wrote Kay a cashier's check. Feeling guilty, she figured that God must have put him into her life for a reason and maybe <u>she</u> was supposed to help him. [TOMI: The tools used by addicts include charm and intimidation, along with promises to "never do it again" and to offer more business/love/whatever. It is suspected Jacob used this combination in the privacy of the bank manager's office, getting the manager to accept blame just to quiet him down. Kay also later learned that the banker knew more about her personal finances and wealth of her family than he should have. Jacob may have promised the banker Kay's business if he would go along with his ruse.]

Pouring on the charm, Jacob asked her to dinner; "A token to beg your forgiveness, I was a total ass, could you ever find it in your heart to forgive?" Over dinner he told her, "I really want to know you," all the while admiring her jewelry. He told her about his family and stated in an obvious attempt to gain sympathy, "My mother is dying," as the tears welled up. Drinking a bottle of wine over a 4-hour dinner, he gradually became more aggressive between numerous lengthy visits to the bathroom. [TOMI: The restaurant bar, not visible from her vantage point, lay between their table and the men's room. It is strongly suspected that he grabbed a "quick one" on at least some of those visits.]

He insisted on going back to his place, "just for coffee." She drank a cup and felt extremely sleepy. After having another, she was out like a light. She slept clear through, waking up at dawn, horrified, but finding no evidence of sexual or other abuse. She apologized profusely for having fallen asleep, to which he responded jokingly, "You must have found me pretty boring." [TOMI: He spiked her coffee with a sedative and managed to inflate his ego by having her sleep over on a first date. More importantly, he placed her in a position to feel ashamed and guilty over the fact that she would even think he had taken advantage of her. He didn't violate her; therefore, he must be trustworthy. He was laying the groundwork for attaining tremendous control.]

Over the next few weeks, with Jacob in pursuit, they began dating. After a time, Kay became Jacob's partner in his store. She was appalled when she realized he carried a fraction of the inventory for which the store was designed; as every retailer knows, you must have inventory to maximize sales (although the cost can decimate cash flow). "I know retail," he'd tell her, "I don't need more inventory." [TOMI: Despite his talk of having had many business interests and current high income from his Florida pharmacy, he couldn't even afford to purchase much-needed inventory.]

In the beginning, while Jacob for the most part behaved, they were very happy together as Kay's initial reticence gave way to romance and love. Kay found Jacob's charm, attentiveness and intelligence extremely attractive. On her mother's birthday (to whom he had sent flowers on every possible occasion), he asked for Kay's hand in marriage. With Jacob's incredibly positive qualities so far overwhelming the negative, she decided to marry him.

Some things, however, were troublesome even before they wed. Once she caught him smoking dope, to which he admitted being an occasional user. When she told him she would not tolerate such drugs, he flushed it down the toilet in front of her. Apologizing profusely, in an affirmation of his love, he promised to never smoke it again. On the rare occasion she saw him drink alcohol, he always seemed to drink the last drop, tilting the glass way back. Explaining that he was "just thirsty," he reached over the table once to finish a friend's drink, even though a glass of untouched water was sitting by his side. She was unaware of how close she would have come to diagnosing addiction, if she only had the tools. [TOMI: She had shared with him exactly how she felt about excessive drinking and other drug use. He used this information to insure she never saw him drink heavily or again use other drugs. She hadn't the faintest idea that a person who uses drugs and doesn't want others to know about it has an amazing ability to creatively conceal the use. Kay, having no cravings for any drug, also had no understanding of what it feels like or the extent an addict might go to satisfy his urges.]

A few things at work also concerned her. Anything that went wrong at the store always seemed to be an employee's fault. Even though sales grew from $40,000 to $120,000 per month (aided by the vastly increased inventory she'd insisted on and for which he somehow found the money), they lost 3 of their 6 employees in just the first three months of working together. The staff told her that he shoved them and was verbally abusive. After confronting him with these accusations, she believed his denials since such behavior would have been out of character for someone so intelligent and charming. She became certain the employees had been wrong; perhaps, they even abused him. [TOMI: He repeatedly intimidated the employees in these ways. Kay had no idea that certain people, especially addicts, have an ability to charm the pants off some, all the while intimidating others.]

Still, these strange behaviors were not enough to change her mind about marrying him. They planned a fabulous wedding, for which Kay's mother shelled out $150,000. When making the guest list, Kay realized she hadn't even heard of most of the people he was inviting. The wedding being a black-tie formal event at a Beverly Hills hotel, she was mortified when he came dressed as Don Juan de Marco. The dozen "Jane Does" he'd invited were (in her opinion) "trashy types." He explained each one's relationship to him. "This one was my dance partner; the other over there worked for me," etc., but Kay gradually realized that they were mostly old girlfriends who came alone. [TOMI: Jacob had to be the center of attention to feel good about himself. Having so many fawning admirers and ex-lovers in the same room together (along with his latest conquest, who is gorgeous) inflated his ego.]

For a wedding gift, Jacob gave Kay the business (in more ways than one). He <u>seemed</u> to be planning a permanent bond, unconcerned about ever losing her. [TOMI: He turned the business over to Kay because he couldn't keep anything in his name for too long due to a variety of legal matters, along with immense private debts. A credit check would have shown his home had been foreclosed upon. A private investigator would have discovered he'd had a felony conviction for personally selling pharmaceuticals years ago. He lost his pharmaceutical license for several years and only avoided serving time by having the "right" connections.]

Kay learned, much later that Jacob had previously been married for eight years. He told Kay he hadn't informed her of this marriage because the ex-wife was violent and the "bitch from hell," not wishing to frighten her with stories of abuse for fear that Kay might be concerned over her own safety. [TOMI: His former spouse worked two jobs to support him and pay for college and pharmaceutical school during those years. He left her immediately after graduating. Not yet employed, the court determined he was unable to pay alimony. He offered nothing in the way of even a token reimbursement for her efforts.]

Kay also discovered that the store's contractor (who did the build-out) and architect (who designed the store) both attached liens for non-payment. Jacob, once again apologetic and embarrassed, claimed only now to realize how under-capitalized the business was from the start. He asked her to entice her mother to loan them $200,000. Reluctantly, wishing only to help her daughter in a marriage to which she was committed, her mother agreed. Once the liens were removed, other creditors began coming by to collect on loans as yet unknown to Kay. [TOMI: Had she known his financial history, she might have figured out he was plotting to gain access to her family's fortune.]

Among such debts was the down payment friends had lent him for his share of the pharmacy. He was so sorry for not telling her; he just hadn't wanted her to worry. Business was very good; he never thought there would be a problem paying his friends. She never deduced that these debts might be among the reasons Jacob insisted on opening all the mail at both home and office. [TOMI: This control of the mail prevented Kay from uncovering his true financial situation, amongst other things.]

Another reason for taking the mail was that he had two Corvettes stolen the year before they met. He was still dealing with the insurance claims. [TOMI: The theft of the Corvettes was an insurance fraud.] Yet another was that letters from Jacob to old girlfriends were occasionally returned. [TOMI: He was engaging in adultery.]

One of the most outlandish reasons for controlling the mail was to prevent Kay from finding out about a credit card scam that enabled him to embezzle from their store. The con went down like this: let's say on a particular day there had been $5,000 in cash sales and he wanted $3,000 of it for himself. (He was smart enough to not take it all, because having no cash sales would arouse suspicions.) He'd go through the last several months' credit card sales, looking for large ones to out-of-state customers. He'd then charge an amount equaling what he decided to embezzle that day in cash between the credit cards of 2 or 3 customers. When the charge was disputed, he didn't argue. Jacob told the accountant that the reversals were due to returned merchandise. Kay never found out because she didn't get the mail. [TOMI: This kind of criminal behavior, along with obtaining cash with which to spend freely on other women, were Jacob's ways of exerting control over Kay, thereby inflating his ego.]

There were many other signs that Kay just didn't understand. She observed mood swings and unreasonable, histrionic and narcissistic behaviors. She saw Jacob's initially restless sleep worsen to the point at which he'd be up and down almost constantly all night. Two years into the marriage, domestic violence began, not coincidentally soon after the money was borrowed from Kay's mother. [TOMI: The loan was so much a control tool that he could really begin showing his true nature.] He always begged for her forgiveness on hands and knees the next morning, promising to reform; he "didn't mean to shake or slap" and oh, he loved her so. When this worsened and became regular, Kay told Jacob she'd go to the police if he didn't stop. He threatened to kill her if she did. She never imagined that shouting at bankers and alleged abuse of employees could ever escalate into threats on her life. Nor did she ever dream that he'd attempt to take out multi-million dollar life insurance policies on both her and her mother when divorce became imminent. Kay learned this through a suspicious insurer who declined coverage, believing that Jacob had no insurable interest in her mother's life. [TOMI: The reason Kay never saw any of this coming is that addicts have an amazing capacity to abstain when needed, appearing moral and honest for extended periods of time when there is something they are after. However, the addict's ultimate goal is controlling others and maintaining access to the substance. They are capable of luring people into relationships where trust and love develops and whom they later betray in horrific ways. This form of control, once again, feeds their ego, especially when the person controlled is admired and respected by others.]

Still, Kay did not give up. She was raised in a family that valued the sanctity of marriage. As a result, Kay insisted that she and Jacob seek help from a marriage and family counselor. They did this every week for the last 3 years of their 5-year marriage. She could not have known that licensed therapists seldom suspect addiction and, of course, Kay had no idea that this was the case. Here was a man who hated the affliction so much that he raged about alcoholics whenever there was any mention of it on television or in conversation with friends. Nor would she have ever thought that a man who ranted about gays would later be seen at gay bars; or one who boiled over sexual immorality would masturbate while watching child pornography. It should not surprise that the words "contradiction" and "addiction" come from the same Latin root.

When the break-up finally occurred, Kay found boxes of books in the attic. Dropping one of the boxes, bags of pills fell out, scattering all over the floor. On her lawyer's advice, the police were summoned. One hundred pounds of morphine, opium suppositories, amphetamine-like substances, strychnine and other drugs were found hidden in numerous boxes underneath Jacob's books. Jacob, the pharmacist, had apparently been bringing his work home with him.

Kay has been awarded the business in exchange for their home, but without compensation for what she estimates to be $100,000 in embezzled funds in their final year together, not to mention the years prior. Because Jacob was no longer working and despite the fact that he could earn $150,000 a year as a pharmacist, the judge determined he has an earning capacity of only $1,000 per month and awarded him $5,000 per month alimony. Kay's tragic error was her failure to report abuse to the police, along with hiding the evidence of that abuse and other trouble in their fractious relationship, even from all her friends. The result has been zero recognition by the authorities that Jacob is dangerous; on top of which, she has been forced by the courts to continue enabling him with alimony.

Kay, like you and I, had never been taught that she needed to look for substance addiction in others. She was not told that anyone suspected of addiction must be forced to bear the consequences of their own misbehaviors. She never learned the signs and symptoms of addiction, or the extreme harm that could come if not identified. It was a taboo subject, never discussed in school or by friends and family. This may have been due to the stigma associated with the idea that people should simply learn to control their drinking and using. When she heard stories like her own once or twice, it was either "just a movie," or, "There must have been plenty of obvious clues given before someone could be so stupid as to get involved with one so clearly dangerous to others." Kay learned that these were clues to addiction only after she and I met. She now pays for her ignorance, both in support payments and constant fear, as Jacob stalks and makes repeated threats against her.

Employers, employees, co-workers and advisors

Employee addicts can be every bit as dangerous to one's financial health as partner addicts. An example was Anne, who employed a supposedly recovering addict, Harold. Upon getting involved romantically after working together for a year, they had a wonderful period of fun and amorous adventures. Then, things slowly deteriorated. Catching Harold in several lies, Anne sought counsel. With the support of her therapist, she cut off the personal relationship. While appreciating Harold's good work and considering maintaining the working relationship, she was concerned that the deceit might spill over into the business. The therapist told her, "While you apparently can't trust him personally, he'll be fine at work. Just put all agreements, instructions, etc., in writing."

Anne happened to mention her predicament to me. I suggested she could not trust him at all. He lied (not to mention having other signs and symptoms) and had, therefore, likely relapsed. While the recovering addict must live a life of rigorous honesty to stay sober, there are no boundaries for the practicing addict between work and play. Unfortunately, Anne trusted the therapist. She figures $20-40,000 in yearly income was forfeited for the rest of her career, due to the loss of long-standing clients from Harold's ineptitude, rudeness and other alcoholic behaviors. Especially tragic was the loss of a valued friend and client of over 15 years, who suffered serious repercussions from mistakes that Harold had made. The client told Anne, "Lucky for you I'm only leaving and not suing you." These were just a few of the consequences of Harold's undetected relapse.

Addicts are independent sorts. Being told what to do is ego deflating. They not only rather enjoy the ego inflating power that exists in controlling others, but also use it to fuel their addiction. In addition, they like the freedom of being able to come and go as they please, increasing opportunities for using. As a result, they are frequently self-employed and (until the latter stages of the disease) sometimes function very well. They can create thriving enterprises that employ many people. When the collapse occurs, victims often include these same employees, occasionally suffering consequences far worse than the mere loss of work.

There is little that is less fair in life than being assessed by the Internal Revenue Service for unpaid payroll taxes of a company that one doesn't even own. Forbes Magazine[303] reported the case of 28-year-old Nathan Unger, vice president of an advertising agency, where the sole owner was "high on cocaine and alcohol." Unger repeatedly warned the owner that payroll taxes were overdue. The owner told Unger to write checks to everyone except the IRS. In 1994, the U.S. district court ruled that Unger was liable for the $1 million in payroll taxes that didn't get paid, since Unger *could have* written the checks.

Anyone with check-signing power can be held liable for unpaid payroll taxes. Therefore, it's essential that anyone who has such powers be absolutely certain that all payroll taxes are paid before *any* other bills. First-

---

[303] *Forbes Magazine, "IRS nightmares," April 8, 1996, p. 64.*

hand evidence of payroll tax payments should be obtained if there is even one sign or symptom of substance addiction in a higher-up. The fact that taxes are owed gives two clues to a possible finding of addiction. The first one is obvious: the owner has financial problems. The other is less so: there's a willingness (implicit in such an attitude) to take on something almost infinitely more powerful than he (the IRS). Anyone not having a certain healthy concern over going head-on with the taxing arm of the U.S. government has an apparent feeling of invincibility. If evident, we will often find that substance addiction brought this about.

In another case, 25-year-old Ron became victim to his <u>own</u> company's non-payment of payroll taxes. His CPA, Greg, along with other advisers made Ron feel like a young boxer in the ring. He had been advised on doing a leveraged buy-out of a company in what seemed an obvious turn-around and a "no-brainer." Greg became the company comptroller. A small negative cash flow turned into a <u>potential</u> gusher when little jobs turned into big ones. While great for maximizing future income, these jobs required longer work-in-progress time and, therefore, longer billing and collection cycles. Temporarily, the small negative turned into an outpouring of cash by the company. Greg lured vendors into extending far more credit than they would have otherwise by "blue skying" (a term for "exaggerating," which is a euphemism for "lying about") the financial condition of the company, thus forestalling disaster.

In the midst of this cash-flow crunch, Greg, the CPA, talked his way into a company car for his non-working wife. He advised Ron to pay employees and vendors first, the loan for the purchase of the company second, car payments third and payroll taxes last, if at all. He also told Ron, who was swept up in the whirlwind of fast business growth and high finances that delayed payments of taxes should be considered a "high-interest loan from the government." Greg told him he'd better have the stomach for it, whispering, "I could tell you countless stories of multi-millionaires who've gone through this and despite these high-interest loans have gone on to become rich."

When their payroll service company refused to write checks without the cash in the account to pay withheld taxes, Greg said, "We'll just have to do it ourselves." Ron hired a full-time payroll clerk just to figure the $60,000 weekly payroll. The situation soon got so bad he had to run around with $40,000 cash (the net to his employees) in a briefcase between the bank and plant every payday for several weeks.

The brilliant sting was Greg's setting up the checking accounts with only Ron as signatory, making Ron uniquely liable for any unpaid payroll taxes. Greg, no doubt, knew he would be immune from the long arm of the IRS.

Ron went from owning an 80-employee printing company to belly-up in 18 months. It was three years before he had any inkling of the muck he was in with the IRS, when he was hit with a $400,000 lien for back payroll taxes, penalties and interest. (At $20,000 per week, tax liabilities grow fast and, unfortunately, the IRS can be slow to act on such improprieties.) Over the course of the next eight years the liability grew to $1.2 million, all the while leaving Ron unable to move forward in life which, by that time, included a wife and two young children.

Ron, unbeknownst to him, had been given numerous clues to the likelihood of addiction, while seemingly intelligent and successful men twice his age groomed him for "success." Greg was the accountant for a number of companies, including one for which Ron previously worked. Greg and its owner, Jack, frequently drank their lunch together. One of the false confidence builders was that Jack was the father of Ron's best friend. He was also a brilliant craftsman who had taught Ron the printing trade and who gave his blessing when the buyout opportunity came.

Greg carried a flask of brandy for a "tooth problem" which he never had fixed. He'd sit up late with Ron, drinking his dinner and smoking, while Ron ate. Ron had dinner at Greg's home on a number of occasions which, despite his talk and "large clientele," was a modest lower-middle class home in an L.A. suburb. Ron got wind of marital strife during these visits.

After the buy-out, Greg milked the company for his wife's car and, among other frauds, created bogus jobs and got lenders to give advances for non-existent work-in-progress. The prior owner wanted to stay and teach Ron the ropes; Greg insisted that he not only leave as soon as possible, but had Ron take his office just to "show everyone who is boss now." Ron, naïvely going along with this (as he had with everything else), later found that a potential ally had been lost. There would be no deferring payments on the $48,000 per month due for the purchase. The seller didn't benefit either, eventually losing almost his entire $3 million note due to the poor judgments and frauds of addicts causing the company's demise. This was a tragic example of a seller who would have been well served knowing his buyer and, in this case especially, the buyer's advisers.

With the company gradually falling further behind, Greg exhibited additional suspicious behaviors Ron now sees as clues, if only he'd been trained to look for them. There was excessive tardiness, high tolerance for alcohol, intense mood swings, nastiness and rage. He'd blame others for the company's troubles, often stating, "You know how avaricious those people are" (whoever "they" may be at the moment). He'd increasingly pontificate with $24 words, causing Ron to feel trapped. Unable to leave or even interrupt, this was a variation of "live and in person" telephonitis. The ego-based behavior of the addict takes many convoluted forms in its efforts to control and wield power.

Ron was lucky. Twelve years later the IRS accepted an offer in which the tax liabilities were settled for pennies on the dollar. Now 37, an MBA in hand, Ron is able to get on with his life.

With a 50% probability of at least one addict among every 10 or 12 employees (more or less depending upon the industry), even small firms are, at some point, likely to experience the destructive energy of an addict. These businesses are ill equipped to deal with such situations. The addict may be a co-worker, employee or the employer-owner himself. The actions of even one can create substantial hostility in the workplace. This is inevitable, due to the addict's need to inflate his ego through such chicanery as deceit, deviousness, underhandedness, conning and fraud. He may, for example, set up another employee for a fall, or engage in an elaborate embezzlement. Lawsuits from accidents and frivolous discrimination and harassment claims, as well as inventory, tool and supply theft and vandalism may also put the employer at risk for his very survival. Latter-stage addicts may exhibit far greater than average tardiness, absences, requests for time off, lower productivity, wasted materials and volatile mood swings. Regardless of what stage the addiction is in, we can expect the addict to engage in perverse and pathological behaviors at work.

These can so seriously affect others that harm often results from a lack of teamwork and the angry responses of coworkers who become, by our definition, codependents. According to director Billy Wilder, Marilyn Monroe's behavior during the production of *Some Like It Hot*, "demoralized the whole company," through habitual tardiness, absenteeism, and conflicts with co-workers. Difficulties in remembering her lines resulted in tremendous wasted time and resources among a crew of dozens, requiring retake after retake. Wilder let her continue, despite knowing "the thermos she carried to the set contained vodka and orange juice, and that she frequently refreshed herself from its contents."[304] Tony Curtis was so disgusted over Monroe's unprofessional behavior that his response to a reporter's question on what it was like kissing the "sex goddess" was that it felt "like kissing Hitler."[305] Just like Jean Harlow, Judy Garland, Jessica Savitch, Inger Stevens, Natalie Wood, Vivien Leigh, Carole Landis and Marion Davies, Monroe was enabled to an early demise by friends, lovers, co-workers and employers, to the detriment of their own serenity.

Remembering that the behavior of the codependent frequently mimics that of the addict, you get an idea of its potential for destruction in the workplace. Because co-workers, employers and employees are an "extended family" when looking for codependent responses to the addict, such persons can exhibit many of these same behaviors, to the point where it

---

[304] *Robe, Ibid., p. 2, citing Maurice Zolotow, "Billy Wilder in Hollywood."*
[305] *Robe, Ibid., p. 3.*

may be difficult to distinguish between addict and codependent. The old adage, "One bad apple spoils the barrel," applies.

It's difficult to know before hiring that an employee may have this affliction, especially the small employer who can't afford to do a battery of tests, getting to know someone over several interviews. You hire if he has the skills you need and you like him. The clues usually begin later, pointing out the importance of terminating the relationship (if appropriate) at the first sign, or at least putting in every possible precaution and playing hardball to protect oneself.

These behaviors in a codependent could have wiped out my friend, Shelly. A tax professional (an Enrolled Agent like myself), Shelly had an employee of several years, Carrie, whose husband turned out to be an addict who abused her. Carrie sometimes came to work battered, making the usual excuses for her bruises and injuries, such as falling, playing too hard with the kids, etc. In this way, she protected her husband, Scott, from consequences. He'd page her several times each day, "needing" to know where she was all the time, something Shelly attributed to a lack of self-confidence. Scott wouldn't let her work for Shelly when Shelly's husband was at the home-office alone with Carrie. Both of these behaviors were signs of paranoia, symptomatic of stimulant addiction. Coincidentally, Carrie happened to mention once that Scott "used to" use cocaine.

While Carrie was a fairly good employee, to the best of Shelly's knowledge, Scott never held a job for more than four months. He lost consciousness several times behind the wheel, but still managed to get a job driving a construction truck despite a Department of Motor Vehicle's threat to revoke his license. Carrie claimed that he lost jobs because "everyone's ganging up on him and nobody appreciates him," repeating Scott's words.

Shelly knew that the children were out of control. Carrie had a 10-year-old boy by her first husband, also an alcoholic and physical abuser. This child had taken a knife to Carrie and Scott's 4-year old daughter and raped her. We'd think Carrie would have learned, but as a daughter of an abusive alcoholic, she was used to insane behavior. It was, to her, just a normal part of life.

Although Carrie smoked, was somewhat over-emotional at times and the children lacked boundaries, she didn't have the volatile behavior one would expect of an addict. There were no work absences, maybe because this is where she preferred to be. Shelly could detect no work-related problems during her four-year tenure.

However, when one finally occurred, it was a doozy. After tax season, Carrie forced a blow-up with Shelly, gave her two weeks' notice, went home and never came back. In hindsight, it was obvious it had been pre-planned, since Carrie stole the client list and all the tax and accounting software. More potentially damaging to Shelly's livelihood was that Carrie also stole inside, crucial information on a client involved in a multi-million dollar lawsuit, for which Shelly believes Carrie may have been paid $50-80,000. Shelly would have been sued and might have lost everything, were it not for the fact that Carrie missed a few critical documents. Shelly was very lucky that the lawsuit was decided in the client's favor.

While Shelly would have been hard-pressed to fire Carrie for cause, just knowing that she was married to an addict would suggest taking greater precautions to protect oneself. She might not have given Carrie the key to the office or allowed her to work alone. She could have made software theft more difficult by using safes for back-ups and passwords for opening certain files, such as the one for which there was a pending lawsuit.

Shelly learned the hard way that addiction is not "just" a family disease. It is also a workplace and social disaster. It can truly be difficult to distinguish between the behaviors of the addict and close non-addict. The behaviors of the addict will always be manipulative, anti-social and dangerous to others. This is often true in the case of the codependent as well.

One final example of this workplace behavior is Nelly. Nelly believed her alcoholic employee, Brad, when he promised he'd pay back the money she loaned him for a new car (which he claimed he needed to increase his — and hence company — sales). Instead, he gambled the money away. There were plenty of clues to his alcoholism. In the '60s, he lost a million dollar home in Bel Air, along with his wife and apparently everything else that was dear to him. He had serious physical problems, including heart and circulatory disease. His current wife, explaining his gambling, told Nelly, "He relaxes at the race track." Nelly knew that Brad carried alcohol in a cane (they'll carry it any way they can) and Nelly "just wanted to help," figuring if Brad could just make that next big sale he'd get and stay sober. When the sales occurred, there was always another excuse, along with a request to continue to just make payments. Nelly invested $40,000 learning that alcoholics don't always pay their bills and that every "next big sale" only buys more booze and other drugs.

Other business connections

Debtors and investors

Investing with and extending credit or lending money to addicts can be very hazardous to one's financial health. At least half those to whom I've extended credit over the years and whose debts I eventually wrote off were likely addicts. Now if I suspect addiction, I either don't extend credit or I accept the possibility up front that I may never be paid. I frequently do the latter and extend the credit anyway (as long as it's not too large an amount), since even most substance addicts eventually pay their bills, especially if they are addicted to legal drugs. Since I require a deposit prior to initial meetings, addicts who are deep in their affliction generally don't become clients in the first place.

In fact, requiring an up-front deposit has made my life much easier. Tax season is an exhausting ordeal, during which I work 75-90 hours per week for about 10 to 12 weeks straight. I used to allow myself to become miserable several times each season because of truly dreadful people. When I began requiring the deposit and signed agreement detailing how I operate, what I expect of the client and what they can expect from me, the number of new clients demonstrating poor behaviors dropped to near-zero, where it has stayed for 10 years. Looking back, while I couldn't <u>positively</u> identify every "difficult person" as an addict, it's clear that many were. I never dealt with such people in a calm manner, especially if they were those I consider "intellectually dishonest," which addicts often are. I lacked the tools I now have for understanding addiction and achieving serenity regardless of others' actions. I occasionally have difficult situations involving existing clients who have simply slipped deeper into their disease, but now I just let them — and it — go.

One of the most rewarding events to occur in the course of dealing with recovering addicts is when they work the 9th Step of the 12-Step program, requiring that they pay amends to persons they harmed. When done right, this is far more than a simple, "I'm sorry." The addict who really wants to stay clean and sober must voluntarily assume full responsibility for his actions requiring contrition, detailed accounts of his poor behaviors and monetary recompense where appropriate.[306] It's an honest attempt to repair the damages he caused. It's a beautiful process to watch, as an addict becomes the person we somehow knew was held captive by addiction. Unfortunately, a truly honest 9th Step is rare. The addict needs first to recover and stay clean for a period of time. He must get rigorously honest in working the first 8 steps. Sometimes the 9th Step is difficult because he may be so deeply in debt that he could never pay back all his creditors. So, amends in monetary form are sometimes never made. On the other hand, once, I was paid $300 for a debt that I had written off years before. Knowing nothing about addiction and the 12-Step programs, I was puzzled and thought, "How odd." Now I realize that what the addict had done was rare and wonderful.

Let's look at this realistically. Sometimes, it's not just a few hundred

---

[306] *Terence T. Gorski, "Understanding the Twelve Steps: A Guide for Counselors, Therapists, and Recovering People," Herald House/Independence Press: Independence, MO, 1989, pp. 125-132 has a superb discussion of working this Step.*

dollars at stake and, chances are, you won't get your money back. If you're selling a business (like the printing company that Ron bought) and carry a note for 80 or 90% of the selling price, an entire retirement may be lost. Even if only selling a home and carrying paper, it may be helpful to know a little something about the buyer. In one case, an employee of a developer offered to buy a home for $150,000, sight unseen. The owner, Martha, was beginning to get a little desperate, since it was not a good market for sellers. The buyer was unable to qualify for a new loan, the existing loan of $140,000 was not assumable and the buyer had no money for a down payment. This called for creative financing. He offered to make a monthly payment on the full $150,000 purchase price to Martha, who would then make the required payment on the $140,000 loan to the lender (this method is called a "wrap around mortgage," or "all-inclusive trust deed"). With the assurance of the well-to-do developer that his employee had stable employment, Martha reluctantly agreed. This was to go on for no more than three years, at which point the buyer would be required to refinance. Martha was assured the loan would be paid off much sooner, since the buyers' home in another state was for sale and had "plenty" of equity.

The first set of sale instructions from the developer's own escrow company required Martha to carry the paper for 15 years, an error (which she had corrected on the spot) she now sees as a clue to problems that lay ahead. She has received payments late every single time, requiring her to pay the underlying mortgage without the benefit of the buyer's payments. The buyer is now so far behind in his payments that repossession is imminent. The house is, of course, in far worse condition than Martha left it. The convoluted scheme, the lies, the willingness of the buyers to purchase sight unseen and the current condition of the home are all suggestive of addiction. The neighbors reported that police have, on numerous occasions, responded to complaints of loud parties and drug use. A simple credit check, along with verification of the existence of the house for sale in the other state (which proved to be a fantasy) might have provided enough additional clues to have prevented the ordeal that endangered Martha's own credit rating.

Investing in a business run by addicts can also prove to be dangerous to one's financial health. In another story, Jean was luckier than was her best friend, Irma. Irma was a highly successful stock market analyst and astute money manager. Her husband, Tom, was an extraordinary chef. Jean was one of the many friends and family who invested in his new upscale restaurant in Manhattan Beach, California, to the tune of $50,000.

The restaurant was a transient glittering success, just like addicts often are before falling into the maelstrom. Tom began drinking at his own bar and, unbeknownst to Jean, was also using cocaine. Not doing as well as expected, he told his investors he "just needed more time" and asked for one "final" infusion of money. Some gave it to him while Jean, suspecting problems, did not. The restaurant failed, followed by his marriage. Tom disappeared.

Jean's boss had been offered a share of the initial investment and declined, explaining to Jean that he knew Tom smoked his own home grown marijuana. Jean figured, "no big deal, lots of people grow and smoke dope." What she now realizes is that there were signs not only of use or abuse, but also of addiction. Once, Jean heard Tom screaming at his wife outdoors in an uncontrolled rage over some triviality. A number of times, she watched him attack Irma with subtle put-downs and engage in other verbal abuse. There was a previously failed business along with a certain "edge" to his demeanor that, looking back, should have (by her own testimony) raised caution flags. She never dreamed her best friend, as bright as she was, could err in her choice of a marriage and business partner. Even if Jean had diagnosed the disease, she had no idea that chemical codependents can lose their (otherwise) sound judgment in the death spiral of familial addiction, no matter how smart they may otherwise be.

Tom and Irma divorced, but not before they'd filed tax returns on which Tom's income had been substantially understated. Several years of IRS audits (in which many of the records could not be presented due to their "mysterious disappearance") resulted in a tax debt of tens of thousands of dollars. With Tom's vanishing act and joint returns obligating both to pay any tax later assessed, the IRS found Irma fair game. Fortunately for Irma, when a return is old enough (due over 3 years ago) and the tax assessed over 240 days prior, income tax (barring fraud) can be discharged in bankruptcy. With this, along with other debts he had incurred in both their names, she was forced into Chapter 7. Seven years after her divorce, a smart, successful woman, previously worth $2 million, is now restarting her life.

Sometimes, a borrower who doesn't repay his debt can be treated as a swindler and the loss as a theft. Such was the case of an elderly retired couple who invested most of their non-IRA retirement funds in trust deeds. The trouble was, their funds (pooled with those of others by a general partner into multi-million dollar mortgages on commercial buildings) did not comprise the only mortgage for each building on which loans were made. On one $2 million building, there were no less than eight $1.2 million trust deeds, totaling over $10 million. The general partner was a respected church-going family man who belonged to all the "right" community organizations. This made the couple overlook the significance of the DUI and arrest for public drunkenness a few years earlier. The general partner conned his way into dozens of hearts, convincing them he was the world's greatest investor. Taking the couple's $100,000 to "invest" (along with hard-earned money from dozens of others), he used the funds to live the lifestyle of the rich and famous, while his victims struggled to make ends meet.[307]

Tenants from hell

As part of tax return preparation, I've prepared the profit and loss statements for thousands of rental properties over the past 20 years. I've seen mundane yet profitable rental situations turn gruesome, due to tenants almost as callous and venomous as Michael Keaton's characterization of the tenant from hell in the movie *Pacific Heights*. (Anyone seriously pondering the purchase of residential rentals should see this movie, if only to dispel the notion that such rentals are a "can't lose" investment.") Investing in such property should not be undertaken lightly, with its huge potential for emotional and financial trauma. It can be especially risky in pro-bad-tenant states such as California, where it can take many months to evict. I experienced a lightweight version of Keaton's monster early in my investing career. Looking back, there's little doubt my tenants were husband and wife addicts.

I have claimed deductions for dozens of these rental disasters. Rent has gone unpaid for as long as a year, with thousands of dollars of malicious damage to the contents and premises by abusive tenants. There have been toxic tenants engaging in such legal games as, "My buddy here who just moved in with me isn't listed on the eviction notice, so you have to start all over and evict <u>him</u>." Even worse (but by no means unusual) they have played, "Let's do a bankruptcy the day before I'm evicted so the bankruptcy court will protect me." This has often been followed by intentional destruction, including broken windows, holes in doors and walls, broken or stolen fixtures and desolated landscaping.[308]

---

[307] *The loss could potentially be treated as a theft loss (as opposed to a capital loss, subject to a limit of $3,000 per year net deduction). I did this for them, arguing there was no loan, citing several Tax Court cases with similar facts where the IRS lost (including the case of Norma R. Hold, N.D. Okla., 94-1 USTC).*

[308] *The good news is, income not received isn't taxed and the costs of repair are deductible. As much as 40% of these costs are often saved in taxes. However, due to quirks in the law (and depending on the landlord's other income), there may be no tax savings. For example, there isn't any when taxable income is already zero (and the usefulness of what's known as a "net operating loss" is vastly exaggerated in such cases). Nor is there any for losses (for the typical taxpayer, the non-real estate professional) in excess of $25,000 or when other income exceeds a certain threshold (generally, $150,000). On the other hand, a casualty loss is fully deductible due to its business nature (unlike personal casualties, which must exceed 10% of one's income before they begin to help). Such a loss is arguably deductible to the extent of costs for repairing damage due to vandalism, less any insurance reimbursement.*

I've seen widowed retirees, real estate brokers, young couples, developers, police officers and even recovering alcoholics clobbered with such losses (which may be insured; check with your agent). Al, a recovering alcoholic with 15 years' sobriety and his wife Mimi, a real estate broker, had owned rentals for years. You would think this was a couple who would protect themselves. Think again. Another broker (a good friend of Mimi's) recommended a couple as tenants. The hook the parasite-tenants used to lure their host was the pre-payment of four months' rent.

Al and Mimi made one fatal mistake: they didn't run a credit check. Assured by the referring friend that the tenant-husband was to soon receive a large inheritance from a well-known grandparent actor, they were unconcerned. There were no signs hanging around their necks that said, "I am a drug addict," nor were there ice-filled glasses of gin and tonic in hand. Nevertheless, the signs and symptoms of possible addiction did exist, even at their initial meeting. Only in their 20s, neither was working because they were "going to be rich." Living in expectation of wealth without work would be enough to raise eyebrows all by itself. In addition they both bore "a somewhat unkempt and sloppy appearance" and smoked.

From day one the house was a mess. Friends came and went in a seeming never-ending party atmosphere. When the 5th month's rent came due, there were the usual excuses, from "the check's in the mail," to "I thought I told my wife to mail it," "we'll get it right out," "there are unexpected legal difficulties in the probate" and "the check from the inheritance bounced." All the while, their apologies sounded truly sincere, and oh, how they loved the home and they thought Al and Mimi were the nicest people in the world and told their mutual friend how wonderful they were, ad nauseam. The niceties and seemingly sincere apologies resulted in deferring eviction for three months.

The tenants then used every trick in the book to stay put for another seven months, including declaring bankruptcy. When they were finally booted out, the gorgeously manicured grass yard was just a pile of dirt, there were holes in almost every door and wall in the house, burn marks in every carpet of every room, with broken porcelain and tile all over. There was an enormous mound of trash in the middle of the garage that was charred, obviously having been set on fire and, luckily, burning out. The dozens of bottles of alcohol in the middle of the heap were empty. The cost to repair the damage was $20,000.

Al was fooled because many recovering addicts don't realize what their brethren are capable of and they haven't been trained to look for addiction in others. Al's alcoholism didn't drive him to be <u>as</u> purposefully destructive of others. Just as non-addicts, as James Graham puts it, "develop their own sets of attitudes toward the drug based on their own experience with it,"[309] addicts develop their attitudes toward other addicts based on how destructive <u>they</u> were when using. The mindset they develop from their own experience contributes to their "inability to see alcoholism."[310] Al got sober after hitting what we call a "high bottom" when, years earlier, a girlfriend left, he was "overlooked" for a promotion and was hit with a wage garnishment for taxes due, all at the same time. This would explain why he became victim to a scam by addicts who went far deeper than did he.

Another case involved Cory's mother, Sarah, who rented rooms in her home to "down-and-out" types. One of her tenants, 37-year-old Nicole, told Sarah that she wasn't working, despite having a Ph.D. in music, due to the need to get over an extremely abusive relationship in which her life was threatened. Cory met her twice, noticing only that Nicole never made eye contact, her mood seemed a bit erratic and sentences in conversation were not always complete.

Unfortunately, Sarah died. Since there's no evidence Sarah ever received any rent, financial abuse may have already been occurring. We know for sure that such abuse (along with abuse of the usual emotional kind) began when Cory went to retrieve a few of his mother's personal items. Nicole prevented him from entering, even calling police and accusing Cory of intruding. As eviction proceedings began and dragged on, he received occasional horrifying reports from neighbors. Nicole harbored formerly homeless people who swam naked while neighbors' kids peered over backyard walls. Police responded numerous times to reports of lewd behavior and disruptive parties. Finding evidence only of alcohol but no illegal substances, they could do nothing other than issue citations. Cory also learned from neighbors that the constant parties included drinking and drugging to the point of everyone passing out. Such times were the only quiet ones the neighbors had during these months. The mayhem got so bad that police, unable to bust someone for possession of the drug alcohol, finally (literally and illegally) threw Nicole out.

Nicole had been reported selling Sarah's furnishings at swap meets. The few furnishings left were destroyed. None of his mother's personal effects were found. The carpets were ruined with urine and human feces. There were countless holes in walls and almost all the fixtures had been removed, including bathroom vanities, towel racks and anything else that could be sold. The cost of repairs was almost $10,000 and the estimated value of the stolen and ruined furnishings was $6,000. The mortgage payments during this period along with the cost of eviction amounted to over $12,000. The home's equity wasn't much more than the $28,000 in costs, but Cory was

[309] *Graham, Ibid., p. 34.*
[310] *Graham, Ibid., p. 34.*

just glad to get her out and get the home sold, with all its recent bad history.

Cory later found that Nicole knew full well how to abuse the system, having been evicted a number of times. Over two years later, she called Cory's employer (the local telephone company), accusing him of wire-tapping her phone and treating her horribly as a tenant.

There wasn't much else Cory could do in the addict-tenant enabling state of California. Instead of personal treasures, his mother left a legacy of heartache from making a decision to be kind to a woman whose stories of abuse were, in hindsight, the perfectly believable lies of an addict.

8

Financial Disenabling

Uncompromising disenabling

We know that pain provides the inducement required for the addict to get clean and sober, yet the level necessary can be greater than the non-addict observer can bear. Addicts shrug off pain, which to non-addicts (without benefit of chemical distortions) is staggering.

Yet for sobriety to be possible, the observer must unilaterally and uncompromisingly disenable. He must cut the bonds, the umbilical cord, which drains the observer and feeds the addict's disease. He must always be open to the possibility that a person's seemingly inexplicable destructive behavior really is quite understandable, a result of the action of chemicals operating very differently in the brain of an addict. He must persevere and never forget, especially when dealing with younger addicts or family, that what may seem to be harsh, mean-spirited and uncaring responses are, in the cold light of reality, the only helpful ones. Therefore, this degree of disenabling is far from being harsh; it is as pure a love as can be offered. The fact it is so painful to watch makes it all the more so.

We can sometimes observe the effect on a young person at first gulp. Over half of all recovering alcoholics remember the first drink they ever took. While this is remarkable to non-addicts (who would never recall this event), it is a clue to the extraordinary importance of the occasion to the addict. Many report that, for the first time in their lives, they felt powerful and their "world changed." This can result in the witnessing of an altered personality and sudden appearance of confidence indigenous only to those afflicted. We may see the "little God" behavior even after just a drink or two. If he drinks so much that a normal person would be hammered and yet he appears to be barely tipsy, he has the tolerance that many addicts say they had from the start. If he gets so drunk he vomits, has a hangover and yet steals more alcohol at the first opportunity, one may be reasonably certain that they are observing an alcoholic in the earliest stage. No normal person suffers such apparent pain only to quickly do it all over again. If the pain is observably great, the pleasures of using must be monumental. Yet, in many instances we will not see the subsequent drinking and using because, as many tell us, they somehow knew to conceal their use of alcohol even before their first drink. For this reason, it is essential that we carefully scrutinize behaviors to tentatively diagnose addiction.

Sometimes addiction takes hold more gradually and insidiously. Alcoholism expert E.M. Jellinek found five different kinds of alcoholism, each occurring at its own rate and degree of severity.[311] These varying degrees are the reason we may find addiction in a person who qualifies under one set of indicators in the Substance Addiction Recognition Indicator (often exhibiting only a few obvious signs and symptoms of addiction), with another registering under an entirely different set. We are not in control of the speed with which a slower form of addiction sets in, nor can we predict which child will not process alcohol normally and how poor the processing will be. Nor can we know, with current medical technology, who has acceptable levels of the various neurotransmitters and who does not. Therefore, to avoid enabling the most helpless and important person in our lives, our own child, we must not give large gifts a budding young addict may squander at his first opportunity, or in any other way fuel his possible addiction.

Money as an enabler

Money inevitably results in such enabling. Alcoholism expert Stanley E. Gitlow, M.D., states, "If you have two alcoholics who seem about equal, the one with lots of money has a lesser chance of recovering than the one without money."[312] As Lucy Barry Robe put it, "money insulates rich alcoholics from alcohol related problems that cannot be so easily avoided by the less affluent...."[313] In addition, money that can buy better medicine for the treatment of other diseases generally doesn't seem to buy better medical technology for treating addiction. The dollar-a-meeting AA program seems to provide as good a chance for recovery for many as a thousand-dollar-a-day program. Notable exceptions include the latter-stage alcoholic, polydrug users or others deep in the affliction, all of whom may need medical care to get through life threatening withdrawal or overdose. There may also be exceptions for the wealthy. Many well-known celebrities have died of their disease, or a related cause. Unfortunately, they are often unable to run out of money. Yes, an expensive recovery treatment center could at least assist them in doing this, but someone like a John Belushi needed to lose far more than the expensive program could ever cost. Those who would hire wealthy stars or otherwise assist them may

---

[311] *E.M. Jellinek, "The Disease Concept of Alcoholism," Hillhouse Press: Piscataway, NJ, 1960.*

[312] *Cited in Robe, Ibid., p. 149.*

[313] *Robe, Ibid., p. 85.*

wish to reconsider their role as employer, friend or adviser "helping" them to better handle their finances. Contrary to the usual goal in financial planning, they often <u>need</u> to lose it all.

Young people get money of an enabling quantity from three primary sources: their own work, inheritances and large gifts. Judy Garland was enabled by money from working while very young. Barbara Woolworth Hutton inherited $28 million at age 12. She was enabled while still a teen, with access to $300,000 of the earnings per year. Married seven times, she lived a life of extravagance fueled by her addiction. Others are enabled in less obvious ways. More than one couple lets their 20-something-year-old addict child live with them, knowing (even while disapproving) that he does drugs every day. Understandably, they don't want him living on the street. Yet for some, that is the path to sobriety.

Many parents give large amounts of money to children as gifts, with the goal of shifting taxation on the earnings to a lower tax bracket, assisting in funding a future college education and reducing the size of the parents' taxable estate. Yet, we have seen that addiction is genetic. If a child inherits and then triggers a genetic predisposition, these benefits may not only never be realized, but also cost the child his life. Trusts can help prevent this. While costing more in legal and accounting fees, these can have control features regulating payments and even prevent known addicts from gaining access to funds.

Roughly one out of 10 of us is destined to become a practicing substance addict. Parental and other environmental influences have proven irrelevant in determining the likelihood of addiction to alcohol. Environment is instrumental in predicting propensity to abuse, but remember, abuse is not addiction. Further studies may show that such influences are irrelevant in determining the likelihood of addiction to other psychoactive drugs. Only unavailability (or possibly education) prior to the potential addict first using can keep an incipient addiction from activating. Attempting to restrict access to drugs doesn't seem to work, since addicts always find a way to get their drug or a suitable substitute.

There <u>appears</u> to be more addiction in families where there is child abuse. Many experts attribute the addiction to this early mistreatment. This does not explain addiction among those who not only have not been abused, but who also may have had excellent upbringings. Nor does it explain why, so often, child abuse fails to result in addiction. The reason for addiction being so common among those abused as children is that the parent is probably an addict. While child abuse does not beget addiction, a parent's addiction genetically increases its likelihood in their child, as Dr. Goodwin's studies suggest. While we can never be certain it will or will not occur, one should be <u>extra</u> cautious in doling out family funds or engaging in other potentially enabling behavior, if substance addiction runs in the family.

Once money is placed into the account of a child under the Uniform

Transfer to Minors Act, the money is the child's. The parent cannot legally take it back. When it becomes available, usually at age 18, 21 or 25 (depending on the terms of the gift and the state of residency) the money is theirs to do with what they will. If the child is an addict, the money might not be used for the college education for which it was intended. If it is, it will still add fuel to the fire of addiction (remember Martha Morrison's story). The parents will have become unwitting participants in the enabling of their child's addiction, regardless of social status.

There's little benefit in having earnings from gifts of invested funds taxed at a child's lower rate, since earnings in excess of a low level are taxed as if they belong to the parents until the child reaches 14. Since alcohol and other drugs are readily available at school even at that age, the particularly perceptive parent may, by this time, have a fairly good idea of a child's predisposition to addiction. In the meantime, there are numerous tax-advantaged alternatives to saving for a child's education in which the parent maintains control over the funds.

For example, many investments, including growth stocks, municipal bonds and real estate may earn little or no taxable income. These can be kept for the child in the parents' names at little or no additional cost in taxes. The investments can later be gifted to the child, when we may know whether or not a child has inherited addiction, often in tax-advantaged ways. For example, parents can do this with appreciated stock or other assets, which can then be sold by the child with the profit taxed at his lower rate. Up to $10,000 a year (indexed for inflation beginning in the year 2001) per parent can be given to each child without adverse gift or estate tax consequences. The grandparents and others, including non-relatives can also gift like amounts. In addition to this, tuition can be paid directly for the child without limitation.

The new Roth IRAs and Educational IRAs are extremely useful tools for funding children's college education. Those with income from working (whose total incomes are under certain thresholds) can stash $2,000 per person per year into Roth IRAs. With these, two parents can have $72,000 invested principal alone in 18 years, which can be withdrawn at any time without tax or penalty (the earnings must remain in the IRA until age 59 1/2). The new Educational IRAs are limited to only $500 per student per year. The beauty of both, however, is that the contributor to the account has total control over the disbursal of funds.[314]

You can see, there are many alternatives to saving money without enabling the child.

[314] *If an Educational IRA isn't used for the child for whom it was intended, the creator of the IRA can substitute other children in the same family as long as the person is under age 30. In the worst case, the donor eventually withdraws the accumulated funds and pays the tax plus 10% penalty on the earnings. This may be the lesser evil if the alternative is providing fuel for a young person's addiction.*

Just say <u>no</u> to addicts

Diagnosing one's child as an addict is, with any other life-threatening disease, the most difficult prognosis for a parent to make, accept and appropriately act upon. At best, understanding addiction makes it only a little easier for parents to do what must be done: uncompromisingly disenable and intervene. Even if a <u>young</u> addict refuses help, he must be offered pure and uncompromising tough love. "I love you and I cannot help you by helping. Every time I do so, I'm only putting you one step closer to your grave. Someday, when you are clean and sober, you will realize how much I love you and that this is truly the most difficult thing I've ever done. When you are ready, I'll drive you to AA meetings and be fully supportive of the primary goal of getting and staying clean. Until then, I must ask you to step out of my life and home [or to have zero benefits of living as a family if under the age at which the child can be forced to leave].[315] When you're ready, I'll be there for you." Parents of young addicts report that only when such extreme measures were taken, was there any progress made on the road to sobriety.

Recognizing that one's partner in a committed romantic relationship is an alcoholic-addict is perhaps the second most difficult such finding to ever acknowledge and respond to properly. A person in love with an addict can more easily step out of the situation while unmarried, physically if not psychologically. However, if married, enabling may continue involuntarily because of the constraints of one's religion or the results of divorce. Yet, it is imperative that any codependency to an unrecovered addict be ended as early as possible in order to minimize the duration of alimony and hence enabling. As bad as it is to have been deceived into enabling prior to and during marriage, it's even worse to be required to continue the enabling after a marriage has failed due to addiction.

The spouse has likely griped numerous times, "You drink too much." He should instead be pointing out that there is possibly addiction, informing the addict that she simply can't ever drink or use again. He should explain the effects of the addiction on close persons. It is likely that the spouse (along with others) have also "accused" the addict of ruining ev-

---

[315] *The precise formula for the treatment of the child-addict is beyond the scope of my expertise and of this book. Woodward, Ibid., and Poulson, Ibid., are highly recommended to assist the parent, along with a local chemically certified therapist who understands that addiction is the primary affliction and that nothing else can be done for the child until in a program of sobriety. Woodward suggests absolutely no hiding of the affliction from others, something that should be suggested for adults as well. She argues persuasively that there should be zero privacy allowed for such a child, with not even a finger raised to help him.*

eryone else's life. However, this is not the same as explaining the destructive, genetic and deteriorating nature of the disease in a formal intervention, with the addict being offered a choice of divorce, separation or sobriety.

Professional interventions should always be attempted. If they fail, maintaining a relationship with a person diagnosed as an addict will only help him to his grave. The disease only gets worse, perceptions become more distorted, judgments more impaired and brain damage more severe. By remaining, we also perpetuate abuse. Given the totality of the effect on the addict's life and its psychological manifestations, at the very least children become victims of neglect and verbal abuse; at worst, their lives are endangered.

I can personally relate to this. My mother has asked if she should have left my father. Without the knowledge contained in this book, I certainly can't blame her for not having done so. A very bright man, Dad spoke three languages fluently. When sober, he truly cared for his family, staying up all night with my one-year old ill sister and gently caring for me after an operation when I was just a toddler. I grew up with Dad for 20 years and Mom stayed with him for almost 40. Mother, in classic enabling fashion, learned to protect Dad from the consequences of his actions, believing she was doing what was best for the family and not wanting his drinking to pull us all down. If she had left him, we would have been children from a broken home, of which there are all too many. Instead we lived in an alcoholic home with some of the usual manifestations of craziness and psychological dysfunction, although probably not as bad as most.

On the other hand, Dad was a type who <u>might</u> have experienced a high bottom and who, if the brain damage wasn't too severe, may have gotten sober with the temporary loss of family and job. This would possibly have caused his pain to quickly become greater than the pleasures of use (the necessary precondition for sobriety). It's really too bad, for he really could be a great guy and terrific father when he was sober. As a burgeoning young alcoholic, he was more of a Nick Charles character right out of *The Thin Man* story. He was very amusing, very competent early on at both work and even (at times) child rearing. Shortly after they met, he patiently taught Mother to drive. He taught me to read at age four. Instead of bottoming out, he was financially and psychologically enabled, never allowed to fully experience the consequences of his addiction. His affliction cost him his life at age 60.

He was not as destructive a drunk as are many. He never even received a traffic ticket, let alone getting into an accident. He was pulled over only once for driving under the influence and allowed to drive home (undoubtedly due to his British accent and smooth alcoholic charm). While he never embezzled funds from an employer, he told me once he received money inappropriately for having directed business to one of his employer's suppliers.[316] He didn't engage in the violence that many addicts commit. I would suggest it is possible that if my mother had temporarily separated, we might have instead grown up with a sober father, whose life expectancy would have been greatly increased, by far the better alternative.

We can greatly improve the odds of sobriety through intervention. Whether or not an addict immediately seeks rehabilitation, he will often go through many attempts prior to achieving long-term sobriety. As long as the addict is using or slipping, there is physical, psychological and financial risk to the family that lives with him. Separation, with visitation rights for children and "dating" (if eventual reconciliation is the ultimate goal) is appropriate and generally essential, in treating an addict. Protection from his unpredictable actions, or from the actions of one in very early recovery (who is really nothing more than in-between drinks) is of primary importance. Many addicts turn out to be relatively benign, but we don't know which. If we think we know, just think back to the murder of Phil Hartman by his wife, Brynn. We are safer thinking "unpredictable" and accepting that we cannot predict how destructive an addict's behavior may become.

The view that separation is essential seems contrary to that held by many members of Al-Anon and the therapeutic community. Many codependents continue to live with the addict long after they are aware of the addict's condition. Many believe the addict's behavior is something we should just ignore and that we must simply learn to mind our own business. But why should we subject ourselves to any kind of abuse or even the risk of such mistreatment, or worse?

My mother's concern was that divorce could have resulted in financial disaster and a feeling that my sister and I would have hated her for having "driven" our father away. While this is a real concern when dealing with young children, a greater one is the psychological abuse the children invariably experience and the potential for physical abuse. Proper counseling for the children could help circumvent any hatred for the adult taking a position of tough love, while eventual sobriety may render it irrelevant.

Many alcoholics commit far greater abuse of their children. Many physically violate or drink and use with them. Some become their "buddies," as inappropriate as it is in the area of raising children. The fact of substance addiction in a parent means there is abuse occurring; it's only a question of kind and degree. At the very least, a parent-addict abandons his children

---

[316] *Knowing his likely innate psychological style, I wonder if this set him on a path to greater self-destruction, unable to live with himself for shirking his duty and responsibility to his employer. The effect of these violations of one's personal values will be discussed in depth in the chapter, "Improving the Treatment of Drug Addiction." His Psychological Type was "ISTJ," a Guardian ("SJ") in Temperament, whose core needs include being dutiful and responsible toward others.*

and spouse for a relationship far more personal, significant and secret than he is capable of carrying on with another human being. The relationship with their substance is an all-encompassing one. In the long run, its manifestations in terms of abusive behavior toward others far outweigh in importance any love they may show for family.

If there is <u>any</u> physical abuse, separation and restraining orders are imperative. If one stays, it should be only with a commitment to sobriety and with the knowledge that we cannot predict the behaviors during early sobriety or in relapse. We should be prepared to witness bizarre and even criminal behaviors during these times, which are common to recovery.

Protecting yourself financially

Separating the finances is an essential first step in helping an addict spouse to experience the full consequences of his own addiction without further sharing pain. One way to do this is to file separate tax returns. Under old law, either spouse could be held fully responsible for the entire tax, regardless of who earned the income. The liability could extend to an original, amended or audited return and might, therefore, emerge years after an original filing. This is supposed to have been changed by 1998 tax law revisions, but it is early yet to see how fairly the law will be applied.

One concern is that the addict may have income about which the spouse, tax preparer and/or government are not being told. If the addict holds a regular job, there is less risk of this, although even those who hold regular jobs may have unreported self-employment income from drug deals, money laundering, bribery, special favors performed with related cash payoffs or even legitimate side work. If the "innocent" spouse "should have" known about such illicit activities or unreported income, liability for tax, interest and penalties may be impossible to avoid even under the new law. It can be difficult proving the negative to such an allegation and can become very aggravating, not to mention costly. We already subject ourselves to enormous risks by the very act of unknowingly dealing with addicts at any level. Additional risks, such as filing joint returns, are often best avoided.

The trouble with separate tax returns (SRs) is that a plethora of deductions and credits become far more limited than would be expected by simply splitting incomes.[317] Nevertheless, where there may be unreported income, overstated deductions or a complex business in which the records may or may not exist, SRs may be recommended. Even if no tax is currently owed, this may be appropriate due to the possibility of subsequent assessment of additional tax. SRs are essential if tax is owed that cannot be currently paid. Even in community property states (in which income and deductions must be divided equally until the couple makes a decision to permanently separate), these may be beneficial. In such cases, the non-addict spouse can be assessed tax on no more than half the income. If the addict spouse doesn't disclose the income to be reported by the due date of the tax return, the Internal Revenue Service may allow the other spouse to report only his own on a separate return, helpful if the non-addict is the lower income spouse.[318] While one can amend (re-file) from separate to joint returns within the statute (usually three years), one can never re-file separately after a joint return is filed.

It is also important to gain access to all financial records. The addict may get careless or seek revenge by making such records disappear. All tax and financial records should be removed or copied. This includes bank and credit card statements, receipts supporting deductions claimed on all prior and current tax returns and calculations of income along with supporting documentation. All insurance policies (check that all premiums are up-to-date), deeds, paid bills, marriage and professional licenses, passports and birth certificates should also be removed or copied. Your attorney's office may provide safe haven for these documents.

Everything possible should be done to prevent his possibly bankrupt finances from further impacting yours. All joint credit cards should be cancelled and any new credit, applied for separately. All joint bank and

---

[317] *Examples include the elimination (or partial elimination) of the $25,000 loss allowed for rental real estate and the IRA deduction for those in employer and self-employed pension-type plans. Also, 85% of Social Security is taxed regardless of income, instead of being phased in at $32,000 of "modified" adjusted gross income. The only fair way to change the law is to allow married couples to file their returns as if they are legally single, or as heads of household if with children. This option would in one fell swoop eliminate all the "marriage penalties" built into the structure of the tax code as well as responsibility for another's tax. (These penalties are usually created because the various credits, phase-out levels, deductions and maximum income thresholds for couples are not doubled over those for individuals. They include the level of income subject to various tax rates, standard deductions, earned-income credits, capital loss and rental loss allowances, social security taxability threshold, child and child care credits, deductible and Roth IRAs and the new educational credits.) However, the federal government would lose, by some estimates, over $100 billion in tax revenue a year by allowing such a choice (which is the true cost of the marriage penalties to married couples when both have income). Since this would so drastically cut into government revenue and additionally burden the IRS (with perhaps 30 million additional tax returns to process and audit each year), the marriage penalties, despite the talk, are unlikely to be repealed in their entirety anytime soon. Therefore, an option of filing legally single even though married is not likely.*

[318] *Internal Revenue Code section 66(b) states, "The Secretary may disallow the benefits of any community property law to any taxpayer with respect to any income if such taxpayer acted as if solely entitled to such income and failed to notify the taxpayer's spouse before the due date (including extensions) for filing the return for the taxable year in which the income was derived of the nature and amount of such income."*

investment accounts should be separated according to an attorney's instructions. Real property should be divided (if possible) by transferring joint property to each spouse in equal amounts, "equalized" with other assets. For example, if two rentals are owned, one with $100,000 equity and the other with $75,000, they can be split if the one receiving the lower equity gets cash or other assets for the difference. If there is just one property or properties with disproportionate values that cannot be "equalized" with other assets, they should be transferred to each as equal tenants-in-common. Unfortunately, tax considerations should be taken into account (as in any divorce). Properties have different tax attributes and cost bases for purposes of reporting taxable gains on later sales. Professional advice is a must.

Joint tenancy property automatically succeeds to the survivor upon death. If you predecease the practicing addict, your ultimate heirs will be unlikely to receive their proper bequest since joint assets may be spent, lost or wasted by the survivor. On the other hand, the assets of property owned separately or as tenants-in-common are disbursed according to one's will or trust. These likely name your addict-spouse as heir, so it is essential to immediately change the terms of these instruments to insure your assets pass to non-addicts in the event of death. If the addict achieves long-term sobriety, you can always re-combine the assets and change your will or amend your trust.

A trust can be designed with the addict in mind. A survivor's trust can limit support to the practicing addict, while it can provide whatever level of support you wish for the addict in advanced recovery. This may be important for the disabled or retired addict who has long-term sobriety.

Beneficiary designations should be changed on life insurance policies, annuities (including Tax Sheltered Annuities), IRAs, 401-Ks, Keogh and other retirement and pension-type plans whether employed or self-employed. Whomever you named as beneficiaries receives these funds upon your death. You likely named your addict-spouse. Unfortunately, designations for certain retirement plans cannot be changed to a non-spouse without his consent. For this reason, in some cases divorce proceedings should be started even if you hope to avoid having to go through with it. You can always change your mind later, while avoiding additional contributions and growth of assets in plans proliferating for the benefit of an addict.

All cars, motorcycles, boats and airplanes should be transferred to one spouse or the other. Separate motor-vehicle insurance should be purchased. The additional cost of separate policies is minimal compared with the potential cost of a serious accident (something for which the practicing addict is at far greater risk). Obtain plenty of liability insurance on items that cannot be divided, for assets that the addict refuses to cooperate in separating, or in instances of continued cohabitation. The cost of protecting your own interests may be as little as purchasing additional liability coverage for both you and the addict (check with your insurance agent and attorney for specifics). Although hesitating to suggest pre-emptive strikes, collectible art, coins, stamps, antiques, jewelry or other valuable personal property you may feel is yours should be taken or placed with a neutral third party. You can always return it if appropriate or by agreement pursuant to a marital dissolution. You are likely more trustworthy and reliable in keeping (not losing or selling) and returning such property than is he. Besides, if you don't take it, he might.

We cannot believe anything the addict says. We can't rely on the addict to do anything he says he will. He will promise anything, yet deliver only what he remembers and feels like. For your own sake and in the hope he will suffer the consequences, separate the financial assets as much and as soon as possible. Obtain the services of a lawyer if your financial arrangements are at all complex, preferably one enlightened about addiction (but be careful of practicing addict lawyers!). Being pro-active in separating the assets is much safer than trusting and waiting, only to find the assets have all but disappeared.

Do not help him financially in any way. Even in early sobriety there should be no aid given, since there may be difficulty in determining whether he's really clean and sober. In addition, financial enabling may give him the funds needed to begin using again. When tempted to help, remember that the addict who goes without stands a greater chance of recovery than one with money and credit.

Do not tell anyone else what you are doing before you do it. Assume the children, neighbors, family, co-workers and friends will tell the addict everything you say and do. As is suggested in court and IRS audits, do not volunteer anything. If you are an extrovert, introvert yourself. If you need to talk, attend support groups such as Al-Anon and/or call your attorney. Those in support groups are more likely to provide psychological support to your tough-love decisions than those outside. Support groups are less expensive and there is usually another member you can call at any time, day or night. They can help you understand the consequences of communicating threats or planned actions, utterances of which you might later regret.

Do not trust anyone else to help you to carry out your plans. Regardless of how obvious the situation seems, the addict is probably more persuasive and charming than you could ever hope to be. He will convince everyone else that you are the source of his problems, just as he already may have for many years. Therefore, expect everyone to help and side with the addict. You will avoid disappointment.

Preventive measures are imperative. More than once, a person has unknowingly married another with prior tax debts. The IRS may take tax refunds from a joint return to pay a tax debt of a spouse incurred prior to this marriage, something you'll end up fighting over to get back. While we expect our loved ones to be honest about such obligations, we have learned that we cannot rely on this with addicts, with whom we must expect dishonesty and/or omission of material facts. Hopefully, the behavioral signs and symptoms of addiction elucidated here will now be enough to put you on notice. Background searches ranging from credit checks to full private investigations should not be ruled out if there remains any unconfirmed suspicion. Preventative medicine is the best medicine, especially when dealing with possible addicts.

Figure 10 - Disenabling Checklist: Protecting Yourself from the Addict Spouse

Seek competent legal, insurance and tax assistance for direction and approval regarding some or all of the following:	
1.	Filing separate income tax returns.
2.	Remove or copy all tax and financial records. These include: Bank and credit card statements; Receipts supporting deductions claimed on current and prior returns; Calculations of income; Insurance policies; Deeds; Paid bills; Tax returns as far back as you have; Marriage and professional licenses, passports and birth certificates.
3.	Cancel joint credit cards.
4.	Close joint bank and investment accounts, separating assets per legal counsel's instructions.
5.	Separate real property if possible, or re-title from joint to tenants-in-common.
6.	Change beneficiaries of all life insurance polices, annuities, IRAs, Keoghs, 401-Ks, profit sharing and all other pension plans.
7.	Change your will or amend your trust.
8.	If appropriate, set up a survivor's trust to support your addict if and when he is in advanced recovery.
9.	Transfer title to all cars, motorcycles, boats and airplanes to appropriate spouse.
10.	Purchase separate insurance coverage, especially motor vehicle.
11.	Obtain additional liability insurance on those items not put in separate names.
12.	Remove collectibles, jewelry and any other valuable or easily saleable property that you feel is yours.

9

Predicting a Predisposition to

Substance Addiction

Ancestry

Alcoholism is known as a "family disease" because of its impact on and the fact that it runs in, families. Dr. Goodwin's study of Danish brothers showed that the rate of alcoholism is unrelated to environment and is instead heavily influenced by alcoholism in one's parents. But why has it apparently been passed down through the generations in some families, yet not others?

It turns out that the ancestors of the Mediterranean peoples have had access to large quantities of alcohol for at least 500 generations.[319] Yet, such quantities only became available to northern Europeans less than 50 generations ago. North American Indians had their first taste about 10 generations ago, with American Eskimos just in the past three. There is an indisputable correlation between these time frames and rates of alcoholism. Those of Mediterranean ancestry (such as Italians, the Southern French and probably those of Jewish descent) have very low rates of alcoholism (estimated at 5%), while Northern Europeans (the Irish, Scandinavians and northern Russians) have higher rates (approximately 20%). Eskimos and American Indians experience epidemic rates of alcoholism. The less time a people have had access, the greater its prevalence. Alcoholism authority James W. Smith, M.D., who was Chief Medical Officer for the former Schick Chemical Dependency Center, theorizes that "the difference in the incidence of alcoholism, by race, appears to be another instance of the evolutionary process of 'natural selection' at work. Those Mediterranean peoples

---

[319] *James W. Smith, M.D., Schick Programs booklet, "An Orientation on Alcoholism," Ibid., pp. 25-27. This section would not have been possible were it not for this little noticed booklet.*

most susceptible to alcoholism tended to die out over the many generations during which alcohol was consumed. North American Indians, on
the other hand, have had very few generations during which to develop
an alcoholism-resistant racial strain"[320] and, in fact, seem to have developed little or no additional resistance since the colonists traded brandy
and rum for skins, pelts and land.

This could easily be confused with culture. A close Russian friend has
told me of parties where 50 Russians consumed 50 liters of vodka. Surely,
you might say, this sort of apparent alcoholism could be the result of 70
years of totalitarian socialism on the culture. While there are no hard and
fast statistics to disprove this, there are two arguments against. One is that
while the Soviet people lived in fairly uniformly abysmal conditions north
to south, the rate of alcoholism appears to have been far less in the south.
For example, Georgia, Russia (a southern region) is reported to experience
minimal levels of alcoholism, even though its people are heavy wine drinkers.[321] Northern Russia, on the other hand, has apparently experienced far
greater levels. This is consistent with Dr. Smith's theory.

The second argument against culture as a cause is actually an "I'll grant
you this" response. Just as abuse of children may result in greater use of
alcohol (but not addiction), abuse of a people can result in similar increased
use. There was nothing truly productive for people to do in much of the
former Soviet Union and its colonies. A criminal element held (and still
holds, albeit in different form) the reigns of power. Non-addicts, unable
(without great difficulty) in a totalitarian socialist economy to achieve self-
esteem, self-actualization or economic success by their own labors, believed
they may as well get drunk and did so. Addicts would feel little compunction to get sober, since it didn't pay, thus maintaining a high rate of active
addiction. Those with actual addiction comprise possibly 20% of the Soviet population, while those who abuse may amount to an additional 40%.
This results in what appears to be a rate of alcoholism as high as 60%,
which is the level my Russian friend estimated.

There is evidence of this in the monumental increase of alcohol consumption by the Soviets. Spending on alcohol in 1929 by the average Mus-
covite already exceeded his Berlin counterpart with similar income by a
factor of five.[322] This is astonishing, because in 1930, Stalin decreed that
the Central Committee "'aim openly and directly for the maximum increase
in output'" of alcoholic beverages.[323] It was reported that, "By 1940 there
were already more shops selling drink than meat, fruit and vegetables put

[320] *Smith, Ibid., pp. 25-27.*
[321] *White, Ibid., p. 68 and 52.*
[322] *White, Ibid., p. 22.*
[323] *Perhaps so his own drinking wouldn't be so noticeable.*

together."[324] Although Soviet official statistics were hardly a model of reliability, the official production of alcoholic beverages increased by 400% from 1940 to 1980.[325] By the late 1970s there were cities "where the average consumption among working adults was as much as a bottle a day" and we're not talking wine.[326] Women alcoholics are estimated to have quadrupled during the same period, with 99.4% of all men and 97.9% of all women at least occasional drinkers.[327] The level of consumption is mind-boggling. My Russian friend's numbers may not be far off, since according to one Soviet estimate, "at least 50-60 million of the population [of 300 million] were alcoholics" as of 1985 and "a further 110-110 (sic) million 'cultured drinkers' were alcohol-dependent."[328]

Since alcoholism requires both the genetic predisposition and actual drinking, in more temperate societies and cultures some of those pre-disposed will not become alcoholics, since many will not have or take the opportunity to drink. When there's as much drinking going on as there was in the former Soviet Union, we can get a good idea as to how many alcoholics there really are, since just about everyone who is predisposed will trigger alcoholism. Culture, then, can lead to greater abuse and touch off more alcoholism.

A measure of these grotesque levels was found in the workplace. An official Soviet report in 1982 found that of every 100 workers surveyed, an average of 30 were absent at any given moment[329] and "as high as ninety per cent of such absences were connected with alcohol."[330] Another investigation "found that in some cases no more than ten per cent of the workforce were still at their places during the last hour of the shift."[331] One scholar, Boris Segal, calculated that over 30% of the Soviet labor force were alcohol "abusers" and "an average alcohol 'abuser,' according to Soviet investigations, lost about forty working days annually."[332] Anything approaching such a rate of absenteeism smacks of alcoholism and not just abuse. By the early 1980s "'alcohol plus adult' had replaced 'children plus matches' as the most important single cause of" fires (two-thirds of them) and by 1985 "more than ten per cent of all Soviet males were involved *every year* in a

[324] *White, Ibid., p. 27.*
[325] *Ibid., p. 41.*
[326] *Ibid., p. 40.*
[327] *Ibid., p. 40.*
[328] *Ibid., p. 184.*
[329] *Ibid., p. 62.*
[330] *Ibid., p. 49.*
[331] *Ibid., p. 62.*
[332] *Ibid., p. 50. That certainly sounds like "addict" to me, but how can we differentiate in a totalitarian socialist country where people really didn't give a damn?*

criminal offense" relating to alcohol (emphasis added).[333]

The example of American Indians is, in some ways, even more instructive. They have suffered enormously since Europeans brought rum, brandy and other alcohol to their nations in the 1600s. Deaths among Indians today directly attributable to alcoholism are four times greater than for the U.S. population as a whole, while an astounding 70% of all treatment provided at Indian Health Service clinics are for <u>obvious</u> alcoholism-related illnesses.[334] Many view alcohol as more destructive of the Indians than communicable diseases subsequent to first contact with Europeans. The governor of Maryland in the 1680s stated that "'the Indians of these parts decrease very much, partly owing to smallpox, but the great cause of all is their being so devilishly given to drink.'"[335] The Swedish naturalist Peter Kalm wrote in the mid-18th century that brandy killed more Indians than epidemic diseases and had heard Indians proclaim that "'to die by drinking brandy was a desirable and honorable death.'"[336]

Despite the ubiquitousness of drunken violence among the Indians, after tasting rum and experiencing its mind-altering effects, they would crave more. The Indians would trade their most valuable skins and furs in its pursuit, leaving nothing with which to buy tools and clothing for their families, sinking into abject poverty.[337] Once they began to drink, Indians would rarely stop until the booze ran out, resulting in loose morals and bacchanalian scenes. In at least one instance after a 10-day blowout affair, sobered up Indians pawned "'every thing they were in possession of, for a mouthful of spirits to settle their stomachs....'"[338] One instance of seemingly one-sided treaties (and perhaps many others) can be explained by alcohol. The Indians gave away lands while being plied with "'liquor for several days'....[persuading] the Cherokees to agree to cede their claims 'to the lands they claimed towards the Mississippi to the Crown of Britain'"[339] in exchange partly for rum and brandy.

Long ago the North American Indians complained about liquor depopulating their nations and making them "'poor and foolish,'" recognizing "'there are Some among us So disorderly by reason of rhum [original spelling] that we are unable to keep them in any Regulation."[340] This is a clear

---

[333] *Ibid., p. 48.*

[334] *Peter C. Mancall, "Deadly Medicine: Indians and Alcohol in Early America," Ibid., p. 6.*

[335] *Ibid., p. 92.*

[336] *Ibid., p. 93.*

[337] *Ibid., p. 86, 97 and 116.*

[338] *Ibid., p. 88.*

[339] *Ibid., p. 48.*

[340] *Ibid., p. 117.*

description of the anti-social rule-breaking behavior so often a trademark of addicts. Despite the destruction the new drinks wrought, a Jesuit missionary wrote in the 1630s, "'They cannot abstain from drinking, taking pride in getting drunk and in making others drunk.... [give them enough bottles of brandy and] they will sit down and, without eating, will drink, one after the other, until they have emptied them.'"[341] We have a host of indications to addiction for practically entire tribes, including the children.

This behavior was clearly not learned from the colonists, most of whom were far more restrained in their drinking. The Indians' conduct was out of control, undertaking "with vigor and bravado [while drunk] almost any evil action such as anger, vengeance, or impurity...[providing an] excuse for any evil which they might commit in such a condition.'"[342] Even Indians recognized that colonists could apparently control their own drinking, while they themselves, could not. This baffled observers of the time, since Indians never drank that much, certainly not as much as the colonists who downed (by one estimate) an average of 7 shots of hard liquor per capita per day. Although perplexed at the quantity the Indians downed when drink was available, it was not how much they drank that concerned the colonists, but rather how they behaved when they drank.[343]

Their symptoms of addiction did not end there. Drinking was the social and economic ruin of entire villages due to alcohol's erosion of civility and order.[344] They didn't drink on account of the taste, but rather "'simply to become intoxicated, imagining, in their drunkenness, that they became persons of importance, taking pleasure in seeing themselves dreaded by those who do not taste the poison,'" feeling "more powerful when they were drunk."[345] One British official unknowingly reported ego-based belittling by active alcoholics when he described drunk Indians telling "'the persons they most Esteem *that they are Cowards, that they will put them to death, that they are the Lords of the Ground they live upon,'*"[346] etc. This sort of behavior stems from what is easily diagnosed as alcoholism. Even today, in one Native American community "three-fourths of the men and over a third of the women [have] been diagnosed at some point as abusers of alcohol or dependent on it."[347] It is baffling to many Native Americans that they have such an enormous problem. Yet it shouldn't be, any more than having a susceptibility to sickle cell anemia should be baffling to Afri-

---

[341] *Ibid., p. 68.*
[342] *Ibid., p. 69.*
[343] *Ibid., p. 14-16.*
[344] *Ibid., pp. 84 and 86-87.*
[345] *Ibid., p. 75.*
[346] *Ibid., p. 70.*
[347] *Ibid., p. 6.*

cans. It's in the genes.

The tendency to alcoholism may be in the genes of African-Americans as well. Like Native Americans, Black Africans seem to have had little or no exposure to fermentable grains until their contact with Caucasians. Interestingly, both "Native Americans and enslaved Africans were the only groups [early American] colonialists recognized as stimulated to violence by alcohol."[348] While this may understate certain affinities to violence by some of Caucasian and other ancestry, there is little question as to the reasons colonists made such a concerted attempt at enforcing temperance on both Native Americans and African slaves. They largely succeeded in prohibiting slaves from "producing or consuming alcohol except with their owner's permission,"[349] in what was, possibly, the most successful Prohibition ever.

Furthermore, the behavior of perfectly sane, considerate and even wonderful people turning into monsters is similar in descriptions of both Native and African-Americans. A priest noted in 1750 that the Indians, "especially the Illinois who are the gentlest and most tractable of men — become, when intoxicated, madmen and wild beasts" (emphasis added).[350] Similarly, slave-holding Southerners, in calling for prohibition of the sale of alcohol to African slaves, observed that "alcohol brought out what they saw as the bestial nature of the African" (emphasis added).[351] While some would suggest this was self-serving on the part of the White Southerner, it should be pointed out that "brought out" implies the African was also among "the gentlest and most tractable of men," as are most non-addict African-Americans. Indeed, the observation among missionaries in Africa that the plight and wretchedness of the "African Negro" was due not "to colonial abuses...but to overindulgence in alcohol,"[352] was not likely a self-serving observation. There were reports of drunkenness in the late 19th century that sound amazingly similar to that of American Indians, including missionary reports of "four hundred blacks lying drunk in the streets.... Thirty girls under sixteen lay drunk, even parts of their clothing bartered for drink.... Germany and America export eight million gallons of rum to the Congo yearly, with the result that the Negro has degenerated morally and mentally.... Remember as you go next Sunday morn to church that the

---

[348] *Robert Nash Parker with Linda-Anne Rebhun, "Alcohol and Homicide: A Deadly Combination of Two American Traditions," Albany, N.Y.: State University of New York Press, 1995, p. 9, with several cites.*

[349] *Cited in Parker and Rebhun, Ibid., p. 9.*

[350] *Cited in Parker, Ibid., p. 10.*

[351] *Cited in Parker, Ibid., p. 10.*

[352] *Edward Behr, "Prohibition: Thirteen Years That Changed America," New York: Arcade Publishing, 1996, p. 53.*

Congo native, his wife and children lie in their hovels drunk."[353]

As we have seen, the effect substance addiction has on others is monstrous and wide in scope. The multiplier effect of addiction has contributed to the devastation of entire cultures. To get an idea of it's potential, consider the effect addiction has on society if we assume each alcoholic seriously adversely impacts four people at a time (a number suggested as reasonable by many recovering alcoholics). If the rate of addiction among Jews in a closed social structure is 5%, 25% of the Jewish population is negatively impacted at a particular moment (the alcoholic and four others equal 25%). If the rate of addiction among American Indians is only 20% (it's probably far higher), those negatively impacted at any moment is virtually 100%. Consider the fact that the typical addict, particularly the single drug user of alcohol, may wreak havoc for 30, 40 or even 50 years and you begin to get an idea of the devastation this affliction can cause. The four people that are being affected today are often not the same four persons affected 5 or 10 years later. This is why the rate of addiction in a particular people may explain not only the relative success and failure of cultures, but that of entire civilizations.[354]

The sort of addictive drinking in Africa described above resulted in a breakdown of order and the social structure, including destruction so great that tribes were no longer distinct entities. Social commentators have long been perplexed that a land so rich in natural resources has remained to this day, so unbelievably dirt-poor. This is easily explained by free-market economists, who point out that where there is little market-based capitalism, nations remain poor, while countries with mostly free markets (even such countries as Japan and Hong Kong, with few or practically no resources) become tremendously wealthy. What hasn't been explained by either economists or social commentators are these questions: why didn't Africa adopt free market capitalism once it was introduced and why did it end up with numerous tin-pot dictators, destroying the lives of so many? We now have a clue. Among North American Indians and central Africans we can see the effects of the introduction of large quantities of a new (then) psychoactive drug (alcohol) to which there was no inbred resistance. De-

---

[353] *Behr, Ibid., p. 54.*

[354] *This may partially explain the history of ruinous tax policies destroying nations. Politician-addicts, in their quest to exercise capricious power and inflate their egos, may well support destructive governmental policies. Charles Adams demonstrates in his "Fight, Flight and Fraud: The Story of Taxation" that the most destructive policies involve taxation, often used to redistribute income from the rich, who are often (in another version of the "blame game") blamed for the plight of the poor. (Curacao: Euro-Dutch Holdings, NV, 1982.) See also Adams, "For Good and Evil: The Impact of Taxes on the Course of Civilization," Lanham, MD.: Madison Books, 1993.*

veloping into mass addiction, the "multiplier effect" insured that practically every member of every tribe was seriously affected. Viewing the signs and symptoms of addiction as a list of behaviors commonly observed among addicts and even codependents could explain the failure of civilizations when such conduct is epidemic.

Making things worse is the fact that political power attracts addicts. Exacting power over others is easier in government institutions than in private ones, where market forces may more easily result in the loss of such positions of control and power. The need to insure and maintain such positions by addicts, then, may account for the fact that free markets (far superior in every way to other systems in satisfying the demands of consumers and increasing overall wealth) have had great difficulty gaining even a toehold in some cultures. This may be the root of the poverty among not only American Indians, but also the African nations.[355]

While there are few statistics showing that African-Americans have a higher incidence of substance addiction than the general population, there is additional strong anecdotal support for it. (Bear in mind throughout, addiction is a genetic and not moral issue.) We have seen that incarcerated criminals suffer a rate of addiction on the order of 80%. African-Americans comprise about 12% of the U.S. population and yet 40 to 50% of prisoners, far out of proportion to their numbers. The chance of a Caucasian going to state or federal prison during his life is 4.4%, while that for an African-American is an astonishing 28.5%.[356] While there is certainly prejudice in the criminal justice system, a low resistance to alcoholism (and other substance addiction, although alcohol is almost always the first drug of choice among addicts) is consistent with this alarmingly high incidence of incarceration. In a moral sense, there is no evidence that a particular race of people is innately better or worse. However, physically speaking, since there is clearly a pattern of criminal (and criminal-like) behaviors among those afflicted with substance addiction, it is likely that African-Americans are at far greater risk for addiction than Caucasians and most others. Prisons, then, do not house (for the most part) innately bad people, but rather an entire class of undiagnosed and untreated substance addicts.

---

[355] *Jared Diamond, in "Guns, Germs and Steel: The Fates of Human Societies," New York: W. W. Norton & Company, 1997. Diamond provides compelling reasons why civilizations fail to develop on their own in areas such as Africa, but does not explain why democracy and free markets failed to take hold when the seeds were planted by Europeans, or when the various African nations became independent.*

[356] *The Wall Street Journal, "Prison Is All Around For a Girl Growing Up In Inner-City Baltimore," by Jonathan Kaufman, October 27, 1998, p. A18 (Justice Department's Bureau of Justice Statistics). The overall chance at being incarcerated in state or federal prison at some point in their lives is about 9% for all men, not dissimilar to our estimate of 10% as the rate of substance addiction across race and gender in America.*

Another statistic that may support this view is that Washington, D.C. has the highest rate of alcohol consumption in the U.S., with almost double the national average.[357] Although politicians, bureaucrats and lobbyists may experience a high rate of alcoholism, not even Washington, D.C. has a majority of its citizens holding such positions. Instead, the vast majority of the citizens are African-Americans.

The subject is sorely lacking studies that could shed light on which racial groups and descendents are at the greatest risk. Acknowledging that substance addiction is the source of most criminal behavior would greatly increase the odds of treating the proper affliction. With addiction treated, the rate of repeat offenders would collapse. We must recognize that the environment, poverty and physical abuse do little to explain long-term criminal and other destructive behaviors. The disease of substance addiction explains far more.

If the genetic component to addiction were taught to children and parents, it's just possible the first or second drink would be avoided by at least a few who are at great risk. Obviously, we have a long way to go, but skeptics should be reminded that hardly anyone expected the Berlin Wall to be torn down. Certain Psychological Types, properly educated and guided, may well be lifelong abstainers. I know several individuals who have determined they are at risk and chose early on to never take their first drink. Others took the first drink and, recognizing their own at-risk responses to the drug, stopped while the stopping was easy. Properly educated, it may be easier to avoid succumbing at or near the start of such use.

Knowing one's ancestry may assist in preventing early use that could turn into addiction. If we are in a high-risk population, we can educate families of that risk. Once the first drink is taken and we observe behaviors consistent with a diagnosis of addiction, we can immediately act to insure that negative consequences are experienced (just as Bossu did early on, with his Indian hunter). We can also educate close persons to never enable and thereby improve the odds that the early-stage addict never suffers, along with family and friends, the debilitating effects of later addiction.

Totalitarian socialism precludes people from profiting by their own efforts. This likely prevents many from achieving desirable levels of self-esteem, self-actualization and economic success. Such lack of freedom to pursue one's dreams may cause some to repeatedly violate their values. This may perpetuate substance addiction in those genetically predisposed, while triggering heavy abuse in others. Just as addiction (or heavy use) may result in repeated personal failures, a nation of drunks may result in a

[357] *The New York Times, June, 1985, reported by Robe, Ibid., p. 290.*

failed culture. Evidence for this is found in the former Soviet Union.[358]

Conversely, we may be able to decrease the level of both abusive and extended addictive substance use by having the freedom to pursue dreams and personal goals. Freedom is not the license that the addict may prefer. Freedom requires each person to take responsibility for his actions. This is the antithesis of allowing people to abrogate responsibility through what we now know as "enabling" or "bailouts." The great Austrian economist Ludwig Von Mises, in "Human Action,"[359] argued that the maximization of human happiness, creativity and productivity requires each person to be free to act, yet obligated to experience all the consequences of those actions. Values may be more strictly adhered to in a system where one must accept responsibility for one's own mistakes and errors of judgment.

A brief unexplained comment commanded my attention during my early reading about addiction: Vernon Johnson's observation "that alcoholism cannot exist unless there is a conflict between the values and the behavior of the drinker."[360] While violation of values cannot precipitate addiction (due to the genetic nature of the disease), addiction causes violation of values. This can put addicts with deep core values at greater risk in terms of the depths of despair to which they are likely to sink. Repeated violation of values may serve to keep addicts drinking and using. We will now explore which Psychological Types may be at greater risk for this. We will also describe the differing values the recovering addict must live with to get clean and sober, staying in a program of recovery. We will also find some Types that may be more likely to pay heed to warnings that show they may be at great risk.

---

[358] *This could explain the failure of other cultures in which drugs other than alcohol are used. Western society has its social drinkers and its alcoholics. Other cultures, with different drugs of choice, may have their social users and addicts. This could explain the insanity existing elsewhere that is so similar to ours, without which madness on such a massive scale might not exist. The Middle East has hashish and Southeast Asia has opium. It may be questioned whether warfare and dictators as destructive as a Joseph Stalin would exist to anywhere near the degree that they do in an absence of psychoactive substance addiction.*

[359] *Ludwig Von Mises, "Human Action," Auburn, Alabama: Ludwig Von Mises Institute, 1998.*

[360] *Johnson, Ibid., p. 2.*

Personality Type and addiction

Just as substance addiction may explain 80% of unhealthy human behavior, Personality Type and Temperament could explain 80% of behavior that is healthy.[361] The mother-daughter team of Isabel Myers and Katherine Briggs expanded upon the theories of the great psychologist, Carl Jung, in devising a personality system now known as the Myers-Briggs Type Indicator. This system presents the idea that people think and function very differently by nature. We'll talk about Personality Type first, since it is related to what <u>appears to be</u> a predisposition to addiction.

One's Personality Type describes inborn "preferences," which explain behaviors that we lean toward, in four areas. It's important to note that these are <u>preferences</u> in terms of behavior and are not carved in stone. However, they are a great indication of how people, for the most part, behave and think. The four preferences are:
1. how we interact with and relate to our environment
2. how we collect and generate information
3. how we make decisions
4. which of the latter two behaviors are most obvious to others

Each of the four areas has only two different preferences. To keep it simple, we'll stick to the last one, which tells us who (and who doesn't) have a tendency towards novelty seeking, experimentation and play.[362] These, in turn, may be the greatest personality predictors to extended and destructive addiction.

Those who are more obvious in their **collection and generation of information** are called Perceptives ("Ps"). They tend to give information rather than directions. For example, instead of saying, "Let's go to the movies tonight," they're more likely to say, "Gee, honey, a great movie is opening this weekend," (implication being, they want to see a movie.) They <u>appear</u> to be externally unstructured, but appearances can be deceiving. While their desk may be a complete mess, they know exactly where everything is. Generally, Perceptives would rather play before work, postponing unpleasant jobs. Preferring to explore all options by keeping them open, they also tend to delay decisions. "Ps" are process oriented, with little need for closure. For them, it's the journey, not the destination. Whenever possible, they just "let life happen." What's important for our pur-

---

[361] *Integrating an understanding of Personality Type and Temperament with an understanding of substance addiction, virtually all human behavior (heretofore often inexplicable) becomes not only understandable, but also logical.*

[362] *A detailed description of all four preferences and other insights as predictors of extended periods and deeper levels of addiction is found in Appendix 4.*

poses is that Perceptives are novelty seeking, flexible, spontaneous, experimental and impulsive, able to quickly accept some degree of risk.

Their opposites, Judgers ("Js"), are more obvious in their **decision-making**. They are more direct when communicating with others and comfortable giving directives. In other words, they tend to get right to the point.
They also appear to be more outwardly structured, preferring to have everything in its place. "Js" tend to get the work out of the way before allowing themselves time for play. Comfortable once having made decisions,
they are "outcome" oriented. Significantly, Judgers are more rigid, planned,
careful and deliberate. Type and Temperament expert Alice Fairhurst points
out, they are more likely than "Ps" to focus on risk containment.

Because of these obvious differences, we might predict that Perceptives
would slip into active and more obvious addiction at an earlier stage than
do Judgers. They may also be more resistant to treatment. Due to their
preference for novelty seeking and impulsiveness, they tend to be more
experimental with alcohol and other drugs. Because they were born as
Perceptives, experimentation often begins at an earlier age. Experts in Type
and Temperament have noted this from stories related by the two disparate Types. Studies of college students and substance-related problem behavior[363] support these ideas, with a statistically significant number of
Perceptives being represented over Judgers. While split about evenly in
the general population, "Ps" with such problems outnumbered "Js" 3 to 1
in one study and 4 to 1 in another. In addition, Native Americans may be
far more Perceptive than Judging. Recall that probably no other group
exceeds their tendency to addiction. A study of Native-American high
school students found three times the number of Perceptives as Judgers.

On the surface, it could be argued that these findings suggest some Personality Types are more likely to be addicts, which would contradict the
disease theory of addiction; but it doesn't. As we have shown, most addicts are not diagnosed as such. The studies are simply measuring obvious addiction. The seeming correlation between Type and addiction is
due to some other reason or reasons. These may include a predilection
among Perceptives to (a) go deeper into their addiction, (b) remain active
addicts for longer periods, (c) engage in more destructive behaviors and
(d) be more likely to "experiment".

"Ps" may go deeper due to their propensity to play. After all, who is
less likely to stop the progression of one's life falling apart? One who is
more play- than work-oriented seems less inclined to do so. Due to this,
"Ps" may also be more likely to remain active addicts for extended peri-

[363] *"Tracking Freshman Difficulties In the Class of 1993," Judith A. Provost, Journal
of Psychological Type, Vol. 21, 1991, and "The Type to Drink: Undergraduate Alcohol
Policy Violators and Personality Type," Phil Barrineau, Journal of Psychological Type,
Vol. 41, 1997.*

ods. Those who "go deeper" are more obvious addicts and more likely to be counted as such. Also, addicts who remain active for long periods of time may skew the statistics, making it appear that some Personality Types are at greater risk for addiction than are others. For example, if a "P" Type's average period of active and easily observable addiction is 30 years (partly due to an earlier start) and a "J's" is only 10 years, "Ps" will statistically measure three times as likely to be addicts. This would be true even if they may otherwise have an equal initial inclination to addiction. "P" addicts also tend to engage in more destructive behaviors[364] and, therefore, have a greater likelihood of standing out.

There is also a possibility some Personality Types are more likely to "experiment" with drugs than others, especially when young. Some Perceptives are extremely experience-driven and innately hedonistic, craving excitement.[365] Others are intensely curious and experimental.[366] However, without a predisposition to addiction, experimentation eventually declines or ceases. Extended periods of experimentation are more likely to result in a dependency on drugs that are physically addictive. It is doubtful that Judgers who are not at risk for addiction would engage in extended experimental use to the degree required for physical addiction to take hold.[367]

If we can develop models that have some predictive value as to who is at greater risk for addiction, we may help some budding addicts avoid or limit what is otherwise unavoidable in our drinking and using culture. By predicting the unique problems an addict might create both for himself and his victims, we may better zero in on where to concentrate our offer of uncompromising tough love. This helps to more efficiently set the stage

[364] *This is due in particular to one Temperament (the SP or "Artisan," discussed in the next chapter) which always shares this preference and who, when unhealthy, can play very destructive "survival games."*

[365] *See SFPs and STPs in the Appendix.*

[366] *See NFPs and NTPs in the Appendix.*

[367] *For example James A. Inciardi, professor and director of the Division of Criminal Justice at the University of Delaware, points out that it takes months to become addicted to heroin. He reports on one addict snorting heroin for several months, who was not physically addicted. The same addict "skin popped" (injecting into the muscle just beneath the skin) for the next three months. Still, he was not physically addicted, sometimes going for a week without the drug and not getting sick. Only after two months of "mainlining" (injecting directly into the vein), did he finally become physically addicted. The same addict also reported that withdrawal from heroin is not the big deal it's made out to be, with many recovering addicts comparing it to "a good dose of the flu." (James A. Inciardi, "The War on Drugs: Heroin, Cocaine, Crime and Public Policy," Mountain View, CA: Mayfield Publishing Company, 1986, pp. 61-64.) As has been pointed out, psychological addiction, rooted in the biological differences between addict and non-addict in processing the drug, is a far graver concern than physical addiction and its withdrawal.*

for successful intervention.

Psychologist David Keirsey integrated human Temperament, which had been theorized by many philosophers and sages for 2,500 years, with the Myers-Briggs Personality Types. Temperament goes further than Personality Type in refining a person's different innate interests, skills, behaviors, abilities and roles. It also describes varied core values and needs of the individual. More significantly, Temperament describes differing sources of self-esteem, an understanding of which may assist the addict to both bottom and recover. But first we must discuss the role of deflating the ego and rebuilding self-esteem so that one can see how Temperament might help in this process.

10

Improving the Treatment
of Drug Addiction

Deflating the ego

There is a vast difference between ego and self-esteem, although the observer can easily confuse them. Ego is egotism, an inordinately large sense of self-importance. Concomitant to this is that whatever one does is OK, even though it may violate another's obviously less important space. This may account for much of the criminal and unethical conduct we observe in addicts.

The 12-Step programs work because they are designed to deflate the ego while suggesting Steps to help rebuild self-esteem. Bill Wilson and Dr. Bob Smith, co-founders of AA, knew that "deflating the massive ego of the alcoholic" had to be a fundamental objective of the program. The first three steps of this program, i.e., admitting "we were powerless" over a substance, recognizing "a Power greater than ourselves," and handing "our will and our lives over to the care of God" (or other "higher power") do not come easy to a practicing egomaniac. The 4th Step, that we conduct "a searching and fearless moral inventory of ourselves," suggests that there is work to be done on one's character. This is not an acknowledgement made by one who views himself as god-like. Admitting to wrongs (in Step 5) is a clear admission of imperfection, something that must, by definition, deflate the ego of those with a bloated sense of importance. "Ready to have God remove all these defects of character" implies they cannot do this themselves, something an egotist would not admit to, as is true of asking "Him to remove our shortcomings" (Steps 6 and 7). Making "a list of all persons we had harmed" and offering "direct amends to such people" (Steps 8 and 9) are truly humbling experiences. The suggestion to continue "to take personal inventory" (Step 10) implies continuing imperfection, once again ego-deflating for one who thinks he can do no wrong. "Praying only for knowledge of His will for us" and "having a spiritual awakening" (Step 11) is the culmination of this ego-deflation. The fact that these Steps are impossible for the practicing addict to take, hints at the sense of helplessness and experience of devastation required before becoming ready to attempt recovery. He must be at the point of "*willing to do anything.*"

Recall that Vernon Johnson identified "euphoric recall" as the most destructive of the distortions. The fact that this makes the addict remember everything he does in a favorable light could not only inflate one's ego, but it may be the inflated ego's primary cause. While abstinence is the first step towards recovery, this by itself yields only a dry drunk. The ego, although no longer being pumped up, is not being <u>deflated</u>. Ego deflation is imperative for healthy sobriety, even if it is not the fundamental cause of <u>all</u> the other bizarre conduct and appearance of psychopathological disorders. Sometimes, bewildering actions are engaged in due to the need to insure availability of the substance. At other times, such behavior is a result of extreme mood swings and other dysfunctions, which have the appearance of mental disorders. Eventually, addicts fall to the effects of latter-stage addiction, including financial difficulties and secondary diseases. Physiologically based blackouts may explain much of the most bizarre and destructive conduct. However, once the bloated ego begins to be deflated, the most consistently destructive behaviors begin to subside. Only then can the rebuilding of self-esteem commence.

Self-esteem and responsibility

<u>Self-esteem is regarding oneself with respect and having a favorable view of self.</u> Ask any recovering alcoholic-addict how they viewed themselves while they were using and they will tell you, it was with total disdain. While some may confuse ego with self-esteem (as I did in my addict-ex), make no mistake: the self-esteem of the addict while using is zero. For recovery to occur and sobriety maintained the ego must be deflated <u>and</u> self-esteem restored. Deflating the ego without rebuilding self-esteem will ultimately cause the addict to self-destruct. Understanding his source of self-esteem, then, is exceedingly important for both him and us if we are to provide real help in recovery.

The "suggested Steps to recovery" of the 12-Step program are no more suggestions than the advice to not drive over a cliff if one wants to live. Each Step is essential to recovery. Since each builds on the other, it is important that they be "worked" in order. While the process of deflating the ego is begun in Steps 1 through 3 and continues in Steps 4 through 9, these latter are also geared towards helping the addict rebuild self-esteem. Providing the core of recovery, these Steps require the addict to get and stay honest with both himself and others. Crucially, they admonish that he face up to and experience the consequences of his poor decisions and behaviors.

These Steps assist the addict in recognizing his character flaws and personality defects, helping him to take responsibility for his behavior. Milam and Ketcham point out the danger this poses to the addict in leaving him with guilt and shame of massive proportions. They also suggest that some may incorrectly interpret this to mean, "Once his personality problems are fixed, he can return to normal drinking."[368] AA could do more to inform members of the biological basis for the affliction, thereby extinguishing this interpretation. Despite these concerns, Milam and Ketcham agree that AA is "far and away the most effective program in the world for helping alcoholics to stay sober."[369] It likely works as well as it does because Steps 4 through 9 are designed to both deflate the ego <u>and</u> assist in the renewal of self-esteem. Acknowledging one's flaws, admitting one's wrongs and paying amends to others in truly penitent fashion require ego deflation. Taking responsibility for one's behaviors, living consistently with one's values and core needs, while getting (and staying) honest, begins the process for the restoration of self-esteem.

Those who believe in either the Mental Health Model or "excuse" models of addiction may not accept this. The Mental Health Model, as previously discussed, hypothesizes that other psychopathological disorders precede, explain and cause the addiction. If true, addicts could overcome their disorders through psychological counseling and later resume drinking or using non-addictively. Telling them they have a psychopathological disorder gives them an excuse for their behavior. Counseling is reported by addicts themselves to <u>never</u> result in a cure for substance addiction, but instead to <u>always</u> enable their use. They later find that, once in recovery, the behaviors giving rise to the incorrect diagnosis of behavioral disorders or mental illness have diminished and usually disappear.

The "excuse" model suggests that the addict cannot be held accountable for his actions and behaviors, since he is either diseased or mentally ill. This flies in the face of the addicts' own view on the subject. By their own testimony, recovery from their disease is impossible without taking responsibility. This, along with the consequential rebuilding of self-esteem, is the only way by which the disease can be kept in remission.

---

[368] *Milam and Ketcham, Ibid., p. 156.*
[369] *Milam and Ketcham, Ibid., p. 55.*

Temperament and recovery

Johnson has never observed alcoholism in a person whose behavior was consistent with his values. However, Gorski believes for addiction to exist, all that is required is for the genetically predisposed individual to drink. If this is true, violation of values does not cause addiction. Rather, addiction causes one to violate values.

The addict has no choice about his disease and, initially has no understanding of it. However, as Milam and Ketcham point out, once comprehension sets in, "a moral obligation does enter the picture" and that "if he willfully or carelessly deviates from the program, he will drink again and inflict the illness on himself and others."[370] Since the program is designed to restore self-esteem, the addict must live within his values to keep from relapsing.

Johnson's observation is suggestive of the possibility that the addict drinks, uses and violates values in a circular fashion. This can be headed off with intervention and a recovery program that supplies the tools necessary for the addict to understand his own core values. Once he knows these values, he is better able to avoid violating them. That's where Temperament comes in. It determines one's core values, needs and source of self-esteem. If the trigger for relapse and/or extended active addiction is the violation of such values and needs, Temperament can be used to predict these triggers. Therein lies the usefulness in knowing an addict's innate Temperament: it can help him stay sober.

Family and schooling frequently teach others' values and needs during childhood and adolescence. This should not be confused with morality or other fundamental truths of right and wrong. Values are intensely personal, without which we cannot meet our own psychological core needs. Since many do not understand nor truly know themselves (least of all, the addict) the therapist's and codependent's goal may be to assist the recovering addict in this discovery. He can then learn to meet his needs in ethical ways and reduce the risk of relapse. If properly identifying an addict's Temperament increases the chances of recovery by helping him live within his values, misidentifying Temperament would greatly reduce these chances. The premise that Temperament is fixed and does not deviate is crucial in both helping us in its discovery[371] and the approach we must take in treating the recovering addict.

No other system of psychology provides such a plethora of information about what drives people. If we understand our values, needs and source

---

[370] *Milam and Ketcham, Ibid., p. 152.*
[371] *Childhood behaviors prior to onset of addiction may give powerful clues to one's Temperament.*

<u>of esteem, we know what will provide pleasure and pain.</u> All human energy is directed at maximizing pleasure and avoiding pain. The confusion here is, most of us think it's whatever drives "me." Psychologists have based their entire system of psychology on the belief that people are fundamentally alike in having a single basic motive force.[372]

Unfortunately, these psychologists seem to have had us driven by the force that drove <u>them</u>.[373] They were partially correct in describing what may have been their own Temperament and fitting the world into their own style. However, there is not just one, but four of these fundamental drives and sets of core needs and values, defined by one's Temperament. We can learn to recognize each of these as readily as subspecies of clouds or cats. Knowledge of Temperament gives us tremendous power to predict behaviors, natural skills, values, needs, intelligences (not IQ, but rather the type of mental or physical processes at which one excels) and, most significantly for our present discussion, one's particular source of self-esteem.

It's easy to be who you really are. It takes work to be someone you're not. Write with your opposite hand and (unless you're ambidextrous) you'll feel childlike, slow, plodding, uncoordinated, messier and far more prone to error. In the same way, violation of one's values results in a contradiction between beliefs and actions (cognitive dissonance), which may serve to keep the addict medicating once he starts.

Temperament is genetic. This explains the fact that children a year apart in age, living in the same environment for 20 years, are often so radically different. This also tells us why identical twins, genetically the same, separated at birth (raised in families not only unknown to each other but sometimes speaking different languages in different cultures), have similar personalities in every fundamental way. We learn, adapt and change as our Temperament would, in different environments. Thus, such change is superficial, not fundamental. Individuals of the same Temperament living in different environments are very similar in basic fundamental attributes, values and core needs, far more so than siblings close in age but of different Temperaments, raised in the same home.

We know far more about the inner needs and values of a person whose Temperament is known than we ever could through chance, interaction with him or an awareness of the environment in which raised. If values are learned or enforced that are not innate to his natural Temperament, he will be living (what he knows down deep to be) a lie. Core values are as

---

[372] *Derived from Keirsey, "Please Understand Me – II," Ibid., p. 2-3.*
[373] *Harry Sullivan theorized social solidarity as our primary basic motive. Alfred Adler saw us driven by a need for superiority over nature. Carl Rogers and Abraham Maslow had us all seeking self-actualization. Freud claimed we are driven by instinctual lust and all other motives stem from this.*

fundamentally inborn as alcoholism or its absence. Therefore, we cannot mold an addict to our likeness. We must instead create treatment programs that take his inborn Temperament into account, treating him as he would want to be treated in sobriety.[374] In addition, recognizing Temperament's genetic roots removes judgment from the fact that some Temperaments may have a greater predisposition to experimentation, a need for excitement and other behaviors. He may experiment and make new and wonderful scientific discoveries or, through such experimentation, trigger addiction.

The Temperaments, summarized

David Keirsey refers to the Temperaments as Artisan, Guardian, Rational and Idealist. In the Myers-Briggs paradigm, these are Sensing Perceiving or SP, Sensing Judging or SJ, iNtuitive Thinking or NT and iNtuitive Feeling or NF. The following are the Temperaments' different core needs and values, reason for being, brief word descriptions, intelligences and innate natural gifts. As you read, try and identify your own primary Temperament.[375] One means by which to do so may be to determine which of these describe a need that, when met, could give rise to a natural "endorphin" rush. This exercise will help you learn the four styles. Knowing these will help to identify the addict's Temperament, which could prove crucial in recovery, as we help to replace the artificial with a natural "high" using Temperament as a tool.

Artisans, or "SPs," need to be free to act on impulse and have an almost overwhelming desire to make an impact. They value aesthetics and the ability to gracefully vary the next move, as well as a skilled performance. They seek excitement, action and stimulation. Their innate nature calls on them to live each day to its fullest, eschewing rules and taking risks.[376] As Type and Temperament experts Alice and Lisa Fairhurst put it,[377] "To do is to be;" Nike's slogan "Just do it!" is clearly an Artisan slogan. AA's suggestion to take things "one day at a time" is consistent with the Artisan's need

---

[374] *The Golden Rule of Type and Temperament is, "Do unto others as they would have you do unto them."*

[375] *For many, the primary Temperament will be obvious. Others will have difficulty in immediately distinguishing between the primary and what some might call "secondary" Temperament. This confusion will diminish over time.*

[376] *This is the temperament Freud most closely described.*

[377] *Alice Fairhurst and Lisa L. Fairhurst, "Effective Teaching, Effective Learning," Palo Alto, CA: Davies-Black Publishing (Consulting Psychologists Press, Inc.), 1995, pp. 11-16.*

to live for today. They are at ease when afforded the opportunity of demonstrating their highly developed tactical intelligence, knowing what to do and when,[378] a form of which other Temperaments can only admire in their facility of use. To the Artisan, this tactical intelligence is mere play (and play they must!). Myers described "SPs" as "adaptable, able to see the needs of the moment, having no use for theories, wanting first hand experiences and enjoying life."[379] These abilities and preferences, combined with a predilection to "just do it," often results in his developing extremely fine eye-hand coordination. They comprise probably about 35% of the population. Both John F. Kennedy and Bill Clinton are prototype Artisans, along with Marilyn Monroe and Mel Gibson. So are most craftsmen, dancers, great athletes (such as Michael Jordan), surgeons and mechanical types. They also comprise the vast majority of more easily typecast actors and actresses, as they seek to make an impact through performance (including, for example, Jack Nicholson, Burt Reynolds and Liza Minelli).[380]

Guardians, or "SJs," have a strong need to belong. They must have obligations, duties and responsibilities to feel fulfilled. They value legal and proper methods, tradition, hierarchy, structure, stability and security. They have a deep respect for rules.[381] For Guardians, "To serve is to be." David Keirsey points out that they are most at ease when using their highly developed logistical intelligence. Myers described "SJs" as "conservative, stable, routinized, unimpulsive, dependable and hard-working." They make up 40 to 45% of the population. Florence Nightingale, George Washington, Harry Truman and Richard Nixon were all classic Guardians, as are most in the military, law enforcement, banking, insurance, accounting, founders of professional and service organizations, teachers, nurses and doctors.

Rationals, or "NTs," must develop and acquire new ideas and knowledge, striving to tame nature and be competent at whatever they choose to make an area of expertise. They value intelligence, logical consistency, ideas, theories, scientific inquiry (and progress) and basic, simple truths.[382] "To know is to be;" they have strategic and integrative intelligence. From the point of view of the other Temperaments, they are totally at ease when using this intelligence to learn and generate new ideas. Myers described

---

[378] *Derived from Keirsey, "Please Understand Me II," Ibid.*

[379] *The descriptions are from Myers, "Gifts Differing," as reported in Keirsey, Ibid.*

[380] *Obviously, the celebrities and historic figures used are "best guesses" as examples of the various Temperaments based on available evidence — their behaviors.*

[381] *They most closely resemble Sullivan's lovers of "social solidarity."*

[382] *They are perhaps closest to Adler's notion that we need "superiority," specifically in the area of ideas and in terms of power over nature (not people, a power for which healthy NTs have disdain).*

"NTs" as "analytical, abstract, theoretical, intellectual, independent, curious, scientific and research-oriented." They are natural skeptics who question authority but (in deference to competent authority), do not openly flaunt it, as will the Artisan. Rationals are rare, comprising only 6 to 12% of the population. Ayn Rand, Thomas Edison, Thomas Jefferson and Albert Einstein were all variations of Rationals, as are most scientists, inventors, computer nerds (such as Bill Gates), other techies and deep, original thinkers in many occupations.

Idealists, or "NFs," have a driving need to find their own unique identity, meaning and significance, while helping others do the same. They may even engage in a lifelong search for self-identity and their reason to exist.[383] They value ethics, personal relationships, empathy, self-actualization, idealism and authenticity. "To become is to be," means being genuine and true to self. They have a natural diplomatic intelligence that becomes far and away more developed than the other Temperaments. Idealists find using this intelligence to bring people together spiritually and cooperatively as instinctually as a fish takes to water. They are described by Myers as "humane, sympathetic, creative and insightful." Idealists represent only 10 to 14% of the population. Mahatma Ghandi and Oprah Winfrey are clearly magnificent examples of Idealists. Because of their need to help build interpersonal relationships, they develop great communication skills and may use these in writing, teaching, therapy and other people-helping-people professions. They are often the greatest actors and actresses, having the ability to place themselves into the shoes of others empathically (e.g., Dustin Hoffman and Meryl Streep). Because of their openness and interest in both the fanciful and fantastic, Idealists are more likely to be "new age" and mystical types.

---

[383] *They are clearly described by Rogers' and Maslow's self-actualization seeking personality.*

Figure 11 – Core Needs of the Temperaments

Temperament	Core Needs
Artisan SP	Be free to act on impulse; enjoy an ability to make an impact and be noticed
Guardian SJ	Maintain membership, belonging, obligation, duty and responsibility
Rational NT	Develop power over nature, acquire knowledge and perfect competencies
Idealist NF	Find meaning, significance and one's own unique identity

Matching Temperament to recovery

How does this relate to recovery? Recovering addicts acknowledge that each person must work the 12-Step program in his own way. This means, the style used to work the program must be consistent with one's personal values and core needs, which vary with Temperament. We can assist the addict in understanding these if his inborn Temperament can be identified. If he is consistently true to his core values, it is possible he can more easily stay sober.

Figure 12 – Values and Intelligences of the Temperaments

Temperament	Values	Intelligences
Artisan (SP)	Aesthetics, graceful action, performance with skill, excitement and stimulation	Tactics
Guardian (SJ)	Stability, structure, hierarchy, rules and regulations, tradition, security and law	Logistics
Rational (NT)	Intelligence, logical consistency, ideas, theories, scientific inquiry and progress	Strategy
Idealist (NF)	Self-actualization, ethics and morality, authenticity, personal relationships, empathy and idealism	Diplomacy

An Idealist addict in recovery who violates his values of morality, ethics and authenticity (which require honesty and genuineness) is more likely to relapse. Give us an Idealist who is Perceptive (i.e., one who is novelty seeking, impulsive, externally unstructured and prefers play before work) and we've got an addictive minefield. This Idealist (which Myers calls the NFP), in a vicious circle will possibly lie and use, then use and lie. A Rational recovering addict who lands himself in a dead-end job in which he is unable to make use of his prodigious mental faculties may relapse (particularly the Perceptive novelty-seeking Rational, NTP). A Guardian addict in recovery but not acting responsibly within proper channels or unable to provide stability and security for his family, may fall off the wagon. The cycle of use leads to poor judgment, resulting in yet further irresponsible behavior, the bane of the Guardian. The Artisan recovering addict, who fails in his quest for healthy excitement, action and stimulation, may well return to addictive behaviors. A risk-taking free-spirited Artisan may be prevented from having the freedom he needs to "just do" by more rigid and structured Guardian teachers and parents. This may set the stage for the Artisan to begin excessive partying while young, finding excitement and stimulation through drugs and, if predisposed to addiction, never looking back until his life is a total shambles.

We would think people know themselves. Most are not so introspective.[384] When we combine this general lack of introspection with the brain damage the addict has inflicted upon himself, we have a person in a state of confusion about who he is. Considering this, the idea that we can assist the addict in staying sober by helping him understand his core values doesn't seem so arrogant.

This concept has powerful support in the matching (or pairing up) of alcoholics with the style of recovery program and therapist most consistent with the addict's own Temperament. The recovery rates in one study[385] that compared matches and mismatches between alcoholic, therapist and "aftercare setting" were far greater with matches than without. Researchers rated the drinker's personality as one of the following:

1. poorly socialized, egocentric, impulsive, cognitively simple
2. dependent and compliant
3. independent, questioning, self-assertive
4. interdependent, empathic and cognitively complex

The therapists were rated using the same descriptions, with none classified as the first. Aftercare setting was rated similarly. Ignoring the likelihood that the recovery rates following were impossibly high, the magnitudes of difference are probably valid and certainly illuminating. With matched alcoholic and therapist or alcoholic and setting, there was a 70% and 71% recovery rate respectively; without the matches, the recovery rates were 50% and 49%. With all three matched, the recovery rate was 77%, while with all three mismatched the recovery rate was only 38%. Can you see the pattern here? The more matches, the higher the rate of recovery.

Because the study was published several years before David Keirsey wrote "Please Understand Me" (which popularized Psychological Type and Temperament), we can only hypothesize which Temperaments can be linked to each personality style rated. However, the possibilities are intriguing. The first, "impulsive," best describes the Artisan, who may appear more egocentric than others due to his need to be seen and "make an impact." He can appear poorly socialized because of an anti-authority attitude (which can become extreme while a practicing addict) and be seen as "cognitively simple" as a result of "having no use for theories." The Artisan's maladaptation to alcoholism is the most dangerously egocentric of all the Tempera-

[384] Keirsey, in "Please Understand Me – II," suggests that barely over 15% of the population is truly introspective.

[385] McLachlan, John F. C., "Therapy Strategies, Personality Orientation, and Recovery from Alcoholism," 1974, Canadian Psychiatric Association Journal, 19:25-30, reported in "Heavy Drinking: The Myth of Alcoholism as a Disease," Herbert Fingarette, Berkeley: University of California Press, 1989, p. 117-118. The irony of finding this extremely important study referred to in Fingarette's work (in which it is believed that addicts should just learn to control their drinking) has not escaped me.

ments. The fact that none of the therapists matched the style further supports the case that this describes Artisans, since few therapists are this Temperament, uninterested as Artisans are in theories such as those common to human psychology.

"Dependent and compliant" is closest to the Guardian, the Temperament that most values compliance with rules and law, while comfortable doing so. "Independent, questioning and self-assertive" describes the analytical and abstract rational. "Interdependent, empathic and cognitively complex" almost perfectly define the humanitarian Idealist.

Temperament and occupation

Another excellent clue to Temperament is occupational choice. Graham has given us additional tools by his suggestion that addicts pursue professions in which they can inflate their ego.

Many if not most addicts have their first drink (thus entering early-stage addiction) long before they select a career. If they can inflate their ego by becoming supremely successful at a chosen occupation, they may stave off latter-stage addiction. People are far more likely to be successful at work that fits their Temperament. Therefore, we can predict that many Artisan addicts (employing their tactical brilliance, excellent coordination and need to have fun) might become entertainers or professional athletes. This allows them to exercise power over their audience and fans. Or, they may become top business executives and politicians, exerting power over employees and constituents. Rational addicts may exercise their strategic and integrative intelligence by becoming philosophers, lawyers or politicians, employing power over minds and people rather than nature. Idealist addicts may become actors and therapists, because such professions not only allow them to use their innate empathic and diplomatic intelligence to their fullest, but also offer the ability to feed their ego through the exercise of power over audiences of many or one. They, like Artisans, may also become con men through their brilliant use of such innate intelligence. Guardian addicts might seek positions in law enforcement out of the conflicting desires to both enforce and violate the law in ways that allow for ego inflation.

Figure 13 - Ego-Inflating Professions for the Early-Stage Addict

Temperament	Profession	Gives Power Over
Artisan (SP)	Entertainers, athletes, politicians	Audiences, fans, constituents
Guardian (SJ)	Police, judges, prosecutors	Criminals, citizens
Rational (NT)	Philosophers, lawyers, politicians	Minds, juries, constituents
Idealist (NF)	Actors, therapists	Audiences, patients

Author James Graham discusses the Charles M. Fickert and Charles Whitman cases (cited earlier), in which these two alcoholic District Attorneys falsely accused innocent men of heinous crimes. What might not seem obvious is the possibility that other areas in law enforcement may be attractive to early-stage addicts, particularly those of the Guardian Temperament who use only the legal drug alcohol, along with Artisans who may stick to legal substances out of practical necessity.

Police have one of the highest divorce and suicide rates of all professions. Several policemen have confided that they believe addiction (especially to the alcohol in beer) is epidemic among officers. One, a recovering addict retired from a small police department in the Northeast, thinks a least half of his 30 fellow officers were alcoholics. Another, a Drug Recognition Expert in a department of 50, thinks about 35 to 40% are practicing, not just in his department but in most. Other officers concur. The lowest estimate is from an aware and sober officer in a large police department in the Southwest, who estimates that a third of the police on his force are either active or recovering addicts. The reports from recovering former inmates (who hold no identifiable grudges) are that half of prison guards are practicing alcoholics. At least some former guards agree. Addicts guarding addicts could certainly explain much of what goes down in prison. Obviously, statistics do not (and may never) exist that will prove these assertions. It bears repeating: when the afflicted will not and cannot self-diagnose or agree with a diagnosis offered by others, we can't obtain reliable statistics, particularly of early-stage highly functional and over-achieving addicts.

If we observe addict-like behaviors of a prison guard, we would do well to consider the possibility he may be a Guardian addict who would best be served by offering a treatment program consistent with this inborn preference. Take two addict politicians, one of whom seems to have an unmatched strategic ability to engage in corrupt activities, another with unparalleled tactical brilliance repeatedly under investigation for corrupt practices, yet always able to slip through the noose. We can assist their life-affirming interests by helping the former consider a Rational-based recovery program and the latter an Artisan-based program. If destructive behaviors are found in a carpenter, there is a high probability an Artisan type of recovery program will help him stay sober, while if such behaviors exist in a writer, the odds are, an Idealist style program will best help. Knowing this can give us a tremendous edge in helping the addict.

Temperament and "bottoming out"

Knowing core needs may help us predict what it will take for an addict to hit bottom, and how deep that bottom might be. The greatest difficulty in making such a prediction is the degree of brain damage the addict has inflicted upon himself. The greater the damage, the greater the difficulty in gaining and achieving permanent sobriety.

The sorts of things perceived as costs and benefits is based (at least in part) on one's Temperament, particularly at fundamental levels. The loss of ability to meet one's core needs is a cost, while the opposite is a benefit. The sort of pain required for motivating an addict to get clean and sober may be predicted from his Temperament (even though the degree of that pain is largely unpredictable). Because Judging types need external structure, it's possible few Judgers allow the affliction to create total disarray in their lives before seeking sobriety. Alternatively, they may be quicker to recover, once they see their lives in turmoil. Because they are work oriented, the bottom may be the loss of their job, not allowing their lives to slide to the depths that a play-oriented Perceptive might.

We need to do everything possible to help raise that bottom which addicts must experience. Guardians have a desire for stability arising from their need for duty, obligation and responsibility, while Artisans need to act on impulse. Anything giving rise to perceptions (even though numbed and distorted by euphoric recall and memory repression) of instability, such as a loss of job or spouse, may cause a Guardian to hit bottom. An Artisan may bottom through loss of freedom. An Introverted and sensitive Idealist may feel little pain from loss of memory, while a Rational, requiring a clear mind for the nurturing of ideas and knowledge, might bottom out at the first hint of suffering a blackout. The independent-minded Rationals are far less likely to experience pain from loss of friends and family than might an Idealist, who would likely feel enormous pain from such loss of connections.

Those who have been identified as Rational recovering addicts provide testimonials to higher bottoms than do other Temperaments, with less of a need for AA and therapy in recovery. When one Rational (an INTJ) was asked what caused her to bottom, she responded, "I'm not a good example." After persisting, she told me she had heard herself drunk on an audiocassette. I asked, "Was that all?" to which she responded, "I told you, I'm not a good example." Asking if she ever relapsed and how often she went to meetings, she again insisted that she just was not a good example. Pressing further, she told me that when she remained abstinent for three days, she never drank again. She attended AA for only a year and went to a meeting maybe once a week. I pointed out to her that, for her Temperament, she was a terrific example.

Another Rational was threatened with divorce. He quit using and, although never attending an AA meeting has not relapsed in 12 years. Yet another Rational (an INTP), Gus, snapped at his wife and complained about everything. (A common thread often seems to be "bitching" only to those with whom the addict has a committed relationship.) He was extremely negative, unforgiving and intolerant of errors either in himself or others. His wife walked on eggshells and "fixed" everything for fear of irritating him. Told by a doctor that drinking would kill him, he stopped cold turkey only to smoke more dope. When warned that his employer was beginning random drug tests, he simply stopped using. Six months later, the arguments were a fraction of what they were before and Gus was so improved in terms of behavior that I thought he was a new man. Addicts usually go far deeper and require greater tragedies before successfully attaining sobriety. Some would ask if these Rationals are really addicts; all except Gus consider themselves so. All the behaviors changed in spades.

Ulysses S. Grant, the only Rational U.S. President identified as an alcoholic, stopped drinking after the Civil War. He apparently abstained for the rest of his life, including during his Presidency.[386] That this occurred at all is even more remarkable in an age without AA, other recovery institu-

---

[386] *Graham, Ibid., p. 138. Keirsey and Ray Choiniere identified the Presidents' Types in "Presidential Temperament: The Unfolding of Character in the Forty Presidents of the United States," Del Mar, CA: Prometheus Nemesis Book Company, 1992.*

tions or any basic understanding of the disease; a time during which the founders of AA estimated as few as 2% of alcoholics ever achieved permanent sobriety. The other alcoholic Presidents who James Graham has identified, Andrew Johnson (a Guardian) and Franklin Pierce (an Artisan), remained active alcoholics during their respective Presidencies.

Vernon Johnson noted that "people who appear phlegmatic seem less likely to become addicted to alcohol or other mood-changing chemicals."[387] Phlegmatics are Hippocrates' Rationals.[388] As we have seen, they may be less likely to succumb to latter stage addiction, accounting for Johnson's observation.

Guardians, although along with the structured Idealists (NFJs) the greatest enablers, may also have an ability to spontaneously get clean and sober. One (an ISFJ) looked at the chaos in her life and proceeded to attempt to clean up. A 30-day visit at a rehabilitation clinic failed upon release. Three years later she tried again. This time, she went to a couple of AA meetings a week for 2 or 3 months and has been clean for 2 years. An introvert, she tells me she did better on her own, reading AA literature, than by sharing (an extroverted task) at meetings and therapy. Another (an ISTJ) never identified with the group sharing, yet stayed clean and sober on her own. As Guardians, they are both structured and outcome-oriented in the world around them. Once on the right path, this may have helped them in staying the course.

Artisans may be at the opposite extreme. A disproportionately high percentage of incarcerated prisoners are probably Artisans, according to Type and Temperament professionals. In some studies, such prisoners more often measure SJ (Guardian) on the Myers-Briggs Type Indicator. However, these studies are believed to be in error, due to both the difficulty of accurately typing an addict and the fact Artisans frequently score anything but SP.

Linda V. Berens, a former student of Keirsey and a Temperament expert, has studied Artisans in depth. She explains that they are chameleon-like and extraordinarily adaptable to the situation at hand. They are brilliant tacticians and opportunists in every sense of the word. They will become whomever they must, in order to survive. Berens moderated a panel of seven Artisans at the 1993 International Convention of the Association for Psychological Type. Five had previously scored not only as Types totally different from that which they determined years later to be accurate, but also as different Temperaments. Discovering their true Type and Temperament was reported as a "liberating" experience for each of

---

[387] *Johnson, Ibid., p. 3.*
[388] *NFs are Choleric, SJs Melancholic and SPs Sanguine, in Hippocrates' terminology of human Temperament.*

them.[389]

The Artisans are novelty seeking, action and excitement-oriented people, who in their extreme form need constant stimulation. They may also be the least understood of the Temperaments. They are not left to their own devices from the earliest ages when, in school, they are given Ritalin (a drug for hyperactive children) just because they can't sit still. However, put them on the playing field or give them tools to master (or clock radios to take apart and put back together, which they may well do at age 3 or 4!) and you'll have a healthy Artisan living his dream. By giving him Ritalin, we may set the stage for cocaine addiction, because Ritalin can be a lead-in drug to cocaine and give the impression that what others perceive as behavior problems are solved with drugs. More importantly, perhaps, we set the stage for extended use in the Artisan with a predisposition to addiction. He seeks excitement, yet has been drugged into sitting still, thus forcing him to violate his own core needs and values.

Artisans would be expected to go deeper in the affliction than do others, even left to their own devices. They enjoy play, having sometimes-wild fun, acting on impulse while seeking action, excitement, stimulation and freedom. What have alcohol and other drugs signified from time immemorial? All the above. Levels of neurotransmitter activity that other Temperaments may experience as adequate, may not be for the pleasure-seeking Artisan. As extroverted Sensory Types in the Myers-Briggs paradigm, they may appear hedonistic. They love the texture of things soft and velvety, the taste of delicious foods, pretty sights, lovely sounds and the smell of a wonderful aroma. Since substances (at first) seem to magnify these senses, they are likely to experiment to a far greater extent than are others. Endowed by nature with an inclination to "test restraints on their action"[390] (which may be experienced as an aversion to authority), Artisans are more likely to gravitate toward illegal substances, resulting in a greater likelihood of incarceration. Guardians, in contrast, often stick with the legal drug alcohol and doctor-prescribed drugs (gravitating toward the legal opioids and downers, possibly in an effort to reduce stress, according to Alice Fairhurst). Guardians, along with Rational and Idealist Judgers (NTJs and NFJs), have been generally observed to stay more within legal

---

[389] *For advanced Type theorists: in addition, the questions on the J/P dichotomous preference are, in my opinion, flawed, particularly for introverted types. Questions asked are so vague that if a J chooses to read them in an internal (or introverted) way, he may score P and if a P reads them from an external (or extroverted) point of view, he may score J. We are all both Perceptives and Judgers, displaying to the world the opposite function of our internal preferences. Since the J/P scale is supposed to report our extroverted function, the questions should be revised so they can be read strictly from this point of view.*

[390] *From an interview with Temperament expert Alice Fairhurst.*

constraints in their use, while Artisans, along with Rational and Idealist Perceptives (NTPs and NFPs) may stray more outside the law.

Temperament and the games addicts play

Artisans are also more likely to engage in "survival" games ("coping strategies") that are dangerous to others. Another of Keirsey's students, Eve Delunas, describes the Keirseyan Game Model in *Survival Games Personalities Play*.[391] People typically engage in destructive games when they feel "their sense of self-esteem, self-respect, and self-confidence is in jeopardy."[392] These usually occur when under intense internal pressure due to unmet core needs or violation of internal values. As Johnson pointed out, the latter is symptomatic of addicts.

Coping strategies vary by Temperament and are manifestations of addiction. Therefore, while psychologists cannot treat the addict (since the addiction must first be arrested), we may be able to determine an addict's Temperament by observing the survival games played. This may help us predict the sorts of crises and intervention he needs to help hit bottom. We can then assist in recovery by offering guidance in meeting his particular core needs in non-addictive and responsible ways.

Coping strategies are "people's desperate attempts to defend themselves in overwhelmingly threatening social environments."[393] While appearing absurd, self-defeating and destructive to the observer, they are a person's perceived solutions to difficult situations. The only way to make sense of the fact that the "perceived" solutions are really not solutions at all (yet still tried) is to go back to addiction 101, recalling that the addict's perceptions are distorted.

Graham points out that the egomaniac-alcoholic does not like rules. Neither do sociopaths. Artisans, even healthy ones, also don't like rules, but they put up with them. Now, picture an Artisan addict who, due to his disease, has become an out of control egomaniac exhibiting sociopathic behavior. Get the picture?

Other Temperaments can demonstrate destructive behavior, but usually not to the extent of the Artisan. For example, in a 1989 letter of apology to his wife, Nicole Brown Simpson, O.J. Simpson (an Artisan) wrote,

[391] *Eve Delunas, "Survival Games Personalities Play," Carmel, CA: SunInk Publications, 1992.*
[392] *Ibid., p. 19.*
[393] *Ibid., p. 19.*

"...I'm not going to blame being drunk [for having struck you] that's (sic) no excuse. (But I have decided to stop drinking and will go to AA)"[394] (parentheses in the original).

Survival games have a number of unconscious psychological purposes, including resolution of the fact that the social environment, <u>from the game player's point of view</u>, is preventing him from meeting core needs. If Artisans are unable to follow their impulses (remember: impulses increase when under the influence), they are likely to begin playing these survival games. For the Artisan, this can occur when still young and sober. If they are not seen as impressive in both their own and others' eyes, even non-addict Artisans may play the games as a means of masking inadequacy or to put "others in a one-down position"[395] (a means of gaining the upper hand). A sub-conscious ego inflating tool, they control their relationships with others, all the while denying taking such control. Delunas points out, the player is not really enjoying himself and may be doing others great harm. Yet they play and pay the price, "in order to protect the tiny remnants of self-worth that they have left...."[396] This sounds remarkably similar to the addict with zero self-esteem who inflates his ego.

The most dangerous games are those Delunas calls "Blackmail," most frequently played by Artisans. The player blackmails another with threats of taking or destroying a valued item, if they can't get what they want. The valued item may be their own self by suicide, self-mutilation or a drug binge. However, it could take the form of physical or psychological harm to another person, or "might even be the other's reputation."[397] The latter appears amazingly similar to Graham's "false accusations" of which addicts are often guilty, whether accusing one of adultery or sexual child abuse.

The variations of Blackmail clearly tend toward the criminal. These include *Delinquency, Con Artist, Binge* and *Outrage*. In *Delinquency* the player may lie, cheat, steal and do anything else considered immoral or illegal. Delunas describes what a *Delinquency* player does if caught: they "usually deny any wrongdoing, often blaming someone else for their misbehavior. For example, the Delinquency player who has stolen a car and gotten caught may be quick to point out that the theft was the fault of the owner, who left the vehicle unlocked."[398] This is euphoric recall at work, distorting everything in some self-favored way.

Interestingly, most if not all addicts blame others for problems that are

[394] *Graham, Ibid., p. 99.*
[395] *Delunas, Ibid., p. 21.*
[396] *Ibid., p. 23.*
[397] *Ibid., p. 28.*
[398] *Ibid., p. 28.*

their own, their group's or one in which they have a vested interest. Artisans are probably more likely to engage in overtly criminal acts and then
blame others for such deeds or for having themselves acted criminally or
unethically. Many who are politically motivated blame society for their
ills, poverty and plight. They blame other races and immigrants for their
own problems. This may be a social game of *Delinquency* in which the scope
of the alcoholic's blaming is expanded to accuse people they don't even
know. This may be explained by hypothesizing that the most sanctimo-
nious and zealous advocates of what some call "The Blame Game"[399] are
alcoholic-addict Artisans. The followers, who are less ostentatious and bla-
tant, are more likely to be addicts of other Temperaments or naïve non-
addicts. Remembering that addicts are the greatest salesmen, we should
never underestimate their ability to lure non-addicts into doing things they
normally would not. However, chances are, these followers are more likely
addicts than the societal norm.

In another variation of Blackmail called *Con Artist*, the player "evokes
pity, guilt, or sympathy from others when it is to their own advantage to do
so, such as in the case of...the perfectly healthy adult who manages to collect disability payments."[400] They always have a good excuse for doing
what they do and are expert at gaining the confidence of others. This player
may be the master of financial fraud.[401] A subcategory of lying, con-art-
istry is clearly an observable symptom of alcoholism. The implications in
selecting those with whom to entrust one's money, including the selection
of companies, mutual funds and financial advisors with which to invest,
may be profound. It should be noted that both *Delinquency* and *Con Artist*
mimic anti-social personality disorder. Those playing these games are dangerous people.

In *Binge* (yet another variation of Blackmail), the player "may persis-

[399] *ABC News Correspondent John Stossel hosted a 1997 special depicting people who assign blame throughout the legal and political system.*

[400] *Delunas, Ibid., p. 29. This player is almost invariably the ESTP, which can be discerned by reading Keirsey's description of this Type, reported in the next footnote.*

[401] *The Psychological Type that may compete for the honors of "world's greatest salesman" is the ESTP. If psychologically healthy, they will tell you, "Yes, we are great salesmen," a skill that could be used for evil, if they so desired. When unhealthy they may be the source of many of the world's greatest financial scams. A reading between the lines of Keirsey's description of the ESTP in "Please Understand Me," Ibid., is revealing: "ESTPs are socially sophisticated, suave and urbane and are master manipulators of the external environment....uncanny at observing people's motivations....masters at using these observations to 'sell' the client." Combined with Keirseyan Game Theory, it could be argued on a theoretical basis that the psychologically unhealthy ESTP could con the greatest substance addict con-artists. Reading from my extensive files of financial scams, the descriptions of the perpetrators almost always appear to be the ESTP or substance addict. I now believe that the best are likely both.*

tently over-indulge in substances such as food, alcohol or other drugs, or in activities like spending, speeding, sex, or gambling....often [vacillating] between periods of great excitement and periods when they are feeling empty."[402] Delunas feels that Artisans (while not alone in the ability to binge) are more likely than the other Temperaments to binge, purge, and "abuse" both alcohol and illegal drugs. What she may have observed is that Artisans have a propensity to carry such use to extremes.

The Artisan "SP" is the person who most wants to appear graceful to others. Although the cost of playing Blackmail is appearing disgraceful, the payoff is excitement and revenge. The need to acquire and abuse power can overwhelm the egocentric addict-Artisan. The game of *Delinquency* is a means of over-powering others <u>overtly</u> through destruction, while the Artisan game of *Con Artist* is a means of controlling others <u>covertly</u> through seduction.[403] *Outrage* is another game Artisans play more often than do the other Temperaments. This is where the player abuses and controls others by harming them physically or mentally through violent outbursts.

Delunas's wonderful work in Keirseyan Game Models has been cited extensively because of the fact that there is an obvious correlation between addiction and Game-playing behaviors. Others have either failed or have been fearful of making this connection due to what might be perceived as unfair labeling. Yet, the taboo must be broken if we are to better understand addiction in its many different forms. This helps make identification easier and makes sense of the nonsensical. The effect of addiction varies by Temperament. When addiction is superimposed over the sorely misunderstood Artisan, the result can be catastrophic. Yet, healthy Artisans are able to teach those of other Temperaments how to play more and "live for today," while living life to its fullest.

By way of comparison, the games other Temperaments tend to play are relatively benign. While they may be psychologically destructive, they can be more harmful to the addict himself. If we are not too close to a person, they could be just annoying. According to Delunas,[404] Guardians play the "Complain" games. These include *Invalid* ("I'm suffering"), *Worried* (fear of things going wrong), *Doormat* (allowing themselves to be stepped on), *Poor Me* ("look at the heavy burdens I must bear"), *Depressed* ("there is no hope") and *Nag* ("you should feel, think and do" this or that).

[402] *Delunas, Ibid., p. 30.*

[403] *For Type theorists: it may be interesting to note that the Introverted Artisan is most flagrant in the overt game of Delinquency, while the Extroverted Artisan is the most frequent player of Con Artist. The reasons for this may be related to the "shadow" functions, which are less developed than the dominant ones. This is particularly true for the STPs. The "shadow" of Introverted STPs is extroverted Feeling, while the Extrovert's is introverted iNtuition.*

[404] *Delunas, Ibid., pp. 25-43.*

The purpose is to make others feel obligated to take care of them. The end result is, the Guardian, whose core need is to be responsible, becomes irresponsible. Observing such games is a clue to addiction and Guardian Temperament. Rationals play the "Robot" games of *That's Illogical* ("your emotions, values and intuition are illogical"), *Super-Intellectual* (cold, distant and devoid of emotion), *Nitpick* (not getting the big picture and nothing is ever good enough), *Superstition* (going to extremes to avoid germs, people, places or things), *Blanking Out* (can't remember names, words or numbers) and *Haunted* (unable to make unpleasant thoughts go away). The point of these games is to distract, so that others won't notice the Rational's failures. The paradox is, the Rational becomes irrational. Again, such games often signify addiction (or codependency[405]) in a person whose Temperament is Rational.

Idealists play "Masquerade" games. These include, *Mind Reader* ("I know what you're *really* thinking or feeling!"), *Martyr* ("I'm sacrificing myself for you"), *Grasshopper* (avoiding one topic by hopping around in conversation), *Statue* (loss of motor or sensory functioning in inappropriate places or times), *Forgetful* (forgetting whatever may be unpleasant[406]) and *Twitch* (increase in motor activity or verbal outbursts, pouring out all their repressed feelings accumulated over time). The motive for these particular games is deception and keeping others' attention off the Idealist's unethical behavior by getting them to focus on some other "problem." The paradox is the Idealist, who to esteem himself must be ethical and real, becomes the opposite. I would hypothesize that the addicted Idealist playing these games may become as dangerous a con artist in financial and other scams as the Artisan addict. Once again, these are clues to both addiction and Idealist Temperament.

[405] *Remember, codependent behaviors can mimic those of the addict.*
[406] *This can, in extreme cases, result in multiple personalities and/or memory repression.*

Figure 14 – Games Addicts Play and Psychopathological Disorders for Which They May be Mistaken

Dangerous Games or Descriptors		Psychopathological Disorder Mimicked
Artisan	Blackmail, Con Artist, Delinquent	Manic, Sociopath (Psychopath)
Guardian	Complain, Poor Me, Nag	Depressive Illness
Rational	You're Illogical, Over Intellectualize, "Nit-Pick"	Obsessive-Compulsive Disorder
Idealist	Masquerade, Mind Reader, Avoiding the Subject	Hysteria, Catatonia, Schizophrenia, Dissociative Disorder

The distorted perceptions of substance addiction make it easy to self-delude and believe that these games can accomplish their intended purpose. Therefore, if any survival games are observed, antennae should go up. At least they should have for me, since my addict ex- played all the Idealist games right under my nose. Eventually, recognizing the games proved to be the clues I needed in confirming her true Temperament. Had we stayed together, this might have proved instrumental in intervention and recovery.

I have previously noted amazement that any addict ever achieves permanent sobriety. Their behavior is so perverse that, once remembered, any sober individual could be driven to drink. The recognition, acceptance and overcoming of defects and harmful behaviors are a process of replacing negatives with positives. When positives are powerful enough, negatives cannot survive. When action is taken to rectify the wrongs committed, the commitment to stay clean and sober can more easily be kept. The addict must become honest and remain that way, knowing that he must stay clean and sober to do so. The cycle of lie and use must be replaced with truth and sobriety. We can help trigger the need for sobriety by standing aside as crises occur, or even by helping them come about. With our understanding of Temperament, we can help the addict in sobriety understand the values with which he must live to stay sober. But first, we must intervene, to forge the connection between his problems and his drinking and using. We must also inform him that we will no longer enable.

Intervention

"The real reason we intervene is that spontaneous insight is impossible."[407]

Substance addiction is a multi-faceted disease that eventually affects every area of an addict's life: physiological/biological, psychological, sociological and financial. The treatment must be as multi-faceted, with a holistic approach that leaves no stones unturned. Most of these treatments can overlap in time.

Figure 15 – Time Lines for Taking Action

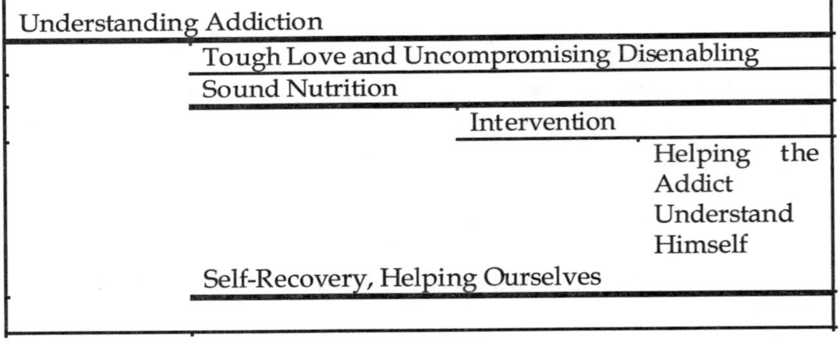

Understanding Addiction

Tough Love and Uncompromising Disenabling

Sound Nutrition

Intervention

Helping the Addict Understand Himself

Self-Recovery, Helping Ourselves

Recall that the addict is incapable of seeing that he has a problem with a substance until there are multiple crises in his life. Non-addicts and recovering addicts can (as newly trained Drug Addiction Recognition Experts™) tentatively diagnose the disease. It is up to them to inextricably link the problems in the addict's life with the use of substances. In confirmed sobriety (i.e., with blood and urine testing, if necessary), the diagnosis will be proven correct as the destructive behaviors gradually sub-

[407] *Johnson, Ibid., p. 65.*

side.

Intervention is best done sooner than later to prevent nervous tissue damage and irreversible chemical changes in the brain's ability to produce its own neurotransmitters. We have seen that children can be full-blown addicts. The parents' job (or society's if the parent is an addict) is to intervene at as young an age as possible within the constraints of a necessary build-up of crises.

A formal intervention is a frank depiction of specific destructive incidents for which addict was responsible. The most meaningful people in the addict's life (family, friends, co-workers, employers, teachers, doctors, clergy, etc.) should make the presentation, in the presence of an intervention-trained professional. The presentation must be conducted in a non-judgmental fashion, with an undercurrent of deep concern. The addict is informed, in a loving way, that he has the disease of substance addiction, which is causing him problems and resulting in adverse impacts on both close and, often, not so close persons. He must be told this because, as we have shown, he cannot see it himself, thus making him incapable of linking his troubles or behavior to the use of substances.

The intervention must be done when the addict is most likely sober, so a weekday early morning may be the best time. For maximum effectiveness, it must be when the addict is experiencing pain from a crisis, or preferably from a confluence of such crises (for example, loss of job, a DUI or other arrest, impending divorce and/or other calamity). He needs to be shown that the deadly, progressive disease of addiction is affecting his entire life. Facts are presented non-accusationally, leaving out personal opinions about his use of the substance, yet tying that use to as many specific problems in the life of the addict as possible.

Please keep in mind that when intervening there must be a united front among all the participants. One weak link can break the chain and destroy what would otherwise be a successful intervention. For example, in the movie *Stewart Saves His Family*, the whole family intervenes in the father's alcoholism. Everything was going well until the mother caved in by saying, "Maybe he could just cut down on his drinking." This effectively ended the intervention.

It is likely each participant in the intervention will hear stories that will be surprising. While many witness the bizarre and destructive behaviors of the addict, in classic enabling fashion, they tend not to share the stories of such behaviors with others, since that "might hurt them." We have all been guilty of being silent about the developing condition, thereby supporting the affliction's progress.[408] Expect to hear stories that will rattle or shock and try to avoid expressions of surprise or judgments of what others

---

[408] *Johnson, Ibid., p. 52.*

reveal.

Make <u>perceptions</u>, not judgments. Addicts don't want advice and, besides, their ego renders them incapable of receiving it. Since euphoric recall causes them to believe everything they have done is good or right, they cannot believe they need help. Since you and close others are the source of their problems, <u>you</u> are the one who needs counseling and psychotherapy and, indeed, "you" may be the addict.

Promises of future actions that will be taken if the use continues should be made matter-of-factly <u>and must be kept</u>. (We know what those tough love decisions, harder on us than on the addict, must be.) A choice of a specific rehabilitation program or AA should be offered, allowing the addict the dignity of being involved in the decision-making process in order to maximize the probability of successful intervention and later minimize the chance of undetected relapse. A therapist assisting in the intervention and follow-up counseling should be a Certified Chemical Dependency Counselor, Certified Alcohol and Drug Counselor, or other similar professional who is an expert in intervention and substance addiction. The follow-up therapy may be more for the close person to keep them on a non-enabling track, since the addict cannot yet be treated for psychological disorders that may exist independently of the addiction.

Early interventions are far easier and superior in every way, except one. Due to the fact that there are fewer (if any) crises in such early stage addiction, it may be impossible to convince the addict he has a problem. This is the reason we must help to create a number of crises as quickly as possible. Contrary to the apparent belief of many during the presidential impeachment hearings of 1998, friends should indeed assist friends in experiencing consequences (as with the Linda Tripp-Monica Lewinsky-Bill Clinton connection). The earlier in the progression of addiction in which massive levels of pain are experienced, the greater the likelihood intervention will accomplish its intended purpose of recovery and eventual long-term sobriety. A lengthy period of psychoactive drug use eventually causes brain damage so severe that post-acute withdrawal makes it only more difficult to get and stay sober.

Although difficult, intervention can take the form of private confrontation. The confronter explains to the addict he has a disease and offers him an answer to the problem. Recovering alcoholic Father Joseph C. Martin points out, "It is absolutely amazing how many alcoholics have never been told that [they have this disease], so they go along merrily drinking themselves to death and hurting others in the process, many of them wishing subconsciously, desperately, that somebody would approach them with help."[409] Confront with love, concern and a solution, an offer to take the

---

[409] *Father Martin, Ibid., p. 97.*

addict for help. Show no sympathy about their other problems, remembering their origin <u>and the primary issue</u> is addiction. We <u>cannot</u> know differently until abstinence and a modicum of recovery is achieved.

Without the power of numbers in more formal interventions, along with the expertise of an intervention specialist, the defense mechanisms of the typical addict will overwhelm all but the toughest, most tenacious and knowledgeable non-addict (even if, one-on-one, everything is done right). The story of the Ford family's successful group intervention with Betty Ford stand in stark contrast to the millions of unplanned and failed interventions (which are usually merely accusations and threats) that some repeatedly attempt. Successful intervention requires cooperation (the addict would call it "conspiracy") on the part of those who love and care about him. For sober individuals to engage in this without guilt, they must be absolutely convinced addiction is the source of virtually all his problems. If you're still not certain of this, head straight back to <u>another</u> dozen AA meetings, re-read this book and pick up several from the bibliography. Successful intervention requires getting past the point of minimizing the problem by telling the addict "you really are drinking too much lately," "you really ought to think about stopping" and "you aren't young anymore; then you could handle it, now you can't." Total abstinence from all psychoactive drugs is the <u>only</u> goal.

Since the likelihood of overt hostility on the part of the addict is great, do not let your suspicions be known until you're virtually certain of your position. This serves another purpose: it maximizes the manifestations of addiction, including both grotesque and other bizarre behaviors, along with necessary crises (remember the Graham-Heisenberg principle). Such indicators may be essential in providing additional evidence you or others may still need to prove that addiction is the root problem. Besides, as soon as the addict knows you suspect, he might make promises to clean up his act in a non-addictive fashion—i.e. "I won't drink *so much* any more," etc., all the while claiming he doesn't have *that* problem. As we've learned, his superhuman ability to improve *for a while* can fool even those very knowledgeable about the disease.

The aware and mindful observer is in a better position to provide specific incidences of problems associated with addiction. Since drawing on specific events is so important to successful intervention, you shouldn't hesitate to pull a "Tripp," in which the addict is video- or audiotaped while under the influence.[410] For some, hearing and/or seeing oneself behaving like an incoherent, stuttering, slurring and nonsensical idiot, telling lies, or engaging in other perverse behavior will be enough to create that bottom. Then, there can be little argument over the facts (I'd say "no argument,"

---

[410] *Don't do this in Maryland.*

but remember with whom we are dealing). It <u>may</u> prove to the addict, once and for all, his memory cannot be relied upon, particularly if we ask for a description of the events that were taped before viewing or listening to it with the addict (and perhaps taping the description as well!). We must use every tool possible to prove that the addict's use of alcohol and/ or other drugs is the root source of innumerable problems in and around him.

Remember also, motivation is furnished by the pursuit of pleasure and the avoidance of pain. What is perceived as pleasure and pain differs by Temperament and is radically different from that which the non-addict experiences. Consequences that the sober among us would experience as excruciating, may be hardly felt by the addict. As Father Martin points out, pain is a positive force in the life of an addict, eventually allowing him to get well. That is why uncompromising disenabling is of supreme importance, greatly increasing the odds of successful intervention. The addict who has not been at least partially disenabled by the beginning of the intervention stands close to a zero chance of achieving sobriety because, quite simply, he will fail to see the need to seek further help. The Oriental tenet, "there is opportunity in crisis," holds true more for the addict than for anybody else. Still, expect nothing and you won't be disappointed. With expectations, more likely than not you will be frustrated, since even if intervention accomplishes its short-term goal of abstinence, long-term sobriety may still prove elusive.

There are some instances in which more extreme measures may be warranted, but with great risk of reprisal if there is failure. One writer suggests, in some states, "You can go to the Supreme Bench's Court-system's Medical Division and get him picked up for a psychiatric evaluation. You should explain that you want him committed to an alcoholism treatment center."[411] We've already recounted numerous stories in which the addict conned everyone, including the psychiatrist. Unless there is latter-stage addiction or a psychiatrist well versed in the affliction, this strategy may not only fail, but could result in the addict making false accusations against <u>you</u>. Extreme caution is advised, since an addict's lies are almost always more believable than your truths. For example, false accusations by the addict that you have engaged in vile or illegal acts with children are commonly made, especially in custody battles.

---

[411] *Toby Rice Drews, "Getting them Sober, Volume 1: A Guide for Those Who Live With an Alcoholic," South Plainfield, NJ: Bridge Publishing, Inc., 1980, p. 66.*

Nutritional support

Contrary to the belief of some recovering alcoholics that we should be able to drink in front of them, this should not be done. This is particularly true for early recovery, always tenuous at best. The Pavlov factor should not be underestimated. There is no reason to add temptation to the tremendous difficulty in overcoming the disease. Lucy Barry Robe lends support to this in discussing alcoholic Carson McCullers and her husband Reeves, an alcoholic who committed suicide. Although he intermittently tried to stay sober, "There are no reports that Carson ever stopped drinking, which must have made her husband's attempts all the more difficult for him."[412] Robe later matter-of-factly states, "A recovering alcoholic has a tough time staying sober if his or her alcoholic spouse continues to drink."[413] There is no difference in principle whether the spouse is alcoholic or not (and if not, it's so much easier to stop drinking). Ludwig's research on alcoholics, craving and Pavlovian connections lends additional support to this thesis.[414] One can imagine an addict's brain connecting the non-addict's drinking to his own and to the good times he remembers associated with the drinking or other use.

You might be asking yourself, why is this in the category of nutritional support? It's simple. If we maintain contact with the addict, we can help with sound nutrition by both setting an example and actually bringing home healthy food. Doing this provides the nutritional support needed to rebuild his damaged brain, along with the psychological support by not tempting with reminders.

As late as 1983, Milam and Ketcham were bemoaning the fact that although nutritional therapy is crucial to successful treatment, it was a "neglected or slighted feature of almost every treatment program in the country."[415] Unfortunately, according to chemically certified therapists and recovering addicts, it hasn't gotten much better. By definition, alcohol is food because it provides calories, containing nearly as much energy per gram as pure fat or oil. However, alcohol contains virtually no vitamins, minerals or proteins. At 170 calories per ounce of alcohol, it is the ultimate empty-calorie junk food (second only to Twinkies). Drinking, then, results in a decreased requirement for calories from other, more nutritious foods.

---

[412] *Robe, Ibid., p. 226.*
[413] *Robe, Ibid., p. 273.*
[414] *Ludwig, Ibid.; see my footnote number 187.*
[415] *Milam and Ketcham, Ibid., p. 152.*

In addition, it disrupts the absorption of vitamins and minerals from food. Therefore, even if the alcoholic is eating well, "alcohol denies him the full nutritional value of what he eats....Thus all alcoholics develop malnutrition regardless of what or how much they eat."[416] The alcoholic bingeing on alcohol is therefore (by definition) malnourished and, with chemical poisoning of a brain deprived of the proper nutrients, brain damaged. Worse still, damage to both brain and liver may reinforce the craving for more alcohol and other drugs.

Terence Gorski suggests that up to 40% of alcoholics are hypoglycemic,[417] the result of eating excessive amounts of sugar and other refined carbohydrates. Milam and Ketcham found that over 95% of both early- and late-stage alcoholics experience a spike, then a rapid plunge in blood sugar, when given the 5-hour glucose tolerance test.[418] This is a sugar "rush" and subsequent "crash," inevitably leading to a craving for yet more sweets (to relieve the symptoms of the crash). This is the reason alcoholics crave junk food, such as donuts and other sweets or simple, processed carbohydrates, especially in early recovery. AA meetings are terrific, but check out the sugar-laden, high artificial carbohydrate, serving table. These may be major contributors to relapse. The addict seems to know instinctively that alcohol is quickly converted to sugar. The early recovery alcoholic may reach for the bottle in lieu of donuts when they need a rush. Most authorities believe the odds of achieving permanent recovery are increased by avoiding the types of foods, including processed carbohydrates, that inevitably lead to a sugar crash.

The addict needs all the help he can get in stabilizing blood sugar. A sugar "crash" results in symptoms of irritability, fatigue, stress, mental confusion and hunger. Such crashes may be occurring in between drinks, accounting for the behaviors. No wonder we are confused about when the addict is using and when not. According to authors Saul and Jo Anne Miller,[419] other behavioral symptoms of low blood sugar include depression, agitation and erratic behavior. Depression includes listlessness, whining and "crying the blues." Agitation includes excitability, impatience, insomnia, irritability, nervousness and tantrums. Erratic behavior includes acting irrationally, blackouts, confusion, delusion, memory lapses, an inability to concentrate and violent outbursts. These are behaviors that appear suspiciously similar to those of addicts.

Alcohol is a big sugar producer, with many alcoholics developing dia-

---

[416] *Milam and Ketcham, Ibid., p. 29.*
[417] *Terence T. Gorski, "Understanding the Twelve Steps," Ibid., p. 23.*
[418] *Milam and Ketcham, Ibid., p. 154.*
[419] *Saul Miller, with Jo Anne Miller, "Food for Thought: A New Look at Food and Behavior," Englewood Cliffs, NJ: Prentice-Hall, 1979, p. 89.*

betes.[420] Because they often eat poor-quality carbohydrates and sugars, many alcoholics are also overweight. One very aware person, who is both a recovering compulsive-overeater and substance addict, estimates that as many as half of those in the eating disorder 12-Step programs may be cross-addicted to psychoactive drugs. The first chemical addiction is often to sugar, which continues through alcoholism and back into sobriety (AA meetings are filled with compulsive eaters).[421] Other drugs, too, may cause large swings in blood-sugar levels. Stimulants cause the adrenals to produce epinephrine, which in turn stimulate the pancreas to secrete insulin, lowering blood-sugar levels. The Millers point out that the effect of marijuana on these levels can be observed in the food cravings the user experiences (otherwise known as the "munchies"). It matters not whether blood-sugar changes are produced by sweet or non-sweet foods. These changes result in increased emotional volatility and seem to be another biological component to addiction (in at least some substance addicts).[422]

The Millers write that liquor and other drugs have a more marked effect on blood sugar levels than even plain white sugar.[423] These effects may contribute to the criminal behavior in addicts. They report on an Argentinean study in which only 13 apprehended delinquents out of 129 had normal blood sugar levels.[424] Although not reported, it can be predicted, with a high degree of certainty, that 80% or so were addicts. It's possible that addiction to alcohol and other drugs is, in part, a manifestation of blood-sugar imbalances.[425] A diet of complex, unrefined carbohy-

---

[420] *Eating too much sugar or refined carbohydrates "teaches" the pancreas to overproduce insulin, which is responsible for sugar absorption into the cells. Too much insulin results in lowered blood sugar levels, accounting for the paradox of too much sugar resulting in too little blood sugar. The craving for sugar, then, is a result of having eaten too much of it.*

[421] *It's interesting to note that while an alcoholic can choose never to drink again, an overeater must still eat. For this reason, compulsive overeating (even while not as dangerous to others) may be more difficult to overcome than is substance addiction. When it comes to the substance itself, Compulsive Eaters Anonymous has a saying: "A substance addict can lock the tiger in a cage and throw away the key. The compulsive eater must walk the tiger 3 times a day."*

[422] *Miller and Miller, Ibid., p. 86-87.*

[423] *Ibid., p. 88.*

[424] *Ibid., p. 91, from a study by N. Rojas and A. F. Sanchi, "Archives of Legal Medicine," 11, p. 29, 1941, reported in "Natural Health, Sugar and the Criminal Mind," by J. I. Rodale, New York: Pyramid Books, 1968.*

[425] *The three biological traits of substance addiction, then, may be sugar imbalance problems, lack of neurotransmitter activity (or an innate desire for more than God gave) and a slower than normal processing of alcohol into acetaldehyde.*

drates, consisting largely of grains, rice and corn, generally results in balanced blood-sugar levels due to the body's slower and more steady breakdown into simple sugars. This leads to more stable behavior. We may diminish volatile behavior patterns by encouraging the addict to take their food in the form of complex carbohydrates or, some suggest, high quality protein and very limited complex, unrefined carbohydrates. Some alcoholism experts can be interpreted as suggesting we might be "setting up" our children for drug dependency by feeding them sugar and refined carbohydrates. It may be argued alternatively that sugar cravings in children might be an early precursor to possible substance addiction.

Bill Wilson, co-founder of AA, "was interested in the connection between his drinking and his 'enormous' sugar intake....He got rid of sugar, 'stabilized his blood sugar and achieved a sense of well-being.'"[426] Susan Powter reports that two M.D.s discovered that between 75% and 95% of alcoholics tested had low blood sugar.[427] She also points out that the "dry-drunk" and person with low-blood-sugar problems have identical symptoms: "irritability, depression, aggressiveness, insomnia, fatigue, restlessness, confusion, desire to drink and nervousness."[428] An essential nutritional program for recovering addicts includes balancing the sugar so that the craving for it stops. This could prevent a recovering addict's digression from a gallon of ice cream to a quart of vodka. All refined sugar must be eliminated, along with radically decreasing levels of sugar by its numerous other names, including corn syrup and any ingredient ending in "-ose." Because simple or refined carbohydrates are so readily converted to sugar, these, too, must be eliminated.

Ironically, I was given a book by my parents for Christmas, 1985, supporting the idea that humans have evolved to function best on an unadulterated non-dairy vegetarian diet (complex, unprocessed carbohydrates).[429] I read most of the book the next day, took one look at my alcoholic father, whose health at 55 years was rapidly crumbling before my eyes and decided I never wanted to become so frail. I went on the diet recommended

---

[426] *Powter, Ibid., p. 208.*
[427] *Ibid.*
[428] *Ibid., p. 208-210.*
[429] *John A. McDougall and Mary A. McDougall, "The McDougall Plan," Clinton, NJ: New Win Publishing, 1985.*

in the book for the better part of 10 years, following it less religiously only recently. I felt 1000% better[430] and, despite having no real understanding of alcoholism, somehow connected my father's addiction to his very poor diet. I even suggested to my mother that his cravings might be reduced with the right foods. She pointed out that when she prepared such food, he wouldn't eat it. Knowing about proper diet alone will not get an alcoholic sober; the desire must be there. Crises in the life of the addict help cause the pain needed to create the desire. Intervention can connect the pain to the use, often triggering an immediate need to get clean and sober. Nutritional support may help provide the means. Also, aerobic exercise, vigorous walking, spiritual and psychological support (as opposed to standard counseling) may also be extremely helpful.

Alcohol causes malnutrition by making the body think that it's filling needs by supplying the heat energy provided by calories. Alcohol also causes dehydration by trickery. It makes the body think that it's getting water. This is similar to drinking salt water. If we were getting water, we would not experience dehydration. Water must be taken in its pure form, not as alcohol or seawater. Furthermore, water is an essential part of the cure for many diseases.[431] Chronic malnutrition and dehydration are the reasons other chronic illnesses may be a clue to substance addiction. The toxic effects of alcohol combined with lack of proper nutrition and hydra-

---

[430] *I still couldn't reduce occasional high blood pressure. I finally read a book on MSG by George R. Schwartz, M.D., "In Bad Taste: The MSG Syndrome," (Santa Fe, New Mexico: Health Press, 1988) which pointed out "natural flavors" usually includes hydrolyzed vegetable (or soy, corn or anything else) protein (HPV), which always includes MSG. I'd already suspected MSG as the source of this condition; eliminating foods with "natural flavors" finally solved the problem. I wonder how many of the 30 million people in the U.S. suffering from "essential hypertension" (meaning they don't know its source) may be allergic, as I apparently am, to MSG in all its forms. I mention this only suggest that not only have we not learned everything there is to know about how our bodies work, but also that it's possible such isolated observations of non-medical individuals could lead to breakthroughs in medical science. Such observations should not be discounted simply because they were made by untrained persons.*

[431] *F. Batmanghelidj, M.D., in "Your Body's Many Cries for Water," Falls Church, VA: Global Health Solutions, Inc., points out that many diseases are a result of a lack of water. I have increased my pure water intake since I read the book and have virtually eliminated repeated sinus problems that I'd had all my life. Batmanghelidj provides testimonials in which patients have cured everything from ulcers and hypertension to high cholesterol by increasing their water intake. This might be a valuable part of a nutritionally based approach in treating addiction.*

tion result in all sorts of disease and maladies.

Without nutritional support and supplementation, the addict may never stay in recovery. Nutritional imbalances, when corrected, have been reported to result in vastly decreased cravings for alcohol.[432] Since alcohol replaces nutritional food, impairs the function of the digestive tract and inhibits absorption of any nutrients ingested, this makes sense. It should not be surprising that if we replace alcohol with real food, the craving for empty calories laced with sugar (or something readily converted to sugar) may decrease. Our bodies tell us what we need. Unfortunately, we sometimes misinterpret the message. This is especially true if (a) we have the genetic predisposition to addiction, (b) we've triggered addiction with use and (c) exacerbated that addiction with behavioral violations of our own internal values. Proper feeding of both body and mind may help reverse this.

An intriguing aid to the feeding of the mind in early sobriety may be caffeine. Recall that one of the triggers to addiction may be a lower level of neurotransmitter activity than normal. Use of drugs, while artificially stimulating neurotransmitter activity (the addict's goal), further impairs the ability to produce neurotransmitters on one's own. Caffeine, by blocking the brake in the brain that slows down neurotransmitter activity (adenosine), allows the activity that remains in the addict's impaired brain to run loose.[433] It may be hypothesized that this may help to prevent the craving that results in relapse. Perhaps this is the reason AA meetings find pots of leaded coffee brewing even late at night. Addicts may have somehow learned that coffee helps them stay sober.

The recovering addict must be extremely careful when he quits smoking. Because "smoking 'rev's up' the liver's caffeine-destroying enzymatic machinery...the half-life of caffeine among smokers" is half that of non-smokers.[434] This would explain the reason for smokers drinking alot more coffee than do non-smokers. When the smoker quits, the effective doubling of, his caffeine intake could aggravate the anxiety, insomnia and irritability endemic to nicotine withdrawal, which could easily help cause the recovering addict to relapse. Smokers should therefore cut their caffeine intake from all sources by half when attempting to quit smoking.

When caffeine was introduced to Europe in the mid-1600s, James Howell wrote, "This coffee drink hath caused a greater sobriety among the Nations. Whereas formerly apprentices and clerks used to take their morning's draught of ale, beer or wine, which by the dizziness they cause in the brain

---

[432] *Reported by Powter, Ibid., p. 155: Stephen Langer, "Addicted: How to Get Relief Naturally," Better Nutrition for Today's Living, May, 1990; Janet Reid, Journal of American Dietetic Association, April 1991.*

[433] *Braun, Ibid., p. 130.*

[434] *Braun, Ibid., p. 121.*

made many unfit for business, they now play the good-fellows in this wake-ful and civil drink." Stephen Braun points out, "The caffeine in coffee, tea, and chocolate-all of which were introduced to Europe at about the same time-neatly dovetailed with the ideals and values of Enlightenment society."[435] The recovering addict sipping his coffee mimics human history in his own, as he moves from the irrational drugs to the rational.

The addict remains muddle-headed in early sobriety (often for long periods) from the poisoning of his brain. He often feels incompetent at his normal employment. Anything he can do to improve his ability to think clearly may help him regain the self-esteem necessary for permanent so-briety. Caffeine, inducing both physical and mental energy, makes "the genius quicker, and in doing so may help transform the addict's own dark ages into his personal enlightenment.[436]

Other approaches that appear to have helped some newly recovering alcoholics stay sober are the use of herbs and acupuncture. Herbs that detoxify and strengthen the liver may be especially helpful, including milk thistle, golden seal, dandelion and a Chinese herb, bupleurum. Another herb, kudzu, has been used for centuries by the Chinese for the treatment of alcohol-related illnesses. Yet another, Xing-Jiu-Ling (XJL) may actually help reduce alcohol intake.[437] Acupuncture has also been reported to sub-stantially reduce cravings for alcohol and other drugs.[438]

---

[435] *Braun, Ibid., p. 124*

[436] *Caffeine is, perhaps, better taken as tea of diet soft drink than coffee. Cofee has a hundred other chemicals in it, at least one of which may impair digestion, causing diarhea, interfering with the assimilation of nutrients. In this, coffee may do greater damage than good.*

[437] *"Complementary Therapies for Alcoholism," Jill Kelly, Ph.D., Alternative and Complementary Therapies, June, 1997.*

[438] *"Demythologizing Acupuncture," Ralph Alan Dale, Ed.D., Ph.D., C.A., Dipl. Ac., Alternative and Complementary Therapies, April, 1997.*

11

Public Policy

Prohibition or choice

"It is dangerous to be right in matters on which the established authorities are wrong."

— Voltaire

The addict, left to his own devices, will eventually sink of his own weight, if we but say no every time he asks us to bail him out. Preventing him from using his drugs through force, however (whether individually or collectively), does nothing but make him more defiant, secretive and creative in obtaining and using his drugs. This has been proven time and again through the ages.

The observant reader may have noticed throughout, never once has the term "alcohol and drugs" been used. Purposely and with intent, only "alcohol and other drugs" has been described simply because many fail to acknowledge that alcohol is a drug. It is, in many respects, the most dangerous one of all. It seems to cause more violence than all other drugs combined.[439] The others can result in violence, but generally not due to their intrinsic action. It is, rather, because they are illegal. But before discussing the current illegality of certain drugs, let us explore the history of various prohibitions.

We have seen that Native Americans are at enormous risk of developing

---

[439] *Parker, Ibid., and Roy, Ibid. Recall that Roy cited studies in which 85% of domestic violence is rooted in alcohol. Parker, describing the relationship between alcohol and homicide, points out that the area is bereft of studies. The trouble is, rarely is the killer diagnosed as an alcoholic. Graham, Ibid., demonstrates many about whom extensive biographies have been written, went undiagnosed as very likely addicts. These include such notable mass and/or serial murderers as Richard Speck, Ted Bundy, John Wayne Gacy, Henry Lee Lucas, Wayne Henley and Jim Jones. According to Graham, only a few, such as Dr. Sam Sheppard and Jeffrey L. Dahmer, have been properly diagnosed as alcoholics by their biographers.*

alcoholism, due to an unavailability of alcohol prior to its introduction by Europeans. Although the sober among them tried, Native Americans failed in their attempt to use religion and law to stigmatize and punish those "who violated commonly held views on the proper consumption of liquor...[and] few were able to develop effective means for limiting alcohol-related problems."[440] Their error was in failing to understand alcoholism and that its incidence differed from those of European ancestry by magnitudes.

Significantly, rather than impose just and proper consequences on those who violated others' rights as a result of alcohol-induced behaviors, Native Americans attempted to control the drug. In many Indian communities, it was common practice to exonerate "anyone who committed even the worst crimes [while] under the influence of alcohol."[441] As early as 1690, some would get drunk on purpose so they could satisfy their urge to gain revenge against enemies, knowing punishment by the tribe could not be inflicted for committing acts of violence, mayhem and even murder while drunk. The enabling was so great, one observer reported that Indians would not mourn for the victim "'for fear of causing pain to the living [perpetrator] by reminding him of his crime.'"[442]

Despite repeated and numerous attempts at control, the flow of alcohol was never arrested. There were many statutes prohibiting the alcohol trade with the Indians. Since there were always buyers with great desire, willing to pay whatever price the black market commanded, there were always sellers willing to accept the risk of being caught.[443] Some Indians would do anything to get alcohol, loving it "'more than their life.'"[444] The craving was compared with that for a desirable woman. A Choctaw explained, "'When a man wanted her — and saw her — He must have her.'"[445] Even well-connected colonists ignored statutes prohibiting the sale of liquor to Indians[446] and some Indian women prostituted themselves for rum, which they then resold to members of their own villages.[447] If this is a reminder of today's drug trade and its participants, it may be considered as evidence that the use and trade in alcohol and other drugs will never be constrained by force of law.

There have been repeated instances of attempts at Prohibition of other

[440] *Mancall, Ibid., p. 120-121.*
[441] *Ibid., p. 121.*
[442] *Ibid., p. 80.*
[443] *Ibid., p. 44-47 and numerous other cites.*
[444] *Ibid., p. 70.*
[445] *Ibid., p. 119.*
[446] *Ibid., p. 52.*
[447] *Ibid., p. 60.*

drugs throughout human history. A viceroy in Peru, the Marques de Canete, from 1555 to 1560 "promulgated land reform measures designed to limit the number of acres devoted to coca cultivation" and instituted "creative financial incentives to encourage the substitution of crops for coca."[448] In the legal markets of 1886, 158,000 pounds of cocaine were produced.[449] This had changed little by the 1930s, having been made illegal in the U.S. in the early 1900s. However, despite four different international treaties and countless billions spent in a futile drug war since, the estimated production in 1996 was 1.5 million pounds.[450] The addict, whatever his stripe, always obtains his drug of choice—or replaces it, often with something more dangerous. With the possible exception of total enslavement, laws have never prevented addicts from procuring and using. There is always a corrupt official, an enabler, a supplier with his eye on the bottom line or a scientist inventing a new psychoactive brew to meet demand. Cocaine became difficult and expensive to obtain, leading creative types to put the "meth" into amphetamine. Science may yet find a new source for cocaine. Author Steven Karch points out, "It should not be that difficult to decipher the DNA codes for [cocaine's] production, manufacture copies of the DNA instructions, and insert them in some innocuous plant such as corn or soybeans. The genetic manipulation necessary to produce spoilage resistant tomatoes were probably more difficult."[451]

Prohibition of drugs has had a long history of perverse and unintended consequences, as so often results from governmental attempts to regulate trade among willing participants. Royce and Scratchley report that opium had only limited acceptance in China (where it was eaten) for hundreds of years. On the other hand, tobacco smoking caught on so quickly after its introduction, a backlash quickly resulted in its prohibition in 1644. In its place, smoking incorporated opium and quickly gained in popularity,[452] with a nation of opium addicts the unintended result, along with a decline in the relatively advanced state of Chinese civilization.

The former Soviet Union experienced many attempts in its sordid history to stem the flow of alcohol (alternating with Stalin's turning on the spigots). Despite massive internal controls on people, alcohol use became epidemic. There was a concerted campaign in the late 1980s to effect a decrease in alcohol use through the imposition of an attempt at reducing production. It utterly failed, not for lack of trying to get people to drink

[448] *Steven B. Karch, "A Brief History of Cocaine," Boca Raton, FL.: CRC Press, 1998, p. 3.*
[449] *Karch, Ibid., p. 49*
[450] *Derived from Karch, Ibid., p. 86 and 169.*
[451] *Karch, Ibid., p. 169.*
[452] *Royce, Ibid., p. 20.*

less, but rather, because addicts always find a way to get their substance of choice. In lieu of this, they find or create something else that gives them approximately the same high, no matter how dangerous the substitute may be.

When the anti-alcohol campaign began, the Soviet people were forced to turn in their homemade stills, apparently cooperating because they knew their homes could be searched at any time by secret police. In one region of 6,000 homes, 5,115 stills were turned in, while another 400 were found discarded in a nearby forest.[453] In another location, several thousand were of "a hundred different designs, some of them 'real inventions.'"[454] This made illegal brewing safe only for Communist Party regulars, leading to greater corruption than otherwise prevailing in the former Soviet Union.[455] The Communist Party headquarters in Tartarstan contained an entire underground liquor factory. Party members became the suppliers because, with stills having been made illegal, only such members could safely own them. High local officials who were members of the Party-sanctioned Sobriety Society frequently met demand, including one who was found with 240 liters of moonshine at his home.[456]

Soviets attempted to drink as they had before the campaign, only now less openly. While the fishing fleet had officially gone dry, a single cabin in one trawler contained 576 secreted bottles of vodka.[457] The price of liquor had been ratcheted upwards in an attempt to diminish demand. Now, those who would do anything for their substance of choice would sell the services of female members of their family to obtain illegal drink. Toxic substitutes were quickly found. Instead of universal sobriety, they had, according to one correspondent, "'a muddy wave of homebrew, eau de cologne, toothpaste [the toxic effect of glycerine having symptoms that drunks confused with intoxication] and shoe polish and, horrible as it may sound, trichlorofon and dichlorofon, as well as [other] drug addiction and addiction to [other] toxic substances, with the inevitable result—poisoning.'"[458] Colognes, alcohol-based perfumes, lotions and mouthwashes began to disappear from stores to such an extent that sales had to be rationed. One store refused to accept glue deliveries because customers fought over it.

The trouble is, when drugs are illegal, if an addict isn't already a criminal, he becomes one by definition. While the use of alcohol by Soviet con-

---

[453] *White, Ibid., p. 122.*
[454] *White, Ibid., p. 97.*
[455] *The greater the power of government generally, the greater the corruption.*
[456] *White, Ibid., p. 112.*
[457] *White, Ibid., p. 118.*
[458] *White, Ibid., p. 115.*

scripts was forbidden, the struggle to obtain alcohol in the armed services was described as an "obsession" by the conscripts themselves. Making alcohol more difficult to obtain was dangerous not only for the addicts, but also for non-addicts, in unique ways. Soviet defector Viktor Belenko reported in 1976 that his fellow pilots and ground crew "'were drunk most of the time.' According to Belenko, ground crews in particular would drain the de-icing fluid from the aircraft, distill it, and then drink it. They often covered up the theft by the dangerous practice of replacing the de-icing fluid with water."[459]

The amazing ability of addicts to procure drugs starts at a young age. Many teenage alcoholics independently learn to add water to their parents' liquor so that nobody notices the sneaking of drinks. They steal money from mom's purse. They get someone to buy booze in exchange for money, or worse, for sexual favors. Yet, because it's legal and controlled, it's apparently more difficult for kids to get liquor than illegal drugs. One of many 15-year-olds who have come forth in the media says it was "easier to get LSD at my junior high school than it was to buy a bottle of wine on the street."[460] Even in other cities they've never before visited, addict kids find the drug merchants. Most state categorically, they can find any drug in any city in the country within 30 minutes.[461] Those in jails get drugs. Those living in the giant Soviet concentration camp could get alcohol or some suitable substitute. One would think that the most tightly controlled areas are schools. Yet, 60% of high school seniors in America use drugs two or three times per week and 25% of all high school students are stoned most of the time.[462] As Father Martin points out, because drinking is made exciting, kids (especially little Artisans) steal drinks. Since illegal drugs are made even more exciting, kids steal to buy and try them. If soft drinks were illegal, kids would do whatever needed to obtain those, too.

The fact is, alcohol is our number one drug problem for those whose problem is addiction. Adults discuss the drug problem while they drink. Many deny using drugs, apparently not understanding that legal psychoactive substances such as barbiturates and alcohol are drugs, too. Most are well aware that Prohibition didn't work, resulting in substantially increased levels of crime, especially affecting third-party bystanders. Not only did the usual addicts commit their crimes (which they often do while practicing); other people got caught in the crossfire as battles waged over bootlegged gin. Watch practically any drug-based movie or TV show today and you'll see innocent people getting killed due to the illegality of drugs

[459] *White, Ibid., p. 54.*
[460] *Poulson and Newton, Ibid., p. 62.*
[461] *Poulson and Newton, Ibid., p. 62.*
[462] *Poulson and Newton, Ibid., p. 47 and 159*

and the artificially high price this creates. To paraphrase Mark Twain, art does not mimic reality; reality is far worse.

Free individuals make mistakes. When we deal with drug addicts we are dealing with adolescent mind-sets, regardless of chronological age. Adolescents understand swift and sure punishment for transgressing on the rights of others. They do not understand, nor will they tolerate, punishment for experimenting on themselves. If alcohol or other drugs are not available, the young addict will eat morning glory seeds for a mild hallucinogenic experience. He'll dry banana peels, crumble and smoke them for a little high. He'll smoke tea leaves, poppy seeds, rosemary, oregano and bay leaves. He'll boil nutmeg in water and drink it. He'll drink Nyquil and sniff nail polish, nail polish remover and correction fluid.[463] We are not going to stop him. "Just say no to drugs" doesn't work. We're preaching to the choir.

The morality of drug use has been argued from the beginning of time. One argument is that it's not a moral issue at all. For example, as an inanimate object, a gun is neither moral nor immoral. It can be used in moral or immoral ways. If used to violate someone else's rights, the act is immoral, for which punishment should be swift and sure. Like guns, alcohol and other drugs are inanimate and therefore also amoral. Each can be used for good or evil. If used immorally (i.e., driving or working while intoxicated, assuming it violates the rules of the road or workplace), the punishment should be sure, immediate and appropriate. Those committing violence, theft, fraud or violation of contractual obligations need to be held accountable and brought to justice. Those using drugs and committing no crimes, should not be our concern. Those acting in criminal and unethical ways due to drug use are the people in need of our uncompromising tough love and intervention, hopefully before becoming defendants and wards of the criminal justice system.

Sooner or later, almost all kids will drink and/or use. It has been an exercise in futility to try and stop experimentation. What can be done is to halt <u>addictive</u> use early on. Even delaying this is potentially beneficial. Once addictive use begins, so does damage to a brain that, if not fully formed, may be catastrophic for the young person. Regardless of whether it begins early or later, if there is a predisposition to addiction, the incipient disease is activated. Once this happens, destructive, criminal and/or unethical behaviors will often begin. The addict must <u>know</u> he will experience consequences for any resulting deviant behaviors. He must have the link between such behavior and drug use forged for him. Yet, this is rarely done. Rather than learning the truth, that some can use drugs with impunity while others cannot, they learn all drugs are bad. Ironically, some of

---

[463] *Poulson and Newton, Ibid., p. 128.*

those who teach this go home to their six-packs or vodka-martinis. Many of the kids go home to parents, who sip their wine, gulp their scotch and pop their Valium.

In the meantime, we have the "newsworthy" item, "To Control 'Meth,' Authorities Curb Cold Pills."[464] Yet the absurd attempt to control the growth of coca plants across millions of acres in foreign countries led to the inexorable demand for a new drug. Making methamphetamine is a process that requires no tropical climate (or any climate at all) and no land outside that contained in a laboratory. Meth is cheaper, longer lasting than cocaine and more dangerous both to the user and (probably) to those with whom he comes in contact. Suppliers will always meet demand, whether legal or not. Today, bulk sales of Sudafed, Actifed and Tylenol Cold are controlled, as are Contac 12-Hour Cold and Triaminic Syrup. All can be used as active ingredients in methamphetamine,[465] along with battery acid and red phosphorous from road flares. One must be diseased to have an insatiable craving to ingest this junk. We cannot control the diseased by controlling the substance.

Temperate humans have been trying to control the addicts' tendency to use drugs for hundreds of years. China is said to have tried prohibition 17 times. England tried it six times. Russia has attempted various degrees of prohibition and failed, as have Finland and Iceland. Even the Muslim countries have their alcohol users and their substitute drug, hashish (apparently not as strictly proscribed).[466] They've also attempted to scare children into staying abstinent. Today's D.A.R.E. (Drug Abuse Resistance Education) and similar programs had numerous antecedents. The National Woman's Christian Temperance Union (WCTU), established in 1874, compelled all public schools to teach a course on the evils of alcohol. Their demonstrations are startlingly similar to some of today's advertising about the evils of drugs:

> *"Teacher would place part of a calf's brain in an empty glass jar. After discoursing on the nature of the brain and the nature of alcohol, she would then pour a bottle of alcohol into the jar. The color of the calf's brain would turn from its normal pink to a nasty gray. And that, the teacher would conclude in sepulchral tones, is what would happen to her pupils' little brains if ever they drank Satan's brew."*[467] *Nowadays, we use eggs instead of calves' brains, but the message is the same.*

D.A.R.E. and numerous other authority-based programs attempt to

---

[464] *The Wall Street Journal, August 25, 1998, p. B-1.*

[465] *The first group for their pseudoephedrine; the second for their phenylpropanolamine.*

[466] *Royce and Scratchley, Ibid., pp. 31-32.*

[467] *Edward Behr, Ibid., p. 40.*

guide kids away from drugs. According to studies,[468] along with some aware and knowledgeable police officers, such programs have no measurably significant long-term affect on drug use. There have been a few promising approaches, using interactive and peer group teaching, which have been underutilized. Researchers Linda Dusenbury and Matheo Falco note, "Most of the money spent in this country on drug education has not been spent on promising programs."[469] Stop teaching that drugs are bad, which cannot be true of inanimate objects. Instead, teach the fact that while most can, with relative safety, use some drugs for medical, social or recreational purposes non-addictively, a portion of the population cannot, without causing great harm both to themselves and/or others. Nor should we misleadingly suggest that we "use alcohol in moderation." There is no such thing as moderation to an addict.

Although the 19th and early 20th century temperance movement may have had some effect on overall drinking, it seems to have had none on levels of addiction. The mandatory classes did nothing to stop the behaviors of alcoholics, resulting in a perceived "need" for Prohibition. While reducing total alcohol consumption, Prohibition had no apparent effect on the level of alcoholism. The demand created by the unquenchable thirst of the addict instead led to a violent and corrupting black market in alcohol. The same craving to fine-tune the effects of non-alcoholic drugs on various neurotransmitter activities has, with today's version of prohibition, led to even greater destruction.

The crime spree precipitated by Prohibition's Volstead Act began within the hour of its taking effect on January 17, 1920. In Chicago, "Six armed, masked men made away with whiskey earmarked for 'medicinal use,' worth $100,000 in 1920 dollars."[470] Limited amounts of liquor were allowed for such use, resulting in a staggering increase in liquor "prescriptions." Prescription drugs are not much different today in relation to their illegal alternatives, there being a legally <u>prescribed</u> drug of "abuse" for practically every illegal one. Licenses to sell "medicinal liquor" in Chicago alone were applied for by many thousands of doctors and retail druggists.[471]

---

[468] *Dennis P. Rosenbaum and Gordon S. Hanson, "Assessing the Effects of School-Based Drug Education: A Six-Year Multi-Level Analysis of Project D.A.R.E.," Journal of Research in Crime and Delinquency, Vol. 35 No. 4, November, 1998. The authors point out that the studies reporting positive results for D.A.R.E. are not longitudinal, which would measure the long-term success rate for the program. The eventual failure of these programs is predictable since, sooner or later, most young people experiment, thereby triggering addiction in the predisposed. On the other hand, delaying the onset of such use may be beneficial, thereby allowing the brain to fully form before addiction takes hold.*

[469] *"Eleven Components of Effective Drug Abuse Prevention Curricula," Journal of School Health, Dec., 1995, Vol. 65, No. 10.*

[470] *Behr, Ibid., p. 83.*

[471] *Behr, Ibid., p. 84.*

As occurred in the former Soviet Union in the late 1980s, there were runs on anything containing alcohol, including embalming fluid and antifreeze, resulting in far more dire consequences for the user than the formerly legal drug alcohol. Just as recipes for illegal drugs today can be found by children on the Internet, recipes during Prohibition for producing alcohol were not-so-surreptitiously offered by attractive young women acting as demonstrators in large stores. They warned people not to place raisin cakes, sold with a warning label that read, "Caution: will ferment and turn into wine," into jugs with liquid and "put it aside for twenty-one days because it would turn to wine...and not to stop the bottle with a cork because this is necessary only if fermentation occurs."[472] We wouldn't want that to happen.

Obviously, Prohibition didn't succeed. Instead, it generated corruption among police, bureaucrats and politicians. It made it possible for bootleggers (who were criminal types, attracted to an industry that had been turned into something criminal) to become wealthy. It resulted in tens of thousands of deaths from poisoning by wood alcohol or moonshine.[473] The greatest bootlegger of them all, George Remus (after whom alcoholic F. Scott Fitzgerald's fictional Mr. Gatsby may have been patterned) estimated half his gross was spent in bribes,[474] even including the U.S. Attorney General under Warren Harding, Harry Micajah Daugherty. The Prohibition Bureau itself was victim to massive corruption, having had over 13,000 agents (out of a force of 18,000) separated for suspicion of criminal involvement from 1920-1930.[475] Not all agents were corruptible, just as many are not today. But many must have been, since just one clean agent, Izzy Einstein, was responsible for 20% of arrests for violating the Volstead Act in Manhattan from 1920 to 1925.[476]

Who doubts that Daugherty's heirs lurk today in or near the highest echelons of power? The rate of interdiction of bootlegged alcohol is estimated to have been about 5%, not dissimilar to the estimated rate of interdiction for today's illegal drugs. The intuitive reader might infer that today's level of corruption, including volume of bribes to well-placed officials, might be no different.

Hopefully, today's drug Prohibition has its benefits, just as alcohol Prohibition had its good sides. Jimmy McGhee developed speedier boats than would have been at such early dates due to his supplying bootleggers with engines that could easily outrun the Coast Guard patrols. This self-taught

---

[472] *Behr, Ibid., p. 86.*
[473] *Behr, Ibid., p. 222-223.*
[474] *Behr, Ibid., p. 103.*
[475] *Behr, Ibid., p. 153.*
[476] *Behr, Ibid., p. 154.*

mechanical genius subsequently became well known in car racing and as an advisor to Grumman, the maker of fighter aircraft, during World War II.[477] In addition, the effort to break the bootleggers' codes aided in advancing the science of cryptoanalysis in ways that later proved to be instrumental in breaking German and Japanese codes.

However, the current drug war has its travesties of justice, as did the more renowned Prohibition. Today, some are given 10 year, 20 year and even life sentences for simple possession or sale of illegal drugs. In the 1920s "Fred Palm of Lansing and a mother of ten elsewhere in Michigan got life sentences for possession of a pint of gin."[478] The law is incapable of distinguishing between those who may commit transgressions against others and those who do not, prior to such harm occuring. While damage will occur almost every time when there is addiction, it will not in instances of use and even abuse. Let the law address actual instances of harm quickly and surely. Let codependents, acting in their own interests, protect themselves against the ravages of the addict from the earliest transgressions. Let them discriminate by not hiring, by firing and letting or leading the addict out of their lives when he does not accept the alternative of sobriety.

As do the drug lords today, Moonshiners favored Prohibition. Without it, they wouldn't be in business. There is no market with profit margins so great as when the product of trade is illegal. This results in such profits accruing to, by definition, criminal elements. Increasing the punishment to adults for engaging in such trade merely increases the incentive to involve juveniles, who can earn a lot more in crime than by flipping hamburgers. After repeal of Prohibition, the bootleggers disappeared from the schoolyards, with drinking among children declining dramatically. Just as there is some likely selective enforcement today against drug offenders in the poorer sections of society, there was similar discriminating enforcement during the 1920s' Prohibition. New York Congressman Fiorello La Guardia told a constituent, Prohibition "'was only enforced among the coloured population'." A survey of the police blotter in the *Easthampton Star* from 1920 to 1933 revealed that no "respectable" wealthy socialite was ever arraigned on violating the Volstead Act.[479]

Unfortunately, most haven't seen the connection between the current illegality of certain drugs and alcohol Prohibition. To review, a drug is a drug to the addict. Abusers and users pose little threat to the public welfare and purse, when compared with the addict whom we can't keep from obtaining his drugs. He will do anything ("and I mean anything") to get it. We must instead concentrate on stopping the damage he does while in-

---

[477] *Behr, Ibid., pp. 140-141.*
[478] *Behr, Ibid., p. 165.*
[479] *Behr, Ibid., p. 172.*

flicting sure consequences for the destruction he wreaks. We must forge the link, one that he is otherwise incapable of seeing, between his addiction and behaviors, while offering a path to sobriety.

Furthermore, drugs have been part of the human condition for thousands of years; as Aldous Huxley is reported to have said, "Pharmacology antedated agriculture." Drugs will never be eradicated. Substitutes will always be found and/or manufactured. We cannot eliminate something that can easily be obtained by children, incarcerated prisoners and Soviet citizens.

Royce and Scratchley observe that "48-ounce bottles of Listerine disappear very fast in some prisons" and many are able to ferment hoarded raisins and prunes into wine (making "pruno").[480] One recovering addict who spent four years in jail told me she believes 30% of prisoners use drugs daily. Recalling the high rate of alcoholism among police officers and guards, we have, in many instances, addicts arresting addicts, guarded by addicts.

The following are suggestions for dealing with the criminal element in lieu of Prohibition. Recovery and nutritionally balanced food programs are desperately needed in jails. A matter-of-fact correlation should be drawn between destructive behavior toward others and time served. Independent agencies should supervise, monitor and perform regular drug and alcohol testing of all guards, other prison staff and prisoners who want their freedom (I would suggest the same for all law enforcement personnel.) A condition of getting out of prison at any time should be at least two years (or the length of their prison term if less) proven drug and alcohol tested sobriety, with another such period during parole. It matters not whether we give drugs to addicts who never want to leave jail. Bringing the opium dens of China to our jails doesn't seem so bad, given the alternative. It is essential that these addicts be given the opportunity and choice of sobriety. Their addiction likely made "them feel like they are superman," resulting in the commission of criminal acts. If they commit a crime against others, they should go to jail. If they want to use drugs, let them — it can't be stopped, so bring it above board. Segregate and allow those who have violated the rights of others to stay in jail until and unless they successfully complete a program of recovery. An irrefutable link between their use and criminal behaviors must be drawn for them.

The fact is the addict, often soon after his first taste of the drug, knows the resulting behaviors are atrocious. However, he does not correlate the two, as he provides excuses for himself in the fog of distorted perceptions, especially euphoric recall and subsequent obliteration of good judgment. The job of the legal and social services establishments, from police to courts

---

[480] *Royce and Scratchley, Ibid., p. 33.*

and from prisons to welfare services, should be to forge this connection. It should be made clear at the outset that the behavior that likely got him in touch with these agencies was probably a result of an addictive use of psychoactive drugs. In the alternative, it should be suggested that there might be a close familial and/or business relationship with someone who uses such substances addictively that caused the non-addict to engage in criminal behavior. They need to be told that they or someone close may have the *disease* of addiction, something that has likely never before been suggested.

The idea that sellers of drugs are the cause of addiction should be eradicated. By blaming the supplier, we remove the responsibility for addiction from the addict. Former Michigan Drug Czar Bob Peterson recently said of the drug dealers, "These people are getting people addicted."[481] Carol O'Connor, having lost his son to addiction, publicly blamed the dealer for his son's death. Throughout history, governments have attempted to restrict sellers from selling goods to buyers at prices mutually agreed upon. Such restrictions of trade have only created black markets, engendering a climate of corruption from the lowest to the highest levels of government.

We can learn from the Arabs, from whom the word alcohol may have originated. The Arabic al-kuhl means "finely divided spirit of wine," while the Arabic alghul means "evil spirit." The Arabs, perhaps recognizing it as the former for some and the latter for others, possibly intended for this double entendre to serve as one of the many paradoxes about which I have written. We can also learn from the Chinese, whom in 500 B. C. wrote in the *Shu Ching* under an entry on drunkenness, "To prohibit it [beer] and secure total abstinence from it is beyond the power even of the sages. Here, therefore, we have warnings on the abuse of it." But the clearest lesson comes a thousand years prior to the Chinese acknowledgement of the impossibility of successful prohibition. The Egyptians described disenabling, prescribing that if one drinks beer, "If thou fallest down, and thy limbs break, there is none to hold out a hand to thee."[482] If we would but heed these ancient words by offering pure tough love through uncompromising disenabling at the earliest stages of substance addiction, the addict would likely experience far earlier and more permanent recovery. Instead of being the victim, society may become the beneficiary of the recovering addict's creative genius.

[481] *"The Charles Grodin Show," CNBC, May 29, 1998.*
[482] *Nancy Hyden Woodward, Ibid., p. 50.*

Other public policy considerations in the cessation of enabling

Alcohol, with over $1 billion in advertising a year, is portrayed as sexy, exciting and fun, essential to enhancing one's virility, wealth and success. It is, quite simply, glorified. This advertising is blamed by many for the overuse and abuse of alcohol. The glamorized image makes non-addicts underestimate the problems caused by alcohol. However, there's an inexplicable contradiction with the belief that such imagery lures alcoholics into drinking more than they otherwise would: it does not square with what happened in the former Soviet Union.

The former Soviet states have probably the greatest alcohol problems known on so vast a scale, yet there was no advertising allowed for over 70 years. Alcoholism is not an advertising-created problem. It's a biological and genetic one. Its treatment calls for uncompromising tough love, not a ban on advertising.

Intervention is possible at the public level when the addict's behaviors attract public attention. According to *The Los Angeles Times* (January 17, 1998), an estimated 120,000 of California's 154,000 inmates have substance problems. Yet, only 3,000 are being treated for addiction. The rate of recidivism is at least 65% in the untreated addict-prisoner. It has been less than 16% for inmates who've completed an intensive prison and parole drug program pioneered at San Diego's Richard J. Donovan Correctional Facility. This obviously demonstrates that when addiction is treated, there is a vastly reduced rate of repeat offenders. While it costs about $28,000 per year to house one inmate, comprehensive alcohol and other drug treatment adds only about $3,000 annually per prisoner. Relapse prevention expert Terence T. Gorski believes that this would be money well spent.[483]

Accepted public policy mandates that society attempt to save people from the consequences of their prior decisions and actions. We now know that this just doesn't work. We can only lay the ethical and legal framework that helps people experience proper consequences.

Viewing the practicing addict as an adolescent and treating him as such

---

[483] *Terence T. Gorski, "Sentencing Guidelines for Chemically Dependent Criminal Offenders," Independence, MO.: Herald House/Independence Press, 1995, p. 10. Gorski reports that the long-term re-arrest rate of those who completed an intensive rehabilitation program was about one-third the rate of those who didn't. He makes a compelling case for requiring ongoing treatment as a condition of release and probation, suggesting a contract between the court and the criminal defendant addict.*

is not something that should be dismissed out of hand. According to those in recovery, the emotional age of the addict is frozen from the first moment of addictive use (usually when very young). Author Nancy Hyden Woodward suggests we not hide a child-addict's addiction from others. This argument could be extended to adult addicts, who, if not known, can usually do far more damage to third parties than can children.

What do we do when we rescue children? We stunt their growth. Children must be allowed to experience what Rudolf Dreikurs called "natural consequences," barring severe physical endangerment.[484] Addicts could be allowed to experience some physical harm before intervention, since a reasonable amount of such pain may well set the stage for sobriety. Unfortunately, public policy often protects addicts from themselves, preventing natural consequences from being experienced. Worse yet, as alcoholism expert Toby Rice Drews writes, "Rescuing someone keeps them dependent on you."[485] In a perverse sense, keeping someone addicted through repeated rescues is a form of control that prevents personal growth. Drews states, "It may make you feel comfortable for a time, but that person will grow to resent you later."

Consider the resentment by the hard-core welfare addict. He resents the rich, even though in a free market, one person getting rich results in others becoming better off.[486] He views welfare as something to which he is entitled, a view that found its way into the common lexicon, turning a legalized taking from others without the specific approval of those who bear the cost of such takings into an "entitlement." No wonder the welfare recipient resents. All substance addicts resent others who help them.

What is true of individuals is true for groups and entire societies. Foreign aid is a case in point. According to the Cato Institute,[487] such aid has often enabled recipient governments to continue poor policies that keep their citizens (except for the elite whose pockets are lined) in poverty. Just as we must leave the addict to his own devices so he can learn whatever it is he has to, we should leave entire societies alone as well. By "helping," we only protect them from the consequences of their own policies and behaviors, preventing them from experiencing the pain needed to inspire improvements.

---

[484] *Rudolf Dreikurs, MD, "Children: The Challenge," New York: The Penguin Group, 1990.*

[485] *Toby Rice Drews, Ibid., p. 100.*

[486] *I won't attempt to support this broad assertion here for fear of turning this into an economics text. Suffice it to say in overly simplistic terms, if someone gets rich by selling you products voluntarily purchased without being defrauded, you became richer by virtue of having spent money on something valued more highly than the money spent.*

[487] *The Cato Institute, Washington, D.C.*

Welfare handouts destroy self-esteem by preventing people from picking themselves up by their own efforts. In the opinion of a number of addiction-aware social workers, close to 90% of welfare recipients are substance addicts. Such handouts should be eliminated to allow people to rebuild self-esteem and, to quote the Army slogan, "be all they can be." Alcoholism authorities Royce and Scratchley report the success of the Alkali Lake Village people in north-central British Columbia, "in which a nearly all-alcoholic [Intuit] village became 95 percent nonalcoholic through a strictly grassroots effort with no help from authorities."[488]

Additional public policy changes should include those that allow society and its members to uncompromisingly disenable the addict, consistent with protection of life and the derivatives of such in the form of both tangible and intangible (ideas, copyrights, etc.) property. One particular policy might be to track 911 complaints against reckless motorists and to give authorities the ability to immediately trace the kind of car reported based on the license plate (since some find getting the plate number is easier than determining the make and year of car). Letters could be sent to the dangerous driver and the owner could be the recipient of a visit by police, if reported twice.[489] Another policy might be to require all participants in traffic accidents in which there are any injuries, to be tested for alcohol and other drugs. To eliminate the problem of defending oneself by arguing "I drank after the accident," have the law assume whatever the testing finds in the blood was there immediately preceding the collision.

---

[488] *Royce and Scratchley, Ibid., pp. 179-180.*
[489] *Apparently, some jurisdictions are doing a variation of this. Complaints sent to the Highway Patrol in Woodland Hills, CA, result in a letter to the registered owner reporting a possible infraction. This needs to be taken much further.*

Figure 16 – Time Frames for Blood and Urine Drug Testing

To prevent relapse, require random urine testing*

	Blood-Plasma Duration	Urine Duration
Alcohol	.015 BAC decrease/hr	-------------------
Marijuana	-------------------	Ten-Thirty Days
Cocaine	2-5 Hours	24-36 Hours
Amphetamines	4-6 Hours	48-72 Hours
Heroin	4-6 Hours	48-72 Hours
PCP	12-24 Hours	48-72 Hours

Marijuana, Valium and some other drugs convert to different ones in the body, called "metabolites", which last longer than the source drug. Addiction expert Dr. Forest Tennant explains, "Physical addiction may be to a metabolite rather than to the source drug. This accounts for the fact that users of these drugs develop the need to re-use at varying time intervals." Keep in mind, it is psychological addiction that is far more powerful and devastating, accounting for high rates of relapse.

Civil libertarians argue that some of these proposals are violations of privacy. They should be reminded that decriminalization would allow the use of substances in one's home. Private use should fall to the owner. (You may or may not allow, for example, the use of drugs on your property.) Once substances are used on public property (for example, most roads), private becomes public. This is particularly true in instances of elevated blood-plasma levels, resulting in reduced reaction time (depressants) and/or reckless and excessive risk-taking behavior (stimulants), either of which can cause impaired judgment. When an accident occurs, it may be argued (since about 50% may involve an intoxicated person) that there is probable cause to test for drugs.

The same principle should be extended to sporting activities. Fortunately, alcohol has recently become recognized as a major cause of boating accidents, resulting in the strengthening of laws. This has not been true for other sports, including skiing and surfing. The percentage of serious sporting accidents due to intoxication, especially those involving more than one person, is probably not much less than those of automobile or industrial accidents. Fortunately, Sonny Bono didn't take out any others, but the tree he hit skiing while, according to Mary Bono, under the influence of pain-killers to which he was addicted, could have just as easily been another skier. Laws should be toughened so that anyone who injures someone else in an "accident" must be blood tested and, if legally intoxicated, bear the same consequences as a DUI. The following warning could be placed, for example, on all ski lift tickets and posted conspicuously:

"If you have a skiing accident that results in injury for either yourself or another, you will be blood tested for alcohol and other drugs. If legally intoxicated, you will be charged with reckless endangerment of others. If another is injured, you will be charged with assault. If another is killed, you will be charged with manslaughter."

The chart showing BAC levels at various weights with various amounts of liquor consumed could be posted at all bars in sporting areas. While, as we've learned, addicts are not likely to pay attention to this, non-addicts might, both for limiting their own intake and to help them diagnose others as possible addicts.

Private owners should have the right to control who works for them or determine who enters or leases their property, including whatever testing for drugs they wish. This is particularly true for landlords and renters. The difficulty in evicting the non-paying and often destructive addict-ten-ant is one of his greatest enablers. The stories recounted in the chapter on the financial abuse of others are so common, it defies credulity; the sad part is, we don't help these tenants by "helping" them avoid the conse-quences of their financial difficulties and/or outright destructive behav-ior.

Employers in all industries should have the right to test for alcohol and other drugs and set their own standards. Some may set none, yet could be held liable for employees' abusive, reckless and dangerous behaviors in the courts of both consumer demand and law. Others may have a zero tolerance policy for any psychoactive drug, doctor prescribed or not. Pub-lic entities should have zero tolerance, with the choice of rehabilitation or termination offered. Hawaii might have quite a change in the level of pub-lic services: under current law, public employees must be caught drinking on the job four times in a two-year period before even being *asked* to re-sign.[490] Bear in mind, money is the addict's biggest enabler and being fired may be exactly what the employee needs to begin looking at his use of substances as the source of his troubles, especially when combined with intervention.

[490] *The Economist Magazine, June 20, 1998.*

The war on tobacco is as misplaced as the war on drugs. While tobacco does tremendous damage to those who smoke, it pales in comparison to the damage inflicted by alcohol and other psychoactive drugs on non-addicts. While smoking is now banned inside buildings, according to one recent study, 50 to 60% of employers, clergy and family members avoid addressing alcoholism, even when apparent. Worse yet, over 80% of doctors avoid addressing a suspected problem with their patients.[491] Since early to middle-stage alcoholism is so difficult to detect, these statistics likely apply only to latter-stage alcoholics. If it were measurable, it would likely be found that alcoholism is hardly <u>ever</u> addressed. Yet, the average age at death among alcoholics is said to be 4 to 8 years earlier than among non-alcoholic smokers. This is supported by reports that the average age of death in the former Soviet Union is suspected to be about 60.

Adoption is another area of public policy that needs comment. Most adoptions may be of children with at least one biological addict-parent. The adoptive parents should be educated about addiction and given the tools needed. Only then will they have the knowledge to educate their adopted children about the genetic risk factor and the wherewithal to offer the appropriate tough love, should the child fail to heed the warning of genetics and trigger his own addiction.

While bankruptcy is a necessary and humane option for some, many addicts have dug their financial hole due to the distorted perceptions and impaired judgments resulting from substance addiction. Once again, we only harm the addict by removing responsibility and shielding him from consequences. While eliminating the bankruptcy code might seem too extreme, we have gone way too far creating "exemptions," for property the bankrupt can keep. One absurd example is Florida's unlimited exemption for equity in one's home. More typical is California's exemption for household furnishings that are "'necessary' if the items are appropriate to the station in life of the owner and manner of comfortable living to which they have become accustomed.... Items which have been held necessary household furnishings include stereos, video equipment...or musical instruments which are held primarily for personal...use."[492] Bear in mind, the addict's ego must be totally deflated to help insure long-term sobriety. Allowing the bankrupt addict to maintain his "station in life" may be all that's needed to prevent full ego deflation. Again, addicts are better able to get and stay sober without money.

One additional proposal is to teach parents, teachers and law enforcers the physical signs of use and addiction in addition to the behavioral signs

---

[491] *In Tobacco War, Alcohol Escapes The Heavy Fire," by Gerald F. Seib, The Wall Street Journal, April 29, 1998.*

[492] *Merritt and Hagen, "The Basics of Bankruptcy for Accountants and Attorneys," Woodland Hills, Ca., 1996.*

expounded here. Physical signs of pupil constriction and dilation, more obvious in non-tolerant users are useful for identifying young and early-stage addicts (with the caveat that pupils in children tend to be larger than in adults). Although the behavioral signs are more meaningful, physical signs may serve as solid evidence for some that a problem lurks.

12

Recovery for the Non-Addict

A new path to serenity and empowerment

"God, grant me the serenity to accept the things I cannot change, the courage to change the things I can, and the wisdom to know" that this is me, and only on a good day.
— Rheinhold Niebuhr,[493] with author's variation of the "Serenity Prayer"

"As with the creation of a diamond from coal, transformation in the human being usually requires sufficient time and sufficient pressure."
— Robin Norwood[494]

In this chapter, we will be discussing God. The term, as used here, doesn't necessarily refer to an entity in a religious sense. The words "Higher Power" can easily be substituted, as can "reality," "nature," or the phrase, "The Laws of Nature." These Laws include what science has labeled "Chaos Theory."

The 12-Step Program is the path to recovery from addiction created by the founders of Alcoholics Anonymous, Bill W. and Dr. Bob. It consists of basic principles by which addicts and non-addicts alike can live. Practicing the many applications of these principles results in increased serenity.

The idea of analyzing the 12 Steps contradicts the suggestions of many in the Program. However, each must work the Program in their own way, consistent with one's core needs and values. Some, like myself, need to know and understand. For me, "To know is to be," so I find it helpful to

---

[493] *According to Dr. Douglas Talbott, St. Thomas of Assisi, often credited with this piece, is said to have generated the thoughts that went into it. The actual prayer ends, "and the wisdom to know the difference."*

[494] *Robin Norwood, "Why Me, Why This, Why Now: A Guide to Answering Life's Toughest Questions," New York: Carol Southern Books, 1994, p. 26.*

analyze.

Clarity

Several actions resulted in finding the clarity of thinking needed to recover from my own personal experience. As mentioned earlier, I learned all I could about addiction, attending dozens of AA meetings and interviewing scores of recovering addicts. For a time, I attended 4 or 5 Al Anon meetings every week. Since physical health improves mental health, I began taking mega-doses of vitamins and supplements, followed a non-dairy complex unrefined carbohydrate vegetarian diet and engaged in vigorous, regular exercise. I listened to Tony Robbins' "Personal Power" tapes and read numerous self-help books. Within six weeks of beginning this multi-faceted "holistic" approach to recovery, I went through an astonishing metamorphosis.

I also discontinued the use of alcohol. I grew up with alcohol and watched it being consumed as a normal part of everyday life by many adults around me. Due to this environmental influence, I became an occasionally heavy social drinker, partially accounting for my ignorance and naïveté of the distinction between abusive and addictive drinking. The improved health and increased clarity from abstinence was, in retrospect, an essential ingredient to my speedy personal recovery. But because nobody suggested that I take this action, I quit drinking for an entirely different reason.

One might think, experiencing alcoholism would be enough to get any codependent to stop drinking. Instead, I drank more, as otherwise normal drinkers sometimes do in similar situations. Some may drink with their addict in a perverse attempt to control the overall level of drinking. Others drink to excess in a vain attempt at numbing the pain of dealing with this kind of relationship. This is an exercise in futility, since non-addicts can't experience the same "benefits" from heavy drinking that addicts derive.

Six months after the break-up with my addict, I met another intelligent and attractive woman. The second evening together, we shared wine over a romantic dinner. Halfway through the second bottle, I watched a caring, wonderful and sane human mutate into a malicious and irrational demon. I was spellbound as I studied her transformation, occuring over a period lasting no more than 10 minutes. This type of behavioral change, while not alien, had previously appeared isolated and unconnected with a substance, or had occurred over a period of several hours' drinking. It never before made any sense. This time, it was immediate and, with my elementary understanding of addiction, comprehensible.

By now I had learned that to argue with a drunk is to argue with a chemical. As my date began foaming at the mouth, I realized that for the first time in my life I understood the event and simply kept quiet. The few times I did speak were to answer her berating attacks on a mutual friend with the classic response appropriate to any practicing addict: "you may be right" (followed by a silent "and you may be wrong"). Because I stepped out of the ring, leaving her no one with whom to fight, she left. The next morning, when I realized that I'd had enough of this affliction to last dozen lifetimes, I decided to do everything in my power to insure that I would never again allow an addict in my personal life. I also decided to make sure that I would never be as overtly vile and abusive toward others. To do this, while still not understanding the behavioral differences between the addictive and non-addictive drinker, I decided to stop drinking.

Selfishness vs. self-centeredness

My abstinence empowered me to ponder my experience from a more clear-headed perspective. Not drinking, at least for a period of time, should be standard procedure for all codependents. Listening to tapes by Tony Robbins, the motivational speaker/coach, provided me with several additional tools to control my mental state. Two of his methods were particularly helpful.[495] I linked motion to positive emotion, in which you move your body as if were doing something that you love. Your brain, not knowing the difference, makes you feel like you're engaging in that activity with the associated positive emotions. For example, I feel fabulous when I snow ski down a very steep and smooth run, so I physically recreate those movements and start to feel that same rush, creating a natural "high." The other tool, transforming one's vocabulary, calls for softening such harsh words as "angry" to ones less emotionally charged, like "concerned" or "curious." This makes having and keeping negative feelings very difficult.

I then embraced the Al-Anon variant of AA's first step, "I am powerless over other people." While we can seemingly control, influence and change many things, we do not decide when such control is effective and when it is not. Therefore, <u>ultimately</u>, we do not control anything in our external world. Understanding this helps shift focus from others, including the alcoholic, to oneself. By degrees, I realized that the basic underlying prin-

---

[495] *Anthony Robbins, "Personal Power," original audiotape series, San Diego: Robbins Research International, Inc., 1993.*

cipal of the 12-Step Program is, in a sense, a "selfish" ideology: we must be responsible for taking care of ourselves, yet held responsible for our behaviors as they negatively affect others.

As there is an infinite gap between abuse/addiction and self-esteem/ego, so it is with "selfishness" and self-centeredness. Self-centered behavior relates to taking care of self by violating others' rights. As those in recovery will testify, the addict is the most self-centered of the species (due to the actions he takes to inflate his ego). On the other hand, enlightened "selfish" behavior is about taking care of oneself without overstepping boundaries. There is nothing wrong or immoral about being "selfish," in the way used here. However, because the word has such a negative connotation, some may prefer to call this "responsible self-interest." It requires that in taking care of self, we must accept responsibility for our own actions. There is an enormous long-term benefit in this since, as we've learned, experiencing consequences is the greatest teacher of all.

Unfortunately, nothing else decimates self-esteem in people more quickly than taking responsibility for them or making others suffer the results of their actions. Rendered incapable or unable to accept responsibility, they cannot build (or rebuild) self-esteem. Without this, the addict cannot recover. Therefore, we must engage in rational, responsible self-interested behavior not only for us, but also for the addict.

We cannot change man's instinctive self-interest any more than we can his innate Temperament. A system that harnesses man's pre-existing nature for good is (in the long run) to his greater benefit, whether at the macro- or micro-economic unit.[496] This is the reason self-responsibility works at all levels of human interaction.

---

[496] *Ayn Rand wrote in The Virtue of Selfishness that a system channeling self-interest under a fixed set of rules, the rule of Law (as opposed to the capricious rules of the King or other government official), works best to maximize human potential and happiness. She argued that the economic system of free market capitalism best harnesses and directs this channeled energy for the good of all by allowing consumers to reward those who satisfy their needs with a profit, while offering the pain of loss to those who don't. This results in Constant And Never-ending Improvement (what Tony Robbins calls "CANI," or "I Can") on the part of producers in the rational and efficient allocation of scarce resources. The 12-Step Program applies this concept, grounded in self-responsibility, to the microcosm of family and workplace.*

Chaos

The 1st step of the 12-Step Program ("We admitted we were powerless over alcohol...") initially makes no sense to most non-addicts, because they are not powerless in this way. Instead, they eventually accept that they have no power over others' alcohol, behaviors or anything else addicts do. This is later broadened to an awareness and acceptance of the lack of control over all other people, places and things.

If we add "events" to the equation, this "powerlessness" can be integrated with a branch of science known as "Chaos Theory." This states that the more distant in time, the less predictable are outcomes,[497] because the most seemingly inconsequential events can escalate into major changes over extended periods. The range of effects to which such events can lead, are practically limitless. This makes long-term prediction of results impossible except within the confines of known physical law and probabilistic estimates.

Chaos (as defined here) is pervasive throughout nature. Very evident in weather forecasting, it gave rise to the classic example of the effect the flapping wings of the butterfly may have on the wind and hence, weather. In many instances, such an insignificant "initial cause" has no perceived affect. Yet, who is to say it isn't a single flap of a butterfly's wings in Los Angeles that set off a series of events (the movement of air currents), eventually resulting in an Atlantic hurricane? Despite the fact that the hurricane can't be linked to the butterfly any more than the outcome could be predicted from his movement, the implications in both the physical and human sciences are profound and far-reaching. The fact that there are too many tiny variables that can cause massive change is the reason so little in life goes according to "plan."

This does not mean that one should never set goals. We accomplish most of these, especially those with short time horizons. However, while we generally will achieve a goal of having dinner tonight at a specific place and time, we are not as likely to reach our 20-year plan. While we increase the chances of achieving our goals when implementation is planned and outcomes are visualized, Chaos Theory explains why the best-laid plans sometimes go awry. High tornado risk can be predicted, but we cannot say exactly where a tornado will strike. In life, tornado-like events whirl all around. We cannot foresee who will experience sudden wealth and success or whose lives may be abruptly snuffed out. Two-lane highways, on which we are only a few feet from almost certain death, serve as a deadly metaphor for unpredictable change. This does not mean we shouldn't make

---

[497] *This is due to the fact that non-linear feedback systems (which include most systems, physical and human) are highly sensitive to initial conditions.*

every effort to effect change that we feel is important, particularly when taking care of ourselves. However, a 12-Step axiom applies here: we can take the action, but must turn the results over.

Chaos and powerlessness[498]

Human life moves forward in countless permutations. Change one of innumerable (seemingly) unimportant events and we progress on a different path. These events can include a chance meeting, a brief observation, a decision to see (or not see) someone or a price change inducing one to purchase (or not purchase) an item. Dozens of such small events are those in an initial system — the first day of the rest of one's life — which can result in life-altering effects of a totally unpredictable nature.

An example from personal experience was running into an old grade school friend at age 20 and my first day ever on skis. Through all the ski gear, he barely recognized me, almost skiing by. We talked, exchanged numbers and ended up renewing our friendship. We partnered up and bought two houses together. I introduced him to his wife and he, to my now ex-wife. If either of us had moved even a hundred feet a moment before, we would likely have never re-met and our lives would have been immeasurably different. Furthermore, there were innumerable chance meetings, observations and events that led each of us to the slopes that particular day. Thousands more were required to put me here today, along with you. What we <u>can</u> do is choose our actions and reactions to these events.

Since events are "Chaotic," we are <u>ultimately</u> powerless over them. While we may sometimes have an influence, these occasions cannot be predicted. However, we should try when we see the opportunity arise, because we <u>can</u> be a tool or catalyst through which to start the process. If the time is right, the attempt will be successful. As Victor Hugo observed, "An invasion of armies can be resisted, but not an idea whose time has come."

Taking action is also important for <u>me</u>. For example, I refuse to enable substance addicts' poor behavior and am pro-active in doing so (e.g., by

---

[498] *See Appendix 2 for a discussion of Parker and Stacey's integration of Chaos and free market economics. This led to my application of Chaos to the 12-Step Program, ultimately resulting in what some may consider an integration of science and spirituality.*

calling 911 to attempt to remove intoxicated drivers from public roads and writing this book). However, I have no idea when such disenabling (or other actions) will make a difference. When we recognize and accept that Chaos Theory dictates that countless initial conditions will evolve unpredictably and, <u>ultimately</u>, beyond our control, outcomes will no longer determine internal happiness and serenity.

The focus, then, must change. The first step of accepting powerlessness becomes the foundation for a rational "selfishness." It's been said, the road to hell is paved with good intentions. We need to instead concentrate on ourselves. The first step of the 12-Step Program and the Serenity Prayer can become fundamental principles of conduct for one's inner life from which self-empowerment follows. This is a particularly important worldview for codependents, crazed from carrying on a relationship with an addict.

Powerlessness and empowerment

"Regret: Realizing you wasted your life worrying about the future."

— Anonymous

The basic idea of ultimately being powerless over events leads to several other tenets. One can start with a question: if (ultimately) powerless, what can we rationally worry about? I can't think of anything, other than oneself. If there's nothing left to fret over, how can we obsess over future events? Concern and worry/obsession are at opposite poles. To be concerned is caring, while to worry/obsess is dramatic and emotionally exhausting, interfering with serenity. This is true for fear as well, which is based on worrying over future unknowns. If we stop worrying, what is there to fear (at least from a logical point of view)? A lessening of fear (or its healthy elimination) leaves a vacuum, with courage filling the void. Increased courage leads to a greater willingness to take rational risks, in turn providing greater opportunities, ultimately leading to greater success. The old salesman adage that for every "no" he's that much closer to a "yes" rings true. One must take risks and experience failures before ultimately finding success. Understanding that failure is essential leads to the acceptance of outcomes. This can be interpreted as a suggestion that, rather than struggling against, one should try standing aside from or simply going with the tide.

An analogy that nature provides is found in rip tides. When swimmers struggle against these, they can drown. Those who swim to the side and get out of their way survive; those who just go with such tides use no energy, simply ending up further out from shore, alive. They also have a wider perspective of the shore.

Worry and fear result from exaggerated concerns over negative outcomes of future events. ("Fear" is defined by some as "False Expectations Appearing Real.") While some can eliminate these from conscious thought, thus obliterating worry and fear, this is not as automatic for everyone. One mental tool may help. A negative thought (imaginary scenario) could be consciously countered with an opposing positive one. Since for many, negative thought-outcomes keep coming, this can be continued, until a multitude of possible positive outcomes have been dreamt up. The negative thoughts eventually cease, helping one to "let go."

Setting goals can cause worry about one's inability to accomplish them. This can also cause anger over anything that gets in one's way. Comprehending Chaos Theory helps to understand that whatever our sights, we may end up with unexpected and, sometimes, fascinating results. Using these tools, we can quickly become serene and accepting of most outcomes. A progressive flowchart of this logic is found in Figure 17.

Figure 17 – Chaos and Personal Empowerment

Chaos and Personal Empowerment Flowchart 1

Chaos → Powerless over others and events → tough to worry about anyone or anything else → makes it difficult to obsess about future events → leaves nothing to fear → gives one greater courage → provides greater willingness to take rational risks (emotional and otherwise) → opens one to greater opportunities → increases success in life → makes one more accepting of outcomes → greater serenity

Chaos and Personal Empowerment Flowchart 2

Chaos → powerlessness → won't be upset → won't be angry or bitter → eliminates resentment → eliminates hatred → increased serenity

Emotional upset requires worry over events and other people's actions. Now that we accept our ultimate powerlessness over these, try getting upset. If you still can, let's review: we are not in control of other people or events. We can control ourselves, at least to a certain extent. By re-focusing, we have far greater ability to master our own emotional states. Anger, bitterness and resentment all create inner distress. These result from people's behaviors and actions we find objectionable. How could we let such emotions affect us so greatly if we have no final control over the perpetrators of these actions?[499]

Some may object, seeing anger not only as an important human emotion, but as one that should be perpetuated. We could instead ask, why not harness or control this emotion, thus eliminating the need to stay in it for any longer than needed? We might also ask, is remaining in an angry state a useful response to events or actions over which we lack control? Since hatred results from a cumulative series of angry responses to someone, some persons or their actions and we are finding it difficult to be angry, how can we hate? There goes another impediment to serenity.

Chaos and Personal Empowerment Flowchart 3

Chaos → powerlessness → can't hold to expectations of others → non-controlling world-view → focus on oneself → greater self-improvement → greater self-potential

If powerless over others, even though we can try to influence and hope that it takes, we cannot logically expect it to. As the old saying goes, "expectations are disappointments under construction." Therefore, we can decide that we just won't hold on to expectations (even though we may

---

[499] *According to the "Big Book" of Alcoholics Anonymous, resentment destroys more alcoholics than anything else, from which stems "all sorts of spiritual disease...." From, "Alcoholics Anonymous," Ibid., p. 64.*

hold others to moral standards and the rule of law). The second stanza of the Serenity Prayer tells us what we <u>may</u> do: we can allow <u>ourselves</u> the courage to change. This means, for example, that if we don't like someone's behavior, we can choose not to live or otherwise be with him. We can even inform him of our choice. We can't (rightfully) tell the other person not to smoke in the privacy of his own home or on the property of others who may allow it. We <u>can</u> say, "You may smoke; however, I choose not to live with smoke or with one who smokes." This approach alters interaction and communication with others to non-coercive non-controlling statements of perceptions, along with one's own decisions. Taking the helm of self makes such interaction with others far more pleasant and even-keeled.

If we can't hold to expectations we may have of others, we cannot logically try to control them. This is another way of taking the focus off others and putting it on oneself, providing greater opportunity for self-improvement and, therefore, an increased ability to fulfill one's own potential.

Chaos and Personal Empowerment Flowchart 4

Chaos → powerlessness → can't hold to expectations of others → greater patience with others → eliminates anger → we feel better

---

Taking the logic further, if one doesn't stick to expectations of others, how can one be impatient? Anger is thereby converted into patience. This doesn't mean we don't inform authorities about transgressions when appropriate, or don't discuss the poor behaviors and help to mete out consequences. However, we can now do so with patience, accepting of one's inability to control another. We can remember that we have choices (often many), regardless of others' actions or transgressions.

Chaos and Personal Empowerment Flowchart 5

Chaos → powerlessness → no holding to expectations of others → non-controlling of others → increased personal growth in others → greater creativity by others

---

Expectations can result in an attempt to control others, which can serve to prevent them from experiencing consequences of their own judgments and behaviors. If failures are necessary for our own success, it is so for others. If we impose expectations, how can others make the mistakes they need? Few learn without making errors and living with the consequences. Moreover, mistakes for one are not necessarily mistakes for another.

Many great "discoveries" have been made by accident, or were "mistakes," if you will. Great inventors disconnect themselves from expectations. They are able to ask what happened, why, what new opportunities came about and what does this unexpected result offer? Trying to invent a new form of super-glue at 3M was deemed a failure by some when the product didn't stick well; however, the "failure" led to Post-It notes.

Chaos and Personal Empowerment Flowchart 6

Chaos → powerlessness → no holding to expectations of others → no disappointments → increased opportunities

---

As humans, even with all these tools, we'll still get angry or upset from time to time. This is a good thing, since anger leads to passion. Passion is the most powerful of all positive human emotions. However, it need not be driven by anger; it can instead be <u>triggered</u> by it, then continuing on its own. Yet, we will have what alcoholics call "slips," staying in a negative emotional state for longer than needed. While this cannot be eliminated by most, we can learn to limit the duration of such negative states. After repeatedly experiencing positive results from powerlessness, we can eventually learn to accept and deal with our emotions appropriately, more quickly moving into "serenity" mode.

Letting anger (and other negative emotions) go does not mean we must forget or not act. Dealing with those who have not kept their promises, as in the case of alcoholics, can be treated as reminders to reset or redefine one's boundaries. If someone breaks an agreement, we may refuse to make new contracts. When lending money or extending credit, we can decide that we will not allow our happiness and serenity to be affected if not paid, or can choose to avoid the situation. This is not to say, don't try to rectify wrongs. It should just be done serenely.

Remember, since we are not in control of others, we shouldn't hold to expectations. Without these, it's difficult to be <u>disappointed</u>. Without being afraid of disappointment, what seemed risky before now spells opportunity. Sometimes the results will knock us around for a while. These are merely messages redirecting us to new paths, if we'd only listen.

> ## Chaos and Personal Empowerment Flowchart 7
>
> Chaos → powerlessness → no holding to expectations of others → eliminates codependency and other-dependency → independence

If we cannot control others, then the reverse must be true: others cannot control us. It follows that they can't be responsible for our happiness. If we recognize this, we eliminate the bizarre attributes of codependency that the addict brings out (controlling, for example). It also eliminates what many call "codependency," but which I refer to as "other-dependency." This is where we allow someone else's actions to determine our level of happiness. If not dependent upon others for happiness, we are in dependent. This is not to say we shouldn't have a desire to be with someone else. It's just that not being involved in relationships should not prevent us from being happy, content and serene.

Perhaps the most important aspect of accepting one's ultimate powerlessness over others is the inward re-focusing of energies. When we live the reverse of the first step through a belief that we are powerful over others, the focus is outward. By accepting ultimate powerlessness, the time and energy that was expended on others becomes re-focused on oneself, providing far greater opportunities for self-improvement.

We have the right to take care of ourselves first, so long as we don't infringe on anyone else's rights. If we earn money by performing services for others, thereby enriching their lives, our motive doesn't matter. If we choose to play and earn nothing, we make no one else poorer and commit no harm to others. Some may protest that by not working, I may be harming my family. In this case, I likely infringed upon my family's rights by violating a contract, express or implied, requiring that I provide for their financial, emotional, or other support. Others may object that we harm ourselves, but that is not their business. While this would seem to make one an island unto himself, this is true only to the extent that people wish. As evidenced by human interaction in the marketplace and the creation of families and other voluntary associations, most choose to build not just interconnecting bridges, but even entire metaphorical landmasses between those islands.

Taking care of oneself includes finding a life's work that seems like play. Whatever it is, if it's within one's "self-interest," it's something enjoyed. If it's enjoyed, it will generally be done well. This benefits everyone. "Do what you love and the money will follow," because work becomes play.[500] This is the virtue of "selfishness," or responsible self-interested behavior.[501]

Chaos and Personal Empowerment Flowchart 8

Chaos → powerlessness → no holding to expectations of others → non-controlling world-view → I'm responsible for me → focus on me → greater sense of self-responsibility → more responsible behavior → maximizing potential for self-improvement

---

Which Leads to the Ultimate Paradox:
Powerlessness→Self-Empowerment

Acceptance of reality is not fatalism. We <u>should</u> set goals. The crucial distinction is one's response to failure. Acceptance = serenity. Occasionally, however, there is an event so terrifying, tragic or senseless, even acceptance of powerlessness fails, for a time, to empower. This leads to a question raised by the third step of the 12-Step Program: the curious one of "why."

Curiosity and serenity

"Life is what happens to you when you are busy making other plans."
—John Lennon

The 2nd Step says, (we) "Came to believe that a Power greater than

---

[500] *"Do What You Love, the Money Will Follow," Dr. Marsha Sinetar, Dell Publishing: New York, 1987.*

[501] *Market-based economies, built on voluntary human interaction, provide many wonderful benefits. One overlooked benefit may at first seem harsh: the opportunity of being driven out of business, if service or products are not efficiently provided at prices consumers are willing to pay. Far from being harsh, it does one an enormous favor: it tends to redirect a person into a life's work more consistent with one's innate Temperament. The acceptance of powerlessness over others, then, resulting in focusing on oneself, may eventually lead to the discovery of what spiritual writer Doctor Deepak Chopra and others call one's dharma, or purpose in life. This maximizes both happiness and wealth for everyone.*

ourselves could restore us to sanity." However, this can only be accomplished if one allows it. This means, we should accept what Chaos (or one's God) offers rather than struggle against it. The 3rd Step, (we) "Made a decision to turn our will and our lives over to the care of God *as we understood Him,*" suggests that we would do better entrusting the *care* of our will and lives to God (or other term—reality, the Law of Chaos, Higher Power, etc.) than to ourselves. When faced with one of life's difficulties, those not trusting may ask, "Why me?" A better question might be "What opportunities have I been given?" [502]

Obstacles frequently sidetrack us. However, they can result in personal, professional and/or spiritual growth by leading us to new paths. The speed with which such growth occurs is correlated to the degree that we accept these re-directions. Acceptance can result in quick growth, while fighting may result in none.

The martial art of Aikido teaches its students to use the opponent's strength against himself. Rather than blocking a punch or striking back, students guide the opponent in the direction of the punch, making it less likely for the student to be hurt. He uses his opponent's own energy against him by causing him to travel further than intended. It is a metaphor for dealing with obstacles. Instead of struggling against them, they can be used to further one's growth.

Regardless of our action and goals, Chaos Theory predicts that we often end up other than where we intend. Struggling "against" obstacles, saps energy that might be more productively used dealing with "what is." Borrowing from Aikido, we can use obstacles to fuel growth.

Rather than seeing these as brick walls, we can get curious as to where they lead. We can view them as guides to possible alternate paths, offering lessons, insight and knowledge. Just as lifting weights strengthens muscles, as Anthony Robbins points out, resistance in the form of obstacles improves

---

Curiosity and Anger Cannot Co-Exist

Not our will → acceptance of reality → we always learn from obstacles → we can't be angry at something that instructs → gets us curious (what will we learn this time?) → difficult to feel anger when curious

---

[502] *Anthony Robbins' "Powertalk" tape series was instrumental in my understanding and embracing the idea of converting problems into opportunities.*

character, knowledge and wisdom, leading to personal growth.
This brings us to a profound question:

How can we be angry or upset with someone or something that forces us on a path not intended, but from which we invariably acquire knowledge, wisdom and improved character?

Eventually, a faith in reality is engendered from observing that barriers, even if painful in the short run, are repeatedly turned into lessons or other benefits. The presence of these obstructions affords us an opportunity to learn something; however, we must be open to it. Try feeling anger, when curiously asking the reason for an obstacle. The anger <u>will</u> eventually dissipate.

Mindful of the fact that we are led to goals we don't anticipate, we should look for reasons. When attempting to keep on track while being steered elsewhere, we risk staying emotionally hurt, just as blocking the punch is often painful. While sometimes "blocks" are appropriate, rolling with the punches diminishes struggle and hastens life's lessons. This puts an entirely new light on so-called "bad" events.

Story after story of people involved in tragedy has told of overcoming seemingly insurmountable roadblocks and becoming better for it. Instead of venting anger at the perpetrator of the event, we can get curious about who we will meet, what new path we've been led to, what new discoveries a personal crisis may lead, etc. Obviously, in extreme cases, this is difficult. However, if we turn initial anger at a negative event into a curiosity about what will happen next, actively looking for positive interpretations or outcomes, problems may be converted into opportunities. Doing just that led to this book. Curious, with anger dissipated, I was open to opportunities. It is this attitude that provides a level of serenity never dreamed.

How "Bad" Things Become Good

Not our will → acceptance of what is → acceptance of obstacles → always learn something of value, eventually deriving benefits → builds "faith" → always given opportunities → then obstacles are good → there is little offered that is truly "bad" → eliminates "problems" → serenity

There are negative events that seemingly have no lesson or rational reason for having occurred. Obviously, we do what we can to prevent such catastrophes. However, once these have happened, let's look for a reason and make do with what is.[503] We can almost always convert these to some level of good. If mindful of this, we can accomplish such conversions more quickly and effectively. Inevitably, with the right attitude, good can be derived from such tragedy.

When we see that problems inevitably lead to learning and other ensuing side benefits, it is difficult not to develop a certain faith in the events that unfold. Out of every previous obstacle, knowledge and lessons have been derived. Although not certain, there is no reason to believe that this time will be different. One may develop a greater faith in events from such experiences. Ultimately, we can view problems as a grab bag of possibilities. Again, this allows us to deal more easily with events in a serene way.

Acceptance of reality leads to serenity. It allows for a truer and more all-encompassing love, including accepting all people for who they are, while at the same time not necessarily sanctioning their actions. Acknowledging that one is powerless over others, we can more easily detach with love, which is essential when dealing with an alcoholic.[504]

Turning problems into opportunities allows one to turn anger at the alcoholic-addict into a chance for personal growth. Addiction can thereby be converted from personal devastation to a Phoenix rising.

---

[503] *An example of such tragedy was Candy Lightner's daughter, who was killed by a drunk driver. Lightner was herself an alcoholic, who then got sober and went on to found Mothers Against Drunk Driving (MADD).*

[504] *Deepak Chopra in "The Way of the Wizard: Twenty Spiritual Lessons for Creating the Life You Want," Harmony Books, 1995, explains how acceptance of reality can lead one to a greater feeling of personal freedom. As an aside, the 3rd step is a way by which to approach many of Chopra's tools for living.*

Epilogue

The challenge of dealing with an addict has taught me to offer only tough love. I had the opportunity to offer such love to my addict long after she left, one day a few months into one of her periods of sobriety. She asked that I return several music books in a piano bench she had sold to me. The piano and music, it turns out, were her parents', but all she asked was that I return the music. Saying I would not, she pleaded with me not to make her parents pay for her addiction. I again responded no, I would not help her avoid the consequences and return something she sold improperly while under the influence of alcohol and crack cocaine. She hung up abruptly, still unable to accept consequences. When the ego remains inflated (as evidenced by the reverse telephonitis), it means that she's either in early sobriety, about to relapse or using again. I would have taken a different tack if there had been good, solid recovery, but there wasn't at this juncture.

I mulled over my own response for a few weeks, wondering whether it was appropriate. I decided that refusing to aid a recovering addict in negating the consequences of actions while practicing was important for me. Having been fairly close to them, I decided that her parents deserved an explanation of the reason I would not return the music. I called them and explained that we <u>cannot</u> know which event in the life of an addict will get and keep her sober. We must, therefore, <u>uncompromisingly</u> disenable in all areas, regardless of what may be appropriate in similar situations with others. This holds true even in areas where some would suggest we should show "compassion" by moderating our response. That the subject of the following letter to my addict's parents seems so mundane and seemingly insignificant is a testimonial to the importance of not compromising to <u>any</u> degree in our disenabling. It would be presumptuous and arrogant to pretend we can know which memory of which event in the life of an addict may cause her to get and stay clean and sober, no matter how seemingly insignificant. We must disenable even in the small areas. It is a reflection, as well, of the importance of doing what is right for us. This too, leads to serenity.

June 23, 1997

Dear Saul and Maxine,

I hope you are both doing well. I miss you both and the family I once had. At least what I sometimes think it could have been. Turns out, I now understand, it was not meant to be.

I have learned a tremendous amount since we last met. I've converted the obscenely destructive power of alcoholism into a lesson of immeasurable benefit. It was touch and go, but I survived. I say this not to be pompous, destructive of Patricia, or to seek revenge. I say it, rather, to suggest that while this disease can be fatal to addict and non-addict alike, it can be used as a turning point to convert the sourest lemon into the sweetest lemonade.

Nor do I feel anger toward Patricia. Yes, she again chose the first drink. By this time in her life, she knew better. However, the confluence of her own self-destructive behavior, desire to drink wine with me and hope that she could control her own drinking was over-powering. After that first taste, her disease made it impossible to stop for as long as she was enabled to any degree. I blame no one, including myself, having instead used the pain I endured to learn. I have found that just as body builders increase strength with resistance, we build knowledge and character from adversity. The greater the obstacles the more we build. This was, by far, the greatest adversity I've ever encountered and therefore, the greatest learning experience of my life. As a seeker of knowledge and understanding, how can I remain angry?

Many call addiction a "disease of denial." This is far too narrow a view. The addict's perceptions of reality are totally distorted, which explains far more than mere denial. These distortions cause the addict to hate those whom in her right mind, she would love. At the risk of seeming arrogant, despite Patricia's apparent hatred for me, I believe she loved me more than she's ever loved any man. This is an opinion with which I believe you concur, based on conversations early in our liaison when there were moments of clarity. However, the alcohol sabotaged the relationship and undermined her love for me. In the end, the substance is what the addict loves. These same twisted views led us into increasingly heated arguments into which I allowed myself to be drawn. Starting out innocently, I was blindsided. It gradually and inexorably worsened, becoming habitual only in the latter stages. This, with the alcoholic charm and the truly wonderful person I somehow knew was underneath, is how it trapped me, as it does everyone ignorant of the manifestations of the disease. The children suffered even more because of her addiction. I wonder how they will ever recover and lead normal lives.

The damage the substance addict inflicts on others is awesome in its scope and magnitude. Every addict seriously affects several around him. If there are 30 million addicts in the United States, this would cover most everyone. Curing this horrible disease, or arresting it, would be as great a service to mankind as finding the cure for cancer, heart disease, AIDS and every other disease all put together.

The irony is, there is a cure that works for many. It's simple and is actually well known. However, it's not thought of as a cure, so it is not used rigorously. It's a paradox, since it involves helping and educating the non-addict. It is difficult, because it prescribes that non-addicts offer tough love. However, few consistently offer such love. Rather, most think offering their heart, soul and financial resources will help. Unfortunately, this only prevents recovery. Treat not the addict but rather show his enablers the error in helping in any way, leaving no one left to "help." As long as there is one person willing to enable through kindness and charity, the chances for a cure are greatly reduced. The choice allowed for the addict must be, don't do the deed or, suffer outcomes without compromise. The addict must experience every consequence to the fullest without lessening the impact through the sharing of such results with others. Since the substance numbs both physical and emotional pain, it must be greater by several magnitudes than the non-addict could possibly withstand or endure. Unhappily, this often culminates in crises of unimaginable proportions. It is difficult for we non-addicts to accept, but pain is Patricia's best friend. The sooner she is allowed to fully experience such pain, the sooner recovery can begin. The greater the pain she remembers when sober, the more likely she will, with help from her fellow alcoholics, stay clean and sober the next time she's ready to (yet again) take that "first drink."

Patricia called several weeks ago asking if I would return some papers in the piano bench she sold me as she left Los Angeles, high as a kite, in late 1995. She now tells me it was your piano and your papers. She said even if I don't return the piano, please send you the papers. She pleaded with me not to make you pay for her addiction.

I have paid for her addiction. I paid with thoughts of suicide and a depression the depths of which I didn't know anyone was capable of sinking. I paid with lost business. Several large clients left, after she repeatedly failed to keep promises she'd made to both them and me when she pretended to help me in my work. I paid for it with a stolen computer and erased programs. I paid the deductible resulting from her demolishing the old car, the cost of renting and then buying a new one we otherwise didn't need, along with the cost of repairing damage to this one after two more accidents. How could I not "help," believing she was genuinely "disabled" with a back injury from her first two automobile accidents, suspiciously only weeks apart.

I paid $1,000 for tests to check her hormones. I thought she must have had chemical imbalances because she was at times so hostile and irrational. When we received the negative test results she said, " I told you there were no problems!" She forgot to inform me that while hormones did not cause her craziness, there were alcoholic drinks and other psychoactive drugs. There were also moments in between uses when she experienced withdrawals. This made her appear sociopathic, bipolar, paranoid, borderline and at various times practically all the other psychopathological disorders and mental illnesses. Predictably, I was dragged into the maelstrom of insanity as are so many chemically codependent persons.

I would not have purchased a large family home, overpaying for it, were it not for her and the children. I paid with money spent under false pretenses for her children's' education and her support, while they damaged our home in drug-induced rages. I paid for it by covering her medical bills, far greater than they would have been had she not been using. The $8,000 I paid to a psychologist of her choosing was minimal compared with the damage the psychologist caused from giving incompetent counsel. She knew so little about substance addiction that she never once suggested addiction might be at the root of virtually all the other problems. This turned counseling into the greatest form of enabling the addict knows, as any recovering addict who had therapy while using will admit. According to the counselor, the children and I were the source of her problems and even the reason for her drinking. This gave her all the excuses she needed to keep using and blaming me. I paid for hours of less than worthless counseling with a $175 per hour child psychologist who apparently didn't know she couldn't treat the children until their mother got clean and sober. She didn't even know Patricia had the disease of addiction, despite countless signs that any knowledgeable person would immediately recognize. The trouble is, there are few knowledgeable persons. Instead, the psychologist wanted to institutionalize Patricia for possible manic-depression and try varying doses of lithium to control her "mental imbalances."

I paid for her addiction with an engagement ring, fully intending to live the rest of our lives together. I paid for it with lies and deceit and cover-ups about everything that was going on behind my back and in my own home, including a conspiracy between she and her children to insure I would not discover her surreptitious drinking and using other drugs. She had me absolutely duped (in her alcoholic ability to sell anybody anything) that she would never lie or omit anything of a material nature. I suspected nothing for almost two years, even while she shared her drugs with her 11 and 13-year-olds. I paid for it with concern over sexually transmitted diseases, possibly even AIDS, now knowing that she would do anything for her next drink, hit, snort or smoke. I paid for it by losing the greatest love of my life to the disease of substance addiction.

Long after her move, I received calls from American Express regarding an overdue $4,500 balance. I was a signatory on the card and they threatened to come after me. I was very calm as I explained the situation. I was a model of recovery as I said to myself, if God wants me to pay another $4,500 in addition to the $100,000 I've already put out for lessons in the subject of alcoholism and other drug addiction, so be it. I'll do it with the knowledge that He thinks I need yet one more reminder to never let it happen again.

She now begs me not to let you pay for her addiction. You have been giving her the wrong kind of love and charity all her life. This is not to blame you. You had no more idea than I that this is not only what she didn't need, but that it was harmful in every conceivable way. I enabled her addiction for almost three years with my love, my willingness to be her doormat and $100,000 in net worth, far less of a loss to me than now knowing that it financially and psychologically enabled her.

As petty as this may sound, I calmly and politely told Patricia that it would be about time that she experience a consequence of her addiction. If, in fact, there were papers in the piano bench of sentimental or other value to you, she should experience this pain in order to remember.

Patricia should have gone to jail for many crimes, among them child abuse. Having observed it, I believe substance addiction in a parent is prima facie evidence of such abuse. The parent cannot be emotionally connected with a child, nor can there be any ability to provide the consistency of discipline children need, deserve and desire. She cannot be truly available for the child, when all she cares and thinks about is when and where she will have her next drink. She should have been taken to jail for driving under the influence on numerous occasions, including every time (except perhaps one) she got into an accident. She should have been incarcerated for siphoning money out of me under false pretenses, taking great pains to insure I was convinced she would never withhold anything material about her or our relationship. She apparently believed her drinking was not "material." How could I doubt the woman I loved, believing in her honesty and honor, having the utmost faith in her, having no known reason to disbelieve her? She drank and smoked dope with her then 13-year-old son, and supplied cigarettes (and very possibly dope, and later cocaine) to both him and her then 11-year-old daughter. During this time, I worked as many as 90 hours per week during tax season supporting her, her children and their addictions. She should have been imprisoned and had her children taken from her. It's utterly incredible what the law didn't catch.

It's time Patricia fully experiences the consequences of her addiction. I cannot go back and disenable retroactively. I can and choose to disenable now. I will never again knowingly enable another addict. I now understand this only serves to prolong their agony and that of others around them. I have a terrific advantage here. I've developed the ability to observe it where few others seem able, simply by watching the <u>behavior</u> to determine whether someone has the disease of substance addiction. When possible and if asked, I will teach others. We must all stop enabling. Only then will addicts have the opportunity to experience consequences so horrible that, even through their distorted perceptions, they will be able to see they are the problem, rather than those nearby. Only then, can they get and stay clean and sober. This is an action I take not <u>against</u> Patricia, but <u>for</u> her. She must experience and she must remember. I will do this not only for other addicts, but also (and especially) for the one I once loved.

Frankly, had you requested the papers, I wouldn't have hesitated to return them. In fact, if you still want them, I will send them to you. I would only ask for your promise to never tell her.

I sincerely hope you understand. I wish only the best for you.

I love you all.

                                              Doug

Appendix 1 – The Case for Hitler Being an Addict

The purpose of this appendix is to suggest that if we see the behaviors, we must suspect addiction, no matter how farfetched. My first questions for James Graham included the possibility of substance addiction by the most corrupt, dangerous and destructive rulers in history, past and present. Case in point: Adolf Hitler. I felt that the disease could be responsible for his behavior. Remembering Sherlock Holmes (who despite both his and his creator's cocaine addiction made many sound observations), the theory that best explains the <u>observable</u> facts is usually the right one. Eliminate the impossible and whatever is left, no matter how improbable or how few see it, is the truth.

Graham convinced me that Hitler was not an alcoholic. As repeated throughout this work, not every criminal and unethical behavior is explained by addiction. However, I felt there might be a better reason for his behavior than just his father's alcoholism. I remained alert to the possibility I might find something in this regard on the most reviled person in history.

My perseverance paid off at a thrift store in the beautiful ski town of Mammoth, California, where I found "The Medical Casebook of Adolf Hitler," by Leonard L. Heston, M.D. and Renate Heston, R.N., with an introduction by Hitler's biographer, Albert Speer. The Hestons point out, there was "no evidence of psychiatric impairment up to the middle of the 1930s at the earliest."[505] However, Speer became convinced that the disorders which later appeared (and that he had previously described as manifestations without understanding their source) were "produced by the amphetamines he was being given."[506] Eventually, Hitler declared that he could not live without his favorite doctor, Morell, who administered "a mixture specially compounded for the Fuhrer."[507] This was widely believed to be a multi-vitamin injection.

During WWII, Hitler began having outbursts of rage unlike anything his generals had ever seen, reactions that were "grossly disproportionate to the situation in both duration and emotional intensity." A result of likely

---

[505] *Heston, Ibid., p. 71.*
[506] *Ibid., p. 16.*
[507] *Ibid., p. 16-17.*

"chronic amphetamine poisoning," as Speer put it, was mental rigidity, repetitive, stereotyped and disorganized thinking causing all-night monologues with the same stories told over and over, distractibility, hyper-vigilance, confused syntax and organization, paranoia, increased lying, projecting blame onto others, pathological manic states and severe depression.[508] Readers of this book will now recognize these behaviors as clues to addiction.

The amphetamine addiction led to chronic insomnia, resulting in heavy use of barbiturates nearly every night during WWII.[509] The trouble with psychoactive drugs is that they may have a desirable effect on the addict in the short-term. In particular, these include an euphoric mood, increased confidence and sense of well being. When Hitler was given his daily (and by 1943, more frequent) injections, numerous witnesses attested to the alerting and activating effect, causing Hitler to become cheerful, talkative, physically active and awake late into the night.[510] These results, despite the claim he was given only a "multi-vitamin," are incompatible with any drug other than a stimulant of the amphetamine or cocaine group. Injection is consistent with addiction. Dr. Schenck (another of Hitler's doctors) had gotten curious about Dr. Morell's special compound and surreptitiously had an analysis performed. Schenck confirmed Hitler's use of methamphetamine (in particular, Pervitin).[511]

Between amphetamine uses, there was a gradually worsening depression. An unrealistic optimism and sense of invulnerability took hold, resulting in impaired judgment. Eventually, toxicity became obvious, taking on the appearance of paranoid schizophrenia.[512] As we have shown, addiction lends itself to misdiagnosis, giving the appearance of manic-depression, schizophrenia, Parkinson's disease and hysteria, all of which Hitler has been misdiagnosed as having. The Hestons prove beyond any reasonable doubt it was none of these[513] and they, along with Speer, conclude Hitler's behavior could only be explained by amphetamine poisoning, which we now know can only result from addiction.

I would add one idea, which could explain Hitler's hatred and grandiose plans prior to his foray into amphetamines. Hitler ate caffeine candies (possibly starting as early as the 1920s) in such quantity that the Hestons wrote that he "no doubt got an effective pharmacologic dose."[514] I would

[508] *Ibid., p. 39, 43-45 and 113-115.*

[509] *Ibid., p. 79.*

[510] *Ibid., p. 83.*

[511] *Ibid., p. 85-87.*

[512] *Ibid. p. 101.*

[513] *Ibid., p. 109, pp. 116-117 and pp. 121-122.*

[514] *Ibid., p. 87. They also point out that "caffeine, itself a weak stimulant drug, significantly augments the effects of amphetamine," i.e., potentiates it.*

hypothesize that he may have taken sedatives prior to the war years, perhaps as early as when his heavy use of caffeine began, in order to counteract its effect at night. The barbiturates used by Hitler were of the longer-acting kinds which, according to the Hestons, give "little reason to suspect over-use or any effect other than simple sedation."[515] However, addiction expert Forest Tennant, M.D., told me that such barbiturates could result in large and long lasting mind alterations. Early on, barbiturates (potent sedatives) _may_ have been Hitler's drug of choice. Since sedatives mimic the effects of alcohol in the brain of the alcoholic and alcoholism ran in Hitler's family, he may have been one of Dr. Stanley Gitlow's sedativists. Ironically, in a conscious effort to avoid the alcoholism Hitler saw in his father, he _may_ have unwittingly triggered his addictive propensity in pill form.

[515] *Ibid., p. 79.*

Appendix 2 – Institutionalized Enabling

Welcome to world economics and how it relates to getting high. You may wonder, "What the heck does one have to do with the other"? We are about to show that enabling is the same in principle, regardless of the size of the entity.

We have seen unprecedented levels of bailouts in the 1980s and 1990s of large organizations ranging from financial institutions to entire countries. From the Savings and Loan debacle to the Asian meltdown, mistake after mistake has been absolved. Profits have been allowed to inure to the capitalist or the proceeds of bureaucratic theft to corrupt government officials, while losses have been socialized, spreading them across a population that rarely cries foul. Such is the problem of what economists call "rent seeking" behavior. This is the quest by those who err to spread their losses among countless taxpayers, each of whom pay little toward a multi-billion dollar mistake or subsidy. This gives them little incentive to protect their purse, resulting in the failure to hold responsible those truly accountable.

There are a number of correlations between the enabling of individuals and institutions. Enabling not only harms, but can also destroy regardless of size. Disenabling, on the other hand, helps both to see the need for change. This is more likely to result in survival and prosperity, or failure and recovery.

While there is no difference in principal between bailing out individuals and nations, there is a quantitative one in how many must suffer the consequences of the bailout. The results are similar when those who formulated the failed decisions and policies are protected from experiencing the consequences. Poor judgment continues to be manifested and efforts are concentrated on shifting costs to others. Whether on the level of the micro-family or macro-economic, it is enabling. It is different only in that the latter is more catastrophic, for it affects more people and is institutionalized, lawful and more difficult to change.

Bailed-out individuals generally fail to learn the lessons that are required to induce an effort to avoid repetition of errors. This prevents people from moving on to the next lesson of life, slowing progress, by getting "stuck." If we conceal someone else's personal or professional error by experiencing and paying for the consequence ourselves, the likelihood for continued growth is diminished. If we pay for an organization's mistake (with taxpayers' funds for example), the persons that operate that organization are unlikely to learn the lesson the mistake would otherwise impart. If we pay for a nation-state's foul-up by bailing it out of financial turmoil caused by its own financial or ideological excesses, its leaders are unlikely to learn (or its people are less likely to toss out the culprits). Enabling, then, becomes the reason for collapse of both families and entire civilizations.

It is puzzling to the uninitiated that when we bail out an alcoholic or other drug addict, not only is there no gratitude but, quite often, there is hatred. The distortion of perceptions caused by euphoric recall and other memory failures prevent him from ever seeing any problems in his thinking or actions. He remembers only that what he did was good, or "not so bad." Who, then, is to blame for his troubles? Perversely, those nearby seem the obvious choice, oftentimes even those who bailed him out. *He* did nothing wrong and therefore, we who have "helped," over and over, must be at fault.

The same result seems to occur among nations. Masses of people seem to coalesce into a mass psychology resembling that of the addict and his enabler, sometimes because one or the other rules them. The United States is frequently vilified wherever it has tried to "help." We experienced this in Viet Nam, as well as in numerous other countries in which we've interfered. Not surprisingly, our interventionist policies generally failed, we were hated and little changed.[516] Countries such as the former Soviet Union, which made gross economic and social errors under socialist economic models, eventually collapsed not due to our intervention, but of their own weight.

New Zealand was lucky. Having no resources that are vital to any other countries and isolated geographically, it has little strategic importance. When its economy was failing during the mid-'80s due to its socialist policies, no one bailed it out. This resulted in the embarkation upon one of the most radically free market experiments in human history. It has since evolved from a bleak, stagnant socialist economy to a progressive free market mecca (relatively speaking) in a span of only 10 years. Ironically, New Zealanders actually have alcoholism to thank for the opportunity that precipitated this. Its leader got drunk and, perhaps driven by ego, called for a snap election at what was, for his governing party, a particularly inopportune time.[517] He and his party were thrown out of office, paving the

---

[516] *Historian William Blum has compiled a list of countries that the U.S. has bombed since the end of World War II (usually with the best of intentions), including China, Korea, Indonesia, Cuba, Guatemala, Congo, Laos, Viet Nam, Cambodia, Libya, El Salvador, Nicaragua, Iraq and Yugoslavia. He asks how many of these instances resulted in a democratic government coming into existence, as a direct result of our intervention. The answer is zero.*

[517] *The story, a fascinating one, can be found in Liberty Magazine, March, 1997, p. 13-31 in articles by R.W. Bradford and Sir Roger Douglas.*

way for the Roger Douglas-led free market revolution.

Many Asian countries may not be so lucky. The United States bailed Mexico out of its financial errors in 1994, a lesson apparently not unnoticed by a number of Southeast Asian governments. When we learn we will be bailed out, whether as individuals or as nations, old failed behaviors tend to be repeated for as long as they seem to provide short-term benefits. In 1998, Korea, Thailand and Malaysia were being bailed out of economic policies that rewarded a massive boom-fueled build-up in uneconomic debt, which had led to, among other misfortunes, bad loans as high as 20% of outstanding debt. Bailing out both the creditors and debtors results in neither having learned much-needed lessons. When we allow capitalists to keep their profits but prevent them from failing by socializing losses, they are unlikely to reduce lending risks to more reasonable levels. When we allow debtors to repeatedly cry bankruptcy, giving them (yet again) one more chance, they are less likely to keep their debt at affordable levels.

Some suggest imposing external controls such as maximum levels of risk, maximum debt to Gross Domestic Product levels, etc. Doing this is tantamount to telling the addict he cannot drink, can drink only so much or can use this drug but not that. The trouble is, he will always find a way to get and use what he wants. The International Monetary Fund mandates new and improved lending standards or deposit to loan ratios. Invariably, it fails in its goals of financial conservatism, due to loopholes that men find or create through their own ingenuity. This is particularly true when these men know that they will keep their profits or proceeds of unearned takings while their errors (as those of countless lenders and debtors before them) are pardoned and the pain is dispersed to others.

Similarly, there is always some drug the addict can get his hands on for a price. The addict husband goes out drinking if he can't do it at home. The addict wife hides her bottles to protect her drug(s) of choice. Teenagers have their sources on the school playground, despite the war on drugs, D.A.R.E. and repeated and extremely expensive attempts by adults to keep drugs out of their hands. Even in prison, prisoners subsidize prison guards' salaries (or threaten their families by outside means) and prisoners get their substance(s) of choice. If the price is too high, they wait. They can summon, what is for addicts, a superhuman ability to suspend use until a future date.

There are a few countries where the lessons of excessive government interference or institutionalized enabling seem to have been learned, at least for now. Chile and Argentina, like New Zealand, are not that strategically important, so when they experienced the hyperinflations of the 1970s and '80s, they suffered as few nations ever have. They came to realize that their own failed policies and decisions had led them to the throes of national bankruptcy and ruin. This forced them to change in order to avoid having to experience such catastrophes again. They are less likely to be repeated for as long as those with memories of the failures are alive.

Appendix 3 – For Professionals: Type, Temperament and Addiction

Predictors of extended periods and deeper levels of addiction using Psychological Type

In order to comprehend specific cases of theory predicting longer and deeper levels of addiction for two specific Psychological Types (P.T.s) as measured by the Myers-Briggs Type Indicator (MBTI), we must learn the basics of the four opposing "preferences." They are termed this because, while we all have attributes of both sides, we tend to "prefer" one over the other, just as we feel more comfortable with the left or right hand. We've discussed the last preference (Perception vs. Judging — the novelty seeking vs. risk-avoidant personality); we'll now explore the first three.

The first, how we interact with and relate to our environment, is (I)Introversion and (E)Extroversion. Those who prefer Introversion ("Introverts") tend to be withdrawn or reserved, energizing or "recharging the batteries" more in solitude. Those who prefer Extroversion ("Extroverts") tend to be gregarious or expressive, usually drawing energy by being with other people.

The second set of preferences, how we collect and generate information, are (S)Sensation and (N)iNtuition (which would be capital "I," but it's already used for Introverts). Those preferring Sensation ("Sensates") process and share sensory information. Concrete realists, Sensates are comfortable with what they can touch, taste, see, hear and smell. Those preferring iNtuition ("iNtuitives"), gather information first through their fertile imaginations (using concrete perceptions of reality merely to augment) and excel at sharing whatever abstractions they can conjure up.

Figure 18 – Personality Types and Temperaments

How We Prefer to Interact with our Environment
I = Introvert. Reserved; may be withdrawn or shy and "recharges the batteries" by being alone.
E = Extrovert. Expressive; observes people and things. Can be gregarious, energizing with people.

How We Prefer to Take in Information ("Perceptive" Function)
S = Sensing, or Sensate. Observe concrete reality through the senses—sight, touch, taste, hearing and smell. At one with their physical surroundings and perceive "what is".
N = iNtuition, or iNtuitive. "Observe" through the imagination. Perceive possibilities.

How We Prefer to Make Decisions ("Judging" Function)
F = Feeler. Primarily judges based on peoples' values first, logic second, if at all.
T = Thinker. Primarily judges based on logic first, people's values second, if at all.

Which Function We Show to the World
P = Perceptive. Externally unstructured, non-directive, play first, novelty seeking, flexible.
J = Judger. Externally structured, directive, work ethic, more controlling, planned.

Out of these preferences, we can create sixteen Psychological Types			
ISTJ	ISFJ	INFJ	INTJ
ISTP	ISFP	INFP	INTP
ESTP	ESFP	ENFP	ENTP
ESTJ	ESFJ	ENFJ	ENTJ

Individual Preferences	Temperaments
I or E	SJ Guardian
N or S	SP Artisan
F or T	NT Rational
P or J	NF Idealist

When considering how these preferences differ, we can predict (to some extent) the varying effects of drugs. Addicts exhibit out-of-control behaviors, such as impulsivity, extreme play and excessive experimentation. We might guess that logical (T), externally structured (J) Types (Thinkers and Judgers of both the Sensate and iNtuitive stripes, or STJs and NTJs) are not likely to "let it all go" in drunken frenzies. On the other hand, value-oriented (F), externally unstructured experimental player (P) Types (Feelers and Perceptives of both the Sensate and iNtuitive stripes, or SFPs and NFPs) would be predicted to have a greater tendency to such behaviors.

There is anecdotal evidence that these Psychological Types seem to more likely be addicts. These Types tend to congregate in professions that have a high percentage of addiction. For example, addiction is epidemic in construction and entertainment. If it were only entertainment, one could argue that addicts select occupations in which they can inflate and flaunt their egos. However, construction is not an industry in which one can inflate the ego any more than in banking or insurance. Yet, addiction is probably a bigger problem there than anywhere else (which explains the reverse: why we observe those in construction so often flaunting their egos). To give an idea of the grotesque dimensions of the problem, a large construction firm had a contract with the federal government at a military installation. One of the terms was to perform unannounced alcohol and other drug tests on the employees. The failure rate was an astounding 45%. This didn't count those with prescriptions or strictly alcoholic "weekend warriors" (who, after partying all weekend, get sober for the work-week). Similarly, the failure rate was over 50% for workers at a marine assembly yard that the firm managed.

The Psychological Types that predominate in both entertainment and construction are similar. There are massive numbers of "introverted feelers" (in the great psychologist's Carl Jung's terms) which include "Sensing Feeling Perceptives" (SFPs in the Myers-Briggs paradigm), in both industries. There are also some "iNtuitive Feeling Perceptives" (NFPs, the other type of "introverted feeler") in entertainment. Certain FPs, specifically the INFPs and ISFPs ("dominant" introverted feelers in the Myers-Briggs lingo), are the ones who, after violating their own set of incredibly strong personal values, <u>may</u> sink far deeper into addiction than others. This could result in an extended period of active addiction, making them <u>appear</u> to be at greater risk. More research is necessary to confirm or disconfirm my hypothesis that these include the NFPs.

Another clue to the depths of despair resulting from addiction is found in levels of attempted suicide among different P.T.s. If we show a correlation between addiction and suicide, and another between suicide and Psychological Type, this suggests (even if we can't prove cause and effect) a possible correlation between addiction and Psychological Type. The correlation between addiction and suicide may be as high as 80%,[518] whether by practicing addicts, those in early recovery or those seriously impacted by an addict. According to the National Institute of Alcohol Abuse and Alcoholism, while the suicide rate for women in one recent year was about 9 per 100,000, the rate for women alcoholics was about 207 per 100,000, or 23 times as great. The mathematics of this suggest that 70% of all suicides among women are connected to alcoholism.[519] Alcoholism authority James E. Royce reports the suicide rate among young Eskimos (who suffer a rate of alcoholism of up to 95% in some villages) at 25 times the national aver-

---

[518] *Milam and Ketcham, Ibid. Numerous others have reported the incidence at 20 to 30%, but many suicides are likely "euphemized" into other "problems" the victim was having at the time. My hunch is, with further careful studies, the true number will be proved closer to Milam and Ketcham's estimate, when we include recovering addicts in early sobriety and the co-chemically dependent, crazed from dealing with an addict in a committed relationship.*

[519] *Cited in Robe, Ibid., pp. 383-384. If the rate of women alcoholics is 10%, then we can equalize by using 90 out of 1 million for the overall rate (there are 1 million non-addicts for every 100,000 addicts, if the rate of addiction is 10%). Therefore, we can calculate about a 70% correlation (297-90 = 207; 207/297 = 70%). Note that since this rate does not include other substance addicts, the correlation between suicide and substance addiction calculable from these statistics is likely understated.*

age, supporting this calculation.[520] The correlation between suicide and P.T. is also compelling. Introverted iNtuitive Feeling Perceivers (INFPs) were found (in a recent study) to have a far higher propensity to plan or attempt suicide than any other Type. They were three times more likely to make such an attempt than would be expected by chance and eight times more than those P.T.s least likely.[521] While we cannot draw definite conclusions from this correlation between addiction and P.T. given the genetic source of alcoholism, it does suggest that some P.T.s go far deeper into addiction than other Types. This points to a connection between suicide, alcoholism and Psychological Type that has, thus far, been grossly understated.

The difficulty in determining the Psychological Type of addicts

The difficulty in accurately determining an addict's Psychological Type using the MBTI should not be underestimated. Attempting to determine how one "prefers" to perceive or absorb information (through concrete Sensation or abstract iNtuition) is difficult to measure due to drug-altered perceptions. Measuring how one makes decisions or "judges" (through Thinking or Feeling) is also difficult, since judgment is, by definition, impaired because of distorted perceptions. Therefore, the practicing addict, or one in early recovery suffering Post-Acute Withdrawal (experiencing much of the same confusion), will very likely be inaccurately typed. The MBTI is likely wrong almost one-half the time. If it is incorrect so often overall, it likely gives erroneous results for almost all active addicts, who are incapable of viewing themselves accurately whether in Temperament or addiction.

---

[520] *Royce and Scratchley, Ibid., p. 178.*
[521] *"Personality Type and Suicidal Behaviors of College Students," Lola Kelly Komisin, Journal of Psychological Type, Vol. 24, 1992.*

Figure 19 – Why it is Difficult to Determine an Addict's Psychological Type

Non-Addict	
Perception:	Judgment:
Sensation	Thinking
iNtuition	Feeling
Addict	
Perception:	Judgment:
Distorted	Impaired

The MBTI can no more measure true Personality Type (P.T.) than the MMPI (the psychologists' tool) can determine true psychopathological disorders in a practicing addict (or one in very early recovery). Both instruments are merely measuring the effect that chemicals have on the brain of the addict; both are taking the temperature of Mr. Hyde. Even a competent feedback session is not likely to determine the addict's innate P.T. without extended observation. Addicts with long-term sobriety report that in early recovery, their perceptions and judgments were so confused and clouded that they did not really know themselves. They often mask their true selves as well from even those trained in Psychological Type and Temperament, unless those so trained keep a very open mind.

My personal addict, Patricia, not only took the MBTI but also (with me) the course that certifies one to give this Indicator to others. She scored "INTP," emphatically agreeing with that assessment. Subsequently, we met David Keirsey, who has been "Typewatching" both professionally and as a hobby for over 40 years. During our meeting, he pulled me aside and asked whether I was sure Patricia wasn't an Idealist (specifically, INFP) rather than a Rational (NT). I defended her self-analysis, but knew Keirsey was telling me, "try again." He also commented that while Myers-Briggs enthusiasts claim that we must accept one's own self-assessment of Psychological Type, we really must observe <u>behavior</u> to determine that person's

[522] *This is not dissimilar to the fact that we cannot rely upon an addict to correctly identify himself as such, and that non-addicts must tentatively diagnose addiction through observation of behaviors. This book might not have been possible were it not for this key insight of Keirsey's regarding Temperament. I extended this idea to the concept of diagnosing substance addiction, despite hearing at both AA and Al-Anon meetings that we should never "take others' inventories," i.e. diagnose addicts or codependents as such.*

knew not to discount Keirsey's views and proceeded to observe behavior.

I watched her for a year before realizing that Keirsey was right. The Rational Temperament, especially INTP, explained little or nothing, while the Idealist Temperament (in this case INFP) accounted for virtually everything about Patricia's behavior, including a far deeper addiction than would be predicted in a Rational.

Incorrect assessments explain nothing of one's behavior. One Internet "expert" has typed John Kennedy as INTJ, who was as clear an Artisan as there has ever been. (He was probably the exact opposite, an ESFP, or almost-opposite ESTP.). Because of egregious errors such as this, Psychological Type and Temperament are viewed by many as "pop" psychology. Yet, when innate Temperament is correctly identified, the power to explain behavior is unparalleled. A deep insight and understanding of both the addict and our relationship with him is gained when we know both our Temperaments. This occurred with my addict, once I understood the nature of both of her versions of Jekyll and Hyde.

We need all the clues to the addict's natural Temperament that we can muster. Fortunately, for purposes of determining core values and needs, along with one's source of self-esteem, we don't need to determine full Type. We need only determine Temperament, clues to which are readily observable, as described in the text.

Temperament, occupational choice and the limits to diagnosis: Using the clue of ego-inflation

One reason why there is so much addiction in certain fields may involve feeling "stuck," due to above-market wages that keep many performing work beneath their capacity. The likelihood of staying in an unwarranted occupational setting increases as the rate of pay rises. For example, a creative genius with a predisposition to addiction delivering mail for a living, may remain in active addiction longer than he would otherwise. This might be due to his failure to fulfill particular core needs. For example, some of these needs may be creative diplomacy if an Idealist or creative strategic thinking if a Rational. Because of family concerns, it may be difficult (on a practical basis) to change occupations when one might (temporarily) earn far less than $40-50,000 per year.

Any occupation can be made interesting for almost any Type if they are free to mold it to their own Temperament. Let's look at each of the Temperaments as Captains of the Star Trek universe were portrayed. Captain Kirk of the original series was clearly an Artisan tactician. Captain Picard ("Next Generation") may have been a Rational strategist (who competently took on his job assignment of being a diplomat). Captain Janeway ("Voyager") was clearly a Guardian logistician and Captain Sisko ("Deep Space Nine") was possibly an Idealist diplomatist. Each managed to perform their jobs competently, in their own style.

A Rational who just wants to do the job to perfection might find delivering mail relaxing, especially if he is into some intense studying or other mind-work during his other waking hours. (The great Rational, Albert Einstein, was a government bureaucrat at the Swiss patent office, evaluating the plans of would-be inventors, all the while creating the first new model of the universe since Isaac Newton's.) An Artisan may find the postal job fun, especially an extroverted one who chats with the residents during his route. Mail delivery may be a wonderful occupation for an Idealist who loves helping people connect, while a Guardian may be very happy simply taking on the duty and responsibility of getting the mail delivered. However, a person who is unable to mold the work to his style will not find it interesting or rewarding. If he doesn't find another endeavor, he may violate his internal set of values and aggravate any predisposition to substance addiction.

This could account for what seems a higher rate of substance addiction in heavily unionized industries, such as postal workers. Union rules often make it difficult to adjust a job to one's preferences, while monopolistic pricing of wages may be tempting to those who find high salaries difficult to resist. Such industries probably don't attract the preponderance of "Introverted Feeler" Types that construction, music and movie making do, nor are they appealing to those who would flaunt their egos. Although ego-inflation is important in helping us to identify addicts, Type and Temperament could explain an aspect of addiction that would make no sense if we limited our diagnosis to those addicts who would inflate their egos through the "right" occupational choices.

Appendix 4 – An Integration of Chaos, Free Market Economics and the 12-Step Program

David Parker and Ralph Stacey, in "Chaos, Management and Economics: The Implications of Non-Linear Thinking," argue that economic planning for organizations is impossible, whether in a planned (socialist) or market-based system.[523] They show that "systems which demonstrate sensitive dependence on initial conditions [i.e., chaotic systems] will not be successfully engineered or planned." Very small changes, frequently undetectable, in the initial conditions radically alter the ultimate course of the system. In addition, there are a multitude of combinations and permutations of initial events, which have in turn, countless initial inputs not within our control. While "members of such a system contribute to its unfolding future ...none can be in control of it."[524]

Because we cannot control these conditions, the path of an organization cannot be determined. Since the economy comprises countless organizations, we cannot determine the path of an economy, whether market or socialist. Parker and Stacey conclude, "instead of long-term planning, the aim should be to create the conditions most conducive to a *process* of continuous change."[525] It is "an advantage that free-market policies allow outcomes to evolve and do not require some prediction of the future."[526] This happens with a system based on the freedom to buy or sell goods and services at mutually agreed upon prices (a cybernetic feedback loop). The foundation for such a system is the freedom to choose, with responsibility for bearing the consequences of these choices.

Because humans have free choice (even within the confines of a totalitarian society and our genetic Psychological Type), all human behavior is subject to the law of non-linearity, the law of chaos. Feedback mechanisms in such systems in which each decision-maker is responsible for the conse-

[523] *Parker, David and Ralph Stacey, "Chaos, Management and Economics: The Implications of Non-Linear Thinking," United Kingdom: Coronet Books, IEA Hobart Paper Series #125, 1994, p. 16.*

[524] *Ibid., p. 14.*

[525] *Ibid., p. 20.*

[526] *Ibid., p. 16.*

quences of his choices (the benefits and costs of his own decisions and actions) tend to result in improved judgment. "Tough love" is part of this. Interfering with or obstructing feedback mechanisms suppresses the evolution of outcomes at both the macro-economic and individual level. While sometimes such control (interference or obstruction) bears fruit, often it doesn't. When it will or won't is not within our power to control or predict. Since the experience of the outcome is the feedback necessary for the decision-maker to improve his judgment (as manifested in decisions and actions), any and all outcomes are a pre-condition to improving such judgment at both the individual and organizational level.

This affords prodigious and indisputable support for the application of a system of non-control to all social units from the economy to the family or other micro-economic unit, such as the workplace. Such a system, by rewarding good judgment and mandating consequences for poor judgment, increases the chances of improving judgment and learning life's higher lessons. This tends to maximize human happiness and potential in both the macro- and micro-sphere of human relations.

Acknowledgements

A tremendous amount of teamwork has gone into the creation of this book. Without the input of numerous others, this work would have been far less comprehensive. The essential early contributions were from two renowned observers of healthy and unhealthy humans, David Keirsey and the late Vernon Johnson. Halfway through my writing, I was fortunate to discover the works of James Graham, James Milam, Katherine Ketcham and Terence Gorski (the latter and Vernon Johnson's works thanks to Wayne Reese, M.A.). Without the genius of these people, I may not have continued out of concern for an inability to make sense of what seemed incomprehensible. The other authors whose shoulders I have stood on are listed in the bibliography, but special gratitude should be offered the Reverend Joseph I. Kellerman, David Parker and Ralph Stacey, without whom I may not have recovered from my ordeal. Special mention should also go to the late Lucy Barry Robe, Martha Morrison, Miller Newton and Beth Polson, each of whom, in their own ways, helped me realize I was on track and, through their works, provided tremendous psychological and intellectual support.

I am particularly grateful to readers of early drafts for their invaluable input. They include my good friends, Melvin J. Kreger, J.D., L.L.M., Stephen Brooks, Joseph C., Jack Cretney, Joseph Sullivan and Barbara Thorburn-Greene (my mother). My editor, Scott Dorfman later helped re-write entire sections. Aside from his having become a great friend, I thank him from the bottom of my heart (as do, undoubtedly, later readers). Other reviewers offering valuable critiques included David Mark Keirsey, Kathleen Repecka, M.A., Linda Thio, C.C.D.C., Jim Hinman, C.A.C. and Type and Temperament experts Alice Fairhurst and Eve Delunas. My friend Sam Shiminovsky provided continuing psychological support throughout. Donna Winiger, Kelly Manners, Harold Peacock, Jeff L. and Mary L. helped me realize, at a personal level that I had stumbled on to something with enormous potential. Important contributions, whether it be their stories, education or other support were generously given by Neil and Joye Adams, Shari Adams, MFCC and Lon Adams, Jennifer Alamdari, Ralph B., Officer Curtis B., George and Cheryl B., Lee Borton, E.A., Al and Mo B., author Stephen Braun, author and counselor Mike Brubaker, Terri Lee Cadiente, author Randy Cassingham, Steve C., Karen C., Sharon R. Cobb, Claire Paul-Cook, Jeanette D., Clinical Psychologist Gabrielle Du Verglas, Ph.D., Joe F., David Greene, David Hagen, Esq., Deborah H., Dennis G., philosopher Fred Groh, Anthony H., Mr. & Mrs. G. Jewzcuk, Richard and Rose K., author and Sergeant Joseph Klein, Bill and J. Lomenick, Gail J., Robert Marcus, Pat Morrow, Marcus Mayes, Kathleen Price, M.F.T., Nancy P., David and Carol R., Thomas E. Page, Sergeant, LAPD Retired, Robert Prechter, Jr., Kathy

Robertson, Janice S., Jean Stinson, Brandon Tady, Dr. Forest Tennant, Bruce Tracy, Ph.D., Indexer, Stephen White and Dr. Aaron Yusem. In addition, there were numerous others who chose to remain anonymous.

Last but not least, I owe a debt of thanks to the addicts in my life, without whom the obstacles I needed for tremendous intellectual and spiritual growth might have never appeared. These challenges have paid enormous dividends, including providing me with the initial impetus that led to this writing, something which will, hopefully, help many others. Without these addicts, none of this would have been possible.

Bibliography

AA pamphlet, "20 Questions," used by John Hopkins University Hospital, Baltimore, MD.

Adams, Charles, "Fight, Flight, Fraud: The Story of Taxation," Buffalo, NY: Euro-Dutch Publishers, 1982.

Adams, Charles, "For Good and Evil: The Impact of Taxes on the Course of Civilization," New York: Madison Books, 1993.

Akst, Daniel, "Wonder Boy: Barry Minkow – The Kid Who Swindled Wall Street," New York: Charles Scribner's Sons, 1990.

"Alcoholics Anonymous: The Story of How Many Thousands of Men and Women Have Recovered from Alcoholism," New York: Alcoholics Anonymous World Services, Inc., Third Edition, 1976.

Amundson, Everett R., "Responsible Driving," Whittier, CA: Everett R. Amundson, 1995.

Backer, Thomas E., Ph.D., "Strategic Planning for Workplace Drug Abuse Programs," National Institute on Drug Abuse, 1987.

Barrineau, Phil, "The Type to Drink: Undergraduate Alcohol Policy Violators and Personality Type," Journal of Psychological Type, Vol. 41, 1997.

Batmanghelidj, F., M.D., "Your Body's Many Cries for Water," Falls Church, VA: Global Health Solutions, Inc., 1997.

Behr, Edward, "Prohibition: Thirteen Years That Changed America," New York: Arcade Publishing, 1996.

Bernstein, M., and J.J. Mahoney, "Management Perspectives on Alcoholism: The Employer's Stake in Alcoholism Treatment," Occupational Medicine, Vol. 4, No. 2 (1989).

Bernstein, Peter L., "Against the Gods: the Remarkable Story of Risk," New York: John Wiley and Sons, 1996.

Black, Claudia, "Children of Alcoholics – As Youngsters – Adolescents – Adults –

'It Will Never Happen to Me!'" New York: Ballantine Books, 1981.

Braun, Stephen, "Buzz: The Science and Lore of Alcohol and Caffeine," New York: Oxford University Press, 1996.

Brown, Jay A. and the editors of Consumer Guide, "Rating the Movies," New York: Beekman House, 1985.

Brubaker, Mike and Ken Estes, "Deadly Odds: Recovery From Compulsive Gambling," New York: Simon and Schuster, Fireside/Parkside Books, 1994.

Campbell, D. and M. Graham, "Drugs and Alcohol in the Workplace: A Guide for Managers," New York: Facts on File Publications, 1988.

Carter, Dan, "The Politics of Rage," New York: Simon & Schuster, 1995.

Cassingham, Randy, internet site www.thisistrue.com

Chopra, Deepak, "The Way of the Wizard: Twenty Spiritual Lessons for Creating the Life You Want," New York: Harmony Books, 1995.

Delunas, Eve, "Survival Games Personalities Play," Carmel, CA: SunInk Publications, 1992.

Diamond, Jared, "Guns, Germs and Steel: The Fates of Human Societies," New York: W. W. Norton & Company, 1997.

Dreikurs, Rudolf, MD, "Children: The Challenge," New York: The Penguin Group, 1990.

Drews, Toby Rice, "The 350 Secondary Diseases/Disorders to Alcoholism," South Plainfield, NJ: Bridge Publishing, 1985.

Drews, Toby Rice, "Getting them Sober, Volume 1: A Guide for Those Who Live With an Alcoholic," South Plainfield, NJ: Bridge Publishing, Inc., 1980.

Duke, Patty and Kenneth Turan, "Call Me Anna: The Autobiography of Patty Duke," New York: Bantam Books, 1987.

Fairhurst, Alice and Lisa L. Fairhurst, "Effective Teaching, Effective Learning," Palo Alto, CA: Davies-Black Publishing (Consulting Psychologists Press, Inc.), 1995.

Fingarette, Herbert, "Heavy Drinking: The Myth of Alcoholism as a Disease,"

Berkeley, CA: University of California Press, 1988.

Frady, Marshall, "Wallace," New York: Random House, 1996.

Goodwin, Donald, M.D., "Is Alcoholism Hereditary?" New York: Ballantine Books, 1988.

Goodwin, Donald, M.D., "Alcohol and the Writer," Kansas City, MO: Andrews and McMeel, 1988.

Gorski, Terence and Merlene Miller, "Staying Sober: A Guide for Relapse Prevention," Independence, MO: Herald House/Independence Press, 1986.

Gorski, Terence, "Do Family of Origin Problems Cause Chemical Addiction?" Independence, MO: Herald House/Independence Press, 1989.

Gorski, Terence, "The Role of Codependence in Relapse," Independence, MO: Herald House/Independence Press, 1991, audio-cassette series.

Gorski, Terence, "Understanding the Twelve Steps: A Guide for Counselors, Therapists and Recovering People," Independence, MO: Herald House/Independence Press, 1989.

Gorski, Terence, "Sentencing Guidelines for Chemically Dependent Criminal Offenders," Independence, MO.: Herald House/Independence Press, 1995.

Graham, James, "The Secret History of Alcoholism: The Story of Famous Alcoholics and Their Destructive Behavior," Rockport, MA: Element Books, 1996. Also published as, "Vessels of Rage, Engines of Power: The Secret History of Alcoholism," Lexington, VA: Aculeus Press, 1994.

Heston, Leonard L., M.D., and Renate Heston, R.N., "The Medical Casebook of Adolf Hitler," New York: Stein and Day, 1980.

Hyman, B. D., "My Mother's Keeper: A daughter's candid portrait of her famous mother," New York: William Morrow and Co., 1985.

Inciardi, James A., "The War on Drugs: Heroin, Cocaine, Crime and Public Policy," Mountain View, CA: Mayfield Publishing Company, 1986.

Jellinek, E.M., "The Disease Concept of Alcoholism," Hillhouse Press: Piscataway, NJ, 1960.

Johnson, Vernon E., "I'll Quit Tomorrow," San Francisco, CA: Harper and Row,

1980.

Karch, Steven B., "A Brief History of Cocaine," Boca Raton, FL.: CRC Press, 1998.

Keirsey, David and Marilyn Bates, "Please Understand Me: Character & Temperament Types," Del Mar, CA: Prometheus Nemesis Book Company, 1978.

Keirsey, David, "Please Understand Me – II: Temperament, Character, Intelligence," Del Mar, CA: Prometheus Nemesis Book Company, 1998.

Keirsey, David and Ray Choiniere, "Presidential Temperament: The Unfolding of Character in the Forty Presidents of the United States," Del Mar, Ca: Prometheus Nemesis Book Company, 1992.

Kellerman, Reverend Joseph l., "Alcoholism – A Merry-Go-Round Named Denial," Al-Anon Family Groups, 1969, pamphlet.

Kissin, Benjamin and Maureen M. Kaley, "Alcohol and Cancer," in The Biology of Alcoholism, ed. Kissin and Begleiter, vol. 3.

Klein, Sergeant Joseph M. and E.W. "Ted" Oglseby, "Street Narcotic Enforcement," Fullerton, CA: Joe Klein Seminars, 1997.

Knapp, Caroline, "Drinking: A Love Story," New York: The Dial Press, 1996.

Komisin, Lola Kelly, "Personality Type and Suicidal Behaviors of College Students", Journal of Psychological Type, Vol. 24, 1992.

LAPD Website, www.cityofla.org/LAPD/traffic/dre/drgdrvr.htm: Tomas E. Page, "The Drug Recognition Expert (DRE) Response to the Drug Impaired Driver."

Ludwig, Arnold M., M.D., "Understanding the Alcoholic's Mind," New York: Oxford University Press, Inc., 1988.

Mancall, Peter C., "Deadly Medicine: Indians and Alcohol in Early America," Ithaca, NY: Cornell University, 1995.

Mann, Mary, "Marty Mann Answers Your Questions About Drinking and Alcoholism," New York: Holt, Rinehart and Winston, 1981.

Martin, Father Joseph C., "Chalk Talks on Alcohol," San Francisco, CA: Harper and Row, 1989.

McDougall, John A. and Mary A. McDougall, "The McDougall Plan," Clinton, NJ: New Win Publishing, 1985.

Merritt, Laurence and David R. Hagen, "The Basics of Bankruptcy for Accountants and Attorneys," Woodland Hills, Ca., 1996.

Milam, Dr. James R. and Katherine Ketcham, "Under the Influence: A Guide to the Myths and Realities of Alcoholism," New York: Bantam Books, 1983.

Miller, Saul with Jo Anne Miller, "Food for Thought: A New Look at Food and Behavior," Englewood Cliffs, NJ: Prentice-Hall, 1979.

Morrison, Martha, "White Rabbit: A Doctor's Story of Her Addiction and Recovery," New York: Crown Publishers, 1989.

Mueller, L. Ann, M.D., and Katherine Ketcham, "Recovering: How to Get and Stay Sober," New York: Bantam Books, 1987.

Myers, Isabel Briggs and Mary H. McCaulley, "Manual: A Guide to the Development and Use of the Myers-Briggs Type Indicator," Consulting Psychologists' Press, Inc., 1993.

National Council on Alcoholism and Drug Dependence, Inc., "Fact Sheet: Alcoholism and Alcohol-Related Problems," 12 West 21 Street, New York, NY 10010.

NIAAA, "Sixth Special Report to U.S. Congress on Alcohol and Health," USDHHS, 1/87, p. 3, reported in NCADD Fact Sheet: "Alcoholism and Alcohol-Related Problems."

National Institute on Drug Abuse, "Research on Drugs and the Workplace," NIDA Capsules, June, 1990, p. 1, reported in the NCADD Fact Sheet: "Alcohol and Other Drugs in the Workplace."

"NCADD Fact Sheet: Alcohol and Other Drugs in the Workplace," National Council on Alcoholism and Drug Dependence, Inc., 12 West 221 Street, New York, NY 10010; National Institute on Drug Abuse, "Research on Drugs and the Workplace," NIDA Capsules, June, 1990.

Norwood, Robin, "Why Me, Why This, Why Now: A Guide to Answering Life's Toughest Questions," New York: Carol Southern Books, 1994.

Parker, David and Ralph Stacey, "Chaos, Management and Economics: The Implications of Non-Linear Thinking," United Kingdom: Coronet Books, IEA Hobart Paper Series #125, 1994.

Parker, Robert Nash with Linda-Anne Rebhun, "Alcohol and Homicide: A Deadly Combination of Two American Traditions," Albany, NY: State University of New York Press, 1995.

Peck, M. Scott, "The Road Less Traveled," New York: Simon and Schuster, 1978.

"Policy Compendium on Tobacco, Alcohol, and Other Harmful Substances Affecting Adolescents: Alcohol and Other Harmful Substances," Chicago, IL: The American Medical Association, 1994.

Polson, Beth and Miller Newton, Ph.D., "Not My Kid: a Parent's Guide to Kids and Drugs," New York: Avon Books, 1984.

Powter, Susan, "Sober...and Staying That Way: The Missing Link in the Cure for Alcoholism," New York: Simon & Schuster, 1997.

Provost, Judith A., "Tracking Freshman Difficulties In the Class of 1993," Journal of Psychological Type, Vol. 21, 1991.

Robbins, Anthony, "Personal Power," original audiotape series, San Diego, CA: Robbins Research International, Inc., 1993.

Robe, Lucy Barry, "Co-starring Famous Women and Alcohol: the Dramatic Truth Behind the Tragedies and Triumphs of 200 Celebrities," Minneapolis, MN: CompCare Publications, 1986.

Rodale, J. I., "Natural Health, Sugar and the Criminal Mind," New York: Pyramid Books, 1968.

Rosenbaum, Dennis P. and Gordon S. Hanson, "Assessing the Effects of School-Based Drug Education: A Six-Year Multi-Level Analysis of Project D.A.R.E.," Journal of Research in Crime and Delinquency, Vol. 35 No. 4, November, 1998.

Rothschild, Michael, "Bionomics: Economics as Eco-System," New York: Henry Holt and Company, Inc., 1990. Originally published as, "Bionomics: The Inevitability of Capitalism."

Roy, Maria, Ed., "Battered Women: A Psychosociological Study of Domestic Violence," New York: Van Nostrand, 1977.

Royce, James E. and David Scratchly, "Alcoholism and Other Drug Problems," New York: The Free Press, 1996.

Schwartz, George R., M.D., "In Bad Taste: The MSG Syndrome," Santa Fe, NM: Health Press, 1988.

Sinetar, Dr. Marsha, "Do What You Love, the Money Will Follow," New York: Dell Publishing, 1987.

Smith, James W., M.D., Chief Medical Officer, Schick Chemical Dependency Programs, "An Orientation on Alcoholism," booklet, no copyright date (probably written in about 1982).

Somers, Suzanne "Keeping Secrets," New York: Warner Books, 1988.

STAND, "Support Training Against Narcotic Dependency," Los Angeles Police Department handout, "Why STAND."

Tennant, Forest, M.D., Dr. P.H., "Identifying the Cocaine User," W. Covina, CA: Veract, Inc., 1997.

Tennant, Forest, M.D., Dr. P.H., "Medical Uses and Legal Identification of Drug Use," videotape series, W. Covina, CA: Veract, Inc.

Twain, Mark, "Pudd'nhead Wilson's New Calendar," from "The Wit and Wisdom of Mark Twain," Philadelphia, PA: Running Press Miniature Edition, 1990.

University of Wisconsin Law School, "Compendium on Drug Impaired Driving," 1996.

U.S. Department of Transportation, "DWI Detection and Standardized Field Sobriety Testing: Student Manual," Oklahoma City, OK: National Highway Traffic Safety Administration, 1995.

Vaillant, George E., "The Natural History of Alcoholism Revisited," Cambridge, MA: Harvard University Press, 1995.

Vaughan, Clark, "Addictive Drinking – The Road to Recovery for Problem Drinkers and Those Who Love Them," New York: Penguin Books, 1984.

Von Mises, Ludwig, "Human Action," Auburn, AL: Ludwig Von Mises Institute, 1998.

White, Stephen, "Russia Goes Dry: Alcohol, State and Society," Great Britain: Cambridge University Press, 1996.

Wholey, Dennis, Ed., "The Courage to Change: Personal Conversations About

Alcoholism," New York: Warner Books, 1984.

Woodward, Nancy Hyden, "If Your Child is Drinking...What you can do to fight alcohol abuse at home, at school, and in the community," New York: G.P. Putnam's Sons, 1981.

Internet site, www.vix.com/men/battery/battery.html.

QUICK ORDER FORM

FAX orders: 818-363-3111
Phone orders: 800-482-9424
E-mail orders: Visit our Website "JustSayNoToAddicts.com"
Postal orders: Galt Publishing, PO Box 7777, Northridge, CA 91327-7777

Please send _____ copies of "Drunks, Drugs & Debits" @ 29.95 each

_____

Sales Tax: please add 8.25% for products shipped to California addresses

_____

Shipping: $5 for one to 100 within the U.S.; $10 outside_____

Total Investment _____

Please send information on: _____ Other Books _____ Consulting
_____ Speaking, Seminars _____ Other Products
_____ T-shirts, mugs, etc. with "Just Say No to Addicts" ™ logo
_____ Quantity prices on book or other product purchases

I wish to pay by: _____ Check enclosed _____ Credit Card:
_____ Discover _____ Visa
Card Number:_____
Name on card:_____ Exp. date:_____/_____
Signature (required)_____

Deliver to: Name_____
                  Address_____
                  City_____ State_____ Zip_____

Telephone (in case of questions about your order): _____

e-mail address (if you would like to be added to our occasional e-mailings,
from which you can be removed at any time) _____

You can help us educate others by telling us where you first heard about "Drugs,
Drunks & Debits" (please be as specific as possible) _____

You could also help by sharing where you first heard about our Website,
"JustSayNoToAddicts.com" (please be specific)_____